PENGUIN CLASSICS

THE JĀTAKAS

SARAH SHAW was educated at Manchester University, where she read Greek and English. She did her doctorate in English Literature there and went on to the study of Pāli and Sanskrit in Oxford. She has written a book about meditation in the Pāli canon, which is being published as part of a series in connection with the Oxford Centre for Buddhist Studies. She is a teacher and writer and is married with three children. A Buddhist for some years, she practises with the Samatha Association in Britain.

THE JĀTAKAS

Birth Stories of
the Bodhisatta

Translated from the Pāli by
SARAH SHAW

PENGUIN BOOKS
An imprint of Penguin Random House

PENGUIN BOOKS

USA | Canada | UK | Ireland | Australia
New Zealand | India | South Africa | China

Penguin Books is part of the Penguin Random House group of companies
whose addresses can be found at global.penguinrandomhouse.com

Published by Penguin Random House India Pvt. Ltd
4th Floor, Capital Tower 1, MG Road,
Gurugram 122 002, Haryana, India

Penguin
Random House
India

First published by Penguin Books India 2006

This translation copyright © Sarah Shaw 2006
Cover image courtesy Bodleian Library, University of Oxford

10 9 8 7 6 5 4 3

ISBN 9780144001477

Typeset in Sabon by Eleven Arts, Delhi
Printed at Repro India Limited

www.penguin.co.in

This book is dedicated to
the memory of my parents,
Hamish and Kathleen Bremner

Contents

Acknowledgements

If Jātakas were being written now there would have to be one about generosity in the giving of time. I have often had the benefit of this kind while working on these translations. So I would like to thank L.S. Cousins, past president of the Samatha Trust and the Pāli Text Society, for teaching me for many years and for helping me out. I would also like to thank Professor Richard Gombrich for his teaching over the last few years. Both have influenced and taught me so much that the debt cannot be covered fully by footnotes. Dr Justin Meiland has also often given a great deal of useful comment, both on points of translation and about Jātakas in general. Other people I would like to thank for reading sections or giving comments are Ven. Dhammasami, Dr John Elsner, Dr Susan Francia, Sarah Norman, Dr Valerie Roebuck, Professor Grevel Lindop and Dr Peter Skilling. My editor, Sumitra Srinivasan, has been very helpful and alert to inconsistencies. The staff and librarians at the Oriental Institute and the Indian Institute libraries have also always been helpful. My greatest thanks are to my family, my husband, Charles, and children, Jeremy, Roland and Lucy. My dog, Bramble, who died while I was completing the script, was a reminder to me that animals can help to keep us human.

List of abbreviations

A	*Aṅguttaranikāya*
Cp	*Cariyāpiṭaka*
CPD	*Critical Pāli Dictionary*
D	*Dīghanikāya*
DhS	*Dhammasaṅgaṇi*
DP	*Dictionary of Pāli*
DPPN	*Dictionary of Pāli Proper Names*
J	*Jātaka*
M	*Majjhimanikāya*
PED	*Pāli–English Dictionary*
PTS	*Pāli Text Society*
S	*Saṃyuttanikāya*
SED	*Sanskrit–English Dictionary*
Sn	*Suttanipāta*
Vin	*Vinaya*
Vism	*Visuddhimagga*
VRI	*Vipassana Research Institute*

A note on the texts

The text I have used is the Pāli Text Society (PTS) transliteration into Roman script compiled by Fausbøll in the nineteenth century, which he based initially on three Sinhalese manuscripts.[1] As work progressed, Burmese manuscripts became available to him. In his 1877 preface, he freely admits he is not happy with the result or his differentiation between commentary and story, which, as we see in the Introduction, is not an easy matter. The very fact we have such a good text, though, is a tribute to a great scholar who was clearly facing all kinds of difficulties, ranging from manuscripts being lost in the post to lack of funds to find other manuscripts dotted around the globe! For this translation I have usually just followed his guidelines, for the most part taking what he puts in large type as story and, following his implicit guidance as to what is story and what later commentary, leaving out the sections he denotes through small type. The exception to this has been in translating 'the story from the present'. This is in small type in his edition but there is no evidence that it is later than 'the story from the past' in the form that we have it now.[2] For variant readings I have also used his denotation at the bottom of the page: B and a letter for the appropriate Burmese manuscript and C for the Sinhalese. While the whole area needs thorough reappraisal, if possible in the light of all available manuscripts, we do at least have a workable text. There is also now a Burmese version of the text, available for free distribution, along with the entire Pāli canon, on CD Rom.[3] This sometimes simplifies and avoids a potentially authentic difficult reading but is very useful where the Pāli is obscure in the PTS version. Many scholars now use this as their working text.

It is surprising that there has been no complete translation of the 547 tales since the late nineteenth-century edition of six volumes was undertaken under the general editorship of E.B. Cowell. So a word of praise should go to this often maligned but heroic endeavour, now over a hundred years old. The style, particularly that of the verses, which were then ambitiously placed in rhyme, is replete with the 'leagues', 'eftsoons' and 'forsooths' that characterized Victorian storytelling. Our taste for archaisms has gone but the very existence of translations for all the Jātakas is a testament to the enthusiasm of scholarship at that time. I do not suppose any university or funding body would support such a project now. The stories are easily obtainable from the Pāli Text Society in Oxford.[4] More recent translations of selections of specific Jātakas are difficult to obtain. H.T. Francis and E.J. Thomas translated 114 in 1916 in an edition that is almost impossible to find, though it includes helpful notes on counterparts to the stories in other cultures.[5] I have not translated the last, Vessantara, because the job has been done well so recently. For anyone who would like a modern translation of Jātaka 547, Margaret Cone's is an admirable example.[6] Its introduction, by Richard Gombrich, is also the best short essay available on the background to all the Jātakas.

In my Introduction which follows, I have included the number of the relevant story in parentheses when referring to a specific Jātaka.

Notes

[1] *The Jātaka together with its commentary being Tales of the Anterior Births of Gotama Buddha.* 6 vols. (1877–96; Oxford, PTS reprint: 1990–1).

[2] See M. Winternitz, *A History of Indian Literature* (Srinivasa Sarma revised), 2 vols. (Delhi, Varanasi, Patna: Motilal, 1983), II, p. 120, n.1.

See also M. Cone and R.F. Gombrich, *The Perfect Generosity of Prince Vessantara: A Buddhist Epic* translated from the Pāli and illustrated by unpublished paintings from Sinhalese temples (Oxford: OUP, 1977), pp. xxx–xxxi.

[3] The disc may be obtained free of charge from Vipassana Research Institute, Dhammagiri, Igatpuri 422 403, Dist Nasik, India. See www.tipitaka.org.

[4] In 6 vols, 1895–1907, all reprinted in Oxford in 1990 in three volumes.

[5] *Jātaka Tales* (Cambridge, 1916).

[6] Cone and Gombrich, *The Perfect Generosity*.

Author's note

Epithets for Gotama Buddha, the Bodhisatta in his final life ('the present'), who has attained complete awakening and can teach others:

The Buddha
The Exalted One (*Bhagavā*)
The Fully Awakened One (*Abhisambuddha*)
The Teacher (*Satthā*)
The Ten-Powered One (*Dasabala*)
The Thus-gone (*Tathāgata*)

Epithets for the Bodhisatta, the one bound for, or to, enlightenment, the hero of the tales ('the past'), who is preparing to become a Buddha in his final life:

Bodhisatta
The Great Being (*Mahāsatta*)

The Ten Perfections (*pāramī*s)

The number of a story with a rebirth attributed to a particular perfection of quality, either by an ancient source or the story itself, is given after each. The perfections are discussed in detail in the Introduction and specific perfections are discussed in the introductory essays to tales that are starred.

Generosity (*dāna*) 95, 316*
Virtue (*sīla*) 506*
Renunciation (*nekkhamma*) 9*, 538, 539

Wisdom (*paññā*) 402*
Effort (*viriya*) 1, 55*, 539
Forbearance (*khanti*) 75, 313*
Truth (*sacca*) 75*
Resolve (*adhiṭṭhāna*) 20, 538*
Loving kindness (*mettā*) 75, 385*, 540*
Equanimity (*upekkhā*), 94*, 273*

Introduction

A Jātaka is a story about a birth, and this collection of tales is about the repeated births—and deaths—of the Bodhisatta, the being destined to become the present Buddha in his final life. Written in Pāli, the language of the Theravāda Buddhist canon, the tales comprise one of the largest and oldest collections of stories in the world. The earliest sections, the verses, are considered amongst the very earliest part of the Pāli tradition and date from the fifth century BCE; the later parts were incorporated during the period up to the third century CE. Partly because they arose at a time when literature was transmitted orally and partly because storytelling tends to extemporize, the stories were shaped and developed over this period before the final version became settled. The 547 stories all evolve from one vow: the determination made by the Bodhisatta, at the feet of the last Buddha, Dīpaṅkara, to postpone his own enlightenment and freedom from the endless round of existences until he is ready to become a Buddha himself and teach others. This undertaking, recorded in the *Jātakanidāna*, a lengthy introduction to the Jātaka stories that is regarded as a separate work, sets him apart from other beings.[1] In the many aeons when there is no Buddha to teach the world—for according to early Buddhism such teachers occur only rarely in human history—the Bodhisatta tries to build the strengths, resources and experience ready for his final birth.[2] These endeavours form the basis of the Jātaka stories and confer the unusual abilities that make him in his last life not just an *arahat*, an awakened one, but a Buddha, capable of leaving a teaching behind for others. In the time of the Buddha and for the period in which his teaching (*sāsana*) lasts, others may follow the path that he has left for them.

The idea that birth occurs again and again, widespread through most of the traditions of the Indian subcontinent, does not only provide us with a theme of profound religious and philosophical implications, it also gives an unusually flexible means of linking narratives of many different kinds. Although associated with other Indian traditions of folk tale, drama and epic, Jātakas are unique: they are the only collection of stories in the world in which the development of one central character is tested not just through the events of one lifetime but of hundreds. Through his vow the Bodhisatta is able to experience many different types of rebirth: as animals (such as monkey, fish, elephant, horse and mouse), tree-spirit and serpent king (*nāga*); and when in human form, as many different classes, including untouchable, merchant, cook, archer, forester, warrior, musician, brahmin, minister and king. Sometimes he is a god. According to later commentarial traditions, that soon become incorporated into the Jātakas themselves, he fulfils in these lifetimes all ten perfections (*pāramī*) of generosity (*dāna*), virtue or restraint (*sīla*), renunciation (*nekkhamma*), wisdom (*paññā*), effort (*viriya*), forbearance (*khanti*), truthfulness (*sacca*), resolve (*adhiṭṭhāna*), loving kindness (*mettā*) and equanimity (*upekkhā*). These qualities enable him not only to find a path to enlightenment but to teach others too. In most South-East Asian countries, the last ten lifetimes are treated as particularly significant and are associated with the completion of each one of the perfections in turn.[3]

The popular Buddhism that is embedded in Jātakas still lies at the heart of the living tradition. Countless people in Buddhist countries such as Myanmar (Burma), Thailand, Sri Lanka, Vietnam and Cambodia have grown up with these tales as a main source of teaching, anecdote and imaginative background. Traditionally, children were introduced to their religion through hearing the stories in temples, from monks visiting their house or at festivals, though there is no evidence in the stories themselves that the very young were ever regarded as a specific audience. The artistic creativity inspired by Jātakas in temple art is an impressive testament to the central place these stories held in often non-literate Buddhist settings. They are depicted in early stone relief and paintings at Ajaṇṭā, Bhārhut and Sāñchī in India, at Polonnoruwa and Anuradhapura in Sri Lanka, and later, in temples throughout South-East Asian countries as Buddhism spread. Some portrayals, such as in Bhārhut and caves 9 and 10 at Ajantā, date from the first or second century BCE. In the fifth century the Chinese pilgrim Fa-Hien saw Jātaka illustrations in Gandhāra and a large procession of figures from all the Jātakas in Abhayagiri in Sri Lanka.[4] The stories are shown from the medieval period onwards in paintings around Kandy, Sri Lanka.[5] In Thai temples vast murals focus on incidents from the last ten stories. More recent depictions that surround newer temples in South-East Asian countries have been painted with the brilliant colours and techniques of modern folk art, but the stories depicted are those that are still popular after centuries. 'The story of the hare in the moon' (316), for instance, which featured at the ancient sites of Bhārhut and Nāgārjunakoṇḍa in India, is still found painted everywhere. On a different note, the continued accessibility of the stories can be seen in their depiction in cartoon books throughout the East, popular amongst non-Buddhists too. The Indian *Pancharatna* comic Jātaka series, for instance, shows that Jātaka style, with its succession of dramatic events and encounters between eloquent animals is perfectly suited to the medium.[6] Drama, song, dance and puppetry throughout South-East Asia have all been influenced by Jātakas. In rural areas of Myanmar, the Vessantara story is constantly recited and enacted where the Buddha's own life story is almost unknown.[7] The influence of the stories extended out from the temple into the political and public sphere. The nineteenth-century Burmese king, Mindon, urged his ministers to behave like their counterparts in the Jātakas;

the orders of the time list Jātakas felt to be particularly useful.[8]
In Laos much of the legal system was established on principles
laid down in Jātakas, which are also used as precedent in courts
of law.[9]

It is, however, as a repository of funny incident, drama and
adventure that Jātakas show their peculiar charm and emotional
appeal. Buddhism teaches a doctrine of *anattā*, or not-self, but
the narrator's *ahaṃ*, or 'I', of the stories is the Bodhisatta himself,
the being defined by his commitment to develop enlightenment
for the sake of others. His omnipresent search for the truth unifies
what would otherwise be a very disparate collection of exempla,
fables, anecdotes, romances, dramatic interchanges and heroic
dramas. From the very short tales which begin the collection, often
involving animals in the manner of Aesopic tales (37, 75, 128
and 316), to sustained narratives of immense complexity, which
have affinities with other literary traditions such as epic, drama
and even the novel (538, 539 and 540), we find the resourceful,
alert and ever watchful presence of the Bodhisatta.[10] His actions
are, sometimes, all too human—even when an animal—and he
is even, very rarely, shown with some faults in the character he
adopts for each tale (128 and 539). His behaviour is, however,
largely exemplary and an embodiment of heroic elements suitable
for one learning to teach a way to others. Some of the early ones,
which show the Bodhisatta saving other animals through his
courage or skill, are often funny and irreverent. By the time we
get to the longer stories a more sustained exploration of the struggle
for liberation, accompanied by extensive debate and the use of
dramatic interchange to test the Bodhisatta's motive, produces a
genre that is a kind of Buddhist epic in its own right. The intricacies
of plot, character, discourse and poetry that distinguish these
long tales place some of them amongst the great works of world
literature. While no internal chronological sequence is suggested,
the character of the aspirant Buddha grows in stature and

complexity as part of the preparations for the enlightenment. The stories that make up the last ten (*mahānipāta*) of the 547, from which the last three in this collection show (538, 539 and 540), are epic journeys for him, as, tested through challenge, temptation and debate, he hones and purifies the attributes he needs to teach in his final life.

But in the middle of this diversity, the themes of not-self (*anattā*) and impermanence (*anicca*) are unobtrusively knitted into the very structure of the collection as a whole. Though the Bodhisatta features in all the tales, either as watcher or protagonist, his identity, like that of the other characters, is constantly dissolved at the end of each lifetime with his death. He moves from one set of conditions to another, recognizable primarily by the wisdom and integrity engendered by the Bodhisatta vow. His role in a story is only fully understood at the end of the tale with the *ahaṃ eva* (indeed that was I), the acknowledgement on the part of the Buddha that completes all of the tales. Jātakas embody Buddhism applied through events: at the beginning of each story the Bodhisatta is again reborn, searching once more for the qualities that distinguish him from other beings.

Structure of the stories

So how do Jātakas work? Do they need to be read in order? We do not have specific information about their transmission but it is thought that they were in the first instance memorized for chanting, probably by the *bhāṇaka* tradition of monks who kept other early Buddhist texts alive before the advent of writing.[11] They would probably then have been related to an audience, comprising a mixture of laity and monks, at the kind of festivals where they are told now: full moon or *uposatha* days at temples, or *dānas*, meals given to monks where food is offered and blessings given in return. The first story, as we see, suggests, in its recipients a certain lay orientation. With its extensive homage and introduction to the theme, it is clearly distinguished from the others, but it was probably the case that then, as now, any tale might be chosen for a particular event.

Their use for separate occasions possibly shaped the structure of the tales, for they are constructed in a way that any could be told with little reference to others. With the exception of the first, each starts with an identifying tag that was probably intended as a mnemonic device for the monks chanting it. This gives the first couple of words of the first verse in the tale. This tag is given in the translation here just below the title. The tale proper starts with an incident in the present (*paccuppannavatthu*) called 'the story from the present'. This always involves a collection of people, composed of monks, the laity, or both, who are sitting in discussion with the Buddha. Perhaps a monk asks a question, as in Jātaka 108, or an odd event happens, such as the drought in Jātaka 75. This prompts the telling of a past life, which reflects the situation in the present. This is the story proper, 'the story from the past' (*atītavatthu*), usually the bulk of the tale. The Bodhisatta, the remembered self of the Buddha, appears in each 'story from the past'. He is usually, though not always, one of the central characters and the people he encounters are often his principal disciples such as Moggallāna, Sāriputta and Ānanda, or Rāhulamātā, the Buddha's wife or 'mother of Rāhula', in their earlier lives. His evil cousin Devadatta also features, frequently providing a villainous counterpart to the Bodhisatta. Verses (*gāthā*) feature as an accompaniment to the prose narrative in the past. These vary greatly in quality and function. Thought to be the oldest layer of the text, they are sometimes folk homilies, sometimes comments from the Buddha in the present and sometimes extended eulogies or dramatized interchanges that provide a lyrical or emotional counterpoint to the main action. The stories are grouped into twenty-two sections (*nipāta*s) depending on the number of these verses in the story. Following the Ṛg Vedic pattern of ordering material, the stories with only one verse are in the first section, those with two in the second, then three and so on. There are some variations in this, but the pattern is followed until the final section (*mahānipāta*), which contains the last ten stories, whose verses run into hundreds. The first three of these (538, 539 and 540) are translated here. Each tale finishes with the connection (*samodhāna*), in which the Buddha, in the present, explains who was who in the earlier life and reveals his own identity.

This overall structure provides a sense of continuity from one tale to the next. It also means that any story would have pleasingly familiar elements to someone hearing a particular one for the first time: the action always follows a basic shape, with the standard pattern for the introduction and conclusion enclosing whatever goes on in between. The way that each past life also pertains to one event in the present, however, gives us an unusual perspective when each story is read as a link in a larger process. The Buddha, his teaching and his followers always feature to a greater or lesser extent at the beginning and the end of each story.

The Bodhisatta, the Buddha and the different kinds of enlightenment

A fully enlightened one (*sammāsambuddha*), able to show to others the way to find enlightenment for themselves, occurs only rarely. At the beginning of this selection of stories there is an extract from the introduction to the Jātakas (*Jātakanidāna*). This describes Gotama's predecessor, Dīpaṅkara, at whose feet the Buddha-to-be prostrates himself when he makes the Bodhisatta vow and undertakes to live through many lives developing the perfections. Jātakas occur in the time between this momentous vow and the 'present', when he has achieved his aim as our

Buddha. There are no fully awakened Buddhas in the time in between, when the stories are set. Buddha Gotama is described in the story of the present, is said to tell and remember the past story, sometimes comments from the present through the verses and completes each Jātaka in the first person, making the connections between the births in the present and those in the past. In this way, within the terms of the stories, he is literally omniscient: as their narrator he is the only character who is able to recollect all the incidents, in his own and in others' lives. He does not appear as the Buddha in the story in the 'past', the 'dark ages' in which a teaching that leads to enlightenment is not available, but the verses attributed to him that are sometimes interspersed with others in the tales remind us of his presence. When his interjections occur in the story the narrative always points out that it is the Buddha speaking, not the Bodhisatta in the past, who has yet to find full enlightenment.

A number of epithets are used exclusively for the Fully Awakened Buddha, who describes, interprets and explains the worlds his memory have conjured up for us: the Thus-gone (*Tathāgata*), the Exalted One (*Bhagavā*) or the Teacher (*Satthā*). His earlier 'self' has two titles: the Great Being (*Mahāsatta*), a bit like the English expression 'our hero', or the Bodhisatta, a name which could be taken to mean 'the one bound for enlightenment' or 'the one attached to enlightenment'.[12] The Buddha, whose name means 'awake', is enlightened.[13] He tells the incidents of the stories from memory; the Bodhisatta/Great Being, the self his memory recreates, acts within them. The Bodhisatta, is, like any other being in the tales, completely immersed in what is going on. He experiences desire, hatred and ignorance, but is usually heroic in some way: he finds himself in circumstances which others may find themselves in too. His struggles and aspirations, animated by his vow, are always 'in the past' (*atīte*), an expression a little like our 'once upon a time' which begins the remembered stories.[14] The 'past' is 'measureless', involving oceanic stretches of time. It is also largely undifferentiated: while some stories are set in a specific period (Jātaka 94) and the tradition has tended to assume that the last ten are sequentially near the end too, no obvious order or sequence is given. This interplay of times places Buddhahood within the stories always in the present, for the past stories enact in various metaphorical or parallel ways the dynamics of the 'present' stories. The Buddha, in the text as in his life, is the elucidator of meaning. His fully awakened mind is needed to remember, order, comment and provide connecting links that interpret the events of this unspecified time and relate it to a clearly located and recognizable 'present'. Only he can recollect all the incidents and teach them to others, 'as the moon is released from the clouds' (Jātaka 1). Buddhahood is not only the goal, therefore, but a prerequisite and a guiding principle for the text. We are reminded of this at the start and end of each story. It gives us the 'happy ending' to them all which readers or listeners are intended to assume, and which lends Jātakas their whole momentum and purpose. A Buddha, able to teach gods and men, is said to know all worlds (lokāvidu). Many such worlds are described in the stories.

The text describes two other forms of enlightenment. An option that the Bodhisatta could have taken at the time of his vow, but chooses not to, is that of arahatship: this awakening does not confer the great teaching ability of the Buddha. It is only possible in or after the time of the Buddha, so arahats do not feature in the tales set in the past. Like all forms of enlightenment, this has four stages. At the first, stream-entry, the practitioner abandons doubt and grosser defilements. He or she will experience at most seven more lifetimes, none of which will be in a 'bad destiny', a lower rebirth such as an animal or a ghost. The second stage is once-return. At this moment, more subtle defilements are abandoned and the practitioner is certain to attain enlightenment and *nibbāna* after, at most, one more life. The third stage is never-return, which guarantees that the practitioner will become enlightened in that lifetime and never again take another rebirth of any kind. The fourth stage is arahatship, at which all defilements are removed. The enlightened being passes at death to *nibbāna*, the end of all suffering. When this occurs in the stories from the present, it is called *parinibbāna*, or complete *nibbāna*, as in the story from the present in Jātaka 95. In the 'story from the present' it is quite usual in Jātakas for one or more of the listeners to the 'story from the past' to attain one of these stages of the path. This happens after hearing the story from the past and then the exposition of the four noble truths at the end. The four noble truths, of *dukkha*, suffering (literally: dis-ease) the craving that gives rise to this (*tanhā*), the peace and freedom of the ceasing of craving (*nibbāna*) and the path leading to that (*magga*) are the formulation of the Buddha's teaching that is given in his first sermon, in which he teaches the middle way to the group of ascetics who had been his companions in the severe austerities that preceded the enlightenment.[15] By showing characters in the present obtaining insight on the basis of talks given after the stories, the point is continually reiterated that arahatship and the stages leading to it are possible in the 'present', the time of the Buddha, when they were not possible in 'the past', the time when there had been no fully awakened mind to show the way. People do not become arahats during Jātaka tales, nor, the structure of each tale implies, by listening to them either. This only happens when the Buddha in the final section delivers teaching on the four noble truths and makes his explanatory links. During the aeons of the stories in the past the characters in the tales—and perhaps the listeners too—have to follow the resources that are available to them, or the kind of teachings open to their species and station. 'The story in the past' seems almost like a time of dreams, a preliminary journey to prepare the mind for the end of the tale. Arahatship, or awakening, and the stages leading to it, happen in the 'present', when the Buddha explains who was who, and can deliver the teaching that elucidates the text.

Another form of awakening is that found by the *paccekabuddha*s, now sometimes called silent Buddhas. These figures, who feature for the most part in later Jātakas in the collection, find the path to enlightenment for themselves, without the need for the teaching of a fully awakened Buddha. They can arise at any time. Although they do sometimes teach in Jātakas they do not provide for others the full path to enlightenment. They possibly represent some sort of attempt to integrate and validate other meditative paths within the Buddhist tradition. At any rate, from the evidence of the tales, the excellence of *paccekabuddha*s derives from their embodiment, through posture, manner and bearing, of what it is to live in the world free from defilement of any kind, when circumstances prevent other forms of spiritual teaching and practice.[16] Within the context of the Jātakas, they act as representatives of the spiritual path at times when the possibility of hearing the teaching of a Buddha is not there. A bit like the rising and the setting of the sun, with which they are associated in the story of Mahājanaka (539), they follow tracks that are out of the reach of others, but are silent and even mysterious constants. The *paccekabuddha* is a reassuring presence who is honoured and revered whenever any character is lucky enough to encounter one.

The perfections (pāramīs) in the stories

This collection starts with the vow that sets in motion the Bodhisatta path and defines the character of the Bodhisatta, the Buddha-to-be. This moment, the seed of all the stories, introduces the idea of the perfections, the openings on to the 'great highway' that leads to complete awakening. Making his resolve, the Bodhisatta says, 'So few are all the things in this world that bring awakening to maturation, that bring about Buddhahood and that are to be fulfilled by Bodhisattas. Beyond these ten perfections there are no others. These ten perfections do not exist in the sky above; they do not exist in the earth below, or in any of the directions that start with the East. They are established right in the depths of my heart.'[17] The ten perfections are a post-canonical list describing attributes that should be cultivated by the being who wishes to be a Buddha and teach others. The list is also constantly taught at a popular level to this day. The first perfection, generosity (*dāna*), is the practice of giving through acts of generosity, particularly to holy men. The second is moral restraint or virtue (*sīla*). The third is renunciation (*nekkhamma*), usually the giving up of the lay life, but also, in its metaphoric sense, the giving up of sensory ties. The fourth is wisdom (*paññā*), which is only fully developed at enlightenment. The fifth is effort (*viriya*), which encompasses the four right efforts of ridding the mind of unskilful states, ensuring they do not arise again, arousing skilful states and ensuring that they are sustained. It is also one of the five faculties necessary for the attainment of meditation (*jhāna*). The sixth is forbearance or patience (*khanti*). The seventh is truthfulness (*sacca*), said to be one of the defining features of a Bodhisatta. The eighth is resolve (*adhiṭṭhāna*), the determination made when any vow is undertaken, such as a decision to observe a certain amount of moral precepts for a specified time, or, indeed, to become a Bodhisatta. The ninth is loving kindness (*mettā*), an attitude of mind which can become the foundation for all dealings with others. This is developed further in meditative practice, when it is suffused to all sentient beings. The tenth is equanimity (*upekkhā*), the imperturbability of mind that transcends painful and non-painful feeling. This may also be developed further in meditation and becomes, in the end, one of the factors that lead to enlightenment (*bojjhaṅga*). A separate image is used to describe each one of the perfections. He should practise generosity as a jar that is overturned spills and is unstinting with water; he should guard his virtue as a yak her tail. He should practise renunciation as a man serving a long sentence in prison wishes to leave it; he should practise wisdom, asking questions everywhere, as a monk begging for food goes to everyone to find it. He should practise effort as a lion displays unabated vigour; he should practise forbearance or patience as the earth receives everything which is thrown upon it. He should practise truthfulness as the healing star does not deviate from her course; he should practise resolve as a mountain remains firm. He should practise loving kindness as water cools both the bad and the good, and he should cultivate equanimity as the earth accepts whatever pure or impure matter is thrown upon it.[18] It is these qualities which are explored and found in the time of the stories.

The text as we have it evolved over many centuries and association of Jātakas with particular perfections is probably a later, if deeply creative, development within the tales and popular tradition. It provides a formulation of the work the Bodhisatta sees ahead of him and so a unified way of exploring in greater detail the implications of his vow. A single perfection is cited by name in some stories: 'The story of the one who taught forbearance' (313) shows the Bodhisatta's patient endurance in the face of terrible attack and 'The story of the hare' (316) is clearly associated with generosity. In many cases, however, it is less easy to work out if one perfection alone is being described. *The Basket of Conduct* (*Cariyāpiṭaka*), a late canonical work, gives associations for some of the stories with the first seven perfections. The preamble to the Jātaka collection, the *Jātakanidāna*, links groups of tales to each of the ten perfections. The Thai tradition regards the last ten lives (*Mahānipāta/Thosachat*) as representing each one of the ten: these are constantly depicted in temples throughout South-East Asia as representing the summation of the Bodhisatta's path.[19] This pre-eminence is manifest, for instance, in the continued popularity of little chants that take the first syllable of each of the Bodhisatta's names in his last ten lives to make a mnemonic.[20] This diversity of interpretation means that some stories come to be associated with different perfections in different traditions. 'The story of Temiya, the dumb cripple' (538) is an instance of this, for the story from the present describes its subject as renunciation (*nekkhamma*) while the *Cariyāpiṭaka* and the *Jātakanidāna* associate it with resolve (*adhiṭṭhāna*). Both of these elements certainly feature in the story and it is interesting to consider how the two main qualities are fulfilled in the action, for the Bodhisatta, in his attempt to give up kingship and enter upon a renunciate life, also needs great resolve to withstand sixteen years as a prince, pretending to be a cripple. In many the perfections form a more general part of the assumed background and no particular attribution is made at all. The perfections give the Bodhisatta a range of active and immediately applicable resources to be introduced into any situation. They are a way of describing the nature of his vow. They are, however, dependent upon one another and the difference between them is not rigid. Where a story is associated with one particular perfection this is discussed in the introduction to that tale.

Practise generosity (dāna)*, guard your virtue* (sīla) *and keep the full-moon days* (uposatha)

The first two perfections do deserve particular mention, nonetheless, because they are constantly enjoined throughout all the stories and provide us with a key to understanding the tales as a whole. The first, generosity, is accorded a special emphasis. This is shown on the night of the enlightenment when Gotama is challenged by Māra, the embodiment of the forces that militate against spiritual development, as being unworthy to sit under the Bodhi tree in pursuit of his goal. At this time, the Buddha-to-be describes the perfections both as his shield and as his weapons of attack.[21] They help him to transform all the varied psychological onslaughts, represented by the coals, darkness, fogs and mists sent by Māra, into garlands of flowers. Yet it is in one act of past generosity that he finally takes refuge: a gift of seven-hundredfold alms to monks, undertaken in an earlier life, to which he asks the earth itself to bear witness. When he does this, the earth rumbles its assent. Māra, his armies and his terrors are routed and Gotama is free to pursue his aim.[22] It is a detail in early Buddhist mythology that has a curiously modern, or perhaps more accurately, a perennial, appeal. The lowest point of Gotama's doubt and the last hindrance to awakening is his own sense of a lack of worth to sit where he is sitting and to do what he is doing. The recollection of giving overcomes the vestigial fears and doubts, symbolized by Māra and his armies, which might prevent him from attaining his final goal. Indian lists usually work in an ascending sequence of importance, but it is significant that the subject of the last story, the Vessantara Jātaka (547), is also giving.[23] Hospitality and appropriate generosity are still taught as the starting point of all Buddhist practice.[24]

In the stories generosity is treated as the encapsulation of all the perfections. Giving is also often linked in the tales to the second perfection, of *sīla*, the virtue that is protected by adherence to the five precepts (*pañca sīlāni*), of refraining from killing, stealing, sexual misconduct, lying or malicious speech and intoxication. Throughout the stories these two are accorded a special place for their transformatory power. Whatever the situation and however difficult the rebirth, the injunction is repeated like a refrain: 'practise generosity (*dāna*), guard virtue (*sīla*) and keep the *uposatha*'. The *uposatha* is the full-moon (*poya*), new-moon or quarter-moon day, a time in South-East Asian countries when the first two perfections are cultivated at leisure. Lay practitioners wear white for the day, donate money, give food to monks, and sometimes keep extra precepts, such as undertaking to refrain from ornaments, eating after noon or sexual intercourse, for the time they have taken them. Events or festivals on the *uposatha* are the times in which Jātakas are most often recounted now and, it seems likely, were historically too. They are festive, happy occasions when the whole family can take a rest from work to chant, meditate and not do any harm, an activity which is in itself regarded as beneficial. The atmosphere on such days is magical, complicated and relaxed, all at the same time. People make offerings of butter lamps and flowers, light incense sticks, cook and offer food, chant, chat, eat in a leisurely way, ask monks and nuns questions, meet their friends or just sit and appreciate the atmosphere while listening to talks—and Jātaka stories. It is considered a good time to recharge and take a rest from other activities. The characters in the stories do not have the teaching of a Buddha to help them. Despite this, many keep the *uposatha*, including animals, such as the otter, the monkey, the jackal and the hare in 'The Story of the Hare' (316). The nāga in 'The Story of Campeyya' (506) goes to great lengths to observe it. In 'The Story of Mahājanaka' (539), the Bodhisatta, as a human, does not resort to the hopeless prayers which fail to save his fellow shipmates, but keeps the full-moon day as best he can when swimming for his life after the shipwreck.

There were some obvious social and economic reasons for stressing the first two perfections: people who behave well and act with generosity live together in cooperation, support the *saṅgha*, the community of monks and nuns, and help the continuation of the Buddha's teaching. If they go to temples on *uposatha* days they also contribute to their upkeep. From an individual layman's point of view, the practice of generosity and virtue also brings good *kamma*. It ensures a rebirth in one of the sense-sphere heavens whose beauties and pleasures are particularly associated with the results of such actions in the world. This would bring great reassurance to those who would be listening to the stories, who may have taken time off from busy lives to observe such days. From the evidence of the tales, however, the function of such activities goes far beyond the promise of happiness in this world and the next, important though that is. They also confer a particular kind of inner confidence, as evinced in the Buddha's confrontation with Māra under the Bodhi tree. People who practise generosity and virtue can follow a way of life that is resourceful, creative and attentive to the well-being of others. This is action that is *kusala*, a word that has connotations of goodness, health and skill.[25] It is also sometimes called beautiful (*sobhana*). The one who has this is likely to have skill in means (*kusala upāya*): the ability to act as is appropriate to the moment and conditions of the present. In the first story the skilful merchant, the Bodhisatta, does not follow easy options but reads the situation carefully: his judgment, we are told, is not clouded by greed or hatred. The other merchant, motivated only by greed, makes drastic errors of judgement through lack of skill in means. Likewise, the Bodhisatta, as the sensible pupil in Jātaka 48, strongly recommends against an obvious course of action, able to see the dangers ahead if his teacher employs magical powers without careful forethought. His teacher, however, in terror for his life, uses his great ability at the wrong moment, to disastrous effect. In these instances, lack of skill in means is rather like the Aristotelian notion of error (*hamartia*), the tragic blunder of 'missing the mark', which brings down a peculiarly apt, unhappy outcome.[26] The one who has an unskilful (*akusala*) mind acts inappropriately, at the wrong time and in a constricted, blindly selfish way.

Of course we do not say someone has 'skill' if he or she behaves well; we say he or she is good. In Jātaka terms he or she is can express wisdom and do 'auspicious things' (*puñña*), activities which bring happiness and good luck. For the early Buddhist, however, goodness and a sense of skill in what is wished are linked: the wholesome volition (*cetanā*), or will, is all. 'It is will (*cetanā*), O monks that I call *kamma*; having willed one acts through body, speech or mind'.[27] In Jātakas, when the volition behind an act is not *kusala*, it lacks skill too; it is inept. The wish for immediate gain and gratification is not in accordance with *dhamma* and does not, in the end, produce happiness for anyone. Skilful volition, helped by the conditions of a full-moon day or the presence of those worthy of generosity, gives characters a different perspective on events. It shapes the underlying predisposition of the protagonists so that they have a completely different orientation from those motivated by greed, ill will or vanity. They just have that bit more space. So the Bodhisatta and those that follow his way are, in the stories, what we might call the 'goodies', as opposed to the 'baddies', thus enacting a dynamic we might expect in a film or story now. Included in this is also a more ancient pattern: that of 'the wise man' and 'the foolish man', the lynch pins of traditional folk tale.[28] In the depiction of a clever merchant (1), a skilled teacher (106, 402) and the long-term struggle of a prince avoiding kingship (538), Jātakas combine a portrayal of 'goodness' with the practical wisdom associated with the secular narrative tradition. It is almost a kind of common sense, produced by the skilful volition that is hoped for at a time of a full-moon day but possible at other times too. This produces happiness and, in the end, the path to liberation.

The inherent choice in any situation also gives the underlying orientation of the tales. Any difficulty, however desperate, affords the characters opportunities to exercise volition even when the sphere of action seems limited. One writer praised the way that Jātakas fuse popular beliefs and metaphysics to show how every event has causal links which extend far back into the past. They embody in action the law of *kamma*, whereby 'every being becomes what he makes himself'.[29] A skilful resolve has even greater effect. The Bodhisatta as the monkey king literally makes himself a bridge on which others may cross (407). As Temiya, his curious determination becomes a means of helping others, as he leads the king and his subjects to find happiness in new lands and terrain, in a kind of Buddhist meditative utopia (538). Generosity and virtue do not automatically produce skill in means. Characters who practise them, though, live with good luck and the wishes of the gods in their favour. The worlds of Jātakas are not saccharine or 'unreal': highly varied amongst themselves, they are uncompromising in their description of the risks to health, happiness and life. Fears may be condensed into demonic yakkhas and the uncharted imagination described as wilderness or forest. Human and animal nature are seen at its most stark. According to the Buddhist understanding of the mind, formulated in a series of teachings known as the *abhidhamma*, mindfulness, or alertness, is always present at the moment of appropriate generosity or the wholehearted keeping of the precepts.[30] So characters who act on the first two perfections were regarded in early Buddhism as likely to be just that bit more awake: like the skilled trader in the first story, they are not seduced by easy options and so can take themselves, and others, to safety. For those listening to the stories the implications are clear: the volition made in the present, in our human form, shapes our futures too.

Cosmology and the heavens and hells

Some explanation needs to be given to the cosmological background of early Buddhism, also important in understanding the settings to the tales. In the Buddhist tradition, any rebirth, of any kind, is temporary and the way that characters constantly jostle, speak and interact suggests their consciousness of an underlying affinity between each other. In a Jātaka a human is almost as likely to encounter a yakkha (1, 55) or a shining god (*deva*) as he is another human (316). An animal encountering a human may be killed by him (407) or sometimes have a chat with him, particularly if the animal is the Bodhisatta (385).[31] When the Bodhisatta is an animal he even addresses and admonishes a king (476). This familiarity, both friendly and hostile, between beings from different levels of existence arises out of a curious sense of proximity between all realms of existence in the Jātaka tales. Unlike later Sanskrit drama, which differentiates between the language of the court and the dialects of commoners, all beings in Jātakas speak the same language: there is no difference between the vernacular Pāli of a god or an animal and either is as likely to speak in verse.[32] Each realm of existence, however, is separate and each has its own rules. There are in all thirty-one realms where existence may occur and beings move between them according to their *kamma*. The realms encompass the whole range of possible experience, from the most painful and terrifying punishments of the Niraya and the Ussada hells up to the highest heaven. Lifespans tend to be very long at the lowest and highest levels of the spectrum. Yet, they do not last forever, but are subject to the law of impermanence too. There is something of a 'snakes and ladders' aspect to all kinds of bodily form. However low or elevated its status, and however long or short the lifespan, the balance that sustains any existence is fragile and subject, like all things, to decay. The stories enact the possibilities inherent in this over aeons of time: the Buddha's disciples, for instance, are often born together with the Bodhisatta, as animals or men. Their *kamma* is knitted together by their search for enlightenment in different spheres of existence.

The four lowest realms below the human are the bad destinies (*dugatiyo*), or 'descents' as they are sometimes called, where beings are reborn for unskilful action, such as breaking the five precepts (see 55). These realms are the animal kingdom, the realm of ghosts (*petas*), the realm of jealous gods (*asuras*) and the hells. Lower existences include the edgy, hungry monsters that live in some wildernesses (1), lakes (20) or woods (55). They also include the realms where the Bodhisatta lives as a mouse, a deer, a goose and as a nāga, technically a lower rebirth. The Bodhisatta, in order to complete his great vow and to fulfil the perfections, is born in the animal kingdom many times and is constantly tested in different forms and environments. Although they are lower births, such bodily forms impart to the collection, and hence to the Bodhisatta vow, some of its greatest beauty and animation. As a monkey, he is deft and nimble (407), as a goose spectacularly swift in flight (476) and as a mouse clever and quick (128). We do not see him reborn in a hell, though he recollects such a rebirth (538). According to Buddhist theory, beings in animal realms do not take rebirth with the full potential of the skilful mind.[33] Jātakas, however, do not direct our attention to their misfortune, but to their vitality in providing ground for drama, possibility and satiric humour. It is because the animal realms constitute unfortunate destinies that a compassionate Bodhisatta is reborn in them, in order to understand. Only when the first stage of enlightenment, stream-entry, has been obtained is rebirth in such lower realms impossible (See 'A true story', 1).

Above the human realm are the sense-sphere heavens, the homes of the shining gods ('devas', from root *div*, to shine).[34] Beings are reborn here for acts of generosity and keeping the five precepts. These gods, a bit like those of other polytheistic societies such as ancient Greece and Rome, live a life marked by pleasure and good living. They like to preside over and intervene in the affairs of men, and animals too, though in the Buddhist tradition this is almost always with benign intent, in accordance with the good *kamma* that has brought about their fortunate rebirth. The realm of the Four Great Kings is associated with protection: the kings from that realm are said to guard each

direction when, for instance, the refuges and precepts are chanted
by a Buddhist practitioner (539). Sakka, the king of the Heaven
of the Thirty-Three gods, is likewise alerted when any great act
of virtue is taking place in realms below. When his seat becomes
hot, as when the hare is about to offer his own body (316) or the
queen about to become lost in 'The story of Mahājanaka' (539),
he sometimes visits in disguise to ensure that no harm is done.
Above the sense-sphere heavens are the Brahma or form realms,
where beings are reborn according to their skills in meditation
and the divine abidings (*brahmavihāra*s), the meditations on loving
kindness, compassion, sympathetic joy and equanimity. The
heavens give us an enactment of the deep contentment and calm
(*samatha*) of meditation. They are described in an ascending
sequence that follows closely the pattern of the four *jhānas*, or
stages of meditation.[35] The meditations are described as possessing
specific mental factors: initial thought, sustained thought, joy,
happiness and one-pointedness, features that characterize the
heavens too. As each level is attained, factors are dropped, so
that at the highest only one-pointedness remains. Each Brahma
god fills a universe with his mind and lives for many aeons. Brahma
gods possess only the senses of sight and hearing, and so exist
without the need to search for food. Above these are the four
formless *jhānas* of the formless sphere, where beings exist without
any bodily form at all. The Bodhisatta is, however, never reborn
here as his lifespan would just be too long, even by the standards
of Ancient Indians, who cheerfully included vast, unimaginable
aeons in their estimation of time. The higher the heaven the
greater the lifespan, which can last for many *kalpa*s in the higher
heavens. Despite this, the span of life is always impermanent.

The greatest importance, however, is attached to one realm:
the highly mixed world of humans, where beings are reborn on
the basis of the skilful mind (*kusala citta*) but where the greatest
variety of activities, both for good and ill, is possible. Poised

between the heavens and the bad destinies, it is the meeting place
for beings from other realms and the ground for the greater part
of the action. It is the lowest rung of the realms that constitute
a fortunate destiny (*sugati*). It is also the rightful place for the
Bodhisatta, as the form of existence where he makes his initial
vow.[36] All Buddhas are said to be reborn human, for this rebirth,
neither too happy nor too painful, offers the best conditions for
enlightenment. Because of the mixed nature of this realm, the
beautiful, skilful mind (*kusala citta*) has its greatest scope and
range in this existence. The mind of a human is said to be naturally
radiant, but covered by defilements and difficulties, which are
the 'grit' for the spiritual life.[37] Sense-sphere gods also take rebirth
on the basis of this skilful mind but have too easy and happy
an existence. Their bodily form gives them little experience of
physical pain; their birth and death are spontaneous and they
lead immensely long, leisured lives. They do not grow old.
Therefore, despite their love of *dhamma* discussions and the
inevitability of an—often rather abrupt—end to their sojourn in
a heaven realm, they have little motivation to make progress on
the spiritual path.[38] The animal and other lower realms are fraught
with the hunt for food and the dangers of being eaten, killed, hunted
down, or captured. Animals live in bodies and under conditions
that are fundamentally unsuitable for the full practice of the path.
While this is rarely stated in Jātakas where the Bodhisatta is an
animal, the Bodhisatta says so himself in Jātaka 55, when he is a
human. He also notes this, with some sadness, in those rebirths
where he is another lower form, a nāga, a semi-serpent creature
who lives below the waters. The nāga king in the Campeyya Jātaka
(506) cannot live in the world of men: 'Lord of men, nowhere
but in the world of humans is there purity and self-control. When
I have attained a human rebirth I will make an end to birth and
death' (506, v 39). Naturally enough, our attention in the animal
stories is on the Bodhisatta's heroism or kindness: when in animal

or nāga form he is noble, dignified, delivers *dhamma* talks (476), is generous (316) and observes the *uposatha* day (316, 506). He even ensures honour to the eldest (37). In Jātakas, however, the rules that govern lower forms of existence are scrupulously, if unobtrusively, observed. At no time does the Bodhisatta, as an animal, use his body for the practice of meditation (*jhāna*).

For it is this feature above all that really marks out the realm of humans. A human being has the best bodily form for balanced spiritual growth. He or she can choose to sit under a tree, or in an empty place, cross his or her legs and practise both meditative absorption and insight. A human can experience all the meditation states possible for the development of the mind. This is something no animal can do, despite the great strength, swiftness, deftness and vigour of various animal forms. Animals have the potential for higher rebirths but cannot become enlightened in the form they are. The gods are limited in other ways. The sense-sphere heavens embody the delights of keeping the precepts and generosity. In Jātaka stories, however, the gods of the sense sphere are having too much fun to sit in meditation. The Brahma heavens, the destinies of those who practise meditation as humans, do, it is true, enact the joys of pure *samatha* meditation. The formless beings, higher than these, enact the still higher stages of the formless meditations, the higher *jhāna*s. The problem with existence on the meditative levels is its very blissfulness. Beings reborn there have little grounds for insight—the wisdom granted by understanding the three signs of existence, impermanence (*anicca*), suffering or unsatisfactoriness (*dukkha*) and not-self (*anattā*). Neither do they have routine ways of helping and interacting with other less fortunate creatures. So the Buddhism of Jātakas constantly stresses the great gift of the thoroughly mundane conditions of what would have been the present rebirth of its audience. In the *suttas*, it is compared, for instance, to sitting in the shade under a tree on a hot day, the classic conditions for meditative practice.[39] The ascetic in the Mahājanaka Jātaka (539) reminds the Bodhisatta, 'Sleep, laziness, weariness, discontent, drowsiness from food: for the one living in the bodily frame, there are many dangers' (v 133). The human needs to obtain food from somewhere, to eat, and then gets a bit sleepy or discontent when he or she has eaten too much. It is precisely because the highest heavens, beautiful though they are and worthy destinations in themselves, do not feel the goad of these problems that they do not encourage real change.

The interplay between realms as enactments of mental states can be seen by looking at the famous story of Makhādeva (9). As a human with the most fortunate kind of existence, he has an extended lifespan very like that of the gods and a regal life, like theirs, marked by enjoyment and play. As a king, he would be addressed by everyone as 'deva', or 'god'. Unlike gods, however, he has plenty of time to notice his grey hairs and see in them a mark of change. His is a paradigm of lucky existence: but he ends it with a common and natural conclusion to a Jātaka story in that he leaves the lay life for the practice of the *jhānas*. This is not an existential denial of the world but is perceived as a way of entering into it further. Exploration of the mind—so neatly and commonly expressed in Indian thought by the idea of forests and wilderness— is seen as a kind of adventure, or a pursuit proper to one who is truly human. We are told that his next rebirth, as a result of this, is in a Brahma heaven: but the real aim of the stories rests in the pattern of constant rebirth in the tales and enlightenment, the conclusion and end to the Jātakas as a whole. Different realms map out the bodily implications of different states of mind and their effects. Rebirth in Brahma heavens is essential for the Bodhisatta as a way of exploring different areas of experience and building up the reserves of calm (*samatha*) necessary to teach others. The human world, the measure and basis of them all, is, however, the one to which he nearly always returns. All mental states can be experienced here—and hence understood. Most Jātaka stories feature the Bodhisatta in this form.

It is clear that a vast and spacious universe of many different levels forms the landscape of the action of Jātakas. The workings of *kamma*, and the conditions that govern rebirth in different realms and different kinds of bodily form, are explored in complex and intricate detail through the events of the stories. These realms embody the possibilities of many forms of meditation and different kinds of behaviour. They are in many senses physical extrapolations—one could even say explorations—of mental states. Beings seem to create around themselves not only their mode of existence but the realms they live in too. Each realm was, however, felt to have ontological status. Each has an independent existence and contains creatures which all ancient— and many modern—Buddhists would believe were actually there. At *dāna*s and *uposatha* festivals blessings are chanted to this day to encourage the goodwill of the sense-sphere gods and to extend merit, good fortune and loving kindness to any gods, animals, spirits or ghosts that may be nearby. The *Mettā Sutta*, which extends loving kindness to all beings, whatever their rebirth, is usually chanted.[40] Jātakas, recounted at such events, are vivid and precise in their exploration of the mind through imagery and symbol that derive from many realms. The stories are not just psychological voyages, however. For someone hearing the stories in such a context, the realms are what they are. A god would really be a god, reborn there for past good *kamma*; a demon, a demon reborn there for his bad, and a cat, a cat, for his failure to keep the precepts, such as not killing other beings. In Jātakas animals, gods and men have different bodies: all, however, deserve respect and can in time find their way to enlightenment too.

Folkloric stereotypes

Within the stories there is a great deal of the stereotyping characteristic of traditional folklore. As is often pointed out, women, for instance, can be a bad lot in the Jātakas. They plot, betray (402), henpeck husbands (106) and lure men away from their true purpose in life (539). While there are many virtuous and highly individualized female characters in the stories the underlying ethos, of the shorter ones at any rate, is that women are problematic. A few things could be said about this. First, we need to remember that the tales evolved around Indian folk traditions where certain conventions and stereotypes would have shaped the way all social groups—and animal species for that matter—behave. In this, they are like the conventions of modern story and cinema. I have met Americans who complain that everyone thinks that people from their nation are fast-talking gangsters; English people feel they are always depicted as ludicrously polite aristocrats. In his introduction to the *Pañcatantra* stories, a collection whose stories have some affinities with the shorter Jātakas, Patrick Olivelle has described the way in which different kinds of behaviour are associated with various animal species.[41] A cat in Indian folktale is likely to be a hypocrite, as is the one in Jātaka 128; a monkey playful and cheeky, like the one in Jātaka 273. Such typecasting extends to the human realm. Brahmins in the *Pañcatantra*, as in many Jātakas (402), are often weak, hypocritical comic butts. They are likely to find that their wives are unfaithful or dissatisfied with them in bed. Both sets of stories also suggest that women are fickle, treacherous and sexually voracious: it is just how women in Indian folk tales are.

In practice this stereotype is often transcended and in many stories events are transformed by the saving presence of female characters. Kindly local goddesses often feature: Maṇimekhalā,

a sea deity, forgets her duties for a bit while having fun with a
group of gods, but after seven days her eye alights upon the
Bodhisatta in time to save him from death (539). The goddess
of the Gandhamādana Mountains, Bahusodarī, also forgetful in
her enjoyment of divine bliss, intercedes to save the Bodhisatta,
her son in an earlier existence (540). The goddess that lives in
the royal white parasol (538) is like a wise fairy godmother that
presides over the years of Temiya's grim battle against the
assumption of kingship. On a human level, Temiya's mother in
Jātaka 538 is movingly portrayed, in her bewildered despair at
her son's continued failure to respond to the world. Even the
badly dressed fat lady who becomes a great queen (108) shows
down-to-earth virtues of cleanliness and organization. The past
lives of the Bodhisatta's consort, however, give us the richest
depiction of female motive. In the conclusions of the stories, she
is called, somewhat anonymously and mysteriously, Rāhulamātā,
the mother of Rāhula, Gotama's son in his last life. In the stories
in the past, she appears as Sīvalī, Sumanā and the queen of
Mahāsudassana. Although we cannot assume that a single
authorial intent shapes the diversity of her depiction in various
tales, she is usually a sympathetic character.[42] She is, nonetheless,
no saccharine spouse or the ancient equivalent of a cardboard
cut-out figure. In many tales, she is highly individual, resourceful
and sometimes tempestuous: indeed, her behaviour must have
brought plenty of fireworks to enliven aeons of unfailing loyalty
to her partner. As Sīvalī (539) she is bossy and 'princess' like, in
the worst possible sense, while choosing her husband; then
excessively brahminical in her disdain for leftover food in the
final stages of the tale. She is also capable of great deceit in her
tricks to lure the Bodhisatta back to his kingdom. She is described,
however, as being of great wisdom and accomplishment. She
manages, in a number of ways, to lead her husband to the kingdom
and in these, and the eloquence of her final pleas for his return,

speaks as a moving and glorious embodiment of the splendour of Mithilā, and indeed the lay life itself. As Mahāsudassana's wife (94), she agrees with simple nobility to help her husband leave his kingdom at his death. As Sumanā, a seductive nāga, she latches onto the Bodhisatta on his entry into the nāga's subterranean world (506). Nonetheless, she also goes in pursuit of him to appear, goddess-like, interceding on his behalf with the king and so rescuing him from imprisonment by a snake charmer. In this story she, like the Bodhisatta, fleetingly escapes her watery rebirth, and, in a curiously memorable image, stands next to him for a moment, as a human and his equal, on the solid earth of the human realm, their proper home. In his last life she was said to have been born on the same day as he and to exhibit qualities of great excellence herself.[43] In none of the stories is she unfaithful to him. When fully enlightened he returns to teach her what he has found and she becomes a nun too: this culmination of her long association with him would also be known to those who heard the tales.[44]

This rounded sensitivity in the characterization of some female characters is in part a reflection of other genres that share features with Jātakas, such as Indian epic and drama, where heroines also reveal great warmth, emotional stature and complexity. The Buddhist tradition did, however, differ from others of the time in its treatment of women. The Buddha, like Mahāvira, the founder of Jainism, admitted women into monastic orders and founded the sisterhood of nuns. According to the theory and accounts of the practice of early Buddhism, both women and men were thought able to attain enlightenment in this life, a supposition in striking contrast to the ideas underlying other religious traditions, such as the Digambara Jains. The verses associated with the early nuns give us some of the world's most ancient religious poetry composed by women.[45] Buddhist texts include many talks given by nuns, often to men, which are endorsed by the Buddha.[46] This attitude can be seen in Jātakas too: women are, like men, free moral agents and they too are reborn in heavens and lower rebirths according to their *kamma*.

There is a real sense of the diversity of all human and animal nature that is found in the tales. In Jātakas stereotypes do not predominate. Monkeys can be mischievous (273) but the Bodhisatta as monkey king saves his own tribe by his fearless courage (407), for instance. Animal, men and women characters behave badly but in many cases they rise above their limitations too. No species has the upper hand in terms of villainy. The exception to this is perhaps the male human, for whom the range of evil possible seems more comprehensive and calculated than in any animal rebirth. King Kalābu, an earlier rebirth of Devadatta, the Buddha's jealous cousin (313), is particularly vicious and vengeful, as he is in his last life. There is a crucial counterweight to this: the Bodhisatta is always male and a Buddha always a man. Within the limits felt to confine the male and the female bodily form, however, both sexes in Jātakas reveal themselves as multifaceted. Women, it is true, are often as full of dubious undercurrents and tidal waves of emotion as the ocean of *saṃsāra* itself. As we see in the stories, they do sometimes embody or dimly apprehend a way to freedom too.

Geography and history

The settings for the stories are in the area around the Ganga basin, the geographical location for the origins of the Buddhist tradition. The most common location for a tale in the past is Vārāṇasi. This is often at the time of a king called Brahmadatta, but this seems to be a formulaic opening, and the regal name possibly just a familial label for any king of Vārāṇasi. Cities such as Mithilā and Kusinārā also feature. Taxilā, in Gandhāra, is often mentioned as a centre of learning and pupils seem to have attached themselves to teachers there. This is about thirty kilometres from modern Islamabad and was, historically, home to artisans, scholars, craftsmen and merchants. Characters visit Taxilā in the stories to acquire skills in magic, as is the case in 'The Vedabbha mantra story' (48), or martial arts, as in 'The story of five weapons' (55). The social order conforms to the traditional Indian pattern of four castes: the brahmin or priestly caste, the warrior or *khattiya* caste, the merchant class, the *vessa*, and the lowest caste, the *sudda*. Within his community of monks and nuns, the Buddha ignored caste, taking seniority as a rule of thumb for precedence (37). An important social distinction is made between ascetics and laypeople. Holy men or ascetics seem to have been a feature of Indian life for centuries and the pattern of the movement from the life of a householder to that of *sannyāsin* well established. The Himālayas often feature as the destination of those that wish to pursue spiritual practice in this way (99, 539 and 540).

We do not divine much in the way of a chronology or historical dating from the tales, which were not intended, nor can be seen, as literal records of dates and events. As social documents, however, Jātakas are constantly illuminating. Incidental detail about food, buildings, clothes, social mores and law have made them one of our principal sources of information about the assumptions and practices of ancient India around two thousand years ago. To an interested reader they give an abundance of details about coins, clothes, shoes, decorations, jewels, cloth, hairdressing, food, cooking, provisions, flags, weapons, punishments, vehicles, animals, items considered luxurious, travel, childcare, street life, customs concerning meals, the life of the court, shows, music, ways of address, formalities of interchange, structures of city and palace and attitudes to woods, parks, pools, wildernesses and different parts of the countryside. We cannot necessarily date these features of the tales, or differentiate between those that are

fabular and those that would have been everyday. They do provide
us, though, with a pretty full sense of what a certain group of
ancient Indians hoped for, liked and disliked at some point
around the time of their composition.

Text and authorship

This brings us to the question of dates and authors, subjects on
which ancient Indology can seem bewilderingly vague. Why are
texts not given a year of composition of the kind we can fix to
ancient Greek texts of the same period? Why are some dismissed
as 'late' and some cited as 'early', an apparent term of approbation?
Although some form of the texts were settled in the councils
after the Buddha's death, they do not seem to have been fixed
at that time and were not committed to writing.[47] So they are
multilayered, full of accretions and reworkings inserted sometime
during the period of transmission. Sorting out what is original
and what is a modification is tricky. The difficulty is compounded
by the fact that in Pāli texts early strata are inevitably viewed
with favour as being closer to an original form and hence the
formulation of the teaching given by the Buddha himself. For
Jātakas a clear assignation of dates is even more problematic as
we know even less about how they were handed down than we do
about other early Buddhist texts. Most scholars would agree that
some of the verses are very old indeed. They could be adaptations
of material that predates Buddhism and other canonical Pāli
texts. The latest date for any of the texts is the third century CE.
Between these parameters there is much room for manoeuvre:
archaeological evidence such as Bhārhut and Ajantā indicates
that stories like Jātakas were around from the first or second
century BCE, though we do not know what form they took. The
text that is usually taken for the stories, the *Jātaka aṭṭhakathā*,

is a combination of some extracts from the commentary which provide a prose narrative and the verses, many, though perhaps not all, of which are very early. The verses do not make sense without some prose sections as well, so there must have been some sort of story associated with them from the start.[48] The commentary is also not story alone, as there are all sorts of glosses, explanations, changes, interjections and curious asides in the ancient Indian commentarial manner. It could include features that are very old, but have just become subsumed in later material. These factors make for very complex problems. The stories, however, have at least survived. In the nineteenth century the courageous Danish scholar Fausbøll sifted through all of the material and produced the story text we have now, distinguishing it from commentary by putting this in larger type. As we have seen in 'A note on the text', he himself acknowledges the shortcomings of this approach.

For these reasons authorship is also a complete unknown when dealing with Jātakas: the Buddha is said to narrate the tales, but others from the time of the councils must have composed at least the sections in the third person. Much of the prose has been attributed to the fifth-century commentator, Buddhaghosa, although the subject is still under debate.[49] The composition of the stories and the language of the verses show signs of careful construction but we do not know who was responsible for this. At any rate, if the stories did evolve over a long period, aesthetic and spiritual considerations seem to have shaped this process, perhaps as the tales were told for different audiences. As we have seen, distinct genres can be discerned within different tales, often shaped and governed by length. Shorter tales, with a single verse, follow a pattern we associate with Aesopic fables, culminating in a pithy folk aphorism. Longer Jātakas include set interchanges and verse dialogues that anticipate Indian epic and heroic drama. Many stories exhibit a sense of theatre and a subtlety of construction throughout: changes would not simply be the result of a need for additional doctrinal information or to fulfil a didactic intent. Stories that continue to be told grow, shrink, acquire new slants and develop occasional embellishments in accordance with new historical developments or the creative input of the narrator. This certainly seems to be the case for Jātakas: the problem is that we just do not have the information to find out how this occurred, which elements are innovatory, or who was responsible for any changes.

It is remarkable how little Jātakas changed over a long period. There are certainly differences between details described in the verses, the early layer of the text, and the narrative, an indicator of some sort of evolution, but given the centuries involved in their development these are surprisingly minimal.[50] It seems likely that many hands were involved in the evolution of their transmission. Perhaps some added comments or elaborated a piece of dialogue or description for effect until the form finally became fixed. If the texts were handed down by the order of monks, all of those contributing would have felt they were conforming to the spirit of the teaching. So in reading Jātakas the use of terms such as 'early' and 'late' need not be associated with a value judgement. Some features that are apparently late, such as the delineation of each of the perfections, have added considerably to the success of the collection as a whole.

Choice of stories

The link with the perfections is essential to an understanding of the stories and seems to have been a crucial factor in shaping the composition of many. As only a selection of all 547 can be included here I have chosen twenty-six stories, with at least one story that is linked in one ancient source to each perfection. This policy was suggested by an excellent short Pāli reader that I.B. Horner translated for the Pāli Text Society (PTS), some years ago, which gives just ten short tales or extracts from longer ones, one representing each.[51] In many cases the attributions are also generally accepted throughout most traditions (316 for generosity, 506 for virtue, 9 for renunciation, 402 for wisdom, 55 and 539 for effort, 313 for forbearance, 75 for truth, 538 for resolve, 540 for loving kindness). The last perfection, of equanimity, is represented by two very different stories (94 and 273). Choosing a good sample from a collection of so many is next to impossible, so in addition to this I aimed for stories to make the anthology reasonably varied. The first is a key story in the collection as a whole, in its depiction of a journey across a wilderness, steered and rescued by the skill within the means of the Bodhisatta. 'The story of the partridge' (37) gives a rule of thumb for precedence that is employed by Buddhist *sangha* to this day. 'The Vedabbha mantra story' (48) is particularly important for the history of the transportation of folk motifs and themes as it corresponds so closely to tales found in Chaucer and in *The Thousand Nights and a Night*, both written over fifteen hundred years later. 'The story of the monkey king' (407) has always been amongst the most popular tales. Two of the stories show the Jātakas at their most down-to-earth (106 and 108). 'The story of the swift goose' (476) was chosen for the way that the plot, with the crucial interchange between the king and the goose, is informed by a distinctively Buddhist understanding of the nature of mind and matter. The last three in this collection (538, 539 and 540) are the first of the final ten stories. With their extended poetic comment, eulogies and theatrical interchanges between characters on centre stage, the last ten have a different weight and feel from earlier stories. As so many temples around South-East Asia have depictions of these, and of many of the other stories, sites where there are murals, pictures or friezes that depict a particular Jātaka are noted in the discussion that introduces each tale. Stories have also been chosen that are depicted in major Buddhist sites in India (see Appendix C).

The Pāli canon and other related texts

Jātakas are regarded as one of what are called the nine limbs of the Buddha's teaching.[52] The rest of the canon need not be discussed here in detail, but some words should be said about the texts involved to place the collection in its context. The main body of early Buddhist texts is divided into three 'baskets'. These are the *Vinayapiṭaka*, the rules for monks, the *Abhidhammapiṭaka*, the higher philosophy, and the *Suttapiṭaka*, texts concerning particular occasions and incidents where teachings are given by the Buddha. The latter is composed primarily of the four *nikāyas*, the *sutta*s of middle length (*Majjhimanikāya*), the long ones (*Dīghanikāya*), the gradual *sutta*s, arranged by means of number (*Aṅguttaranikāya*), and the connected *sutta*s (*Saṃyuttanikāya*). The Jātaka verses are part of the *Khuddakanikāya*, another branch of the *sutta*s. All of these texts are in Pāli and regarded as 'canonical', part of the early strata of texts purportedly composed at the councils held in the years after the Buddha's death. At these meetings the texts were committed to memory: different groups of *bhāṇaka*s, or chanters, were assigned different collections. Inevitably, each collection acquired, or had from the outset, its own distinctive features and emphases.[53] It is generally presumed that Jātaka verses were transmitted in this way but we have no direct evidence of this.

Other related texts are useful for understanding the context of Jātakas. The *Apadāna*s, a closely related genre, provide verse accounts of the previous lives of the arahats. *The Story of Gotama Buddha* (*Jātakanidāna*), the introduction to the Jātakas, gives an account of the Buddha taking the Bodhisatta vow, his decision to develop the ten perfections and his life story in his last life, as Gotama, in which that vow is fulfilled. It also associates some Jātakas with each of the ten perfections. *The Basket of Conduct* (*Cariyāpiṭaka*), a late canonical work, relates some of the incidents of the Jātakas to the first seven perfections.[54] These texts, with their discussion of different perfections, can throw some helpful lights on the stories themselves. All of them share the same heritage as the Jātaka stories: many stories are duplicated in them, at least in essentials, and incidents which feature in *suttas* from the major *nikāyas*, for example, often provide the basis of the story from the present. It seems that Jātakas were, from the early days of Buddhism, absorbed into the practice tradition and possibly influenced by it too.

Historically, the tales spread quickly and exerted considerable influence on other storytelling traditions. Buddhism's energetic dissemination around the East can be traced in a trail of Jātakas or tales derived from them. Jātakas feature in the Sanskrit *Jātakamālā* collection, and are told in various forms in Burmese, Chinese, Khotanese, Sinhalese, Sogdian, Tibetan and Tocharian.[55] Their popularity was not confined to Buddhist contexts. Many are found in the eighth-century Persian stories of *Kalilag and Damnag* (Kalilah and Dimnah). In Europe, subsequent retellings or variants of the tales can be found in the works of Boccaccio, Poggio, La Fontaine, Chaucer and Shakespeare.[56] Perhaps the most curious quirk of history for Jātakas in the West was the way their hero was absorbed into Christian folklore. 'Josaphat of India' (Bodhisatta), whose adventures are recounted as *Barlaam and Josaphat* by the seventh-century St John of Damascus, was eventually canonized as a Christian saint.[57]

Language

A word should be said about the language and history of Jātakas. Pāli is probably not the dialect or language of the Buddha, who appears to have spoken an early form of what is known as 'Middle Indo-Aryan'. Jātakas as a whole, including the commentarial prose sections, are regarded as canonical 'Pāli' despite the less authoritative status the tradition has accorded to the later prose parts of the text. It is difficult to communicate the quality of the language in a text in translation. The vocabulary of Jātakas tends to be more Sanskritic than other Pāli texts, partly because the subject matter depends less on technical Buddhist terms. The style of the prose itself is simple. Because it is possible in Pāli, as in Sanskrit, to link a number of consecutive actions by a string of participles that culminate with one main active verb, the prose contains some very long sentences that impart a great deal of information. Many important narrative events, perhaps separated by years, can all be strung together: so the first sentence of a tale may include the birth, childhood and early training of the Bodhisatta over a period of sixteen years. Conversely, a single sentence can include a whole series of actions that take place in a split second, as in the shooting of the arrows in Jātaka 476. Unfortunately, these sentences need to be divided into several shorter ones for translation, so some of the effect is inevitably lost. Sometimes sentences at key points in the action are very short, with one subject, one active verb and one object. This all contributes to a very varied and lively narrative style, suggesting that considerable skill was involved in creating the aesthetic balance which lends Jātaka prose its distinctive nature; it is not really possible to translate this well. The verses often use archaic and poetic forms. They do not rhyme, but are distinguished not only by the choice of language but by the use of metre, an effect that also cannot really be recreated in translation. I have not tried to put the verses into English rhyme or verse form but have numbered them to show where they occur.

Another problem for a translator is created by a tendency towards the repetitive use of language, characteristic of oral literature: the same word can be reused in a way that a modern writer would avoid at all costs. This poses difficulties. It is a convention in the translation of Buddhist texts that the same translation for each word is used each time it occurs. For *sutta*s and technical passages, which require precision in the use of terms, this consistency is sometimes essential. In storytelling and for common words denoting speech such a policy does not always work. In Jātaka 48 the word *dhana* or wealth occurs about thirty-two times. It is only a short story, and it simply is not natural in narrative English to use the same word so many times, so a few variations are used: riches, booty, treasure, wealth, etc. The way speech is treated also needs a bit of adjustment. Frequent occurrences of the words 'he said' or 'she said' are irksome in translation. Plenty of alternatives such as 'reply', 'narrate', 'tell', 'speak' and 'invite' need to be used so that it does not sound boring for the modern reader. The name of the speaker also sometimes needs to be inserted at a late point in the dialogue just to remind me, and I expect the reader too, who is saying what: perhaps ancient Indians had a better memory in this regard than we do.

Some Buddhist terms needed consideration. The word *dhamma* has an immense range of meanings and no English word does it justice. As the second quality of the Triple Gem, the teaching of the Buddha, it is used in a special way, as the teaching given and left behind by him in his last life, which leads to freedom. In Jātakas it also means a more general kind of spiritual and moral teaching, for the period when there is no Buddha. In both these cases the original word has often been kept. In the end 'a *dhamma* talk' (*dhammadesanā*) is just a better translation for a book for a general readership than 'a discourse on the teaching', which sounds a little forbidding. For the hall where the monks meet I have also kept the word and called it a *dhamma* hall: 'teaching' does not cover all the activities that probably went on there, such as chanting and private meditation, and 'assembly' does not really carry the same emotional weight such a place would have had for those who used it. Other meanings of the word are also evident in the stories. Sometimes *dhamma* is simply 'what is right' or 'justice' and in this sense accords with the ancient Indian concept of dharma. It can mean 'how things are' or even just 'things': to leave it untranslated in some such cases would be to lend it a weight that the context does not justify. Another word that is used occasionally in this translation is 'bhikkhu', for a Buddhist monk. This has been translated as 'monk' in the narrative and third person contexts as this is much simpler for a reader new to the term to feel comfortable with the actions of the stories. It has been kept for address, however, as it seems a shame to lose it altogether. The word 'bhante', still used in addressing a single monk, is also retained. I hope that this sort of compromise, which does not exclude the use of these Pāli terms completely, gives a bit of variation in the stories and helps to make them easier for a newcomer to Buddhism to read. There is a glossary at the end for translations of some key words.

Pāli texts are sometimes discussed in the introductory essays to the stories for parallels and explanations of features of Jātaka stories. Because there are now at least two good translations for some of the collections it has become confusing for someone new to the study of early Buddhism to work out which modern translation of any collection of *sutta*s refers to which text. So each has been annotated with reference to the Pāli text. In order to help a newcomer to the subject there is an explanation of how to look up translations and texts in the Bibliography.

Reading the stories now

On the night of his enlightenment, the Buddha, with his mind finally freed, saw the succession of his past lives: 'When my concentrated mind was thus purified, bright, unblemished, rid of imperfection, malleable, wieldy, steady, and attained to imperturbability, I directed it to the knowledge of the recollection of past lives . . . This was the first true knowledge attained by me in the first watch of the night.'[58] We might not remember, or even believe that there were, past lives in the technical sense it is used here. The metaphor is a useful one, however, to describe the potential hidden from us in our present human condition. Telling stories about our past is an activity of the human mind, irrespective of time and place. For the modern reader the dynamic established in Jātaka tales is like the relationship we all have with our own oddly assorted memories and influences that contribute to what we are. We make accounts of our past 'lives' and 'selves' in this lifetime, and try and understand them from the perspective of the present. How can we interpret them in a more spacious way, that does not reduce motive to thwarted drives described in post-Freudian terms, or assign 'blame' to a single event in our childhood development? As in the stories in this collection, the present moment provides the creative chance for those described within the stories as hearing them from the Buddha himself: it is where contact with *dhamma*, the truth, can revive stories in the memory and makes some form of illumination and change possible. The Jātakas challenge us to relate our pasts to ourselves from an entirely different perspective.

As some modern philosophers have observed, the Buddhist teaching of 'not-self' does not so much teach the absence of any kind of self, but an absence of what could be called a permanent, isolated self.[59] The Bodhisatta, by his very movement within different types of existence, enacts this teaching through a new

identity that is defined and 'perfected' by the conditions of each
new testing ground in which he is born. Each new story presents
a new set of governing conditions under which he needs to work
and a way of finding what could be called an authentic self,
created in the moment of his ancient vow to become a Bodhisatta.
This is the teaching that as modern readers we can divine from
the stories, whatever we might feel about the doctrine of rebirth
from life to life. The tales, popular in peasant cultures where loss
of various kinds would be endemic, could well have been told at
all times of great grief and deprivation.[60] Abstract consideration
of the three marks of existence, change (*anicca*), suffering (*dukkhā*)
and not-self (*anattā*), would not always help someone who had
lost a family member or suffered a great setback. The Buddhist
position is not that we do not have a self: most of us feel that we
do. It is that self is created and governed by the choices that face
us in our present, moving and unsatisfactory conditions. Selfhood,
impermanent as it is, is defined by what we are, what we do and
free will. If we choose to be 'unskilful' and think only for advantage
or gain, our choices are limited. The skilful volition (*kusalā cetanā*)
creates new possibilities that can bring happiness and benefit to
ourselves and others. At a time of death, sorrow or indeed of
great personal joy, reminders of selflessness, enacted through
stories such as the monkey who saves his tribe (407) or the young
man who cares for his parents (540), embody Buddhist doctrine
for those who listen to them. They show what it is like not to
have a constricted view of what we are and can be, and to extend
that awareness to include other beings too.

Early Buddhists perceived the universe in their own image.
Gods, men and animals speak with human voice in the stories
and act with motives explained in human terms. The characters
in Jātakas inhabit an intricately meshed network of almost familial
relationships. They are constantly interacting with each other,
discussing their problems and giving advice on how to live. Each

has a solitary destiny of endless cycles of birth and death: but by sharing this they form patterns within a community, repeatedly meeting and finding earlier companions as they take rebirth in different places and various kinds of forms. Links between characters extend far back into the past; events tend to recur as old habits are repeated in later lifetimes. Underneath it all is the assumption of the Jātakas that each being lives as an independent locus of consciousness, capable of choice and of finding enlightenment for him- or herself. It was an unusual and even revolutionary idea at the time. After reading a few Jātakas the universe seems very large: full of birds, cats, fish and deer, unseen presences and humans in all kinds of conditions, each with their own consciousness and destiny to fulfil. The great compassion of the Buddha in the stories is that he does not teach as an outsider, separated from this living network. By describing himself 'in the past', as Bodhisatta, he demonstrates his own participation in these conditions and gives hundreds of instances of how to be free within them. At the end of each story he brings this understanding to the present and reveals his own identity. It is like walking into a Buddhist temple, past the stories of Jātakas shown on the walls. Different selves lead in the end to a human form, the embodiment of stillness in the presence of many. This is the heart of each story too: the place of the Buddha, the knower of all worlds, freed at last from any grasping after false ego, or 'I'-making (ahaṃkāra), at all.

Notes

[1] Translated by N.A. Jayawickrama as *The Story of Gotama Buddha* (Oxford: PTS, 1990). An extract from the *Jātakanidāna* has been translated as a preface to this collection.

[2] Traditions vary as to how many Buddhas there have been before the present one. The *Mahāpadāna sutta* describes six with Gotama as a seventh (D II 1–41); Sri Lankan tradition holds that there have been

twenty-four, with Gotama as a twenty-fifth. The Bodhisatta is often painted in temples paying respects to them all, in the various forms he was at each time, ranging from human prince to a nāga. A South-East Asian chant pays homage to twenty-eight Buddhas, including the present one. The Buddha-to-be, Maiteyya, is common to all traditions, and is said to be waiting for his final birth in the Tusita heaven.

³ This culminates in the final and most famous rebirth as Vessantara. This story is translated in Margaret Cone and R. F. Gombrich, *The Perfect Generosity of Prince Vessantara: A Buddhist Epic* translated from the Pāli and illustrated by unpublished paintings from Sinhalese temples (Oxford: OUP, 1977). The introductory essay (pp. xv–xlvii) by Gombrich gives the best modern account of the place of Jātakas in the Buddhist tradition.

⁴ J. Legge, trans., *Record of Buddhistic Kingdoms* being an account of the Chinese monk Fa-hien in his travels of India and Ceylon (Oxford, 1886), p. 106.

⁵ Some are enacted in continuous registers that depict incidents as a linear narrative, with four or five 'layers' of frieze occupying an entire wall. At Degaldoruwa in Kandy, for instance, Jātakas 313 and 402 are shown in this way, though the surface is a little damaged. For frieze style, see C.H. Holt, *The Religious World of Kīrti Śrī, Buddhism, Art and Politics in Late Medieval Sri Lanka* (Oxford: OUP, 1996), plate 45.

⁶ See Anant Pai, *Jātaka Stories*, Amar Chitra Katha, 1003 in series, India Book House. The stories are remarkably true to the originals. One exception to this is in Jātaka 20, where the monkeys make a long tube out of all the canes and there is no Bodhisatta resolve: perhaps it is too obviously 'Buddhist'.

⁷ See Cone and Gombrich, *Perfect Generosity*, pp. xxxix–xliv. I am grateful to discussion with Ven. Paññavaṃsa and Ven. Dhammasami about the importance of the tales in Myanmar (Burma).

⁸ See Than Tun, ed., *The Royal Orders of Burma, AD 1598–1885*, vol. V: 1788–1806 (Kyoto, 1986), pp. 60–1. Stories particularly popular at this time are the last ten (which include in this collection 538, 539 and 540) and, also in this collection, 20, 75 and 316.

⁹ P. Wongthet, 'The Jātaka stories and Laopuan world view', *Thai Folklore: Insights into Thai Culture*, Siraporn Nathalang ed. (Bangkok,

2000), pp. 47–61; originally published in *Asian Folklore Studies*, 48 (1989), pp. 21–30.

[10] The whole area of Aesopic tales in relationship to the Jātakas and the folk literature of other parts of the world is discussed in J. Jacobs, *History of the Aesopic Fable*, 2 vols. (London, 1889).

[11] For characteristic features of oral tradition see L.S. Cousins, 'Pāli Oral Literature', in P. Denwood and A. Piatigorski eds., *Buddhist Studies: Ancient and Modern* (1983), pp. 1–11. For the place of memorization and chanting in texts see R. Gethin, 'The Mātikās: Memorization, Mindfulness and the List', in J. Ggyatso ed., *Remembrance in Indian and Tibetan Buddhism* (Albany, New York, 1992), pp. 149–72.

[12] I am grateful to Richard Gombrich for his suggestions about these words: that the word *Mahāsatta*, 'Great Being', was originally a *bahuvrīhi* compound meaning 'of great courage'. The Bodhisatta is the awakening being, the 'bodhi-being'; the word seems to have meant originally 'attached to enlightenment'(*bodhisakta*).

[13] The word derives from *bujjhati*, to be awake.

[14] Locative of neuter noun derived from *acceti*, for the passing of time: lit 'in the past', DP I 26; PED 21 gives 'once upon a time'. Jātaka 20 uses 'formerly' (*pubbe*). Jātaka 94 is set 91 aeons ago.

[15] *Vin* I 10–11.

[16] See Garrett Jones, *Tales and Teachings of the Buddha*, pp. 166–70. Stories in which they feature, not translated in this collection, include: 420, 421, 424, 442, 459, 490, 491, 495, 496, 514, 529, 531 and 536 and in this collection, 539. The Pāli *sutta*s place less emphasis on these figures than the later tradition. They are not named in Jātaka verses. On subject in general, see K.R. Norman, 'The Pratyeka-Buddha in Buddhism and Jainism', *Selected Papers*, vol. II (Oxford: PTS, 1991), pp. 233–49 and R. Kloppenborg, *The Paccekabuddha: a Buddhist Ascetic*. A study of the concept of paccekabuddhas in Pāli canonical and commentarial literature (Lieden: Brill, 1974).

[17] J I 25.

[18] Each of these images is discussed in a story in which that perfection features. These are starred in the list at the beginning.

[19] See E. Wray, C. Rosenfield and D. Bailey, with photographs by J.D. Wray, *Ten Lives of the Buddha* (New York: Weatherill, 1972, revised

paperback edn, 1996), p. 16; S. Leksukhum, with photos by G. Mermet, 'The Ten Great Jātakas', *Temples of Gold: Seven Centuries of Thai Buddhist Paintings* (London: Thames and Hudson, 2001), pp. 136–57.

[20] I am grateful to Peter Skilling for this information.

[21] *Story of Gotama Buddha,* p. 96 (J I 72).

[22] *Story of Gotama Buddha,* p. 98 (J I 74).

[23] 'The Treatise on the Pāramīs' works throughout on the assumption that each perfection is better than the one before, but also puts considerable emphasis on generosity. See *Cariyāpiṭaka Aṭṭhakathā*, in *The Discourse on the All-Embracing Net of Views: the Brahmajāla sutta and its commentaries* (Kandy: BPS, 1978), pp. 242–317.

[24] See A III 48–50. For a discussion of the place of *dāna* in the Buddhist tradition see Bhikkhu Bodhi ed., *Dāna: the Practice of Giving; Selected Essays,* Wheel Publication no. 367/369 (Kandy 1990).

[25] See L.S. Cousins, 'Good or Skilful? *Kusala* in Canon and Commentary', *Journal of Buddhist Ethics*, Vol. 3, 1966, pp. 136–64, for a discussion of the development of this word.

[26] *Poetics*, 1453 a 16. See M. Bowra, *Sophoclean Tragedy* (Oxford: OUP, 1944), pp. 166ff.

[27] A III 415. See discussion in P. Harvey, *An Introduction to Buddhism, Teachings, History and Practices* (Cambridge: CUP, 1990), pp. 32–46.

[28] See S. Thompson and J. Balys, 'The Wise and the Foolish', *The Oral Tales of India* (Bloomington, Indiana: IUP, 1958), Motif J.

[29] Robert Graves, *New Larousse Encyclopedia of Mythology* (London: Hamlyn, 1983), p. 355. See also D.V.J. Harischandra, *Psychiatric Aspects of Jātaka Stories* (Galle, Sri Lanka, 1998), p. 8.

[30] The *Dhammasaṅgaṇi*, the first book of the *abhidhamma*, opens with a list of the attributes of the skilful mind, present at any moment of appropriate generosity or active virtue. Skilful consciousness always includes mindfulness. This first *citta* also forms the basis of the mind that experiences the meditation (*jhāna*). The presence of *abhidhamma* terminology in the Jātakas is striking, as we see in stories 55 and 476.

[31] Animals that converse are a feature of Indian literature from the Vedas onwards. See K. Chaitanya, 'The Beast Fable', *A New History of Sanskrit Literature* (London: Asia Publishing House, 1962), pp. 360ff.

³² No Jātaka is set in a Brahma realm for beings there do not speak: when the Bodhisatta descends from one in Jātaka 99 he has to assume a different form.

³³ Rebirth in an animal realm is not based on an underlying continuum (*bhavaṅga*) of skilful consciousness (*kusala citta*), which has its roots of non-greed, non-hatred and, usually in the case of humans, wisdom. Skilful consciousness is possible for animals, however. It is just that it is not innate, as it is with humans.

³⁴ S. Collins writes, 'It is easy to overlook the Buddhist heavens'. As he points out in his admirable discussion opened by this statement, they are not just some sort of holiday destination for those stuck in *saṃsāra* but a means of exploring and describing the mind and existence itself. See *Nirvana and Other Buddhist Felicities: Utopias of the Pali Imaginaire* (Cambridge: CUP, 1998), pp. 297–309.

³⁵ See ibid. and Gethin, *Foudnations of Buddhism,* (Oxford: OUP, 1998), pp. 112–32.

³⁶ The vow for Buddhahood made in a human existence is said to be fulfilled. See *Story of Gotama Buddha*, p. 18 (J I 14).

³⁷ See A I 10.

³⁸ Beings in this realm do not die, but just 'fall away' (*cavati*)—as the Bodhisatta does at the opening of the Mūgapakkha Jātaka (538). Gods do not necesssarily want to chat about *dhamma*. In the depiction of the Nimi Jātaka (541) on the north wall at Wat Suwannaram in Thonburi, Thailand, some gods in the Heaven of the Thirty-Three are shown deep in discussion while others ignore them and delight in the pleasures of their heavenly existence.

³⁹ M I 76.

⁴⁰ Sn 143–52.

⁴¹ See his highly entertaining introduction, *The Pañcatantra: The Book of India's Folk Wisdom,* (Oxford: OUP, 1997), pp. xxii–xxv, for animal types in Indian literature.

⁴² Oddly enough, she is barely mentioned in recent works on the Buddha's disciples or his female followers, perhaps because she features so little after the enlightenment in *sutta*s or the Buddha's life story.

⁴³ In the *Jātakanidāna* she is described as being born on the same day as Gotama (see *The Story of Gotama Buddha*, p. 71; J I 54). For

the most extensive account of her life see Sally Mellick Cutler, 'A Critical Edition, with translation, of selected portions of the Pāli *Apadāna*', D Phil Oxford, 1993, vol. I, pp. 232ff. It would have been assumed by an ancient audience that she too would have made her own undertaking to accompany the Bodhisatta through many lives to be the spouse of a future Buddha. The story taken as an account of the earliest incidents associated with their union is the Candakinnara Jātaka, 485, where, as a mythical half-bird being, she refuses to marry the king who has apparently killed the Bodhisatta (J IV 282–8). Through the power of her love for the Bodhisatta, the poison is dispelled and he is restored to life.

44 Related in 'story from the present' in Jātaka 281 (J III 392–4).

45 See K.R. Blackstone, *Women in the Footsteps of the Buddha: Struggle for Liberation in the Therīgāthā* (Richmond, Surrey: Curzon, 1998), pp. 113–7, and Susan Murcott, *The First Buddhist Women: Translation and Commentary of the Therīgāthā* (Berkeley: Parallax, 1991).

46 C.A.F. Rhys Davids and K.R. Norman, *Poems of Early Buddhist Nuns (Therīgāthā)*, revised joint reprint with section of *Elders' Verses* (Oxford: PTS, 1989).

47 W. Geiger, B. Ghosh trans., *Pāli Language and Literature* (New Delhi: Oriental Books Reprint Corporation, 3rd reprint, 1978), pp. 9–11.

48 See M. Winternitz, *A History of Indian Literature*, (Srinivasa Sarma revised), 2 vols. (Delhi, Varanasi, Patna: Motilal, 1983), II, pp. 115ff.

49 See Geiger, ibid., pp. 19–22, and Oskar von Hinüber, lecture at Oxford, 1997.

50 See for instance the detail in 'The story of the monkey king' (Jātaka 407), and accompanying discussion, where the verse says that the monkey ties the creeper round his legs, while the prose narrative says he ties it round his waist. The Sanskrit version of the tale follows the verse version.

51 I.B. Horner, *Ten Jātaka Stories (A Pāli Reader)*, (London: Luzac, 1957).

52 See Geiger, ibid., pp. 13–14.

53 See Bhikkhu Bodhi's introduction to *The Connected Discourses*

of the Buddha, 2 vols. (Oxford and Boston: PTS/Wisdom, 2000), I, pp. 31–5.

⁵⁴ Published in one volume, I.B. Horner trans., *The Minor Anthologies of the Pāli Canon*, (London: PTS, 1975), III.

⁵⁵ P. Khoroche trans., with foreword by W. Doniger, *Once the Buddha was a Monkey: Ārya Śūra's Jātakamālā* (Chicago: University of Chicago Press, 1989). There is not the space to discuss all of these collections further. See Cone and Gombrich, *Perfect Generosity*, pp. 109–11 for the widespread dissemination of the last story (547). P.S. Jaini has made a translation of the very popular non-canonical Jātakas in *Apocryphal Birth Stories: Paññāsa Jātaka*, 2 vols. (London: PTS, 1985–8).

⁵⁶ This is a large subject which cannot be fully addressed here. The best introduction to this dissemination in the West is still the preface in T.W. Rhys Davids, *Buddhist Birth Stories* (London, 1880). For *Kalilag and Damnag*, see p. xxix.

⁵⁷ See ibid., pp. xxxiii–xxxix.

⁵⁸ Sutta 36, Bhikkhu Ñāṇamoli and Bhikkhu Bodhi trans., *The Middle Length Discourses of the Buddha*, (Oxford and Boston: Wisdom/PTS, 2001), p. 341 (M I 247–8).

⁵⁹ See Sue Hamilton, 'Setting the Scene: We have no self but we are comprised of five aggregates', *Early Buddhism: A New Approach, The I of the Beholder* (Richmond, Surrey: Curzon, 2000), pp. 18–32. And for the brahminical context in which the doctrine of 'not-self' is argued, see R.F. Gombrich, *How Buddhism Began: The Conditioned Genesis of the Early Teachings* (London: Athlone, 1996), pp. 14–21.

⁶⁰ The Vessantara Jātaka is traditionally recited at wakes. See Cone and Gombrich, *Perfect Generosity*, p. xlii.

The Far Past

The Bodhisatta Vow and the Ten Perfections

According to the tradition, four countless aeons (*asaṅkheyyānaṃ*) and one hundred thousand kalpas (*kappasatasahassādhikānaṃ*) ago, the hero of the Jātakas, the Bodhisatta, made the resolve to become a Fully Awakened Buddha. These extracts are from the *Jātakanidāna*, a separate work from the Jātakas, usually regarded as their introduction, that describe this.[1] Catching sight of the last Buddha, Dīpaṅkara, the Bodhisatta is so inspired that he prostrates himself at his feet. Although the possibility of enlightenment occurs at that moment, he chooses instead to make a vow to attain Buddhahood himself, thus showing a path for other beings to follow to find an end to suffering. '. . . I would rather, like Ten-Powered Dīpaṅkara, seek for the highest, complete awakening. I will embark on the ship of *dhamma* and take the great mass of people across the ocean of existence: afterwards I will attain to complete *nibbāna*. This would become me.' In order to prepare himself he must develop, over countless lifetimes, the ten perfections, the attributes needed which will enable him to do this. His determination is interspersed with injunctions from Dīpaṅkara that address the listener as 'you'.

Four countless aeons and one hundred thousand kalpas in the past

125. So then: I search for things that lead to awakening.
     Above, below, in the ten directions, as far as the very element
     of things.[2]

126. Searching, I saw the first perfection, of generosity,
     the magnificent highway walked by the great teachers of
     old.

127. 'If you wish to find awakening, go, making firm and taking
     upon yourself this first perfection, of generosity.

128. Just as a jar filled to the brim, toppled by someone, pours
     forth water,
     and does not hold onto anything that remains there,

129. So you, when you see supplicants, low, middling or high,
     practise generosity, like the toppled jar, with nothing
     remaining.'

130. But these are not all the things that are needed for awakening:
     I will search for other things that ripen awakening!

131. Searching, I saw the second perfection, of virtue,
     frequented and practised by the great teachers of old.

132. 'If you wish to find awakening, go, making firm and taking
     upon yourself this second perfection, of virtue.

133. Just as a camarī cow, with her tail caught in something,
     approaches death and still does not harm her tail,

134. So you, for the fulfilment of the precepts on four levels,[3]
     continually guard virtue as a camarī cow her tail.'

135. But these are not all the things that are needed for awakening:
     I will search for other things that ripen awakening!

136. Searching, I saw the third perfection, of renunciation,
     frequented and practised by the great teachers of old.

137. 'If you wish to find awakening, go making firm and taking
     upon yourself this third perfection, of renunciation.

138. Just as a man who has stayed a long time, painfully afflicted, in prison
      does not feel desire for it but seeks only release,

139. So you too, see all states of becoming like a prison;
      Be one who turns his face to renunciation, for the complete release from becoming.'

140. But these are not all the things that are needed for awakening:
      I will search for other things that ripen awakening!

141. Searching, I saw the fourth perfection, of wisdom,
      frequented and practised by the great teachers of old.

142. 'If you wish to find awakening, go, making firm and taking upon yourself this fourth perfection, of wisdom.

143. Just as a monk, begging for alms, avoids neither low, middling nor high families, and takes his sustenance in this way,

144. So you too, at all times ask questions of wakeful people, and, going to the perfection of wisdom, you will attain full awakening.'

145. But these are not all the things that are needed for awakening:
      I will search for other things that ripen awakening!

146. Searching, I saw the fifth perfection, of heroic effort,
      frequented and practised by the great teachers of old.

147. 'If you wish to find awakening go, making firm and taking upon yourself this fifth perfection, of effort.

148. Just as a lion, the king of the beasts, whether lying down, standing or walking, exhibits unabated vigour and is always courageous,

149. So you too, firmly exerting effort in every state of becoming,
      going to the perfection of effort, will attain full awakening.'

150. But these are not all the things that are needed for awakening:
      I will search for other things that ripen awakening!

151. Searching, I saw the sixth perfection, of forbearance,
     frequented and practised by the great teachers of old.

152. 'You, with an undivided mind, make firm and take upon
     yourself this sixth, and you will attain full awakening.

153. Just as the earth endures everything thrown upon it, pure
     and impure alike, and does not show anger or favour,

154. So you too, patient of all respect and disrespect, going to
     the perfection of forbearance, will attain full awakening.'

155. But these are not all the things that are needed for awakening:
     I will search for other things that ripen awakening!

156. Searching, I saw the seventh perfection, of truth,
     frequented and practised by the great teachers of old.

157. 'Making firm and taking upon yourself this seventh, with
     undivided speech, you will attain full awakening.

158. Just as the healing star, Venus, is balanced for gods and
     men in all times and seasons and does not deviate from
     her course,[4]

159. So you, do not deviate from the course of the truths, and,
     going to the perfection of truth, you too will attain full
     awakening.'[5]

160. But these are not all the things that are needed for awakening:
     I will search for other things that ripen awakening!

161. Searching, I saw the eighth perfection, of resolve,
     frequented and practised by the great teachers of old.

162. 'You, making firm and taking upon yourself this eighth,
     be unwavering there and you will attain full awakening.

163. Just as a mountain, a rock, unwavering, is well established,
     and does not tremble in rough winds but remains in its
     own place,

164. So you too, be unwavering at all times in your resolve,
     and, going to the perfection of resolve, you will attain full
     awakening.'

165. But these are not all the things that are needed for awakening:
     I will search for other things that ripen awakening!

166. Searching, I saw the ninth perfection, of loving kindness,
     frequented and practised by the great teachers of old.

167. 'You, making firm and taking upon yourself this ninth, be
     without an equal in loving kindness if you wish to attain
     full awakening.

168. Just as water suffuses with coolness good and bad people
     alike, and washes away dust and dirt,

169. So you too, cultivate loving kindness for friend and enemy,
     and, going to the perfection of loving kindness, you will
     attain full awakening.'

170. But these are not all the things that are needed for awakening:
     I will search for other things that ripen awakening!

171. Searching, I saw the tenth perfection, of equanimity,
     frequented and practised by the great teachers of old.

172. 'You, making firm and taking upon yourself this tenth,
     be balanced and firm and you will attain full awakening.

173. Just as the earth remains unperturbed at both the pure
     and impure thrown down upon it, and avoids both anger
     and favour,

174. So you too be balanced at all times to the happy and the
     painful, and, going to the perfection of equanimity, you
     will attain full awakening.'

So few are all the things in this world that bring awakening to
maturation, that bring about Buddhahood and that have to be
fulfilled by Bodhisattas. Beyond these ten perfections there are no
others. And these ten perfections are not in the sky above; they are
not in the earth below, nor are they in the directions that start
with the east. They are established right in the depths of my heart.

    (Sections from J I 14 and 20–5)

Notes

[1] It is found, in Pāli, at the beginning of the first volume of the Fausbøll edition. I.B. Horner's notes to *The Basket of Conduct* (*Cariyāpiṭaka* = Cp), (London: PTS, 1975), which contains an almost identical version of the ten perfections, have been a great help in translating this section, as has the clear translation of the *Jātakanidāna*, by N.A. Jayawickrama, *The Story of Gotama Buddha* (Oxford: PTS, 1990).

[2] The 'element of things' (*dhammadhātuyā*) is usually applied to the range of omniscient knowledge of a Buddha (see Franklin Edgerton, *Buddhist Hybrid Sanskrit: Grammar and Dictionary*, 2 vols. (Delhi, Poona, Varanasi: Motilal Banarsidass, 1953) Vol. II, pp. 278–9. It probably refers here to the highest formless realms, the subtlest forms of existence (See Cp 20, n. 1).

[3] Control over the rules laid down for the monks, control over the sense organs, purity of livelihood and reliance only on the requisites of a monk's livelihood (*Basket of Conduct*, p. 20, n. 4). As the vow is being made in the time of a Buddha, all of these would be known to the aspirant Bodhisatta.

[4] Osadhī, supposed to have healing properties: medicinal herbs are gathered when it is in the sky. It seems to be Venus, the morning star. See CPD II 790.

[5] The truths are the four noble truths of suffering, the cause of suffering, the end of suffering and the way leading to that end.

1

A true story
Apaṇṇaka Jātaka (1)

Vol. I, 94–106

Homage to the Exalted One, the Enlightened One,
the Fully Awakened Buddha

After the customary homage given above, the story from the
present starts with a tribute to the Fully Awakened Buddha,
the teacher of the path to freedom and the narrator of the stories
from the past. The majesty of his presence is intended to be self-
explanatory, but mention should be made of some features, found
only in this introduction, which help place his first appearance
and the stories in context. First, there is the extensive description
of the attributes that distinguish the Buddha, the fully awakened
teacher, from other men. He is said to be endowed, for instance,
with the thirty-two marks of the Great Man (*mahāpurisa*), which
include the turban-crowned head and the fine wheels on the
hands and feet, often seen on statues and pictures.[1] His body
and voice are here said to be like those of Brahma, the lord of
the heavens beyond the sense sphere. Although these
characteristics mark him out as heroic and impressive, he is not
considered a god in early Buddhism and is never described as
such: he is beyond the gods (*atideva*). When Anāthapiṇḍika, the
lay follower in this story, pays homage to this man it is to the
possessor of the fully awakened mind, who has fulfilled the
highest potential possible for a living being.

The introduction also makes an assertion not often found in
early Buddhism. It states that the meditation on the Triple Gem,
the Buddha (*Buddhānussati*), his teaching (*dhammānussati*) and

that of his followers (saṅghānussati) can lead the practitioner to
all stages of enlightenment: taking refuge in these is the only
safe refuge. These three recollections number amongst the forty
subjects for meditation recommended by Buddhaghosa in his
fifth-century manual for meditators, The Path of Purification
(Visuddhimagga), and are constantly encouraged in the tradition
as ways of bringing calm (samatha) and confidence (saddhā).[2] They
are not usually accorded such emphasis, however, and their presence
suggests a certain orientation towards laymen. Anāthapiṇḍika,
to whom the story from the past is primarily directed, would
have been the head of an extended family, a 'houselord' or
householder (gahapati), and his friends are laymen. He is elsewhere
praised by the Buddha as foremost amongst his disciples who
support his order of monks and nuns.[3] In these and in other ways
the introduction gives us a key to the tales: the full request is
made to the Buddha to remember the past and to reveal what
has been hidden, which he does, in a formula we do not also
find in other stories. This story from the present is, in part, an
introduction to and validation of this Buddhist tradition: it packs
in a great deal of terminology associated with doctrine and practice
that might be unfamiliar to a reader new to Buddhist texts. Because
of this, and the number of suttas quoted that were presumably
intended to remind listeners of other texts that they had heard,
there are quite a few explanatory footnotes for this section. These
are intended to explain new terms and help the reader find
complementary texts in the Buddhist canon: the other 'stories
from the present' do not need such lengthy explanation.

The events and easy momentum of the first tale in the past,
which introduces the hero of the tales, set a completely different
tone. A straightforward story of common sense and care triumphing
over self-seeking greed, it reveals the pragmatism, native wit and
occasional humour which so often characterize the Bodhisatta
as the one who has skill in means (upāyakusala). The Bodhisatta

is a cautious, shrewd but, in his willingness to offer choice to the other trader, generous hero. The ability not to be seduced by appearances, to exercise authority and to win over his followers through appeal to their own judgement prove vital in the course of the dangers that confront him. Up until the end, when he sells his wares for a good price after staying up on guard all night, he is shown as a reliable and utterly down-to-earth leader of men. Buddhism arose at the outset of a period which saw great mercantile and urban development. It exercised an appeal, which, unusually for the time, crossed all social boundaries. We know that merchants were often the principal donors to temples from the first century CE.[4] It is apt that the first story has such a simple figure as hero, exemplifying virtues that would be valued as those of a reliable and honest 'man of the people'. He is juxtaposed against the foolish trader, who leads his followers into the wilderness of opinions and falsity and so, crucially, lacks skill in means. In the Buddha's last lifetime Devadatta, the Buddha's cousin, continually plots against him, attempting to divide the order of monks and constantly undermining the Buddha's authority amongst his followers.[5] In him we are introduced to one of the main sources of tension in the Jātakas as a whole: a corrupt leader who shares the Buddha's popular charisma and genius for leadership, but is dedicated to jealousy and hatred. His dedication to undermining the Bodhisatta and his followers provides, throughout many stories, a dark parody of the search to develop the perfections.

A story of travel across a wasteland is a fitting starting point to the collection of 547 tales. The treasurer's friends are described as living in a kind of wilderness, in the belief that, for instance, one's fate is predetermined or that actions have no consequences.[6] Elsewhere in the Pāli canon the image is used to express the state of scepticism and the kind of doubt that is unhelpful to the mind. In the *Pāyāsi sutta* an almost identical story is told by the Buddha

to illustrate the ruin and disaster that befalls the one who follows
false views.[7] In the *Sāmaññaphala sutta* the same word, *kantāra*,
is used in a simile that describes doubt, which is considered one
of five hindrances to the meditation practice and the healthy
and skilful mind (*kusalacitta*).[8] The one who doubts, the *sutta*
says, is like a man lost in a wilderness. The one who relinquishes
doubt is like one who has crossed over it, and finds himself safely
returned to the outskirts of his own home territory. The wilderness
can also be taken to describe the condition of all living beings.
Existence itself, *saṃsāra*, the world in which continuous rebirth
takes place, means wandering or continuous movement, from a
verb that means literally 'to flow together, to go about, wander
or walk or roam through; to walk or pass through (a succession
of states), undergo transmigration, enter or pass into': the fate
of all beings until they find release.[9] In the canonical *The Path
of Discrimination* (*Paṭisambhidāmagga*) the Buddha says,
'Worldly life has entered a great wilderness, there is none other
than myself to get it across the wilderness.'[10] There are striking
parallels with the opening lines of two other voyages of
psychological and cosmological exploration. Dante's *Inferno*
begins '*nel mezzo del cammin di nostra vita/mi ritrovai per una
selva oscura/che la diritta via era smarrita*',[11] ('Halfway along
the road we have to go,/I found myself obscured in a great forest,/
Bewildered, and I knew I had lost the way.'[12]) Bunyan's *The
Pilgrim's Progress* starts with the words, 'As I walked through
the wilderness of the world'.[13] One only has to fly over the vast
stretches of wild terrain in India to see the pertinence of the
image for these stories: just as the trader travels with his caravan
from east to west, and from west to east, so the Bodhisatta, with
many disciples, travels from one birth to the next, and from one
identity to another. It is a characteristic of the Bodhisatta's
method that he does not always follow what might seem the
easy path (*magga*), the same word used in Buddhism for the

attainment of the stages of enlightenment, but the way that crosses the wilderness safely. The 'true' in the title of this story, *apaṇṇaka*, is the word used for something that has a certain or safe outcome.[14]

Story from the present

When staying at the great monastery at the Jetavana Grove near Sāvatthi the Teacher gave this *dhamma* talk about being true. And what prompted this story? Well, it was the five hundred friends of the treasurer, who followed teachers of other schools. For one day Anāthapiṇḍika, the treasurer, took a large group of friends of his, who followed other schools, to the Jetavana to pay homage to the Exalted One. He arranged for them to take a large quantity of garlands, perfumes and ointments, together with oil, honey, sugar cane, clothes and robes. He offered the flowers and handed over the medicinal foods and robes to the order of monks. When he had done this he sat down, avoiding the six faults that can be made in taking a seat.[15] The lay disciples from other schools similarly paid homage, sat down next to Anāthapiṇḍika and gazed upon the Teacher: at his face, as glorious as the full moon, at his Brahma-like body, surrounded by light and adorned with all the marks and signs of a Great Man and at the rays of awakening that emanated from him like garlands, pair upon pair.

Then, like a young lion giving a great roar in Manosilātala, in the Himālayas, or like a storm cloud in the rainy season thundering as if bringing down the Ganga from the sky, [96] he gave a pleasing *dhamma* talk, as if knotting a garland of jewels. It was varied and full of detail, and he spoke with the voice of Brahma, endowed with the eight special qualities of speech, pleasant to hear and friendly.[16] They all listened to the talk from the Teacher, and, rising with minds that had become clear, they paid their

respects to the Ten-Powered One, broke their allegiance to other
teachers and took refuge in the Buddha instead.[17] And after that
they used to visit with Anāthapiṇḍika and went to the temple
with perfumes, garlands and suchlike in their hands and kept
the *uposatha* day. They listened to the *dhamma*, made acts of
generosity and guarded their virtue.

Then the Exalted One went from Sāvatthi back to Rājagaha.
But when the Thus-gone had departed they broke their refuge
and went to take refuge in other teachers and established
themselves back in their original position. The Exalted One spent
seven or eight months in Rājagaha and went back to Jetavana.
Then Anāthapiṇḍika brought them again in the presence of the
Teacher, made offerings of flowers and suchlike and sat down
to one side. They also paid homage to the Exalted One and sat
down to one side. Then Anāthapiṇḍika informed the Buddha that
when he had gone on his journey they had broken their refuge,
taken refuge in other teachers and established themselves in their
original position. The Exalted One opened the lotus of his mouth
and, as if opening a jewelled casket filled with various perfumes
and scented with divine smells by the virtue of his having displayed
good speech for countless thousands of aeons continuously, spoke
out with a sweet voice. 'Is it true, what they say, that you disciples
have broken your allegiance and taken refuge in other teachers?'
he asked. And they were unable to hide it, and said that it was.
So the Teacher said, 'Lay disciples, if you made a measure from
the lowest hell, the Avīci,[18] up to the highest level of existence,[19]
or across through boundless world systems, you would not find
such a one as the Buddha, endowed with virtue and other qualities
of excellence: much less a superior'. 'Bhikkhus, whatever beings,
whether those without feet, with two feet, with four feet, or those
with many feet, those with form or without form, perceiving or
non-perceiving, those that neither perceive nor do not perceive:
a Thus-gone, an arahat, a Fully Enlightened One is reckoned

the best of them.'[20] 'Whatever wealth there is, in this world or in the other, or whatever jewel is the greatest in the heavens: it is not equal to the Thus-gone.'[21] 'Of those that have clear minds the Thus-gone is the chief.'[22] He then explained the excellent qualities of the Triple Gem, with a number of *sutta*s and said, 'There is no such thing as rebirth in hells for laymen and laywomen who have gone for refuge in the Triple Gem, which is endowed in this way with the highest qualities.[23] Freed from rebirth in a bad destiny,[24] they rise up to the heavens and experience great glory. Therefore it is not right for you to break your allegiance and go for refuge in other teachers.'

These *sutta*s should be cited here to make it clear that for those who take refuge in the Triple Gem, by virtue of its freedom and its highest good, there is no occurrence of rebirth in the bad destinies:

[97] Those who go for refuge in the Buddha: they will not go to a bad destiny.
When they leave the human body they will fill the ranks of devas, the shining gods.

Those who go for refuge in the *dhamma*, the teaching: they will not go to a bad destiny.
When they leave the human body they will fill the ranks of devas, the shining gods.

Those who go for refuge in the *sangha*: they will not go to a bad destiny.
When they leave the human body they will fill the ranks of devas, the shining gods.[25]

(from the *Mahāsamaya sutta*)

188. Men who are terrified go to manifold refuge: mountains and forests, gardens, trees and shrines.
189. But this is not the safe refuge, it is not the best refuge.
He who has gone to this refuge is not freed from all suffering.

190. But the one who goes to the refuge of the Buddha, the *dhamma* and the *saṅgha,* with right wisdom sees the four noble truths:

191. Suffering, the arising of suffering, the crossing over of suffering and the Ariyan eightfold path that leads to the quelling of suffering.

192. This is the safe refuge, the best refuge. The one who goes to this refuge is freed from all suffering.[26]

(from the *Dhammapada*)

But the Teacher's talk to them was not quite yet complete. As he said, 'Lay disciples, the meditation object of the recollection of the Buddha, the meditation object of the recollection of the *dhamma*, the teaching, and the meditation object of the recollection of the *saṅgha*, the followers of the Buddha: each gives stream-entry and its fruit, the one-return and its fruit, the never-return and its fruit and arahatship and its fruit.'[27] So he delivered the teaching by such methods and said, 'It is not sensible for you to break your allegiance to such a refuge.' Then he spoke about the gift of the paths for those that take these meditation objects: 'There is one thing, bhikkhus, which is to be cultivated, made much of, that leads to complete disenchantment, dispassion, to freedom, to peace, higher knowledge, awakening and *nibbāna*. And what is that? The recollection of the Buddha.' Each recollection is to be elucidated by this and the other associated *suttas*.[28]

So the Exalted One, with various explanations, admonished the lay disciples. 'Lay disciples: in times past men sought refuge in what is not a refuge, taking up opinionated ideas and obstructive misconceptions. In a wilderness possessed by non-humans they became food for yakkhas and fell into ruin. But those who were single-minded and clearheaded met with prosperity in that very same wilderness.' And when he had said this he was silent. And then the householder Anāthapiṇḍika rose up from his seat and paid homage to the Exalted One, proffering an añjali at the head. Offering praises he said, 'Sir, it has been made clear to us that at this time these disciples have broken their allegiance to the highest refuge and fallen into opinionated ideas. Now reveal what is hidden to us: [98] the ruin of those opinionated ones in a wilderness haunted by non-humans and the prosperity of those who adhered to the truth. So, Exalted One, make this matter clear to us, as if causing the full moon to rise in the sky.'

Then the Exalted One said, 'Householder, through measureless time I have fulfilled the ten perfections and I have acquired omniscience for the purpose of the removal of doubt from the world. Apply your ears and listen carefully, as if filling a golden tube with the fat of a lion.'

He produced the arising of memory in the treasurer and, as if breaking open the birthplace of the snow[29] and releasing the full moon, he made clear what another life had kept hidden.

Story from the past

Once upon a time in the city of Vārāṇasi, in the kingdom of Kāsi, there was a king called Brahmadatta.[30] At that time the Bodhisatta took rebirth in a family of caravan drivers, and when he was old enough he travelled plying his trade with five hundred waggons: sometimes he went from east to west; sometimes from west to east. Now at Vārāṇasi there was also another caravan leader who was plain foolish, lacking any skill or resourcefulness. At this time the Bodhisatta procured some merchandise of the highest value in Vārāṇasi, filled up five hundred waggons and made preparations for a journey. The foolish caravan leader then and there did exactly the same thing. So the Bodhisatta thought, 'If this foolish caravan leader travels with me the road will not be able to take a thousand waggons in one convoy. There will not be enough wood and water for people or grass for the oxen. It is better for either him or me to go first.' So he sent for him and talked it over. 'It won't work if the two of us go together: do you want to go first or later?' he said. The man thought, 'It will be to my advantage to go first: I'll go on a road that won't be broken up, the oxen will eat untouched grass, there will be fresh herbs for curries, clear water, and I'll be able to fix the price as I like when I sell'. So he said, 'Sir: I'll go first.' [99] The Bodhisatta saw considerable benefits in going later, and thought, 'If they go first they will make uneven ground level: I'll go on a path that has already been used. Their oxen will have eaten the tough, tangled grasses, while mine will eat new standing, sweet grasses. In a place where there is no water they will dig the ground and get water so we'll drink from wells that have been dug by others. Setting prices is life-destroying work. I'll go later and sell mine when the price has been set.' Seeing these benefits he said, 'You go first, sir'.

'That's fine, sir,' said the foolish caravan trader. He yoked his carts and in due course he went on his way until he left human settlements and reached the entrance into the wilderness. Now there are five different types of wilderness. There is a wilderness of thieves, a wilderness of wild beasts, a wilderness without water, a wilderness of yakkhas, and a wilderness with little food. So in a wilderness of thieves thieves beset the road; in a wilderness of wild beasts the road is beset by animals like lions. In a wilderness without water there is no water for drinking or washing. A wilderness of yakkhas is haunted by yakkhas.[31] A wilderness of little food has no roots and vegetables to eat. This particular wilderness was one without water and haunted by yakkhas too.

So the caravan leader loaded very big water jars onto his waggons, filled them with water and entered into the wilderness, which stretched out for sixty yojanas. When he had gone half way through the wilderness the yakkha who lived there thought,

'I'll make sure they throw out the water they have collected and then, when they are weak, I will eat them all up.'

So he [100] conjured up a delightful carriage yoked up with pure white young oxen, and sat on it just like a powerful baron, with wet hair and clothes and garlanded with blue and white lotuses wreathed on his head. His carriage had mud smeared on its wheels. He also took with him an entourage of ten or twelve yakkhas carrying bows, quivers, swords and shields in their hands. His attendants went in front and behind him, also with wet hair and wet clothes. They too were adorned with garlands of blue and white lotuses, were chewing lotus stalks, while in their hands they carried red and white lotuses. They were dripping with water and mud.

Now when a strong wind blows caravan leaders like to sit in the carriage in front with their attendants to escape the dust; when the wind blows from behind they go to the back of the line. This time, as there was a headwind, the foolish caravan leader went in front. When the yakkha saw him coming, he pulled up his carriage and greeted him courteously, 'So, where are you going?' The caravan leader caused his own carriage to pull up off the road, while giving room for the other waggons to pass, and stood in front of the yakkha. He said, 'Sir, we come from Vārāṇasi, but you come wearing blue and white lotuses, with red and white lotuses in your hands, chewing lotus stalks, and are all muddy and dripping wet. Did it rain when you were on the road and are there pools covered with lotuses?' The yakkha listened to this and replied, 'My friend! Why are you saying that? Over there you can just see a dark streak of forest, and from there on the forest is full of water. It is always raining, the wells are full, and on each side there are pools covered with lotuses.'

Then, while the waggons went on he asked, [101] 'So where are you taking these waggons?' The merchant said where he was going.

'What kind of goods are in that waggon?' The merchant explained what he was carrying.

'What kind of goods are in that last waggon, which moves as if it is carrying a heavy load?'

'Oh, that's the water.'

'Well, it was a good idea for you to bring water from over there, but there is really no need for it from now on: there's plenty of water ahead, and you'll travel more easily if you break the jars and throw out the water.' Then he added, 'Well you'd better get going, we have delayed you.'

The yakkha then went on a little, but when he was out of sight returned back to his own city. The foolish caravan leader, through his own stupid fault, followed the words of the yakkha, had the jars broken and threw the water out, without saving even a handful, and drove his waggons on. But there was not even a drop of water ahead. The men, deprived of water, became worn out. They carried on till sunset and then unharnessed the waggons, rounded them up to form a corral and tied the oxen to the wheels. But there was no water for the oxen and there was not even any rice gruel for the men. The weakened men lay down and fell asleep right where they were. As soon as night fell the yakkhas came out from their city and killed everyone, man and beast, ate their flesh and, leaving the bones behind, went on their way. So, because of this foolish caravan leader they all met their end. Various bits of bones were scattered in all directions while the five hundred waggons remained filled up where they stood.

Now, the Bodhisatta let six weeks go by after the departure of the merchant and then left the city with five hundred waggons until in due course he came to the edge of the wilderness. He filled the water jars, took a good amount of water and had a drum beaten throughout the encampment for everyone to meet together. [102] Then he said, 'Do not use even a handful of water without asking me for permission. There are poisonous trees in the wilderness, so do not eat so much as a leaf, a flower or a fruit which you have not eaten before, without asking me first.' Giving this instruction to his men, he entered into the wilderness with the five hundred waggons. When they came to the middle of the wilderness the yakkha appeared before the Great Being in the road, in the same way as he had before the foolish caravan leader. As soon as the Bodhisatta saw him he knew: 'There is no water here in this wilderness, for it is called the "desert without water". This fellow is brazen and with red eyes and you cannot see his shadow. Undoubtedly, he prevailed upon the foolish caravan leader that went before to throw out his water, and, waiting until his entourage was worn out, ate them up. But he does not know my native wit and skill in means.' So he said, 'Get out of the way! We are merchants: if we do not see water we do not throw out the water we do have. When we do see water to be had we will throw it out, make our waggons light and proceed on our way.' The yakkha carried on a little and when he was out of sight returned to his own city. When the yakkha had gone the Bodhisatta's men said to him, 'Sir, these men pointed out to us a dark streak of forest over there that can just be made out.[32] From there on it is always raining. These men were wearing garlands of blue and white lotuses, were carrying red and white lotuses in their hands, and were chewing lotus stalks. Their clothes and hair were dripping wet, with drops of water streaming off them. Let's throw out the water and we'll go on our way with light waggons.'

The Bodhisatta listened to what they were saying, got the waggons to stop and assembled all his men. 'Right. Have any of you ever heard that in this wilderness there was a pool or lotus ponds?' he asked.

'No sir, we have not,' they replied. 'It is called the "waterless desert".'

The Bodhisatta questioned them again. 'So some men have just told us that it is always raining in that dark streak of forest. But how far does a rain-wind carry?' [103]

'About a yojana, sir' they replied.

'And has this rain-cloud been felt by anyone of you?'

'No, sir, it has not.'

'And how far off can you see the tips of a rain-cloud?'

'From three yojanas,[33] sir.'

'And has anyone here seen the tip of even one rain-cloud?'

Not one of the men had. Not one had seen any lightning, which they agreed should be seen from four or five yojanas away. And not one had heard any thunder, which they agreed should be heard two or three yojanas away.

'These are not humans, but yakkhas,' the Bodhisatta said. 'They will come back, hoping to eat us up when we are worn out after having had the water thrown away. The foolish caravan leader who went on ahead was not skilled in means. After having the water thrown away he will have been eaten when exhausted. There will be five hundred waggons still standing there all loaded up: today we are going to see them. So do not throw so much as a handful of water away, and let's get on our way.' And so he ordered them on.

And as he proceeded he saw the five hundred waggons still loaded up, and the bones of men and oxen scattered in every direction. So he had his waggons unyoked and set in a circle to form a corral. He saw that men and oxen had their evening meal in good time, and ensured that the oxen lay down in the midst of the men. Then, with some strong leaders, he stood guard, with sword in hand, through the three watches of the night, remaining there until the break of day. Early the next day he carried on with his duties, saw that the oxen were fed and then discarded weak waggons for strong ones and substituted less valuable goods for more valuable. Then he went on his way and sold his goods, able to set a price at two or three times the original value. He then returned, with every single one of his men, back to his city.

[104] The Teacher told this story and said, 'In this way, householder, those who formerly took up opinionated ideas came to complete destruction, while those who kept to the truth escaped from the hands of demons, went where they wanted in safety, and returned back to their own homes.' And when he had linked the two stories together, as the Fully Awakened Buddha he said this verse:

§   Some said the true position, those with opinions a false.
     The wise man should take that which is true in order to attain
     perfect knowledge.[34]

[105] In this way the Exalted One spoke to the lay disciples, 'What is called the path of truth confers the three wholesome attainments, the six sense-sphere heavens, the attainments of the Brahma heaven, and in the end, the way to arahatship.[35] [106] The path of falsity leads to the four descents or to the five lower castes of men.' He went on to give a *dhamma* talk and revealed the four noble truths, in sixteen ways. And at the end of this teaching all five hundred lay disciples were established in the fruit of stream-entry.

The Teacher delivered this *dhamma* talk, made the link between these two stories and then explained the connections with the birth. 'At that time the foolish caravan leader was Devadatta, and his followers the followers of Devadatta. The followers of the wise caravan leader were the followers of the Buddha and I was the wise caravan leader.' And he finished his teaching.

Notes

[1] See *Lakkhaṇa sutta*, D III 142–78.
[2] I am grateful to Dr Justin Meiland for discussion about this. See,

for instance, Buddhaghosa, *Path of Purification*, pp. 117–8 (Vism III 121–2).

³ See A I 26. Anāthapiṇḍika, a treasurer or banker, is singled out by the Buddha as the foremost of his lay disciples in the practice of hospitality and generosity towards monks, considered in Buddhism a particularly auspicious kind of giving. He bought the Jetavana for the Buddha's use by spreading out coins that covered its entire surface. As a *gahapati*, he is both head of a household, an extended family, and a man of private means.

⁴ See A.L. Basham, *The Wonder That Was India*, (revised edn, London: Sidgwick and Jackson, 1967), pp. 143–4. Thirty-one Jātakas feature the Bodhisatta as a merchant or trader: four of them begin the full collection.

⁵ See DPPN II 1106–11. Stories in which he appears in this collection are 20, 313 and 407.

⁶For the six ascetics whose doctrines are described and criticized by the Buddha, see D I 52–9.

⁷ That there is no other world, nor beings born not of parents (the shining gods, or devas) nor is there any result of deeds done well or badly, D II 343–50.

⁸ See D I 73.

⁹ M. Monier Williams, *Sanskrit–English Dictionary* (Oxford: OUP, 1899), p. 1119.

¹⁰ *Paṭisambhidāmagga* I 129.

¹¹ Opening lines to the *Inferno* (Milan: Biblioteca universale, 1949), pp. 47–8.

¹² A. Dante, with Introduction and Notes D. Higgins, 'Inferno' in *The Divine Comedy*.

¹³ Opening line of *The Pilgrim's Progress* (1678), J. Bunyan, Introduction and Notes W.R. Jones, *The Pilgrim's Progress*, Oxford University Press, 2003, p. 10.

¹⁴ *Apaṇṇaka*, CPD I 51 'certain, true, absolute' and so DP I 162–3. At first sight, though, the word looks like 'without leaves or foliage', which could have been the original meaning. The main source for it is the *Apaṇṇaka sutta*, no. 60, M 506–19, which also deals with the wrong views and opinions which obstruct enlightenment. The *sutta* was

delivered at Sālā, which lay, according to the commentary, at the entrance to a forest; the varied views presented in the *sutta* suggest metaphoric and literal trouble in the road ahead. The sense of certainty or truth in both contexts could then arise from a description of a path 'without leaves or foliage' that was much easier to follow.

[15] See, for instance, J V 138. These are being too close or too far, with body bent or crooked, sitting too directly in front or behind.

[16] The Buddha speaks with 'a voice of eightfold quality—a voice that was fluent, intelligible, sweet and audible, sustained and distinct, deep and resonant . . . he made himself audible to that assembly by his voice, the sound thereof did not penetrate beyond the assembly' (D II 227).

[17] A Buddha is said to possess ten powers, such as knowing the state of other beings and their future rebirths (M I 68–71). The word *pasanna*, translated as 'clear', means both 'clear' and 'full of faith'.

[18] The lowest hell is reserved for such crimes as patricide or matricide, or causing a schism in the *saṅgha*, the order of monks. Rebirth here may be for a very long time, but is, like all rebirths, impermanent.

[19] The realm of the eighth meditation (*jhāna*), the formless heaven of neither perception nor non-perception.

[20] See Buddhaghosa, *Path of Purification*, pp. 221–2 (Vism VII 47–8). This and the following two texts are quotes from longer *sutta*s in the Pāli canon. This first quote, taken from the *Aggappasāda sutta* (A II 34), is inserted in full, as the abbreviated version in the Fausbøll text does not make sense on its own. The beings listed here are firstly form-sphere gods, who do not have physical bodies and hence no feet, as well as various gods, men and animals who have two, four or many feet. 'Form' refers to beings up the form heavens, 'formless' to those in the highest, formless heavens. The only beings who do not have perception are those who inhabit one of the form heavens (*asaññā sattā*), one of the realms that can be obtained on the basis of the fourth meditation (*jhāna*). The highest heaven, mentioned in the sentence before, is the realm of neither perception nor non-perception. The point being made is that the Buddha is superior to beings in all thirty-one realms of existence, even that of the highest, formless gods. See also S I 139.

[21] This is an extract from the third verse of the *Ratana Sutta* (Sn

223 ff), extolling the jewel of the Triple Gem as the highest blessing. It is one of the most popular Buddhist texts for chanting, used on such occasions as building a new house, moving into one or welcoming a new member of the family.

22 This is an extract from A V 21, which lists the highest in a number of categories. Just as the enlightened being, an arahat, is the foremost amongst living beings, so carefulness or diligence, *appamadā*, is the highest mental state. See also the *peyyāla*, or repetitive section, of S V 29. Possibly some sort of ascending sequence of eulogy is being suggested by these three quotes, culminating in the importance of the quality of attentiveness needed for any particular moment.

23 The Pāli is unclear here. I have kept the phrase *evaṃ uttamaguṇehi samannāgataṃ* ('endowed with the highest qualities') despite its having no obvious object. It seems to be a gloss incorporated into the text at some time in the distant past.

24 The four bad destinies, or descents, are realms lower than the human: the animal, the *peta* or ghost realm, the *asura* realm and the hells.

25 D II 255.

26 *Dhammapada*, 188–92.

27 These are the four stages of enlightenment and the fruit of each. The one who attains stream-entry never again experiences doubt or rebirth in a descent: he will become enlightened within seven lifetimes; the once-returner will become enlightened within the space of one more lifetime, the never-returner will gain enlightenment within this lifetime. The path is fully revealed at arahatship.

28 See A I 30 for the series of ten texts on the 'one things' that lead to enlightenment. The same wording is used for each of the ten recollections of Theravāda Buddhist meditation practice: on each aspect of the Triple Gem, on virtue, generosity, devas, the breath, death, the body and peace. The last three quotes again suggest an ascending sequence of benefits, from freedom from a lower rebirth, to freedom from suffering described in a general sense to, lastly, the four stages of enlightenment. It is not clear if the speaker of these three is the narrator of the story from the present or the Buddha himself.

[29] *Himagabbham*—epithet for the clouds.

[30] In this first, as in many stories, King Brahmadatta is introduced. Nothing is known of Brahmadatta other than the name, possibly generic, which is applied to one king or a line of kings of Vārāṇasi.

[31] A yakkha is a regular feature of Indian folklore. Pot-bellied, with a terrifying face, he appears in some traditions as a supernatural being, with an earthy physical appearance to which a goblin is the nearest Western equivalent. When depicted in the doorways and lintels of Buddhist, Jain and Hindu temples he is often seen as a protective deity, whose power to terrify is employed to keep away other evil spirits. In Jātakas yakkhas are sometimes benign; more usually though they are malevolent towards humans. As this story shows us, they are capable of disguise and supernatural conjuring yet may be detected by the fact that they leave no shadows.

[32] Perhaps an image conjured up by the yakkha—or just a mirage.

[33] The PTS text says 'from one yojana', but the Burmese manuscript give 'from three yojanas', which seems more likely for a rain-cloud.

[34] This is the first example of the oldest layer of the text, the verses that form part of the stories from the past. This one is spoken as comment by the Buddha in the present. All the stories in the first *nipāta*, or section, have just one verse, which, perhaps because of its brevity, tends to be a short adage or homily. Stories towards the end of the collection often have passages of consecutive verse that run into hundreds, permitting extensive dramatic interchange, lyrical description of places and events and prolonged doctrinal discussion. Verses are usually in four *pādas*, or lines, of eight syllables each.

[35] The three wholesome attainments are that of a human birth, a heavenly birth or *nibbāna*, freedom from birth. The six sense-sphere heavens are those where beings may be reborn for acts of generosity and keeping the precepts. The Brahma heavens, the form-sphere realms, are where beings who practise meditation (*jhāna*) may be reborn.

2

The story of Makhādeva
Makhādeva Jātaka (9)

Vol. I, 137–9

The story of King Makhādeva's discovery of a grey hair is the most famous example of the Bodhisatta's practice of renunciation (*nekkhamma*), the third perfection.[1] In Gotama's last life such 'messengers of the gods', in the form of the old man, the sick man and the dead man, prompt his departure from his palace and impress upon him the need for a spiritual path.[2] The single grey hair here arouses a sense of urgency (*saṃvega*). The meditation manuals regard urgency as a precursor or even prerequisite for some calm (*samatha*) practices, such as the meditation on death, and say that if used skilfully it leads to peace.[3]

Although prompted by agitation, Makhādeva's decision to leave the lay life shows that renunciation was regarded as involving great reward and was not just a simple rejection of sensory pleasures. According to Indian practice there were four stages of life. The disciple (*brahmacārin*) follows his teacher in learning sacred duties; the householder (*gṛhastha*) enjoys domestic happiness and public duty; the forest life (*vānaprastha*) is for the time when these duties have been fulfilled and, lastly, the stage of the homeless wanderer (*sannyāsin*) is for the stage leading to the completion of life.[4] When he takes on the ascetic life, the renunciate gives up the active pursuit of the pleasures associated with sensory and sexual fulfilment (*kāma*) and wealth, political power and status (*artha*).[5] Just as the pleasures of youth were thought appropriate to the young and the exercise of authority to the prime of life, going out into the world was considered natural to old age. It was felt to pave the way for a real freedom from sensory ties, at an inner as well as an outer level, to give time for meditation. In Buddhism, the attributes of the first meditation (*jhāna*) are initial thought (*vitakka*), sustained thought (*vicāra*), joy (*pīti*), happiness (*sukha*) and one-pointedness (*ekaggatā*). These factors are said to arise when the meditator practises inner renunciation and finds release from the senses. Two of them, 'joy' and 'happiness', are the same words applied to sexual and sensory pleasure in texts such as the *Kāma Sūtra*.[6] In meditation they are described as occurring in a more refined and intense form, on the basis of a meditation object, without the dependence on sensory hindrances.

This story provides a paradigm of a benign and just king who enjoys each stage of life to the full. This is in striking contrast to the depiction of kingship in the Mūgapakkha Jātaka (538). In that story only the darker aspects of royal office are emphasized and pressing arguments are given against postponing the pursuit of renunciation until late in life. Thousands of years of time, the great by-product and metaphor for heavenly states of mind, do not feature at all. Makhādeva, however, like Mahāsudassana (95), lives for thousands of years in an existence that is—apart from the shock of the grey hair—almost divine. His kingship, presumably, fulfils the ideal of a just king dedicated to the welfare of his subjects.[7] In such stories the king, in the last stage of life, often cultivates the divine abidings, the meditations on loving kindness, compassion, sympathetic joy and equanimity. According to Buddhist theory all of these qualities may be present in daily life, in dealings with other beings. By cultivating them in seclusion, a just king, or anyone with a human rebirth, attains *jhāna* and becomes 'one bound for a Brahma realm'. In this Jātaka the 'happy ending' portrays renunciation and its fruit, meditation, as a natural process in the completion of a single life cycle. Despite the Bodhisatta's rebirth in a Brahma heaven he is committed, however, to renouncing 'all states of becoming', a goal for which the human form is most suitable.[8] After many aeons, the story says, Makhādeva is born again to fulfil the perfections as King Nimi, one of the last of that line of kings.[9] The story is depicted on a roundel at Bhārhut.[10]

Story from the present
'Appeared on my head'

While staying in the Jetavana Grove the Teacher told this story concerning great renunciation. It is already told in the introduction to the Jātakas.[11] At that time the monks were sitting, praising the renunciation of the Ten-Powered One. Then the Teacher arrived at the *dhamma* hall, sat in the Buddha seat and addressed the monks. 'What, bhikkhus, have you met together to discuss now?' he asked them. They replied, 'Bhante, we meet for no other discussion than to praise your renunciation'. He said, 'Bhikkhus, the Thus-gone has not just practised renunciation now. Even before this he practised renunciation.' The monks asked the Exalted One for an explanation of this. The Exalted One made clear the action which had been hidden by a previous existence.

Story from the past

Once upon a time, at Mithilā in the kingdom of Videha, there was a king called Makhādeva who was just and ruled justly. For successive periods of 84,000 years, he enjoyed the play of youth, then acted as viceroy and then was king. A long time passed. One day he called his barber: 'Good barber, at the time when you see grey hairs on my head, you should inform me.' A long time passed and one day [138] the barber saw a single grey hair amongst the collyrium-black locks of the king. He informed the king, 'Sire, a single grey hair has appeared on you.' 'Good man, pluck out the grey hair and put it into my hand.' When he had been asked the barber plucked out the hair with golden tweezers and placed it into the king's palm. At that time the king had eighty-four thousand years of his life remaining. When he saw the hair he felt a sense of urgency and in his imagination it was as if the king of death had arrived and was standing by him or that he had entered a leaf hut that was on fire. He reflected, 'Foolish Makhādeva! In the time up to the arising of this hair you have not been able to get rid of defilements!' As he pondered and pondered at the appearance of the hair an internal fire arose in him. Sweat poured from his body, his outer garments oppressed him and he wanted to pull them right off. 'I have to renounce and go forth as an ascetic this very day.' He gave the boon of a town that yielded a hundred thousand coins to the barber and summoned his eldest son. He said, 'Dear one, a grey hair has come upon my head. I have become old. I have had my fill of human pleasures and now I am going to investigate divine ones. It is time for me to renounce. You take over the kingdom but I will go forth, live in the Makhādeva mango grove and practise the teaching of the one who has gone forth into the world.' As he wished to become an ascetic the ministers approached him and asked, 'Sire, what is the reason for your going forth?', the king held the hair in his hand and spoke this verse to them:

1. 'These messengers from the gods have appeared and grown on my head,
   Taking away the prime of my life: It is the time for me to go forth.'

He spoke in this way and that very day abandoned the kingdom and took the going forth, the path of living as an ascetic. Living in that very Makhādeva mango grove he cultivated the four divine abidings for eighty-four thousand years. He died without abandoning his meditation and then took rebirth in a Brahma heaven. When he fell away from this he was again in Mithilā, as a king called Nimi. He united his diminishing family line and took the going forth in the same mango grove, cultivated the four divine abidings and went again to a Brahma heaven.

The Teacher said, 'So it was not just now that the Thus-gone practised a great renunciation. He did so in the past too.' Then he gave this talk about the teaching and revealed the four noble truths. Some there become stream-enterers, some once-returners and some never-returners.[12] So the Exalted One related these two tales and made the connections between them both, explaining the birth. 'At that time Ānanda was the barber, Rāhula the son and I was king Makhādeva.'

Notes

[1] The story features in the *Makhādeva Sutta*, no. 83 (M II 74–83).

[2] The other deva messenger is a man dressed in monk's robes (J I 59).

[3] Buddhaghosa, *Path of Purification*, p. 248 (Vism VIII 8).

[4] Basham, *The Wonder that was India*, pp. 159–60.

[5] Ibid., 166–73.

[6] See W. Doniger and S. Kakar, *Vatsayana Mallanaga: Kamasutra: A New, Complete Translation of the Sanskrit Text* (Oxford: OUP, 2002), p. lxiv, on range of meanings of joy (Sanskrit *prīti*/Pāli *pīti*) and happiness (*sukha*) in Indian thought.

[7] See stories 95, 539 and the story of King Nimi (Jātaka 541), his later incarnation (J VI 95–129).

[8] J I 21.

[9] Jātaka 541 (J VI 95).

[10] Sir A. Cunningham, *The Stupas of Bharhut* (London: 1879), Plate xlviii. It bears the inscription, in Brāhmī script, 'Maghā deviya'.

[11] This refers to the great renunciation of Gotama in his final life (J I 61ff).

[12] The first three stages of enlightenment.

3

The cane stalk story
Naḷapāna Jātaka (20)

Vol. I, 170–2

This story, particularly popular in Myanmar (Burma), is of a type that gives a folk 'explanation' for a natural occurrence: it could as easily be called 'How the cane reed got its hole'.[1] Rudyard Kipling, a lover of Jātakas, has his Buddhist lama tell one in chapter 9 of *Kim*; tales such as this must have provided him with the inspiration to compose his own fictional explanations for some natural quirks in the universe in *Just So Stories*.[2] A needle is one of the eight requisites described at this period as the basics needed by a monk to sustain life. The list varies historically but at this time the others are usually the three robes, an alms bowl, a razor, waist band and a water strainer.[3] Later items included an umbrella and sandals. Monks were expected to be reasonably self-sufficient and would be expected to do their own darning and mending: in the early days their robes were sewn from rags and pieces of cloth left in charnel grounds. The material was then washed and dyed a saffron yellow or cinnamon brown, or whatever was the cheapest kind of dye. As a reminder of their origins as cast-offs, Buddhist monks' robes are today sewn with a kind of patchwork effect. The fact that a needle case can be found anywhere as a result of the Bodhisatta's resolve reinforces a sense of the monks' freedom from ties and the suitability of the natural environment for their ascetic life.

The miracles described in the story provide a vindication of

the comprehensiveness of a Bodhisatta's resolve through mastery
or transcendence of each of the four elements, though only fire
and water are specified. A mountain is squeezed in the first to
make the imprint of the hare, involving the element of earth.[4]
The absence of rain occurs when the Buddha is so moved by the
potter Ghaṭīkāra's piety that he sees that no rain ever falls on
the spot where his house is located.[5] The element of fire is mastered
when the Bodhisatta, as a baby quail, makes a declaration of
truth that puts out a forest fire and ensures no fire ravages that
place again.[6] This one, the fourth, involves the use of air, which
assumes in this instance the miraculous power to hollow out a
cane. Although mastery of the elements is considered to be one
of the powers (*iddhi*s) that can arise after the practice of the
fourth meditation (*jhāna*), only a Bodhisatta is thought capable
of effecting these four long-lasting changes in the world. Another
miracle traditionally ascribed to a Bodhisatta in his final life, as
the Buddha, is the Twin Miracle, involving the mixing of fire and
water, which can be performed only by Buddhas. The story
here is not attributed to a perfection but does involve a statement
of truth (*saccakiriya*), which we also find in Jātakas 75 and
538. It is also one of the few that feature a resolve, or resolution
(*adhiṭṭhāna*).

Story from the present
'I saw footprints'

While going on a journey for alms in Kosalan territory, the Teacher
came to the village of Cane Drink (Naḷakapāna). When he was
staying at Ketakavana, near the Cane Drink lotus pool, he told
this story about cane stalks. At that time the monks were bathing
in the Cane Drink lotus pool and got the novices to get cane
stalks for needle cases. They found the stalks were hollow and
ready for use and went to the Teacher. 'Sir, we have had cane

stalks picked for needle cases and from tips to root they are
hollow and ready for use; why is this?' they asked. The Teacher
replied, 'This, bhikkhus, was an ancient resolve of mine,' and he
narrated this story of long ago.

Story from the past

Formerly,[7] it is said, this woody thicket was a forest. And in this
pool a certain water demon used to eat anyone who went down
into the pool. At that time the Bodhisatta was a monkey king, as
big as a red deer fawn. He had a retinue of eighty thousand
monkeys, whom he protected as they lived in the forest. He gave
advice to the tribe of monkeys: 'Friends, in this forest there are
poisonous trees and lakes haunted by non-humans. So before
you eat any fruit which you have never eaten before or drink
from any water where you have never drunk before, check with
me first.' They assented and one day came to a spot they had not
visited previously. After a very long day of travelling they searched
for water and saw a lotus pool. They did not, however, drink the
water, but sat down and waited for the Bodhisatta to arrive. The
Bodhisatta came and said, 'Friends, why are you not drinking
the water?' 'We were waiting for you,' they said. 'Well done, my
friends,' said the Bodhisatta.

Then he walked all round the pool, examined the track of
footprints and saw that they went down to the water, but that
none came back. 'There's no doubt about it,' he realized. 'This
is haunted by non-humans'. He said to them, 'You did well, my
friends, in not drinking the water. It is haunted by non-humans.'
The water demon [171] saw that they were not going down into
his territory. Making himself quite horrible to look at he divided
the water in two, emerged with a dark belly, white face and bright
red hands and feet and asked, 'Why are you sitting there? Come
down to drink the water.' Then the Bodhisatta enquired of him,

'Are you the water demon who lives here?' 'I certainly am,' he replied. 'And you take hold of anyone who comes down to the pool?' 'Yes I do. I do not let anyone go who comes to the water, even so much as a little bird. I will eat the lot of you.' 'We'll not see you eat us up,' the Bodhisatta replied. 'Yet, you will drink the water?' said the demon. 'Yes, we will drink the water. And we'll not come down and be under your power either.' 'So how are you going to drink the water?' 'Why do you think we need to come down to drink? We won't come down to the water at all. One by one, the eighty thousand of us will take a cane stalk and drink from your lake as easily as if through a hollow lotus stalk— and you'll not be able to eat us.'

Having understood this matter the Teacher, as the Fully Awakened Buddha, spoke the first part of the verse:

1. 'I saw footprints leading down but did not see them coming back.'

The Great Being spoke the second:

2. 'We'll drink the water with a cane, but you will not destroy my life.'[8]

When he had said this, the Bodhisatta had a cane stalk brought to him and, bringing to mind the perfections, he made a declaration of truth and blew down the opening. [172] The cane then and there became hollow inside so that no knot was left. 'By this method he had brought another and another and blew down each', the commentary says: he could not carry this out one by one for all the stalks that were there, so therefore we need not take it that way. The Bodhisatta circled the pond and made the resolve, 'May all the canes be completely hollow'. Now, because of the magnitude of the saving goodness of Bodhisattas, their resolve is always successful. From that time on all the canes that grow around the lake have had a single hollow right through. In this aeon, or *kalpa*, there are four wonders that last throughout the aeon: the imprint of the hare on the moon remains for an entire aeon, no fire can be lit for the entire aeon in the place where a fire was put out as it is told in the Vaṭṭaka Jātaka; no rain ever falls for the entire aeon in the place where Ghaṭīkāra had his house and at this lake all the cane stalks are completely hollow, also for the entire aeon. These four are called the miracles that last an entire aeon. The Bodhisatta, having made this resolve, sat down and took one cane. The eighty thousand monkeys each took a reed and, surrounding the pool, sat down too. They all, at the moment when he drank, sucked at their reed and drank the water while sitting on the bank of the pool. In this way the water demon got nothing and went very disgruntled back to his own dwelling place. The Bodhisatta then went back into the forest with his troop.

The Teacher said, 'This, bhikkhus, is how these reeds came to be tubular when I made a resolve in times long past.' Then he gave a *dhamma* talk and made the connections for the birth: 'At that time Devadatta was the water demon, the retinue of the Buddha were the eighty thousand monkeys and I was the monkey king who had skill in means.'

Notes

[1] According to See Than Tun, ed., *The Royal Orders of Burma*, AD *1598–1885*, V: 1788–1806 (Kyoto, 1986), pp. 60–1, the most popular stories at the beginning of the nineteenth century in Burma were the last ten and of those found in this collection, this one, 75 and 316.

[2] See *Kim*, *The Writings in Prose and Verse of Rudyard Kipling*, 27 vols (London: Macmillan, 1897–1910), XX, pp. 261–2 and *Just So Stories for Little Children*, Vol. XXI. Such tales feature throughout Indian folklore: see S. Thompson and J. Balys, *The Oral Tales of India* (Bloomington, Indiana: IUP, 1958), 'causes of animal characteristics',

motif nos. A2300–99 and 'origins of plant characteristics', A2750–99.

³ See *Story of Gotama Buddha*, p. 87 (J I 65). The needle case is described in the *Vinaya, Cullavinaya*, V, 11.

⁴ See 'The story of the hare', Jātaka 316.

⁵ See *Sutta* 81, M II 45–54.

⁶ Jātaka 35 (not in this collection).

⁷ This story, unusually, opens not with *atīte* ('once upon a time', or, literally, 'in the past') but with *pubbe*.

⁸ It is unusual to have a verse split in this way, but it illustrates the different perspective of the Buddha in the present, the Fully Awakened One, whose comments are in the past tense, and the Great Being, his past self, who employs the tense demanded by the circumstances of the action, in this case the future. Verse interjections from the Buddha in the present occur throughout the stories: here Fausbøll supplies the second part of the verse from the commentary (J I 171, n.12). There are nine syllables in the third *pāda*: this is adjusted in the modern Burmese version which gives *pissāma*, an alternative future of 'to drink', to make eight.

4

The story of the partridge
Tittira Jātaka (37)

Vol. 1, 217–20

This story of three animals is constantly recounted as an example of the correct mode of behaviour for monks in taking and giving precedence. Precedence in the East tends to have been given to the eldest person in any group or assembly, as is the case in this story. To this day in Sri Lanka it is still customary to pay homage to monks and very old people by giving them pride of place and offering prostrations. In a monastic context the hierarchy of precedence is organized with the period of time since ordination as the standard, not age in years.[1] So, for instance, when food is offered to monks it is usual for those who have been ordained the longest to be offered first: a monk ordained even a few minutes before another takes precedence over him. A monk who has been ordained for a very long time would, strictly speaking, take precedence even over a much older man who is newly ordained. This technicality makes the monastic code slightly different from the principle of honouring an old person described in the story, but the spirit of the ruling, that seniority deserves respect, is clear. The offence that transgresses this code is called *āpatti*. Not as serious as to exclude an offender from the order of monks altogether, it is regarded as warranting confession to the assembly of monks. In popular art the three animals are sometimes shown with the elephant carrying the monkey on his back, who in turn is supporting the partridge.

Story from the present
'Those who honour an old person'

The Teacher told this story on his way to Sāvatthi about the time
when the elder Sāriputta was excluded from a place of lodging.
When Anāthapiṇḍika had built a monastery and sent a message
that he had done so, the Teacher left Rājagaha and went to Vesāli,
where he stayed as long as he wished, and then decided to go to
Sāvatthi and went on his way there. At that time the disciples
of the six errant monks went on ahead and, before the elders
could take up lodgings, took over the available accommodation,
deciding, 'These will be our lodgings, for teacher, for preceptor
and for ourselves.'[2]

When the elders who came later arrived they could not find
any lodgings. Even the followers of the elder Sāriputta looked
around but could not find a place for the elder to stay. As he did
not have anywhere to spend the night, the elder monk passed
the time near the lodging place of the Teacher, sitting and walking
at the root of a tree. At dawn the Teacher came out and cleared
his throat. The elder cleared his throat too. 'Who is that?' he
asked. 'It is I, bhante, Sāriputta.' 'What are you doing here at
this time?' He told him what had happened. The Teacher listened
to what the elder had to say, pondered over it and a sense of
urgency about the teaching arose in him: 'Even while I am alive
the monks are disrespectful towards one another and lacking in
basic courtesy. What are they going to be doing when I have
attained complete *nibbāna*?'[3] So when night had given way to
dawn he called together the order of monks and asked them, 'Is
this story true, that followers of the six monks went on in front
of the elder monks and kept them out of lodgings?' 'It is true,
Exalted One,' they said. Then, reproving the followers of the
six monks, he gave a *dhamma* talk to the monks. 'Tell me, who
deserves the best accommodation, the best water and the best

food?' Some said, 'The one who has gone forth who is from a
noble family'. Some said, 'The one who has gone forth from a
family of brahmins, or a family of householders'. Others chose
variously the keeper of the monastic rules, the one who can preach
or the one who has attained the first, the second, the third or the
fourth meditation.[4] Others chose the one who has attained the
first, second, third or fourth stage of the path, the one with the
three knowledges[5] or the one with the six higher knowledges.[6]

When the monks had each had a say, according to their own
wishes, as to who deserved the best seat and such honours, the
Teacher said: [218] 'In my teaching, bhikkhus, the standard for
one who takes precedence in getting the best seat and suchlike is
not that he has gone forth from a noble family, nor that he comes
from a brahmin family, nor that he is from a householder's family,
nor that he is the keeper of the monastic rules, nor that he knows
the *sutta*s, nor that he knows *abhidhamma*, nor that he has
attained any of the meditations, nor that he has attained any stages
of the path. In this teaching, monks, it is according to seniority
that a rising from one's seat out of respect, the making of an
añjali[7] and the making of a prostration should be made, and the
best seat, water and alms should be received. This is the standard;
and therefore the elder monk is the right one to have these things.
But now, monks, here is Sāriputta, my chief disciple, the next to
turn the wheel of *dhamma*,[8] who deserves, next to me, to have
the best place to stay. He has passed the night at the root of a
tree because he could not find somewhere to sleep. And what
about you: if you lack respect and courtesy even now, how will
you live as time goes on?'

In order to instruct them further he told this story about the
past. 'Once long ago, bhikkhus, even animals concluded, "it is
not right for us to live being disrespectful, lacking in deference
and without common courtesy towards one another. Let us find
out which of us is the senior and pay due respects to him". So

they examined the matter thoroughly and when they had worked out who was the eldest, they paid respects to him and made full the path to the heavenly realms.' And he narrated this story of long ago.

Story from the past

Once upon a time, on the slopes of the Himālayas, there lived three friends beside a single large banyan tree: a partridge, a monkey and an elephant. But they became disrespectful, lacking in deference and common courtesy towards one another. So they then thought, 'It is not right that we live like this. Why don't we live so that we accord due respect to the one of us who is the eldest?' 'But which of us is the eldest?' they wondered. One day as the three of them sat at the roots of the tree they had an idea as to how to find out. The partridge and the monkey asked the elephant, 'Good elephant, what size was this banyan tree when you first knew it?' He said, 'When I was a baby this banyan tree was just a shrub too and I could walk so that it went between my thighs. When I stood over it its highest branch brushed against my navel. So I have known this tree from the time when it was just a bush.' Then the elephant and the partridge asked the monkey according to the same method. He said, 'Friends, when I was a baby monkey I used to sit on the ground [219] and even without having to stretch my neck I could eat the uppermost buds of this young banyan tree. So I have known it since it was just a sapling.' Then the monkey and the elephant asked the partridge in the same way. 'Friends, at one time there was a very large banyan tree at such and such a place. I ate the fruits and then expelled excrement over this spot. This tree grew from that. So I have known it from the time even before it existed. Therefore I am older than both of you.' At these words the monkey and the elephant said to the wise partridge, 'Friend, you are the eldest amongst us. So from this time we will accord you honour, deference, respect, prostrations and veneration. We will make prostrations and rise from our seats, make an añjali gesture, and perform actions of respect to you. We will do what you advise, and from this time onwards you should give us teaching and instruction.' So from that time the partridge gave advice, set them up in good behaviour, and followed this code himself. The three, established in the five precepts, were courteous, deferential and respectful to one another, and at the end of their lives had their next rebirth in a heaven realm.

The undertaking of the three came to be known as 'the holy life of the partridge'. Indeed bhikkhus, even as animals they were courteous, deferential and respectful towards one another. So how can you, who have gone forth in a theory and practice that has been well taught, live without courtesy, deference or respect towards one another? I advise you, monks, from this time forth, to make prostrations and rise from your seats, offering añjalis and behaving in the correct way in accordance with seniority in the matter of the best seats, water and alms. An elder monk should not be excluded from a lodging by a younger. Whoever so excludes an elder commits a serious offence.' When the Teacher had given this talk, as the Fully Awakened One he said this verse:

'Those who honour an old person are wise in the teaching: in this world they receive praise and in the next a good rebirth.'

[220] When the Teacher had spoken of the virtue of honouring seniority, he made the connection with the birth and explained: 'At that time Moggallāna was the lord elephant, Sāriputta the monkey and I was the wise partridge'.

Notes

¹ The *Vinaya* is the code of conduct for the Buddhist monastic order; along with the *Sutta* and *Abhidhamma* it constitutes one of the three 'baskets', or collections, of the teaching. For this rule see *Vinaya* II 161.

² The six errant monks and their disciples recur throughout later Buddhist texts as examples for any wrong course of action.

³ The *parinibbāna* is in early texts an epithet for *nibbāna*, but by this stage comes to be the term used to describe the entering of the Buddha or an arahat into *nibbāna* at death, so it is complete *nibbāna*.

⁴ The first four meditations (*jhānas*).

⁵ *Tevijjā*, which could refer to the three Veda knowledges of the Brahmins (see *vijja*, PED 617–18) or, in a Buddhist context, to the knowledge of the corruptions (*āsavas*), of past lives and insight into the three marks of existence, impermanence, suffering or unsatisfactoriness and not-self.

⁶ The six higher knowledges (*abhiññā*) are the miraculous powers described in the *Sāmaññaphala sutta*. They are: first, the psychic powers, with ability to become many, become invisible, walk through a wall as if it is air, etc.; second, the Divine Ear, that hears sounds far and near, heavenly or human; third, penetration of the minds of others; fourth, memory of past lives; fifth, the Divine Eye, that sees the arising and falling of beings in different conditions; and sixth, the destruction of the corruptions (*āsavas*) (D I 78–83).

⁷ The añjali is a gesture of respect. It means a cupping of the hands, and is thought to have been at one time associated with the offering of water as a form of greeting. This is uncertain, however, and nowadays in India and throughout South-East Asia it is made by placing the palms of both hands together (see also DP 43–4). Sometimes this is done holding the arms up to the forehead.

⁸ See DP I 116, *anudhammacakkham pavattako*. Even as chief disciple Sāriputta, according to this principle, would still defer to, for instance, Kondañña, the first monk to be ordained by the Buddha.

5

The Vedabbha mantra story
Vedabbha Jātaka (48)

Vol. I, 252–6

S kill in means (*upāya*) is the resourcefulness and good planning that enables the Bodhisatta to escape disaster where others, motivated by expediency or simply deficient in common sense, fail. In this story it is the teacher who lacks skill and his pupil, the Bodhisatta, who uses it. Skill in means, aided by the associated quality of wisdom, generates many of the more surprising and creative twists of plot involved in Jātaka stories. It creates solutions for dangerous situations, as in Jātakas 20 and 128, avoids the obvious and apparently more attractive option, as in Jātaka 1, and also helps in the unravelling of the mysteries which perplex others: the one with skill in means reads a situation in a way that others cannot. For the modern reader this means there is something oddly familiar about certain aspects of the tale here. A series of murders, the discovery of dead bodies by another party, deductive reasoning on the basis of external signs left at the scenes of the crimes and the presence of a clearheaded interpreter capable of reconstructing in his own mind the dependency of one crime upon another must make this one of the earliest counterparts to the detective story. The Bodhisatta's use both of deductive reasoning and imaginative reconstruction as a means of teasing out a solution to a puzzle can be seen in 'The story of the barleymeal sack' (402), particularly associated with wisdom.

The story is of special literary interest for another reason. In May 1881, Rev. Dr Richard Morris, writing in *The Contemporary Review*, noted the striking resemblance between the manner of the thieves' end and the events of Chaucer's 'Pardoner's Tale'.[1] There are many parallels between the two stories, most notably the hiding of the treasure at the bottom of the tree, the apparent friendship and collusion that turns to murder, as one goes for food and the other (or, in Chaucer's tale, the other two), guards the treasure. The final device of the mutual murder, one through poison administered earlier and the other by the sword, also features in both tales, though the 'Pardoner's Tale', like other medieval versions of the story, involves three protagonists in centre stage. The most striking similarity is in the use of almost precisely the same aphorism, in both cases delivered by a hypocrite. The thief left to his own reflections as he guards the treasure in the Jātaka pronounces, 'Greed is the root of ruin' (*lobho ca nām' esa vināsamūlam evā*) while the avaricious Pardoner twice makes the pious assertion '*Radix malorum cupiditas est*'.[2] The transportation of tales and motifs from one culture to another is an endlessly fascinating yet contested area of research. One can only speculate as to where Chaucer heard his version, perhaps amongst tales brought back by crusaders from the East. There is a counterpart in a story related in the one hundred and fifty-second night of *The Thousand Nights and a Night*.[3] 'The Merchant and the Two Sharpers' does feature three protagonists, as in Chaucer's tale, but omits key elements found both in 'The Pardoner's Tale' and the Jātaka: it contains no tag about greed being the root of ruin or evil, nor does it feature the motif of the near simultaneous death of one faction by a sword and another by poison. In the fifteen hundred years between the composition of the two stories the story was perhaps popular in a number of places and there must somewhere have been a tale that did include these elements.

Story from the present
'The one who desires profit by the wrong means'[4]

While residing at the Jetavana Grove the Teacher told this story concerning a monk who would not take advice.[5] The Teacher said to the monk, 'This is not the first time, bhikkhu, that you were difficult to speak to. [253] Through just this cause[6] you did not act upon the advice of wise men. And so it came about that you were cut in two by a sharp sword and thrown into the road. And for this one reason a thousand men met the end of their lives.' Saying this he narrated this story about long ago.

Story from the past

Once upon a time in Vārāṇasi, during the reign of Brahmadatta, there was a certain brahmin in a village who knew a mantra called Vedabbha.[7] This mantra, it was said, was costly beyond measure. If at a particular conjunction of the moon someone looked up at the sky, continuously reciting the mantra, the seven different kinds of jewels would rain down.[8] Now, at that time the Bodhisatta took an apprenticeship with that brahmin. One day the brahmin left his own village on some business or other, taking the Bodhisatta with him, and went to the kingdom of Cetiya. In a certain forest situated on the way five hundred men known as 'dispatchers'[9] practised highway robbery. They seized the Bodhisatta and the brahmin who had the spell. And why were they called the 'dispatchers'? Well, it is said that for every two men they seized they would dispatch one to bring back the ransom. So they were called dispatchers. If they seized a father and son they would send the father saying, 'You bring back the ransom and you can go away with your son.' They also used the trick after seizing a mother and daughter, setting free the mother; if they caught two brothers they set free the elder and if they caught a teacher and his pupil, they released the pupil. This time they kept the Vedabbha brahmin and sent away the Bodhisatta. The Bodhisatta paid homage to his teacher, saying, 'I'll just be away for a day or two. Don't be frightened, but just do exactly what I say. Today there will be the conjunction that brings down a shower of wealth. Whatever you do, do not—because you are unable to endure the bad situation—recite the mantra and bring down a shower of wealth. If you do, you will encounter disaster, and these five hundred thieves will too.' So he took his leave from his teacher and went in search of a ransom.

But when sunset came the thieves bound the brahmin and laid him down. And just at that moment the full moon rose in the Eastern world system.[10] The brahmin considered the position of the stars [254] and saw that the conjunction that brings down a shower of wealth had arrived. 'Why should I put up with this suffering, when I could recite the mantra, bring down a shower of jewels, and pay the ransom to the thieves? I could go just as I please.' After he had thought this he addressed the robbers, 'My good men, thieves: what did you want to seize me for?' 'For the ransom, sir,' they replied. 'Well, if that is what you want, undo my bonds as quickly as possible. Have my head washed, have me dressed in new clothes,[11] get me anointed with perfumes and adorned with flowers. Then leave me be.' The thieves listened to him and did this. The brahmin discerned the conjunction and recited the mantra, looking up into the sky. And instantly the jewels fell from the sky. The thieves grabbed together the booty, made a bundle for it in their upper garments, and left. The brahmin followed behind. And then [a new set of] five hundred thieves seized the other thieves. 'What are you kidnapping us for?' they asked. 'For riches,' they replied. 'Well, if it is for the sake of riches, just take hold of this brahmin. He, by looking at the sky, makes it rain wealth, and we were given this by him.' So the thieves set free the thieves, seized the brahmin and said, 'Give us riches'. The brahmin replied, 'Well, I would give you, but unfortunately the conjunction whereby there can be a shower of riches will not occur for another year. If you would just wait until then, I'll see that there rains another shower of wealth.' The thieves were furious. 'You stupid, evil-minded brahmin! You managed to get it to rain treasure for the others, but tell us to wait another year!' They chopped the brahmin in two with a sharp sword, threw him on the road and then quickly followed the other thieves. They did battle with them, killing them all and taking the wealth. They then split into two factions and duly fought with each other, so that two hundred and fifty men were killed. They carried on killing each other, on the same principle, until only two men were left. And so in this way a thousand men came to ruin. The two men left by these means took the treasure and came in the vicinity of a certain town. They hid the treasure in a jungle lair: one sat holding a sword [255] and acted as guard, the other went into the town with some rice in order to have it cooked. 'Greed is the root of ruin!' thought the one sitting by the booty. 'When he comes back there will be two shares of the treasure. Why don't I just kill him the moment he gets back?' So he drew his sword and sat watching for the other dispatcher to return. Meanwhile, the other dispatcher thought, 'There are going to be two shares of that wealth. Why don't I place poison into the rice and get that fellow to eat it and bring him to an end? And then there will only be one person to take possession of the wealth.' So when the rice was ready he ate his own portion, put poison in the rest, took it with him and went back to the jungle lair. But the moment he put the rice down the other cut him in two with his sword and hid him in a secret spot. Then the first dispatcher ate the rice and he too, in that spot, came to the end of his life. In this way, for the sake of the treasure, they all came to a bad end.

The Bodhisatta, however, after a day or two, came back with the ransom. Not seeing his teacher at the spot where he had been, but observing his treasure scattered around, he realized: 'My teacher did not do what I said. There will have been a shower of treasure; this will have brought ruin to them all.' So he set out on the main road. On his way he saw his teacher chopped in half on the road and said to himself, 'Oh no! he did not follow my advice and is dead.' He collected some sticks, made a funeral pyre and burnt the body, making offerings of forest flowers. Then he went on some more and he found the first five hundred dead. Then he went on farther and found two hundred and fifty dead. Going on, in gradually decreasing number, he finally found just two men who had died. 'So a thousand men less two have met their end. It must also be the case for the other two. They will not have been able to restrain themselves either. I'll go and see where they've gone.' So he went on and then saw the path that led to the jungle lair where they had taken the treasure. He saw the heap of bundles of booty and one man dead after having overturned a bowl of rice. He then surmised everything and what these men must have done. Upon investigation he saw the other man thrown down in the hidden place. 'My teacher did not pay attention to what I said and, through being himself unable to take advice, brought disaster not just to himself but to another thousand men. Indeed those who wish for their own profit by the wrong means and without good reason, like my teacher, come to grief.' Thinking this he pronounced this verse:

1. 'The one who desires profit by the wrong means comes to harm. The thieves killed the Vedabbhan, and everyone came to a disastrous end.'

The Bodhisatta continued in this way: 'My teacher put effort into causing treasure to rain down, by the wrong means and at the wrong time, and so brought about disaster to himself as well as being the cause of the destruction of others. Just like him, the one who makes an effort by the wrong means, wanting gain for himself, will not only destroy himself completely, but be the cause of others' downfall too.' When he had given the teaching in this stanza, the forest resounded with the approval of the shining gods, saying 'sādhu', 'very good'. Because of his skill in means he carried the treasure off to his own home and stayed there, for the rest of his life being generous and doing auspicious things. When he came to the end of his lifespan he went to the heaven he had fulfilled for himself.

The Teacher said, 'It is not just now that you are unable to take advice, but in the past you were too. And because of this you came to a bad end.' And he gave this teaching and gave the association with the birth: 'At that time the monk who was difficult to speak to was the Vedabbha brahmin and I was his disciple.'

Notes

[1] *The Contemporary Review*, XXXIX (May 1881), p. 730. See also W.A. Clouston, *Popular Tales and Fictions, their Migrations and Transformations*, 2 vols (Edinburgh, 1887), II, pp. 379–407. The tale is listed by S. Thompson under 'The treasure finders who murder each other', *Motif Index of Folk Literature: a classification of narrative elements in folk tales, ballads, myths, fables, mediaeval romances, exempla, fabliaux, jest-books and local legends*, 6 vols (Bloomington: Indiana University Press, 1957), IV, K, 1685.

[2] 'The Pardoner's Tale', N. Coghill trans., G. Chaucer, *Canterbury Tales* (Harmondsworth: Penguin, 1951, reprint, 2001), p. 241. See also Timothy, 6, 10: 'Greed is the root of [all] evils.'

[3] R.F. Burton, *The Thousand Nights and a Night* (London: Burton, 1885), III, 158. I am grateful to Professor Grevel Lindop for finding this.

[4] Wrong means (*anupāya*) is contrasted with skill in means.

[5] The word *dubbaca* literally means 'difficult to speak to' and describes

someone who does not take advice. Not listening to the advice of others
is an offence in the monks' rules (rule 12: *dubbacasikkhāpadaṃ*,
W. Pruitt, ed., K.R. Norman trans., *The Pāṭimokkha*, 2001, Oxford,
19–21).

⁶ I have followed one of the Burmese manuscripts (Be), which gives
ten' eva ca kāraṇena, as '*va*' seems to have been mistakenly duplicated
in the PTS version.

⁷ A place, literally, 'devoid of *darbha* grass'. This is the name of the
village where, presumably, the mantra originated.

⁸ The *nikkhattayoga*, translated here as conjunction of the moon,
refers to the passage of the moon through any one of the so-called
lunar mansions. During a yearly cycle the moon passes through different
asterisms of the sky in the same way as the sun passes through the
twelve astrological signs. There were initially twenty-seven of these,
later changed to twenty-eight. They are still used by Indian astrologers,
who usually construct charts on a lunar rather than solar basis. The
jewels described are gold, silver, beryl, crystal, ruby, sapphire or emerald
and lastly, all kinds of gems (D II 171). It is all intended to be rather
vague and mysterious.

⁹ I have followed the clever pun in the PTS translation for
pesanakacora, which seems to combine a number of meanings well.
The word means literally 'messenger thief'.

¹⁰ The *pācīnalokadhātuto*: 'the world system facing the rising sun'.
This could be a reference to the idea that there were ten world systems,
one in each direction. The sun and the moon were supposed to hide
behind Mount Meru when not visible.

¹¹ Literally 'unbeaten' and so never washed.

6

The story of five weapons
Pañcāvudha Jātaka (55)

Martial imagery is sometimes used as the means of
expressing qualities needed for a Buddhist monk and
practitioner. In one *sutta*, during discussion with a king, the
Buddha says that just as a king needs good warriors to fight on
his behalf, so the Buddha needs good monks to support his order.[1]
In another, the mind of the disciple is compared to a well-fortified
citadel, with his knowledge of texts being his armoury of spears
and swords and his energy or strength like a force of troops.[2] On
the night of the enlightenment the Buddha-to-be describes the
perfections themselves as his shield and his weapons.[3] In this story
the vocabulary of warfare is also given a spiritual and moral
application, though with a humorous twist: it shows that the
Bodhisatta path needs a bravado that is much more than military
or bodily prowess.

The heroic prince of the title is called Five Weapons and is
given five weapons by his teacher in Taxilā. The idea of weapons
as a representation of wealth or power, particularly for a deity,
was well known in ancient India and the sense of 'attribute' or
'emblem' accompanies the word *āvudha*, employed in the tale.[4]
Features such as the discus, the sword and the conch are part of
the iconography of Viṣṇu, for instance, and represent various
aspects of his nature and abilities. There are commonly five of
these, though the composition varies. For the hero in this story

the physical attributes are bow and arrow, the sword, the bill-hook and the battle hammer. The fifth, though, is a little mysterious. It could be the boy's five limbs, trained in martial arts.[5] The boy himself claims he derives his strength from wisdom, like a diamond. There are five faculties said to be developed through meditation—faith, effort, mindfulness, concentration and wisdom. The same faculties are also called powers in the list of the thirty-seven factors of awakening that lead to enlightenment. Apart from effort, mentioned in the story from the present, no other mention is made of the faculties or powers. But the reference to the last in both lists, wisdom, is perhaps intended as an encouragement to bring them to mind in some way.

Whatever the nature of the fifth weapon, or indeed all five, clearly the number five is considered important in itself. Number symbolism is an under-researched area of Buddhist thought. The number five is often associated with life in the sense sphere and the conditions that govern it. It suggests the human body, in the five limbs, the five 'heaps' (khandhas) that make up any bodily form and the five senses. It features in a number of meditative lists, such as the faculties, the powers and the jhāna factors. Annemarie Shimmel has noted the importance of the number five in many cultures of the world as suggesting protection, often with four outer elements linked by one underlying or hidden quality or strength.[6] If the diamond wisdom were the fifth weapon that would be the case here, with the fifth element being literally 'inside' the body and the other four outside it. Another interpretation of the five weapons is that they lie in keeping the five precepts, the undertakings not to kill, to steal, to indulge in sexual misconduct, to lie or to become intoxicated. When one considers what actually happens in the story it seems more likely that these, rather than wisdom, give the Bodhisatta the strength of heart to enter the forest and confront the yakkha.

The yakkha, who lives in a world governed by different kinds of 'fives', seems a monstrous personification of the 'wrong' way to live. He practises five wrong kinds of behaviour, which could be those described in another context as poverty through laziness, an evil reputation, shyness in company, anxiety at death and rebirth in an unhappy state.[7] It could simply mean here transgressions of each one of the five precepts. Certainly he is told that breaking the first of these five precepts, the undertaking not to kill other living beings, will ensure his continued existence in lower realms. Exhibiting great precision in the use of *abhidhamma*, the Bodhisatta outlines the dangers of a wrong way of life. In Buddhist cosmology these are the four bad destinies, or unfortunate rebirths, below the human realm, from which it is very difficult, though not impossible, to gain a better birth in a later life. There is also the addition of the most unhappy classes of humans, perhaps added to make another set of five for the yakkha to consider. Unskilful action (*akusala kamma*), that is accompanied by greed, hatred or delusion, is discussed in a highly technical way in the story here as the cause of rebirth in the descents. It is typical of the Jātaka world view that, unlike the monster in many ancient stories, the yakkha is not just an obstacle to be overpowered but is treated by the Bodhisatta as another being, capable of listening to argument and finding enlightenment for himself.

The tale is associated with the fifth perfection, effort (*viriya*), in the story from the present. This word, linked to English words such as 'virility' and 'virtue', has connotations of heroism and courage. In the introduction to the Jātakas the Bodhisatta is told to cultivate it, 'If you wish to find awakening go, making firm and taking upon yourself this fifth perfection, of effort. Just as a lion, the king of the beasts, whether lying down, standing or walking, exhibits unabated vigour and is always courageous.'[8] It is because of this great heroism against all odds that the story appeals and is so funny. It is not just the *abhidhamma* that is precise but its way of describing how we all get 'stuck' in tricky

situations. A strikingly similar story, 'The Wonderful Tar Baby',
emerged from the poverty-stricken Deep South of the United
States in the nineteenth century. When Brer Rabbit tries hitting
the annoyingly silent tar baby made by Brer Fox to ensnare him,
he gets stuck first with one hand and then another; then one leg
and another and, finally, the head. One writer on folk stories said
this was 'perhaps the most remarkable instance of the insidious
spread of buddhistic tales'.[9] But perhaps the presence of the tales
in two such different cultures just shows that similar stories can
emerge in different settings: the sense of exuberant vigour is
apparent in both.

Story from the present
'Whoever the man that with a brave heart'[10]

While staying in the Jetavana Grove the Teacher told this story
about a monk who had abandoned his vigour. During discussion
the Teacher asked this monk, 'Is it true what they say, bhikkhu,
that you have abandoned your vigour?' 'It is true, Exalted
One,' he replied. 'Bhikkhu, formerly wise men attained to royal
splendour after making an heroic effort at a time when heroic
effort was needed,' said the Bodhisatta and he narrated this story
about long ago.

Story from the past

Once upon a time when Brahmadatta was king in Vārāṇasi the
Bodhisatta took rebirth in the womb of the king's chief queen.
When the day came for his naming ceremony his parents plied
one hundred and eight brahmins with the pleasures of the senses,
and asked them about the marks on his body.[11] Brahmins who
were highly skilled in reading the signs discerned the splendour
of his markings and explained them, 'The prince, great king, is

endowed with great merit and luck and he will succeed to the
throne after you. He will be wise, the most excellent of men,
and exhibit in Jambudīpa skills in five weapons.'[12] [273] When
they heard the prophecy of the brahmins they gave the prince
the name 'Prince Five Weapons'.

Now when the prince had reached the age of discretion and
was sixteen years old the king told him to go and learn a craft.[13]
'With whom, sire, should I study?' 'Go, son, to the city of Taxilā
in the kingdom of Gandhāra and study with a world famous
teacher there. Pay him with this fee.' And he sent him off with a
thousand pieces. So the prince went and trained in a craft and as
he was saying goodbye he accepted a gift of five weapons from
his teacher. Armed with these he left Taxilā and went on the road
to Vārāṇasi. While he was on the road he came to a certain
forest inhabited by a yakkha called Furry Hug. At the entrance
to the forest people saw him and warned him off: 'Young man,
do not go into the forest, as there is a yakkha there called Furry
Hug, who kills every man he meets'. But the Bodhisatta placed
his trust in himself and entered the forest like a fearless, maned
lion. When he had reached the middle of the forest the yakkha
caused himself to appear, the size of a palm tree, with his head
as tall as a peaked-roof house, eyes the size of bowls, and two
tusks the size of bananas.[14] He showed himself to the Bodhisatta
with a white face, mottled belly and dark hands and feet.[15]

'Where are you going? Stay there. You are my lunch!' he said.
Then the Bodhisatta said to him, 'Yakkha, I came here with trust
in myself. You are careless that you approach me as I will destroy
you right here with a poisoned arrow.' With this threat he notched
an arrow soaked in the deadliest poison and released it. It just
stuck on to the yakkha's fur. Then he shot another and another,
till he had shot fifty. All of these also simply stuck in the yakkha's
fur. The yakkha shook off all the arrows so that they fell off him
at his feet, and then went up to the Bodhisatta. The Bodhisatta,

challenging again, drew his sword and struck at the yakkha. But the sword, which was thirty-three inches long, stuck in the yakkha's hair like before. Then the Bodhisatta struck him with a bill-hook.[16] But it stuck in his hair too. Seeing the yakkha's sticky nature he struck him with a battle hammer. But that stuck in his hair as well.

Recognizing his sticky nature, the prince said 'Sir, yakkha, [274] you have not heard of me before, but I am Prince Five Weapons. When I came into this forest that is under your control I did not put my trust in bows or anything like that but entered with trust only in myself. And today I am going to beat you so that you are crushed to powder!' Showing his resolve he roared a challenge and hit the yakkha with his right hand. It stuck in his fur. So he hit him with his left hand. It got stuck in his fur too. So he hit him with his right foot. It then got stuck. He hit him with the left foot, and that got stuck. He then hit him with his head, saying, 'I'll crush you into powder!' as he bumped him. But that got stuck in the fur too. So with five blows given, he was trapped in five places, and hung suspended: but he was still without fear and quite confident. Then the yakkha thought to himself, 'This is a lion of a man, a nobly born man and not just an ordinary man. In all the time that I have been killing on this road I have never seen such a man to equal him. I wonder why he is not afraid?' Feeling unable to eat him, he asked, 'Young man. Why are you not frightened with the fear of death?' 'Yakkha,' the Bodhisatta replied. 'Why should I be frightened? Death is destined for each life. And inside my belly is a diamond sword.[17] If you eat me you will not be able to digest this weapon. It will chop your bowels into pieces and that will be the end of your life. So we will both perish. Because of this I am not frightened.' For, it is said, the Bodhisatta was talking about the weapon of wisdom within himself.

When he heard this the yakkha thought, 'This young man is

telling the truth. It would not be possible for my stomach to digest a morsel of flesh even the size of a kidney-bean seed from the body of this lion-like man—I'll let him go.' Terrified of death, he let the Bodhisatta go. 'Young man, you are a man like a lion. I will not eat your flesh. You are freed from my hands just as the moon is freed from the mouth of Rāhu, the eclipse.[18] Go and make your circle of relatives and friends happy.' Then the Bodhisatta said to him, 'Yakkha, I will leave you, but you have performed evil. You have been cruel and have blood on your hands. You took rebirth as a yakkha as a result of eating blood and flesh. [275] If you remain here and do more evil you will go from darkness into darkness. But now that you have seen me it will not be possible for you to do evil. The destruction of life produces rebirth in a hell, in an animal realm, in the realm of ghosts or in the body of an *asura*.[19] If there is a rebirth amongst men, then it produces a shortened lifespan.' In this and in other ways the Bodhisatta spoke about the wretchedness of the five bad kinds of behaviour.[20] He gave praise to the five precepts, encouraging the yakkha in different ways, and gave a *dhamma* talk, making him amenable. He established him in the five precepts and installed him as the god of that forest, to whom offerings should be made.[21] Warning the yakkha to be careful, the Bodhisatta left the forest and at the entrance he told people what had happened. Armed with five weapons he then went to Vārāṇasi and saw his mother and father. In the course of time he ruled his kingdom in accordance with *dhamma*, being generous and performing suchlike auspicious deeds, and when he died was reborn in accordance with his *kamma*.

The Teacher gave this talk as the Fully Awakened Buddha and recited this verse:

1. 'Whoever the man that with a brave heart and a brave mind
   Cultivates the good *dhamma* for the attainment of peace:
   In the course of time he reaches the destruction of the fetters.'

In this way he gave a *dhamma* talk that led to arahatship and he revealed the four noble truths. After hearing these the monk became an arahat. The Teacher explained the connections with the birth: 'At that time Aṅgulimāla was the yakkha and I was Prince Five Weapons'.[22]

Notes

[1] S I 99–100.

[2] A IV 109–10.

[3] J I 72.

[4] 'Besides actual weapons, Ayudhas (or, in Pāli, *āvudha*s) include objects such as vessels, manuscripts, flowers and animals.' G. Bühnemann, *The Iconography of Hindu Tantric Deities*, 2 vols., (Groningen, 2000–1), I, 49.

[5] The five factors of initial thought, sustained thought, joy, happiness and one-pointedness, associated with the practice of meditation (*jhāna*), are called the 'meditation limbs' (*jhānaṅgāni*); see *Path of Purification*, p. 196 (Vism VI 66). For the five-limbed first meditation (*pañcaṅgikajhāna*), see *Vibhaṅga* 267.

[6] See A. Schimmel, 'The number of life and love', *The Mystery of Numbers* (New York: OUP, 1993), 105–21.

[7] See PED 100 for *ādīnava* (D II 85).

[8] J I 22.

[9] 'The Wonderful Tar Baby', J. Jacobs, *History of the Aesopic Fable*, p. 136 in discussing J.C. Harris, 'The Wonderful Tar Baby', *Uncle Remus* (1881). See also Francis and Thomas, *Jātaka Tales*, p. 63.

[10] *alīnacitto*: *Sutta Nipāta* v. 68—with an intrepid or brave mind. See also PED 584: [not] clinging, dull.

[11] There are thirty-two auspicious marks of a *Mahāpurisa*, or great man, which may be discerned on the body of one who is to become a Buddha or a universal monarch: they are mentioned in the story in the present in Jātaka 1. It was the custom for seers to read the marks on the body of the baby at birth to describe his potential and predict his fate. I have taken *aṭṭhasataṃ* as 108 rather than 800, which is usually

aṭṭhasatāni (see DP 1 53). It is considered an auspicious number: there are said to be 108 marks on the footprint of a Buddha.

[12] Jambudīpa, the continent of India and hence the known world.

[13] Probably a martial art.

[14] For this last feature one of the Burmese manuscripts (Be) reads *dakalimakuḷa-*, which is perhaps a muddled form of *kadalīmakula-*, bunches of bananas. The whole description is reminiscent of the protective yakkha masks that can be bought in Sri Lankan markets today.

[15] I have followed a Sinhala manuscript (Cv) which gives *seta* (white) rather than *sena* (hawk), as the other two associated compounds are concerned with colour.

[16] *Kaṇaya*: probably some kind of pole arm. In J VI 107 its tip is used to describe the iron beaks of crows. It is perhaps something with a point and a hook.

[17] The word *vajira* (diamond) has a number of connotations and so is tricky to translate: as a thunderbolt it is associated with King Sakka's weapons. 'Adamantine' is another translation. It is commonly linked to wisdom (see PED 593).

[18] Rāhu is the demon that swallows the moon or sun at the time of an eclipse and then releases them.

[19] An *asura* is a jealous god, born in a bad destiny.

[20] See introduction to this story above.

[21] In rural parts of India and Sri Lanka respect for the environment is one aspect of the ancient custom of, for instance, throwing a coconut to the local deity, or the presiding god—often Ganesh.

[22] Aṅgulimāla is an important figure in Buddhist tradition. In the lifetime in which the Bodhisatta attains Buddhahood, Aṅgulimāla is a murderous robber who becomes a convert to Buddhism (see *Theragathā*, vv. 866–91 and DPPN I 22–3). When he becomes an arahat he is constantly reviled by villagers for his earlier misdeeds. The *Aṅgulimāla paritta*, a short set of verses by which he ensured the safe delivery of a baby to a woman who had been in a long and painful delivery, is chanted to this day in Buddhist countries for women in labour. See also R.F. Gombrich, *How Buddhism Began*, pp. 135–64.

7

The story of the fish
Maccha Jātaka (75)

Vol. I, 329–32

The fable of a truthful fish is characteristic of the shorter Jātakas, which often involve an animal rebirth, contain one verse that summarizes or caps the drama and start with a frequently lengthy story from the present that provides a parallel to the one from the past. This is usually overtly Buddhist, whereas the tale from the past is a folk tale, perhaps adapted from others of that kind, with heroic or noble elements that are not necessarily described in Buddhist terminology. The 'present' stories in the very long Jātakas are often terse, providing the barest introduction to the subject of the main tale. In this tale the present story is a straightforward parallel of the events of the earlier life, though, as is often the case, the doctrinal implications and metaphoric meaning of the main story are anticipated and explored with didactic intent: it describes how the Buddha relieves sufferings not just of the body but the mind as well.

The story concerns the power of truth or truthfulness (*sacca*), the seventh perfection, and the *Basket of Conduct* takes it as an example of that—though the monks discuss its present counterpart as an example of forbearance (*khanti*) and loving kindness (*mettā*).[1] In the introduction to the Jātakas the Bodhisatta-to-be is told to cultivate truthfulness, 'just as the healing star, Venus, is balanced for gods and men in all times and seasons and does not deviate from her course'.[2] This gives us some sense of what truthfulness means in practice in a Buddhist context: it is not just a statement of what is not false but also a steady and even inspiring quality, indicative of reliability and excellence of character. It is understood that all bad states in the end arise from a kind of dishonesty.[3] According to popular supposition the Bodhisatta cannot tell a lie. In one rebirth, the Hārita Jātaka (431), the Bodhisatta, after years of ascetic practice, horrifies himself by succumbing repeatedly to lustful passion through an affair with a beautiful woman. When confronted with gossip about this he immediately confesses his sin to the king, her husband. As the narrative comments, a Bodhisatta might lapse in other ways but cannot say what is not true, for this would be a violation of reality that would prevent him from obtaining wisdom.[4] The power of truthfulness in general is evinced by the convention of Jātakas and early Buddhist literature generally that a formal declaration of what is true, usually with regard to one's own virtue, can have a magical efficacy in averting harm or danger to oneself and others. The Bodhisatta also makes one in Jātaka 20, as does the barren queen in Jātaka 538. The story of the fish king has always been popular, particularly as a tale told to children, and features as one of the *Jātakamālā* stories.[5] He is depicted in cave 17 at Ajaṇṭā.

Story from the present
'Thunder Pajjunna!'

When he was staying at the Jetavana Grove, the Teacher told this story about the time when he caused rain to fall. For it is said that the god sent no rain in the kingdom of Kosala, so that the crops withered and all the ponds and lakes dried up everywhere: the water even dried up in the lotus pond at the gateway to the Jetavana Grove. Fishes and tortoises buried themselves in the silt and lay there, but crows and hawks came and pecked at them again and again with their spear-like beaks while they wriggled, and then ate them up. The Teacher saw the ruin of all the fishes and tortoises and, with his heart stirred by great compassion, exclaimed, 'Today I must get the rain god to send down rain'. [330] So at daybreak the Buddha saw to his bodily needs and waited for the right time for the alms round. Then, with all the poise proper to the Buddha, surrounded by his company of monks, he went to Sāvatthi to beg for food. After he had eaten his meal he returned from Sāvatthi back to the monastery and, stopping by the lotus pond at Jetavana, spoke to Ānanda: 'Ānanda, bring me a cloth for bathing. I am going to wash in the lotus pool at Jetavana.' 'But sir,' replied Ānanda, 'the water has dried up in the lotus pool here and only the silt at the bottom is left.'

'Ānanda, the power of the Buddha is very great. Please bring me a cloth for bathing.' So the elder brought it. The Teacher dressed himself, arranging one end over one side and covering his body with the other. 'Now,' he said, standing at the steps of the pool, 'I shall bathe in the lotus pool at Jetavana.' At that moment Lord Sakka, king of the Heaven of the Thirty-Three Gods, saw that his throne of golden stone had become hot.[6] 'What can this be?' he thought, and observing what the cause was, he called upon the great god of the rains: 'Sir, the Teacher is standing on the highest step of the lotus pool at Jetavana, and has announced his intention to bathe. You had better send rain quickly over the whole kingdom of Kosala.' 'Certainly,' agreed the god.

And sure enough, covering himself with one rain cloud as one garment and another as an outer robe, he chanted a thunder song and leapt into the direction of the eastern world system. And in the east he raised a single rain cloud as large as a threshing floor, which grew and grew until it was the size of a hundred clouds, and then a thousand. Then, facing downwards, he gave forth roaring thunder and lightning, until finally, as if pouring water from a jug, he had covered the entire kingdom of Kosala with one flood of rain. The downpour was so unbroken that in one moment the entire Jetavana lotus tank was filled and the water came right up to the top step. At this the Teacher did bathe in the tank, and when he emerged he put on his saffron robes, arranging one robe over his body and putting his Thus-gone's outer robe so that it went over one shoulder. Then, accompanied by his retinue of monks, he went to his own private meditation hut, which was perfumed by the smell of fresh flowers. He sat down at the place that was specially prepared for the Buddha and when the monks had performed the correct duties, he gave them an inspiring talk from the highest, jewelled step and sent them away. After this he entered into the perfumed hut and lay down on his right side, in the lion posture.

In the evening the monks assembled in their *dhamma* hall and discussed it all. 'Just look at the attainment of forbearance and loving kindness in the Ten-Powered One![7] When all kinds of crops withered and the pools dried up the fishes and tortoises were experiencing terrible suffering. But, in his great compassion, he decided to save all these beings from their misfortune: he put on a bathing cloth, stood at the top step of the Jetavana lotus pool, and in one moment he had got the rain god to send down so much rain it was as if it were a complete flood. And when he came back to his monastery, he freed everyone from torments not only of body, but of the mind too.' [331] This is how their talk was going when the Teacher came out of his perfumed hut and went and joined them in the *dhamma* hall. 'So,' asked the Buddha, 'Bhikkhus: what have you been talking about while you have been meeting together?' They told him.

'Well, bhikkhus. This is not the first time that the Thus-gone has caused rain to fall at a time of general crisis. Once, when he took rebirth as an animal, he was at that time the king of the fishes.' And so he told this story of long ago:

Story from the past

Once upon a time, also in the kingdom of Kosala, and in this
very spot, at Sāvatthi, there was a certain natural gully enclosed
by a tangle of creepers, just where there is a lotus tank in the
Jetavana Grove now. The Great Being took rebirth as a fish and
dwelt there with a shoal of fellow fishes. And it happened that,
just like now, there was a drought in the land, crops used by men
withered up, the water evaporated in all the pools and water
places, and the fishes and tortoises buried themselves in the silt.
The trouble was that when the fishes had wriggled into the mud
and hidden themselves in there, crows pecked them out with
their spear-like beaks and ate them. The Great Being saw the
destruction of his relatives and said, 'Only I, and no other, have
the power to release them from this suffering. I'll make a
declaration of truth. This will get the rain god to send down
rain and I'll set my relatives free from this misery and death.'
And so the great fish pushed apart the black mud, and, blackened
like a bowl made from the finest dark wood smeared with
collyrium, he opened his eyes, which were red like well-washed
rubies, and gazed upon the sky. Then he gave a shout to Pajjunna
the rain god, a king amongst the gods.

'Sir! I am thoroughly miserable on my relatives' account. How
can it be that I, who have such virtue, experience terrible suffering
just because you do not cause rain to fall? For even though I have
been born in a condition where it is usual to eat your relatives, I
have never, from childhood, eaten a fish, even the size of a grain
of rice: no living being has lost his life because of me. By virtue
of this truth send down rain, and release my relatives and family
from suffering!'

Saying this, he gave his orders to Pajjunna, just as a lord
would to his servant, with the following verse: [332]

1. 'Thunder, Pajjunna! Spoil the treasure for the crow!
   Just take away our grief, although you bring it to our foe!'

And so, just as someone might give orders to a servant boy, the Bodhisatta made sure that Pajjuna sent a great rain over the entire kingdom of Kosala, and so relieved many beings from terrible suffering. And at the end of his life, he was reborn in accordance with his deeds.

The Teacher said, 'And so, bhikkhus, this is not the first time that the Thus-gone has caused rain to fall. Formerly I took rebirth as a fish and caused rain in just the same way.' And when he had completed his teaching he identified the birth in this way: 'At that time, the followers of the Buddha were the shoal of fishes, Ānanda was Pajjunna, the god of rain, and I was the great king.'

Notes

1 See 'Conduct of the Fish-King', I.B. Horner, *Basket of Conduct*, pp. 41–2 (Cp III.10).

2 'The Far Past' (J I 23).

3 See Bhikkhu Bodhi trans., 'A Treatise on the Pāramīs', p. 271.

4 J III 499.

5 Story 15. P. Khoroche trans., with foreword by W. Doniger, *Once the Buddha was a Monkey* (Chicago: CUP, 1989), pp. 134–8.

6 This only happens when some notable act of virtue is occurring in the world of humans.

7 An epithet for the Buddha, referring to his possession of ten powers, which include knowing how things are, knowing his own past lives and seeing the past lives of other beings (See *Mahāsīhanāda Sutta*, no. 12, M I 69–71).

8

The hair-standing-on-end story
Lomahaṃsa Jātaka 94

Vol. I, 389–91

Self-mortification, a feature of some Indian asceticism, was firmly rejected by Buddhism, as this story shows.[1] In his final life, before the enlightenment, Gotama spent several years in the company of those who practised torments of body and mind as a means of attaining liberation. These practices, thought by many ascetics at the time as the sort of 'toughening up' needed for a truly rigorous life leading to liberation, are gruesomely described in the *Mahāsaccaka Sutta*.[2] After eating at times only one grain of rice a day and allowing himself to become tormented in body and spirit, Gotama eventually decides that such practices only reinforce fear and prevent the happiness of freedom from sense desires. In the end he discards them, takes food and decides upon a course of practice formulated in the first sermon as the middle way between the two extremes of sensory overindulgence and of self-torment. He delivers this teaching to the ascetics who had been his companions before the enlightenment. This sense of the need for balance in spiritual practice persists throughout his discourses. While he certainly allowed and accommodated certain austerities in the monastic order, such as eating only one meal a day or sleeping always in the open, he resisted attempts to make such strictures applicable to all monks, or even to apply them to himself.[3] He at no time sanctions harm to one's own body or the kind of fasts sanctioned by Jainism.[4]

The story from the present here describes a follower of the Buddha who rejects 'the middle way' and embraces the path of self-torment. Sunakkhatta becomes annoyed with the Buddha's lack of display of the psychic powers, criticizes him in terms which inadvertently praise him and becomes a follower of an ascetic called Kora, who has just been reborn in a bad destiny for his practice of self-mortification. A parallel is made with the Bodhisatta's pursuit of the life of a naked ascetic. In the 'story from the past', set ninety-one aeons ago, the Bodhisatta is convinced that by seeking out discomfort he will find freedom from desire. At the moment of death, however, he recognizes that self-torment leads to a rebirth in hell and relinquishes his views. The curiously precise 'ninety-one aeons ago' is, incidentally, the time of another Buddha, Vipassī. The Bodhisatta, like Sunakkhatta, also had the option of following a good teacher at that time.[5] It is the only existence—and perhaps the fact that it is a far distant one also suggests deliberation—where the Bodhisatta features as a naked ascetic. Ninety-one aeons are also supposed to be the extent of a Buddha's memory, perhaps another indication that he regarded it as far removed from his present experience.[6]

Despite the brevity of the tale there are some difficult and important issues that go right to the heart of Buddhist doctrine. It is by tradition linked to the cultivation of the tenth perfection, equanimity, though the association is not made within the tale. Equanimity, as mental state, a concomitant of meditation and as a perfection represents an area of doctrine which is sometimes misunderstood when Buddhism is interpreted in the modern world. It is considered in Buddhism to be the outcome of the purification of feeling, which transcends, but does not reject, happiness and pain. In this way, accompanied by healthy or skilful consciousness (*kusala citta*), it can be present in day-to-day life and is carefully differentiated from its manifestation in unskilful consciousness (*akusala citta*) as indifference or boredom. When equanimity is present, sense impressions, both good and bad, are received and registered without being allowed to pull the mind in many directions. So equanimity is not regarded as involving 'detachment' but rather 'non-attachment': one image used in the *sutta*s compares some sense impressions received by a mind with equanimity to drops of water falling off a lotus leaf.[7] Equanimity may also be present in dealings with other beings. Buddhaghosa, the ancient commentator on meditation, stressing that it is not the same as indifference, compares it to the attitude of a mother to her son as he grows up and follows his own business.[8] In this aspect it may be developed as one of the divine abidings (*brahmavihāra*s), of which the others are loving kindness, compassion and sympathetic joy. The meditator takes as his object other beings, regards them with equanimity and extends the object of his meditation to fill all directions until it becomes immeasurable.[9] This releases the mind from the sense sphere so that the meditator attains *jhāna*—and a likely future rebirth in a Brahma heaven. Equanimity is also the principal factor in the fourth meditation, from which the higher knowledges (*abhiññā*s) are developed. The image used to describe the bright mind of the meditator who has practised this meditation is that of a man sitting covered from head to foot with a pure white cloth, that leaves no part of his body unpervaded.[10] There is an underlying assumption that for the practice of the fourth *jhāna* and the fourth divine abiding other factors, such as joy and happiness, associated with earlier *jhāna*s, should be developed first.

So can this story be associated with equanimity? Does it fulfil any of the criteria that would be expected of the last perfection? In the introduction to the Jātakas and the *Cariyāpiṭaka* one life is described in which equanimity is said to have been developed, which is indeed called the *Lomahaṃsa Jātaka*, the 'hair-standing-on-end story'.

These other versions describe the Bodhisatta in that life living in a charnel ground, being balanced in feeling both when abused by children and receiving homage and offerings of food from others.[11] There are, however, all sorts of problems in linking the main part of Jātaka 94 with these accounts. The *Cariyāpiṭaka* version does not describe the Bodhisatta seeking out suffering deliberately, but practising equanimity when treated in various different ways, both good and bad, in a way that is true to other canonical and commentarial descriptions of the practice of equanimity.[12] The Jātaka story, however, shows him seeking out self-mortification in a manner that is clearly not intended to be the true means to develop the perfection. The Bodhisatta acknowledges this in the verse: despite his austerities he has not eliminated longing. So while some sort of endurance is being developed by these extreme practices, they lead neither to freedom nor to real neutrality of feeling. Both in content and in the treatment of the events the two versions give us quite different 'takes' on austerities.

The story seems to involve a profound examination of the tenth perfection, in a different way from the events described in the *Basket of Conduct* (*Cariyāpiṭaka*). With his deliberate pursuit of suffering, the Bodhisatta practises a hardness that parodies equanimity and produces neither enlightenment nor wisdom. These are the kind of practices criticized constantly by the Buddha throughout his teaching career. As the image of his next rebirth arises, however, he is able to relinquish his false views. It is this willingness, in one moment, to let go of an entire lifetime of misguided ascetic practice, rather than the ability to withstand cold and heat, that gives the real testament to the development of this transformatory quality.

For a very different slant on the last perfection see 'The story of the tortoise' (273).

Story from the present
'Scorched and frozen'

The Teacher related this while staying in the Pāṭikā grove in Vesāli about Sunakkhatta.[13] At that time Sunakkhatta was an attendant of the Teacher and was roaming the country with bowl and robe when he became taken with the doctrine of Kora the Kṣatriya. He gave over the bowl and robe of the Ten-Powered One and became a householder under Kora the Kṣatriya, at the time when that man had taken rebirth as a Kāḷakañjaka Asura. Sunakkhatta declared: 'There is nothing superhuman in the teaching of the sage Gotama. He is not distinguished by truly noble knowledge and vision. The sage Gotama teaches a doctrine hammered out by arguments, connected to investigation and his own native wit. The purpose for which this teaching is given leads to the destruction of suffering.' He spoke berating the Teacher while wandering in the three walls of Vesāli. Now, the Venerable Sāriputta was going on the alms round when he heard him making his slanders. When he returned from the alms round he reported this matter to the Exalted One. The Exalted One said, 'Sāriputta, Sunakkhatta is quick to anger and a stupid fellow. He spoke in this way out of anger. By saying in anger "this leads to the end of suffering" he unwittingly extolled my praise. For he is such a stupid fellow he does not know my special excellence. [390] There are in me, Sāriputta, the six higher knowledges, this is my doctrine that is beyond that of men, the ten powers, and the four bases of confidences, knowledge of the four kinds of rebirth, and knowledge of the five kinds of rebirth after death: this is my teaching that is superhuman.[14] Whoever should say of me, that he is endowed in this way with knowledge beyond the human, should abandon the statement that there is nothing superhuman in the teaching of the ascetic Gotama. He should abandon that state of mind for, not renouncing this view he is bound, as soon as can be, for the Niraya hell.' Having described his own wise mind and the excellence of the teaching that is superhuman in this way, he added: 'They say that Sunakkhatta, Sāriputta, has confidence in the wrongful ascetic practices, that harm the body, of Kora the Kṣatriya. As he placed trust in wrongful ascetic practices it meant that he did not place his trust in me. About ninety-one aeons ago I explored the wrongful ascetic practices of outsiders, wondering if they had any essence. I lived the four-limbed holy life.[15] Yes, even I was an ascetic, practising extreme asceticism. Even I was miserable, practising extreme miseries. Even I was disgusted, practising extreme disgust. Even I was in seclusion, practising extreme seclusion!' When he had said this, being asked by the elder, he narrated this story of long ago:

Story from the past

Once upon a time, about ninety-one aeons ago, the Bodhisatta decided he would investigate a form of asceticism outside Buddhist teaching.[16] He took the going-forth, the path of ascetic life, as an Ājīvaka[17] and became a naked ascetic, living in dirty mud, secluded, dwelling on his own. When he saw men he fled, as if he were a deer. He ate extremely filthy food, and lived off tiny fishes and cow dung and suchlike. In order to keep vigilant he dwelt in a certain forest in a terrifying thicket. When he stayed there in winter snow he passed nights during the coldest time of the year[18] outside the thicket, sleeping in the open air, and at sunrise entered back into the thicket. So he spent the night wet in the snow in the open air and even in the day became wet with the drops of water that dripped within the thicket. In this way, day and night, he experienced the suffering of cold. In the last summer month he spent the day in the open air and entered the thicket by night. So during the day he was feverishly hot through the heat of the sun in the open air and at night time he found heat in the airless thicket. Sweat poured out of his body. And then he uttered this verse, which was new and had never been heard before,

1. 'Scorched and frozen he is alone in the terrifying woods.
   With no clothes, and sitting beside no fire: the sage is filled
   with longing.'

[391] Practising the holy life, that has four limbs, the Bodhisatta, as he approached the time of death, saw the sign of hell.[19] 'This undertaking really has been useless!' he thought. At that very moment he broke away from his earlier theories and grasped right view. He was reborn then in a heaven realm.

When the Teacher had given this talk he made the connection with the birth: 'On that occasion I was the Ājīvikan ascetic'.

Notes

[1] See J. Bronkhorst, *The Two Traditions of Meditation in Ancient India* (Delhi: Motilal, 1993).

[2] *Mahāsaccaka Sutta*, no. 36 (M I 237–51).

[3] See *Mahāsakuludāyi Sutta*, no. 77 (M II 1–22).

[4] For asceticism in Jainism and its relationship with Buddhism see Paul Dundas, *The Jains* (London: Routledge, 2002), pp. 140–3, 206–9.

[5] See D II 11–51.

[6] M I 483.

[7] *Indriyabhāvanā Sutta*, no. 152 (M III 300–2).

[8] See *Path of Purification*, 347 (Vism IX, 108).

[9] See, for instance, *Anuruddha Sutta*, no. 127 (M III 146–8).

[10] See, for instance, *Mahā Assapura Sutta* , no. 39 (M I 277–8).

[11] '1. I lay down in a cemetery leaning against a skeleton. Crowds of rustic children approached me and displayed a great deal of derisive behaviour/ 2. Others, exultant, thrilled in mind, brought (me) offerings

of many perfumes and garlands and a variety of food/ 3. Those who caused me anguish and those who gave me happiness—I was the same to them all; kindliness, anger did not exist/ 4. Having become balanced toward happiness and anguish, toward honours and reproaches, I was the same in all circumstances—this was my perfection of equanimity.' I.B. Horner, *Basket of Conduct*, p. 48 (Cp III.15) and, for her comparison with the Jātaka account, pp. viii–x.

[12] For instance: 'Just as he would feel equanimity on seeing a person who is neither beloved nor unloved, so he pervades all beings with equanimity.' *Vibhaṅga*, 275.

[13] Sunakkhatta seems to have been much taken with spurious teachers and transfers his allegiance on several occasions. Kora practised extreme asceticism and was reborn in a hell (see DPPN II 1206–7). The incident recounted here is described in *Mahāsīhanāda Sutta*, no. 12 (M I 68).

[14] These attributes include ones that we have already encountered in the stories. The higher knowledges are the psychic powers described in the *Sāmaññaphala Sutta* (D I 77–85), which include the ability to make a mind-made body, to walk on water, etc., to hear the gods, to see with the clairvoyant eye, and knowledge of the past lives of oneself and others. The last of the six is the knowledge of the destruction of the corruptions (*āsava*s). The ten powers are those that are possessed by the Buddha, described in the *Mahāsīhanāda Sutta* (M I 68ff), which also involves Sunakkhatta. The four bases of confidence (*vessārajja*, given in full in M I 71) are the highest knowledge, the recognition of the obstacles, recognition and teaching the way to salvation. Knowledge of the limit of the four kinds of birth is whether a birth is egg-born, viviparous, water-born or spontaneous. The knowledge of the five possible rebirths after death are the ability to discern whether rebirth will be as a hell being, animal, peta (or ghost), human or god.

[15] This is fourfold as it involves the traditional four stages of life: as learner, householder, religious practitioner and *sannyāsin*.

[16] The word is *bāhiraka*—'outsider' and, as it is in the time of a Buddha, hence non-Buddhist.

[17] At the time of the Buddha this was community founded by

74   THE JĀTAKAS

Makkhali Gosāla, who is mentioned in the *Sāmaññaphala Sutta* (D I 53)
as one of the six ascetics who do not answer the questions put to them
by king Ajātasattu.

[18] The text refers to the 'eights', probably a reference to the last four
days of the month of Megha (February) and the four at the beginning
of Phagguna (March), which would be very cold. See CPD II 241–2 and
DP I 148.

[19] According to the *abhidhamma*, a sign (*nimitta*) might arise just
before death indicating the nature of the forthcoming rebirth: so a knife
might appear to a murderer indicating his future rebirth in a bad destiny
or light to someone about to be reborn in a heaven realm. As this story
indicates even at this point change is possible.

9

The story of the great king of glory
Mahāsudassana Jātaka (95)

Vol. I, 391–3

The Mahāsudassana story, given here, is a simple account of
the end of the glorious reign of a universal monarch, who
rules by *dhamma*, not force. Its verse was made famous in the
nineteenth century by the great Pāli scholar, Thomas Rhys Davids,
when he said that it distilled the essence of Buddhist philosophy.[1]
The story is told elsewhere in Buddhist texts: the corresponding
Mahāsudassana Sutta (*Dīghanikāya*) describes, just before the
death of the Buddha, the flowering of possibilities of the human
realm and the happiness that can be experienced in the worldly
life.[2] The idea of a 'wheel-turning monarch' may have been
mythical but such a destiny, predicted as a possible alternative
for the Buddha at his birth, was felt to represent the most glorious
kind of lay existence. The emergence of such an ideal was also
reflected in the aspirations of King Aśoka.[3] The *sutta* is composed
just like a Jātaka story, down to the connections made at the
end. It is a visionary description of a utopian city and palace,
constructed with walls, stairs and pools made of the seven kinds
of gems and a populace happy through adhering to the *dhamma*:
a bountiful king produces a spacious, bountiful kingdom around
himself. The extended visualization of the *sutta* also includes
description of the monarch's seven treasures, which are the wheel,
the elephant, the horse, the jewel, the woman, the treasurer and
the adviser. These treasures can be seen depicted at Amarāvati

in a scene showing another rebirth where the Bodhisatta is a
universal monarch, as Mandhātu (Jātaka 258).[4] Two are
mentioned in the story here: the woman treasure, an earlier rebirth
of Rāhulamātā, his wife, and the adviser treasure, his son Rāhula
in an earlier life. The *Basket of Conduct* (*Cariyāpiṭaka*) also
alludes to the Mahāsudassana birth and links it with the perfection
of generosity, describing the king as making great donations to
his people and constantly searching out and helping those in need
of food or water.[5] It is curious that the Jātaka is so different in
tone from both other versions of the story, perhaps through an
assumption that these would be known anyway. It simply evokes
the themes of impermanence and acceptance, which are presented
in a sober and dignified way.

One feature of the tale is the mention of *nibbāna* here at the
end, also in the *sutta*. One might think there would be no *dhamma*
talks about *nibbāna* in the absence of a Buddha but this does
not seem to be the case.[6] Given the parallel in the story from the
present, when the Buddha is about to leave the world of men,
such a teaching is particularly suitable.

Story from the present
'Impermanent indeed are conditioned things!'

The Teacher told this story while lying on the bed in which he
attained his full enlightenment, the entry into complete *nibbāna*.[7]
It concerned a statement that the Exalted One should not be in
such an insignificant village. 'While the Thus-gone has been staying
at the Jetavana Grove the elder Sāriputta, born in Nāla town,
has entered complete *nibbāna* in Varaka during the full moon of
Kattik and the great Moggallāna has entered complete *nibbāna*
in the dark fortnight of the same month.[8] So the pair of my chief
disciples have now attained to *nibbāna*: I will enter complete

nibbāna in Kusinārā,' he said. In due course he travelled for alms, went to Kusinārā and lay down on a northern couch, never to rise again. And then the venerable Ānanda pleaded, 'Sir, the Exalted One should not enter complete *nibbāna* in this rough, insignificant little village, a jungle village, a village in the back of beyond! The Exalted One should do so in one of the other great cities such as Rājagaha.' The Teacher replied, 'Do not say, Ānanda, that this is an insignificant village, a jungle village, a village in the back of beyond! I once ruled this town, in the time of the wheel-turning monarch Mahāsudassana. At that time it was a great city encircled by a jewelled rampart of twelve leagues.' Saying this, at the request of the elder, he told the *Mahāsudassana Sutta.*

Story from the past

At that time, when Mahāsudassana had descended from the palace of *dhamma*, Queen Subhaddā saw him on a suitable bed, made of the seven kinds of jewels, that had been laid out for him near the *khadira* forest.[9] He was lying on his right side with the intention of never getting up again. 'Lord, there are these eighty-four thousand cities, the foremost of which is Kusāvatī, the royal seat. Set your heart here.' When she had said this Mahāsudassana replied, 'Do not say this, queen, but advise me rather: give up your desire for this and do not have longing'. 'Why is this?' the queen asked. 'Because today I am to die.' And then the queen, weeping, wiped her eyes and, with difficulty and in distress, said what he had asked, crying and grieving. And the other eighty-four thousand wives cried and grieved, and not one amongst the ministers and the rest could endure it, and so they all wept too. The Bodhisatta, restraining everyone, said, 'Enough, to be sure! Do not make this noise.' Addressing the queen, he said, 'Do not you cry and grieve, O queen. Even something as little as the fruit of a sesame tree is compounded and not permanent. So all things are impermanent and subject to destruction.' Saying this, he gave advice to the queen and spoke the following verse:

1. 'Impermanent indeed are conditioned things!
   For they partake in birth and old age.
   What arises, ceases;
   Happy is the calming of these things.'

Thus Mahāsudassana brought his talk to its peak with his teaching of the deathless, the great *nibbāna*, and gave this advice to the people who remained: 'Be generous, guard your virtue and keep the *uposatha*.' He then found his end in a heaven realm.

The Teacher gave this talk and made the connections with the birth: 'At that time Rāhula's mother was Queen Subhaddā; the treasure of the advisor was Rāhula,[10] the Buddha's assembly were the rest of the people and I was Mahāsudassana.'

Notes

[1] See discussion of the Hibbert Lectures, C. Allen, *The Buddha and the Sahibs: The Men Who Discovered India's Lost Religion* (London: John Murray, 2002), p. 241. Rhys Davids writes on the relationship between the Jātaka and the *sutta* in his introduction to his translation, *Dialogues of the Buddha*, 3 vols (London, 1st published 1910; 4th edn, 1959), II, pp. 192–8.

[2] *Mahāsudassana Sutta*, no. 17 (D II 169–98). The *sutta* is an expansion of a conversation that occurs in the *Mahāparinibbāna Sutta*, no. 16 (D II 146–7).

[3] On kingship in early Buddhism see Collins, *Nirvana and Other Buddhist Felicities*, pp. 414–96; Basham, *The Wonder That Was India*, p. 80ff and H.P. Ray, *The Archaeology of Seafaring in Ancient South Asia* (Cambridge: CUP, 2003), pp. 133–6. For the application of the ideal of a just kingship in King Aśoka's reign, see the series of essays in A. Seneviratna, *King Aśoka and Buddhism: Historical and Literary Studies* (Kandy: Buddhist Publication Society, 1994).

[4] J II 310–14.

[5] Translated in I.B. Horner, *Basket of Conduct*, pp. 4–5 (Cp I. 4).

[6] As a golden peacock, for instance, the Bodhisatta teaches a king about *nibbāna* in Jātaka 159 (J II 38).

[7] The death of the Buddha is traditionally termed the full enlightenment, or *parinibbāna*, as at this point he relinquishes the body that has sustained the last vestiges of his *kamma*. This has been translated as 'complete *nibbāna*' to distinguish it from the momentary experience of *nibbāna* attained at enlightenment.

[8] For death of Sāriputta and Moggallāna, see Nyanaponika Thera and Hellmuth Hecker, Bhikkhu Bodhi ed., *Great Disciples of the Buddha*, their lives, their works, their legacy (Boston and Kandy: Wisdom, 2003), pp. 47–54 and p. 100.

[9] I have followed a Sinhalese manuscript (Cv) for this. See SED 438 (*tamāla*).

[10] Rāhula, the Buddha's son in his last lifetime, is here the last of the seven 'treasures' of the universal monarch, the adviser (see D II 177).

10

The story of more than a thousand
Parosahassa Jātaka (99)

Vol. I, 405–7

In Jātaka stories the aspect of wisdom (*paññā*) is often explored in a pragmatic way that presents it as a highly developed canniness or common sense. When the Bodhisatta is applying what is called wisdom, he is often making what we would regard as a careful assessment of the situation when others are not. In this case it is Sāriputta who is exhibiting this important quality. In his last life Sāriputta is the Buddha's chief disciple and is foremost amongst his followers in the excellence of his wisdom (*mahāpaññā*).[1] In the Pāli canon his name at the beginning of a talk is usually a key that there will be some precise analysis of the subject in question, explained in great detail.[2] In art he is often shown on the right of the Buddha while the other chief disciple, Moggallāna, whose expertise is in calm meditation (*samatha*), is on the left. In this story his wisdom lies in simply paying attention to what the Bodhisatta actually said. The joke is in the use of the word nothing. The Sphere of Nothingness is, in the Buddhist tradition, one of the highest formless meditations, the seventh *jhāna*.

Story from the present
'Over a thousand meeting fools together'

While staying at the Jetavana Grove the Teacher told a story about a question asked by fools. The incident will be told in the

Sarabhaṅga Jātaka (522).[3] Now, one time the monks met together in the *dhamma* hall. They sat down and discussed the excellence of Sāriputta. 'Friend! Sāriputta, the general of the teaching, explains the meaning of a pithy remark by the Buddha,' one said to another. The Teacher came in and asked them what they had been discussing while they had been together and they told him. 'It is not just now, bhikkhus, that Sāriputta explains in detail something I have said. He used to do it before too.' And he narrated this story of long ago.

Story from the past

Once upon a time in Vārāṇasi, in the reign of Brahmadatta, the Bodhisatta was born into a Brahmin family in the north-west. He learned all kinds of craft at Taxilā and, abandoning sense pleasures, went forth as a holy man and lived in the Himālayan regions practising the five knowledges and the eight attainments. He had a following of five hundred ascetics. His elder pupil took a half of the group of holy men at the time of the rains and went to the places where men lived to obtain salt and pickles. Then the time for death came for the Bodhisatta and his pupils asked him about his level of attainment:[4] 'What excellence have you obtained?' 'It was nothing,'[5] he said and was reborn in the realm of the Gods of Streaming Radiance.[6] For, Bodhisattas, even though they may have attained to the highest state, are never reborn in a formless sphere heaven because they do not go beyond the realm of form.[7] The pupils thought that their teacher had not achieved any attainment and did not pay their respects at his cremation. The elder disciple returned and asked, 'Where is our teacher?' He was told he was dead. 'Did you ask him about his attainment?' 'We certainly did,' they replied. 'And what did he say?' 'He said he had obtained nothing! So we did not pay any respects to him,' they answered. 'You do not understand what he meant by this,' the elder pupil said. 'Our teacher had attained to the Sphere of Nothingness.' Although he explained this to them repeatedly they still did not have confidence in him. The Bodhisatta, knowing what had happened, said, 'Blind fools! They do not have confidence in my chief disciple. I'll make this matter clear to them.' So he came down from the Brahma realm and, through his great powers, positioned himself in the sky, with his feet over the top of the monastery and, explaining the power of his wisdom, he recited this verse:

1. 'Over a thousand fools might, meeting together, grieve for a century;
   It is better to have just one man with wisdom, who understands the meaning of what has been said.'

So the Great Being, standing in the sky, taught the *dhamma* and having woken the gathering of ascetics up he returned to the Brahma sphere. And the ascetics, at the end of their lives, were reborn in heaven realms too.

The Teacher gave this talk about the teaching and made the connection with the story:

'At that time Sāriputta was the elder disciple, and I was the great Mahābrahmā'.

Notes

[1] A I 23.

[2] Other arahats simply emerge from a meditation state. Sāriputta describes in exhaustive detail all the factors that are present in it. See *Anupada Sutta*, no. 111(M III 25).

[3] The story from the present in this Jātaka describes the terrible death of Moggallāna at the hands of thieves; the one from the past also includes accounts of where people have been reborn after death.

[4] It is not customary for monks to speak of their own attainments in meditation, except when reporting on them to a teacher. According

to literary custom the moment of death is a time when such attainments may be made known to one's followers if they ask.

[5] *N'atthi kiñci*. This is not the best translation, but the nearest in English to get the sense of apparent deprecation.

[6] This is the highest of the three heavens in which one may be reborn after the attainment of the second *jhāna*, which is characterized by joy, happiness and one-pointedness.

[7] A rebirth in a formless realm based on Nothingness is 60,000 aeons, which is of an even longer period of time than in the form-sphere heaven, the highest of which lasts 16,000 aeons. The Realm of Streaming Radiance, with a lifespan of eight aeons, would not be considered too long for the Bodhisatta to be away from the round of *saṃsāra*.

11

The story of the draining bucket[1]
Udañcanī Jātaka (106)

Vol. I, 416–7

This is one of a number of stories in which young, impassioned
monks are dissuaded from returning to unsuitable girls by
the Bodhisatta, perhaps an indication that some tales were intended
as entertainment and even consolation for a monastic audience.[2] The
story is one of sixteen Jātakas carved onto the earliest components
of the railing at Bodh Gaya, probably in the first century BCE.
There is certainly an element of misogyny in some Jātaka stories,
which, in common with folk tales from many areas of the world,
seem to act as safety valves of various kinds. This one is surely
intended to be humorous, however, and need not be taken as
social comment or a serious reflection on the status of women:
this would be to dismiss a strain in literature that has produced
such extravagantly comic characters as the Wife of Bath or,
recently, Hilda Rumpole![3]

Story from the present
'A happy life was mine!'

While staying in the Jetavana Grove the Teacher told a story
about desire for a coarse girl. The subject will be explained in
Culla Nārada Kassapa Jātaka in the thirteenth book.[4] Then the
Teacher asked that monk, 'Is it true bhikkhu, as they say, that you
are yearning?' 'It is true,' he replied. 'And where has your heart
been ensnared?' 'For the sake of a certain coarse girl.' 'She is

bringing you harm, bhikkhu. For, once before, you arrived at the destruction of your virtue because of her. Wavering, with a wandering mind, you found happiness only through wise men.' When he had said this he narrated a story about long ago.

Story from the past

Once upon a time in Vārāṇasi, when Brahmadatta was king, events happened which will be related in the *Culla Nārada Kassapa Jātaka*. But this time the Bodhisatta brought fruit in the evening and, opening the door to the leaf hut, said this to his son, the younger ascetic, 'Dear one, on other days you brought wood and water and food and made a fire. But today you have not made one. Why do you lie, sad-faced and pining?' 'O father, when you were away gathering various fruits a certain woman came here. She wanted me and was pleased to go with me. But I would not go until you released me. So I got her to sit down at a certain spot and returned. And now I am going to go.' The Bodhisatta realized that it was not possible to turn him back and replied, 'Go then, son. She will lead you away [417] and when she wishes to eat fish and meat or ghee, or salt or rice and suchlike she'll say to you, "Fetch this and that," and she will tire you out. Then remember our group and run away and come right back here.' So he went off in the ways of men. And when she had got him to go to her house, sure enough she did say, 'Bring me meat, bring me fish!' and got him to bring every single thing she wanted. 'This lady oppresses and treats me as if I were her servant or slave,' he thought. So he ran away and went back to his father and greeted him, saying this verse:

1. 'Happy was my life until this draining bucket of a woman tormented me:
   A thieving woman, a wife with little sensible to say, asking for sesame oil and salt.'

And then the Bodhisatta praised him, 'So be it, son. Now off you go and practise loving kindness and cultivate compassion.' And he told him about the four divine abidings and the preparations for *kasiṇa* practice.[5] And it was not long before the son won the knowledges and the meditative attainments. And through the cultivation of loving kindness towards other beings, he was reborn with his father in a heavenly Brahma realm.

The Teacher gave this *dhamma* talk, revealed the truths, and made the connections for the birth. And at the completion of the explanation of the truths the monk became established in the fruit of stream-entry. 'At that time the coarse girl was the coarse girl now, and the younger ascetic was the fretting monk. And I was the father.'

Notes

[1] CPD II 396 *Udañcanin*: draining, pulling up water. DP I 420 *udañcanī*—a bucket for drawing or ladling out water (used as a term of abuse?).

[2] There is a cluster of these tales: 30, 63, 85, 106, 147, 207, etc. See Garrett Jones, *Tales and Teachings*, pp. 81–7.

[3] See 'The Wife of Bath's Prologue', *Canterbury Tales*, pp. 258–80. Hilda Rumpole presides like a horrifying goddess over her husband's every move (see, for instance, John Mortimer, *Rumpole on Trial*, London: Viking, 1992). For Indian folklore, see 'The shrewish wife', Thompson and Balys, *Oral Tales of India*, motif no. T 251.

[4] Jātaka 477 (J IV 219–23) gives a slightly different version of the story, in which a village girl takes a shine to a monk, invites him to her house and eventually seduces him. This version also explains that 'coarse' does not mean physically coarse, but lascivious.

[5] The four divine abidings are the meditations on loving kindness, compassion, sympathetic joy and equanimity. The *kasiṇa* practice is a meditation using an external device, which is sometimes prepared by the practitioner himself. All of these practices lead to meditation (*jhāna*) and rebirth in one of the highest heavens, the Brahma realm, after death.

12

A rustic story
Bāhiya Jātaka (108)

Vol. I, 420–1

The practice of virtue often confers beauty in Jātakas. In this earthy story good training does not manage to do this but does produce desirable results, by revealing that beauty of character can be concealed in an unprepossessing and, in this case, rather fat lady. The way she finds happiness is surprising but an encouragement to all women struggling unsuccessfully with slimming diets unsuited to their body types! In ancient India the king's courtyard would have many elephants, horses and other animals around, also relieving themselves, so perhaps human urine would not be obtrusive.

Story from the present
'One should train in things to be trained'

While living dependent upon Vesāli and staying in the peaked gable hall in the Great Forest, the Teacher gave a talk about a Licchavi. It is said that the Licchavi king, a man of faith with a clear mind, sent an invitation to a group of monks, with the Buddha at the head, and organized a big meal for the monks at his own house. Now his wife was a lumbering, heavy-limbed woman, dressed in badly arranged clothes, who looked in appearance very much as if she were bloated. The Teacher expressed his appreciation for the meal by chanting an *anumodana,*[1] went back to the temple, gave a talk to the monks and entered his perfumed hut. The monks met together in the *dhamma* hall and started up a discussion: 'Sir, why does the Licchavi king have a wife with such an appearance—so lumbering and heavy-limbed? How can he take any delight in her?' The Teacher came and asked them what they were discussing and they explained. 'It is not just now, but in a past life too, that he has taken delight in a woman with a large body,' he said and told this story of long ago.

Story from the past

[421] Once upon a time in Vārāṇasi, when Brahmadatta was king, the Bodhisatta was his minister. Now there was a certain countrywoman with a massive body, wearing badly fitting clothes, who was working for wages. She had come near to the royal courtyard as she was oppressed by a great deal of urine in her body. So she covered her form with her cloak, squatted down and relieved her body of the water and then quickly got up again. At that moment the king of Vārāṇasi was looking through a window at the royal courtyard, saw this and thought, 'This woman has managed to relieve herself like that even in the courtyard without giving up her modesty and decency. She covered herself with her inner garment, let out her urine and quickly got up again. She must be in good health. Her property must be clean. Any son born in a clean house will be clean too, and virtuous. I'll make this woman my chief wife.' So he made sure that she had not already been spoken for by someone else, sent for her and put her in the position of chief wife. And she was loving and pleasing to him. Not long after, she gave birth to a son. This son became a wheel-turning monarch.[2]

The Bodhisatta saw the success of this woman and took the opportunity of speaking in this way: 'Sire: it is right to be trained in a skill that is to be learnt; why should it not be? As indeed this very meritorious lady, without giving up her modesty and decency, managed to relieve herself in a discrete way. Having achieved this, she delighted you.

1. You should train in the things in which one should be trained: people are so headstrong.
   But a rural lady has, through a modest action, delighted a king.

So the Great Being explained the excellence of those who are correct in their training.

The Teacher delivered this *dhamma* talk and made the connection with the birth:

'In this connection the lady and man of the house now were the ones then: And I was the wise minister.'

Notes

[1] An *anumodana* is usually a blessing and sometimes a talk, during which the order of monks chant for the laity who have given them a meal and transfer the merit obtained to family and relatives.

[2] A monarch who rules many kingdoms, through *dhamma*, not force: a mythical figure exemplifying an ideal of a just monarch. In accordance with his mythical status, he is described as living for multiples of eighty-four thousand years, builds wonderful palaces, gardens and cities and rules a kingdom of happy subjects. When the Buddha was born soothsayers said he had only two destinies: that he could become such a monarch, or be a Buddha.

13

The kusa grass story
Kusanāli Jātaka (121)

Vol. I 441–3

In this eulogy to friendship, the Buddha's disciple, Ānanda, is the spirit of a large, auspicious tree and the Bodhisatta the spirit of a humble clump of kusa grass.[1] His friendship with the spirit of the most distinguished tree around gives a nudge at the Indian notion of caste: the Buddha did not challenge the caste system but ignored it amongst his own order of monks and nuns, as is demonstrated in Jātaka 37. The practice of honouring particular trees, mountains or lakes as possessing an attendant spirit, a *genius loci*, is part of an innate respect for the natural environment that characterizes ancient rural cultures around the world. In Buddhist cosmology spirits who live in trees are loosely associated with the protective Heaven of the Four Kings, and are still honoured in Buddhist countries by the custom of making offerings to the gods of particular woods and mountain areas.

This is one of the few stories in which a male disciple of the Buddha is female in an earlier life.[2]

Story from the present
'Whether as an equal'

The Teacher told this story while staying in the Jetavana Grove about a firm friend of Anāthapiṇḍika's. The relatives, associates and friends of Anāthapiṇḍika said, 'You're a great treasurer, and this man is just not your equal and certainly not your superior in birth, wealth and property and so on.[3] Why do you have a friendship with him? Don't!' They kept on warning him about this. But Anāthapiṇḍika replied, 'Good friendship cannot be based upon considerations of inferiority or equality or superiority.' He refused to accept their advice and, when he went to a revenue village, he appointed him as the guardian of his household.[4] Everything happened in the same way as described in the Kālakaṅṅi (Bad Luck) Jātaka (83).[5] This time, when Anāthapiṇḍika returned to his own house and related what had happened the Teacher said: 'Houselord, a friend that is called a friend is not an inferior. The measure is his capacity to guard the principle of friendship. A friend who does that should not be held as an equal, an inferior or a superior. All friends get one over a difficult patch. You are now master of your house because of a firm friend. Those in times past also stayed in charge of their dwellings because of a firm friend.'[6]

Story from the past

Once upon a time in Vārāṇasi, during the reign of King Brahmadatta, the Bodhisatta was born in the king's pleasure grove as the spirit of a clump of kusa grass. Now in the same pleasure grove, by the auspicious regal stone, there was a beautiful tree, also called 'Mukkhaka', the Foremost, that was greatly honoured by the king. It stood up straight and its branches and forks made a canopy. Here a certain King of the Gods, who was a great friend of the Bodhisatta, had taken rebirth.[7] Now, at that time the king had only a single pillar to support his palace and that pillar started to wobble; so people informed the king about it. The king had carpenters summoned and said, 'Good sirs! My lucky palace has only one supporting pillar and that pillar is wobbling. Take the heartwood of a tree and make one that is

steady.' They said, 'Very good, sire,' and obeyed his order. They
hunted out a tree that was suitable, and, not seeing any other
around, they went into the pleasure grove and spotted the
Foremost tree. They went to the king and, when asked if they
had seen a suitable tree, [442] replied that they had. 'But, sire,
we don't dare chop it down,' they said. 'Why?' asked the king.
'We did not see any other tree and went into the pleasure grove.
We didn't see any there either, except for the 'good luck' tree.
We don't dare chop down a lucky tree.' The king ordered, 'Go
and cut it down and make the palace firm. We'll institute another
lucky tree.' They agreed and, carrying an offering of food, went
to the pleasure grove. They brought out the food and offered it
to the tree, and said that they would chop it down the next day.
The god of the tree, seeing the reason for this, thought: 'They're
going to destroy my home. Where will I take my children?' Not
seeing any place where they could go, the spirit clasped the
children to her breast and grieved. The deities of the wood, the
spirit's devoted friends, [443] came and asked what was wrong.
When they heard the cause they could not see a way of opposing
the carpenters and, embracing the spirit, began to cry. Then the
Bodhisatta went there, thinking he would see the spirit of the
tree. He heard what had happened and said, 'Let it be; do not
worry. I'll see that the tree is not cut down. When the carpenters
come tomorrow you just see what I do!'

The spirit was relieved and the next day, when it was time
for the carpenters to come, the Bodhisatta got there before they
did, assuming the form of a chameleon. He went into the crossing
at the roots of the tree and, working his way up the middle of
the tree came out at the branches, making it look as if it had
holes. Then he lay down, waving his head. The master carpenter
saw the chameleon and struck the tree with his hand. 'This tree
is full of holes and worthless!' he exclaimed. 'We didn't notice it
yesterday when we made our offerings.' He went off berating

the quite solid great tree. Because of the Bodhisatta the spirit of the tree was mistress of her dwelling. A large number of gods met together in order to congratulate the spirit. The tree spirit was delighted that it had kept its home and extolled the excellence of the Bodhisatta amongst the gods. 'Venerable gods, we possess great power but did not know this trick, because of our weak wisdom. The spirit of the kusa grass made sure I was the owner of my home, through his attainment to knowledge. A real friend can be an equal, a superior or an inferior.[8] They all help out with a trouble that has turned up for their friends, according to their own strength, and even make sure they are happy too.' Praising the way of friendship the spirit uttered this verse:

1. 'Whether as an equal, or as a superior, or as an inferior.
   He should behave one and the same.
   People should work for the highest good in troubles,
   As did this spirit of the kusa grass plant.'[9]

'Because of this, those wanting to be free from other misfortunes should make a wise man a friend and not consider whether he is equal, superior or even inferior in status.' The tree spirit gave this teaching through a verse to the assembly of gods and stayed with the spirit of the kusa grass, until they went according to their *kamma*.

The Teacher delivered this teaching and made the connection with the birth; 'At that time, Ānanda was the tree spirit and I was the kusa grass spirit.'

Notes

[1] Kusa grass, used in Brahminical ritual, has lucky associations, despite the low status of the spirit in this story. In the Kusa Jātaka a queen brings back some as proof that she has conceived her child through visiting the Heaven of the Thirty-Three Gods (Jātaka 531; J V 281).

[2] See also Mahānāradakassapa Jātaka (no. 544; J VI 255).

3 The 'great treasurer' (*mahāseṭṭhi*) is in the vocative, but the speech sounds more colloquial this way. A *seṭṭhi* can also be a foreman of a guild, a banker (PED 722).

4 *Bhogagāmaṃ*: PED 509.

5 Jātaka 83 (J I 364–5). In this story a man called Kālakaṅṅi (Bad Luck) is an old friend, who used to make mud pies with Anāthapiṇḍika when they were children. He falls upon hard times and so is taken in by Anāthapiṇḍika, who gives him responsibilities in the house, despite the warnings of friends who do not approve of a friendship they consider unlucky. His trust is justified, however, and one day while he is away some heavily armed robbers surround the house. 'Bad Luck' goes around the house, getting all the servants to make a lot of noise everywhere. This frightens the thieves, who run away. Anāthapiṇḍika is delighted that he had paid no attentions to the warnings, or the bad luck of his friend's name.

6 The word translated as 'dwelling' or 'home', used throughout this story, is *vimāna*, usually used to describe a floating palace, the home of gods in the sense-sphere heavens. As the spirit of a tree is a god associated with such a heaven, perhaps the tree is comparable to such a dwelling place.

7 There is a bit of a problem with this story. At this stage the spirit in the original is clearly male, even after rebirth in the tree. Later on, the feminine form is used, though one MS, Ck, keeps the male form for some parts of the tale. Perhaps the tale is an adaptation of an earlier story. This makes it a rare example of a disciple of the Buddha being a different sex in an earlier rebirth. In canonical Jātakas the Bodhisatta is always reborn male.

8 'Real' is a loose translation for *nāma*, which means 'by name, certainly, truly'.

9 MSS say *ahaṃ*, 'I', which does not fit, so I have emended to *ayaṃ*. This verse is tricky and I have tried to make the best sense of it.

14

The cat story
Biḷāra Jātaka (128)

Vol. I, 460–1

This cheerfully threatening story, told presumably as a veiled warning to the errant monk concerned, is of interest for the 'cat and mouse' theme, reminiscent of a Tom and Jerry cartoon, and the stagey and ruthless finale.[1] Here the Pāli, with its highly technical account of the kill itself, its use of the term *murumurā* ('munch munch'), and its reliance on the evocative 'it is said' to describe the eventual end of the body, uses the same sort of storytelling techniques and emphases we would employ now in a nursery tale. A fine doctrinal issue is raised by the fact that the Bodhisatta does kill the cat, thereby breaking the first precept, the undertaking not to kill. The Bodhisatta has presumably acted according to the *svabhava* of a mouse: it is the behaviour natural and proper to his species and station. As Richard Gombrich writes of this important aspect of ancient Indian ethics, 'everything is in a category which has its own nature, and its duty is to conform to that nature'.[2] Here it is certainly the only sensible course for the survival of the tribe. In 'The story of the fish' (Jātaka 75), however, the Bodhisatta does rise above the limitations of his species and refuses to eat other fish. The issue of the Bodhisatta's actions that produce animal rebirths is not addressed specifically in the Jātakas, though the courses of action that cause rebirth in all the bad destinies (*dugatiyo*), are discussed in other stories in this collection (1 and 55).

Story from the present
'One who makes the marks of dhamma'

While living in the Jetavana Grove the Teacher told this story about a monk who was a cheat. At that time, when the Teacher had been told about him, he said, 'It is not just now, bhikkhus, but before, too, this man was a cheat,' and he narrated this story of long ago.

Story from the past

Once upon a time, when Brahmadatta was king in Vārāṇasi, the Bodhisatta took rebirth in the womb of a mouse. On account of his intelligence and because he had a large body, like that of a little piglet, he lived in the jungle with a retinue of several hundred mice. Now, a certain cat used to wander here and there and saw the troop of mice and thought to himself, 'I'll deceive these mice and then eat them up.' So he stood on one foot, face up to the sun, drinking the wind near where the mice lived. The Bodhisatta, going on his round for food, saw him and thought, 'This must be a virtuous one.' He went up to him and asked, 'Good sir, what is your name?' 'My name is the Righteous One' was the reply. 'Why do you stand on one foot and not put four feet on the ground?' 'The earth cannot bear all four feet of mine standing on the ground, so I stand on just one.' 'Why do you open your mouth when you are standing there?' 'I do not eat food but I do eat the air.' 'And why do you stand with your face up to the sun?' 'I am paying homage to the sun.' The Bodhisatta listened to what the cat said and thought that he must be very virtuous, so from that time on he went, morning and evening, with his troop of mice to pay respects to him. Now, at the time when he was paying respects, the cat used to take the last mouse of them all, eat its flesh, then wipe his mouth and stand still. In the course of time the troop of mice became small. The mice said, 'Before, this dwelling was not sufficient for us and we stood firm without gaps. Now we are few and our dwelling is not even filled. Why is this?' They asked the Bodhisatta about what had happened. The Bodhisatta pondered about why the mice should have come to this diminution. Harbouring a suspicion about the cat, [461] he decided to test him out. When it was time to pay respects he let the remaining mice go first and stayed himself at the back. The cat sprang up to him. The Bodhisatta though saw him springing forward to seize him and said, 'Mr Cat, so this is the observance of vows and your wonderful righteousness! You carry on putting on a show of righteousness just for the sake of harming others.' When he had said this he spoke this verse:

1. 'Whoever puts up a flag of righteousness, but secretly indulges in evil,
   is friendly to beings with what is called "the practice of a cat"!'

The mouse king said this and then sprang up, caught him by the throat and bit his windpipe, just under the jaw, so that his larynx burst and he died. The troop of mice returned to the cat and ate him up with a 'munch munch' sound. Or rather it is said that those who came first did, as those who came later did not get any at all. And from that time the company of mice lived without fear. The Teacher gave this *dhamma* talk and made the connection with the birth: 'At that time the hypocritical monk was the cat and I was the king of the mice.'

Notes

¹ The title of the story and the verse, the older parts of the text, refer to a cat, though the prose speaks of a jackal (*sigāla*). Other Indian counterparts are discussed in M. Winternitz, *A History of Indian Literature*, II, p.122, n.2, who cites a parallel in the *Mahābhārata*, V,

160, 13. Manu notes that 'anyone whose religion is just a flag, who is insatiably greedy, fraudulent, a hypocritical deceiver of people, violent, allying himself with anyone and everyone, should be recognized as a man who acts like a cat' (W. Doniger with B.K. Smith, *The Laws of Manu* (Harmondsworth: Penguin, 1991), p. 92 (4.195).

² R.F. Gombrich and G. Obeyesekare, *Buddhism Transformed: Religion and Change in Sri Lanka*, (Princeton: Princeton University Press, 1988), p. 46.

15

The story of the kiṃsuka tree
Kiṃsukopama Jātaka (248)

Vol. II, 184–5

The Buddha, a long-sighted tactician, made efforts to ensure that there would be minimal grounds for discord about the path after his death. The intention of this story about a tree that appears different in various seasons would have been to defuse potential causes of schism or splits as regards the methods involved in attaining enlightenment. On several occasions in the *sutta*s the Buddha draws attention to the varied qualities of the arahats, or enlightened beings. While each has attained freedom, different qualities of excellence emerge according to the nature of the person involved. Some, such as Moggallāna, are skilled in calm meditation (*samatha*) and the development of psychic powers. Some, such as Sāriputta, his chief disciple, are highly developed in insight (*vipassanā*).[1] This sense of variation within the single system is also reflected in the ways in which arahats attain enlightenment. Although all need some degree of calm, insight and virtue (*sīla*), the extent to which people pursue these at different stages of development varies according to temperament. Meditation subjects are usually given according to temperament, a practice that dates from the earliest texts.[2] Some people are more suited to a way that is principally based on insight first, and then calm, while others might need more calm in the first instance.[3] In one *sutta*, the Buddha notes that once enlightenment has been obtained, it is natural that the one who has a particular quality

of excellence himself will appreciate others who exhibit it too.[4]
So, different meditation subjects are given to the brothers,
according to their needs. Once they have attained enlightenment
they themselves need to investigate to understand how others
have reached the same point: the tree appears different to
different viewers at different times.

With its use of two verses, this story highlights the different
perspectives of the Bodhisatta, commenting in the past, and the
Buddha, in the present, able to compare the two situations.

Story from the present
'You all saw the kiṃsuka tree'

The Teacher told this story while staying in the Jetavana Grove
about the kiṃsuka tree. Four monks approached the Thus-gone
for a meditation subject. Each took a meditation subject and went
back to his night-time and daytime haunts. One of them became
an arahat after exploring the six spheres of contact,[5] one after
exploring the five aggregates,[6] one after exploring the four great
elements[7] and another after exploring the eighteen bases.[8] They
asked the Teacher about their distinctive attainments. Then this
thought arose in one monk. 'Nibbāna is of a single nature for
all these kinds of meditation. How do all these methods lead to
arahatship?' he asked the Teacher. 'This diversity is like the brothers
and the sight of the kiṃsuka tree' he said. 'Explain this matter
to us.' So, asked by the monks, the Buddha narrated a story of
long ago.

Story from the past

Once upon a time in Vārāṇasi, during the reign of Brahmadatta,
the king had four sons. They sent for their charioteer and said,
'We'd like to see a kiṃsuka, a thingumme tree.[9] Show us a

kiṃsuka tree.' The charioteer said, 'Very well, I'll show you one'. But he did not show it to them when they were together. He got the elder brother to sit upon the chariot, took him to the forest and showed him one, pointing out, 'This is a kiṃsuka'. He showed him the tree at a time when there were just buds on the trunk. Another he showed when the leaves were fresh, another at the time when it was flowering and another at the time when it was bearing fruit. In due course the four brothers were sitting down and one said, 'What kind of a tree is a kiṃsuka?' One put forward the observation, 'It is just like a charred stump'. A second, 'It is like a banyan tree'. A third, 'It is like a piece of flesh'. A fourth, 'It is like an acacia'. As they were not satisfied with one another's explanation they went to their father. 'Sire, what kind of a tree is a kiṃsuka?' 'How have you all explained it?' he asked. So they told him the way that each had described it. The king said, 'You four saw the kiṃsuka tree. The charioteer showed you the whole of the kiṃsuka, but you did not question him in detail and ask, "What is it like in this season?" or "What is it like in that season?" So doubts arose in you.' Saying this he uttered a first verse:

1. 'You all saw the kiṃsuka tree, so why are you all confused?
   You did not enquire from the charioteer about all the conditions!'

The Teacher gave them this explanation. 'So, monks, just as the four brothers made distinctions through not asking about the kiṃsuka and generated doubt, so you have produced puzzlement in this matter too.'[10] Saying this, as the Fully Awakened Being he produced the second verse:

2. 'Thus by all the knowledges of which *dhamma*s are not known,
   These men have doubt in *dhamma*s just as the brothers did
   in the kiṃsuka.'

The Teacher gave this talk about the teaching and explained the birth story. 'At that time I was the king of Vārāṇasi.'

Notes

[1] See A I 23ff.

[2] A famous example of the problems of meditating without a teacher is Meghiya, who tries and fails and then is given several meditation subjects to suit his temperament (*Udāna*, 4.1).

[3] See for instance A II 157. On this subject, see L.S. Cousins, '*Samatha-Yāna* and *Vipassanā-Yāna*', G. Dhammapala et al. eds, *Buddhist Studies in honour of Hammalava Saddhātissa* (Nugegoda 1984), pp. 56–68.

[4] See *Mahāgosiṅga Sutta*, no. 32, M I 212–19.

[5] The six spheres of contact are the six areas in which sense perception occurs: body, smell, taste, sight, sound and the mind itself, considered in early Buddhism to be a sense too.

[6] The five *khandhas* of form, feeling, perception, volitional activities and consciousness comprise the basic components of a being and are a usual subject for insight practice as a means of discerning 'not-self'.

[7] The four great elements are earth, water, air and fire, which may be found in the outside world and within one's own body, with bones and sinews under the category of earth, blood and phlegm water, winds in the body air and warmth fire. Practices involving the four elements are usually associated with the development of calm, *samatha*, which may then be developed to the pursuit of insight, *vipassanā*.

[8] The eighteen bases (*dhātus*) occur in Buddhist *abhidhamma*, or higher philosophy, and involve a breakdown of the six contacts at the spheres of sense. The list comes to eighteen through the three principles necessary for each of the six sense contacts to occur: sight, visible shape and eye consciousness for instance are all required for contact at the eye door to occur, hearing, a sound and ear consciousness for contact at the ear door. In early Buddhism the mind is regarded as the sixth sense (DhS 1333).

[9] The kiṃsuka tree. This literally means 'whatever you like' or 'what do you call it', so denoting a strange tree (PED 213). The English translation 'thingumme' suggests the right air of confusion. It is the popular name for *Butea frondosa*, a moderate-sized deciduous, known as Dhak or Palas. It flowers from February to April. The flowers appear in clumps and are densely crowded on branches which are at that time

leafless. The leaves fall off in spring, when orange-red flowers blossom with the appearance of a flame. Its leaves are used as plates and wrapping, it produces a yellow dye and is regarded as medicinal in ayurveda. Despite the PTS translation, it is not the *Cercis siliquastrum*, or Judas tree. For a discussion of the tree see Bhikkhu Bodhi, *Connected Discourses of the Buddha* (Oxford: Wisdom/PTS, 2000), II, n.204, 1427–8, which explains its name as an ancient Indian joke.

[10] The puzzlement would not have arisen for the monks from doubt, for this hindrance to the mind is completely eliminated at stream-entry. Their lack of real investigation, however, is being heavily criticized through this comparison of their disagreement to the doubts of the brothers.

16

The story of the tortoise
Kacchapa Jātaka (273)

Vol. III, 359–61

In the introduction to the Jātakas the Bodhisatta is told, 'Just as the earth remains unperturbed at both the pure and impure thrown down upon it, and avoids both anger and favour, so you too be balanced at all times to the happy and the painful.'[1] This story of a very mischievous monkey, the only Jātaka that is explicitly assigned within the tale itself to equanimity, tests this in a funny and decidedly undignified way. W.H.D. Rouse, out of deference to Victorian sensibilities, translated the tale in 1895 into Latin. Its humour, however, is characteristic of ancient Indian folk tales. A *Pañcatantra* story entitled 'The monkey that pulled the wedge' involves a comparable situation that lacks the timely intervention of a compassionate Bodhisatta.[2] The ancient editors clearly felt that a little laughter would not go amiss in considering the potentially remote qualities of the last and, by the usual ordering of Indian lists of this kind, in some ways pre-eminent perfection.[3] Equanimity, the aspect of feeling untroubled by difficulties or excitement, is not the same as indifference to the sufferings of others, as the great Buddhaghosa notes and as this story shows.[4]

Story from the present
'Who is this with food that has been collected?'

While staying in the Jetavana Grove the Teacher told a story about the calming of a dispute between two chief ministers of King Kosala. The story from the present is told in the second book.[5]

Story from the past

Once upon a time, during the reign of Brahmadatta in Vārāṇasi, the Bodhisatta took rebirth in a family of Brahmins in the kingdom of Kāsi. When he came of age he learnt all crafts at Taxilā and then, abandoning sense pleasures, he left home to become a holy man. He made his dwelling at the foot of the Himālayas, on the banks of the Ganga, and built a hermitage. Reaching the higher knowledges and the meditative attainments he enjoyed the play of meditation. In this birth, they say, the Bodhisatta reached an excellent state of balance and was fulfilling the perfection of equanimity. Now, while he was sitting at the door of his leaf hut a certain reckless and badly behaved monkey used to put his penis into the Bodhisatta's ears and ejaculate there. The Bodhisatta was not at all perturbed but just sat there in a state of equilibrium. One day a certain tortoise emerged from the water and slept, basking in the sunshine, with his mouth open. When he saw him, the lewd monkey placed his penis into the tortoise's mouth. Now, when the tortoise woke up he bit the penis as if he were closing it in a box. The monkey experienced intense pain and unable to endure the painful feeling the monkey thought, 'O who is there that can release me from this terrible suffering? I'll go to him!' Then he thought, 'There is no one else other than the ascetic who is able to release me from this suffering. I'll have to go to him.' Lifting the tortoise up with both hands, he went to the Bodhisatta. The Bodhisatta, making a joke with the badly behaved monkey, said the first verse:

1. [360] 'Who is the priest who comes with food in a bowl,[6] hands filled?

From where do you bring almsfood?
What faithful person have you approached?'

When he heard this, the badly behaved monkey spoke the second verse:

2. 'I am a witless monkey: I've touched what should not be touched!
   You are able to release me, dear sir, and,
   set free, I may go to the mountain.'

The Bodhisatta then conversed with the tortoise and spoke a third verse:

3. 'The tortoises are Kassapas, the monkeys are Koṇḍaññas:
   Kassapa, free the Koṇḍañña now that you have had sexual intercourse with him.'[7]

[361] The tortoise listened to the Bodhisatta's words and, with a mind made clear because of them, released the monkey's penis. The monkey, freed, paid homage to the Bodhisatta and fled, and never again saw him nor did he return to the spot. The tortoise also paid homage to the Bodhisatta and went back to his own place. The Bodhisatta, not lapsing at all in his meditation, had his next birth in a Brahma heaven.

The Teacher gave this talk, explained the truths and made the connection with the birth: 'At that time the two chief ministers were the tortoise and the monkey and I was the ascetic.'

Notes

[1] 'The Far Past' (J I 24).

[2] Patrick Olivelle trans., *Pañcatantra*, 8. The story from the past of this Jātaka is also translated by John Garrett Jones, *Tales and Teachings*, pp. 194–5.

[3] The importance of laughter is one of the unexplored areas of

Buddhist philosophy. For one helpful study, see Walpola Rahula, 'Humour in Pāli Literature', *Journal of the Pāli Text Society*, IX, 1981, pp. 156–74.

⁴ See *Path of Purification*, p. 347 (Vism IX 108).

⁵ The Uraga Jātaka (154) gives a story from the present where two high-ranking soldiers quarrelled whenever they saw each other. No one could make them agree. The Buddha, seeing that they were both near the attainment of stream-entry, went to the house of one, asked for alms, and spoke to him on the benefits of loving kindness before teaching the four noble truths. He did the same at the other's house. Both attained stream-entry, confessed their faults to one another and ate together that very day in the Buddha's presence (J II 12–14).

⁶ The *Critical Pāli Dictionary* (CPD II 426), following an ancient commentary, reads *vaḍḍhitabhattaṃ*, 'with food in a bowl', for this passage.

⁷ These are evidently two common family names: see DPPN I 553 and 683. Possibly there is a joke using the names of the two chief ministers? At any rate it seems to have the desired effect on the tortoise who is described as clear in mind (*pasanno*).

17

The story of the one who taught forbearance
Khantivādī Jātaka (313)

Vol. III, 39–43

This story is cited in the introduction to the Jātakas as exemplifying the sixth perfection, of forbearance (*khanti*). 'I showed no anger to the king of Kāsi when he attacked me with a sharp axe as though I was an inanimate thing; this is my perfection of forbearance.'[1] Andrew Skilton and Kate Cosby point out, in their discussion of this perfection, that in practice in later texts the word *khanti* sometimes has a rather more positive force than patience or forbearance, its usual translations, being derived from the Sanskrit word *kham*, meaning 'to be pleased, willing to', not the root *kṣam*, 'to be patient, to endure', as was supposed.[2] In early Buddhism it tends to be associated with acquiescence under very difficult conditions, so the word 'forbearance' has been used in these stories.[3] The tale has been a favourite subject for Jātaka art, and depictions of the ascetic are shown in cave 2 at Ajaṇṭā, at Bhārhut and at Nāgārjunakoṇḍa. The tale also features in the *Jātakamālā* collection.[4] It has always been popular in Sri Lanka and was depicted in seven monasteries in the nineteenth century, though only the one at Degaldoruva, near Kandy, remains.[5]

Story from the present
'The one who cut your hands and feet'

While staying at the Jetavana Grove the Teacher told this story about a certain angry man. The story is given below. The Teacher said to that monk, 'Why are you angry during the time of a Buddha who is without anger? Wise men of old, even thought they experienced a thousand blows to the body, and had their hands, feet and nose chopped off by another, still did not become angry.' So he narrated this story of long ago.

Story from the past

Once upon a time in Vārāṇasi there was a king called Kalābu, who ruled the kingdom of Kāsi. At that time the Bodhisatta took rebirth in a family of rich brahmins who had eighty crore rupees. He was called the young man Kuṇḍaka (Red Rice-husk Powder) and when he came to be an adult he went to Taxilā where he received teaching in all kinds of skills. He then set up his own household and after the death of his mother and father considered the pile of his wealth. 'After they produced this wealth my relatives could not take it with them when they went. And neither will I be able to take it with me when I go.' So he distributed his wealth carefully, giving it to whoever was worthy to have it, and then went forth into the Himālayas and stayed there for a long time, living off various kinds of fruit. Then he went down into inhabited regions in search of salt and pickles. In due course he arrived at Vārāṇasi and stayed in the royal park. The next day he went on an alms round in the city and came to the door of the house of the general of the army. The general, impressed with the man's bearing and posture, asked him into the house and gave him the food that had been prepared for himself. [40] The general obtained an agreement from him and persuaded him to stay right there in the royal park.

Then one day the king of Kāsi, intoxicated with drink, came into the park in great splendour with a company of dancers. He had a couch arranged on the auspicious slab of stone and lay upon the lap of a certain girl that was his favourite while the dancing girls, skilled in dances accompanied by singing and music, entertained him. Utterly magnificent, as if he were Sakka, the king of the gods, he fell fast asleep. And then the ladies said, 'The man that we are performing our songs and music for has gone to sleep. What is the point in us singing?' So they dropped their lutes and other musical instruments carelessly and set off for the garden. With minds intent on pleasure they delighted in all the different kinds of fruit and flowers. Now, at that time the Bodhisatta was sitting in the garden under a sāl tree in full bloom; he was like a splendid elephant, passing the time in enjoyment of the happiness of seclusion from the world. As the women were wandering around they saw him and said, 'Come here ladies. Let's sit down and listen to something from the recluse sitting at the roots of the tree until the king wakes up.' So they went and paid respects to him and sat in a circle around him. 'Please tell us something that is worth listening to,' they asked. The Bodhisatta taught *dhamma* to them.

At this point the lady who was the favourite moved her legs and woke the king. As the king woke up he could not see his women. 'Where have those wretched women gone?' he asked. 'Great king, they have gone to sit in attendance upon a certain recluse.' The king was furious and grabbed his sword. 'I'll teach that cheating ascetic a lesson.' He then went off in a rage. Then the women saw the angry king approaching and the more favoured of them took the sword from his hand and calmed him down. He then went up to the Bodhisatta and stood by him. 'So what do you teach, ascetic?' 'I teach the doctrine of forbearance,' he replied. 'And what is forbearance?' he asked. 'It is not being angry with others who are abusive, violent and slanderous,' he replied. 'I'll see now just how real this forbearance of yours is!' [41] And he called for his executioner of thieves.

The executioner arrived bringing an axe and scourge of thorns and wearing the saffron robe decorated with a red garland, his usual practice for his work. He paid homage to the king and

asked what he should do. 'Give a terrible punishment to this thief;
take your scourge of thorns and drag him down to the ground.
Beat him front and back, on both sides: give him two thousand
lashes even on four sides.' So he did this. He tore the Bodhisatta's
body, he tore his skin,[6] and he tore into his flesh so that it was
dripping with blood. Then the king said, 'So what do you preach
about this, bhikkhu?' 'The doctrine of forbearance, great king.
You think that this forbearance only exists on the surface of my
skin, but it is not just skin deep. It is established in the depths of
my heart, where you cannot see it, great king.'

'What shall I do now?' asked the executioner. 'Cut both hands
off this cheating, matted-haired ascetic,' he said. So he put him
on the executioner's block, took his axe and cut off his hands.
Then he commanded, 'Cut off the feet!' and the executioner did
so. Blood flowed from the stumps of his hands and feet like lac
juice from a cracked jug. 'So what is your doctrine now?' he asked.
'It is the doctrine of forbearance, great king. You think that my
forbearance resides in the ends of my hands and feet but it is not
there, it is established in a deeper place.' The king then commanded
that his nose and ears be cut off and the executioner did that.
The entire body was covered in blood. Then he asked, 'So what
is your doctrine called?' 'Great king, it is still called the doctrine
of forbearance. Do not think that forbearance is established only
at the tips of my nose and ears. Forbearance is established deep in
the recesses of my heart.' The king said, 'Then just sit right there,
you cheating, matted-haired ascetic, and extol that forbearance.'
He struck the Bodhisatta in the heart with his foot and left. When
he had gone [42] the general gently sat the Bodhisatta up and
wiped the blood from the stumps of his hands, feet, ears and
nose with bandages made from his clothes.[7] He then paid respects
to him and sat down to one side. 'If you wish to be angry with
anyone who has harmed you, sir, it is with the king and no one
else.' Making this entreaty he spoke the first verse:

1. 'The one who cut your hands and feet and nose and ears:
   Be angry with him, great hero, and do not ruin the kingdom.'

When he heard this the Bodhisatta uttered a second verse:

2. 'The one who cut my hands and feet and nose and ears is the
   king.
   May he live for a long time. Men such as I do not get angry.'

As the king left the park, and at the very moment that he left
the line of vision of the Bodhisatta, the great earth, that is two
hundred and forty thousand yojanas thick, ripped in two, like a
strong, tough garment of cloth. A flame darted from the Avīci
hell and seized the king, as if enveloping him with the bright red
robe of his royal family. And at the gate to the park the king fell
into the Avīci hell and was established there. The Bodhisatta
died that very day. The king's men and the citizens came with
perfumes, garlands and incense in their hands and performed the
funeral rites for the Bodhisatta. And some said that the Bodhisatta
had gone back to the Himālayas, though this was not so.

3. [43] 'In times long past there was an ascetic, an exemplar of
   forbearance,
   Even when the king of Kāsi robbed him of his health,
   He was still endowed with forbearance.

4. There was a terrible result from the scourge of that man's
   actions:
   The king of Kāsi experienced this when he was consigned to
   hell.'

The Fully Awakened Buddha uttered these two verses.

The Teacher gave this *dhamma* talk and revealed the truths,
making the connections with the birth. When the truths were
concluded the angry monk was established in the fruit of never-
return and the others reached the fruit of stream-entry. 'At that

time Devadatta was Kalābu, the king of Kāsi, Sāriputta was the general and I was the patient ascetic.'

Notes

[1] *The Story of Gotama Buddha*, p. 60 (J I 46).

[2] See their translation, P. Williams intro., *Bodhicaryāvatāra* (Oxford: OUP, 1996), pp. 48–9.

[3] 'The Far Past' (J I 22–3). Winternitz notes that this story is not an adaptation of other Indian tales, but 'a genuine product of Buddhism' (*A History of Indian Literature*, II, p. 145, n. 2).

[4] Story 28: Khoroche, *Once the Buddha was a Monkey*, pp. 253–67.

[5] Holt, *Religious World of Kīrti Śrī*, pp. 79–81.

[6] I have read *Chaviṃ*, in the accusative, with a Sinhalese manuscript.

[7] Here the tip (*koṭi*) clearly refers to the stumps left after the limbs have been cut off, rather than the limbs and parts of the body themselves.

18

The story of the hare
Sasa Jātaka (316)

Vol. III, 51–6

In the introduction to the Jātakas the Bodhisatta-to-be is told by the last Buddha to be unstinting in his generosity. 'Just as a jar filled to the brim, toppled by someone, pours forth water, and does not guard anything that remains there, so you, when you see supplicants, low, middling or high, practise generosity, like the toppled jar with nothing remaining.'[1] Generosity, as the first perfection, is the basis for all the others. Throughout Jātakas the first injunction when any discourse is delivered is to give: donations to the poor, food to guests and, most auspiciously of all, food, support and honour to holy men. Stories of the boundless generosity of the Bodhisatta, to the extent that he offers his own body or even parts of it, are frequent in the Jātakas. Among the most famous of these is the Sivi Jātaka (499), where the Bodhisatta offers his own eyes but has his vision restored by Sakka. In the Vessantara Jātaka (547), in which the Bodhisatta gives away his wife and children, Sakka again intervenes and, masquerading as a brahmin, asks Vessantara for his wife, but returns her without committing any violation. The children are bought from the evil brahmin who has enslaved them, by more mundane means of gold; the brahmin then dies from overeating.[2] There is clearly a symbolic element in these stories, borne out by the usual outcome of the acts of giving: the fairy-tale understanding that what is given freely will be found again underlies Jātakas where the Bodhisatta offers himself. Usually he is saved from his own wish to give by Sakka, the lord of the heaven where beings are reborn for practising generosity and virtue: Sakka seems to personify a kind of protective common sense in the world. Sometimes what has been lost is soon restored, as in the Sivi Jātaka. If the Bodhisatta does die through his actions he immediately experiences a heavenly rebirth: generosity is simply felt in Buddhist countries to bring good luck. 'The story of the hare' is cited almost universally as fulfilling the first perfection: the fact that it is generosity offered to a holy man, on an *uposatha* day, renders it particularly auspicious. The comedy of the self-righteousness of the otter and the jackal, who steal so they can offer alms, gives a nice counterpoint to the action.

It is the Bodhisatta's only rebirth as a hare. For this story to be completely effective, one needs to be in the southern hemisphere, where the hare appears clearly upright on the face of the moon on the night of the full moon, the long ears loosely following the line of the upper rim. The generous hare may be seen depicted throughout temples in Sri Lanka: in the Asigiriya temple in Kandy, for instance, he is shown painted in the moon on one side of a standing Buddha figure, with the sun on the other. He is one of the earliest Jātaka figures in Sri Lanka, shown in the vestibule of Tivanka shrine.[3] In India he is depicted at Nāgārjunakoṇḍa among third-century CE sculptures, found on the north wing of the main gallery of the island museum. The tale has counterparts in Indian and Chinese folklore and features in the *Jātakamālā* collection.[4] It has always been popular throughout South-East Asia.

Story from the present
'I've got seven red fish'

While living in the Jetavana Grove the Teacher told this story about a gift of all the requisites. It is said that in Sāvatthi a certain

man of property made a gift of all the requisites to the order of
monks, with the Buddha at its head. He had a pavilion put up at
the door of his house and invited the order of monks, with the
Buddha at its head, asked them to take the very comfortable seats
that he had had prepared in the pavilion and gave a meal to them
of various kinds of the most delicious tasting and abundant food.
'Come again tomorrow, and the next day,' he urged. He invited
them every day for seven days and on the seventh day he gave
all the requisites to five hundred monks in front of the Buddha.
The Teacher voiced his appreciation for the food, the services
given and the shelter. 'Lay disciple: you are right to give this joy
and happiness. For this is the kind of generosity that was the
tradition for wise men of old. They even offered up their lives
for any beggars they encountered, and gave their own flesh.'
And, invited by his host, he narrated this tale of long ago.

Story from the past

Once upon a time, during the reign of Brahmadatta in Vārāṇasi,
the Bodhisatta took rebirth as a hare and lived in the forest. Now
on one side of this forest there was the foot of a mountain, on
another a river and on the third an outlying village. He had three
friends: a monkey, a jackal and an otter. These four wise animals
lived on one side, [52] each on their own patch, each taking their
own feeding ground and then meeting together every evening.
The wise hare gave a *dhamma* talk to encourage the other three
and said: 'Practise generosity, guard your virtue and keep the
uposatha day.' They took heed of his advice and each entered
their own lair dwelling and lived there.

When some time had passed the Bodhisatta looked at the
sky and saw the moon. He noticed that the next day would be
the *uposatha* day, and said to the three others, 'Tomorrow is the
uposatha day. You three had better take up the precepts and be

keepers of the *uposatha* day, for the one who stands firm in virtue and alms-giving has great reward. Therefore you should feed those that you encounter seeking alms from the food that you have obtained.' They said 'very well', took his advice, and each went back to their own abode and remained there. On the next day the otter went out and, deciding to investigate a feeding ground, left and went out to the banks of the Ganga. Then a lone fisherman raised seven red fish, threaded them upon a creeper and took them and buried them in the sand beside the Ganga and went downstream. The otter scented the odour of the fish, dug up the sand, saw the fish and took them out. 'Who is the owner of these?' he asked. When he had shouted three times, and had not seen an owner, he took the creeper between his teeth and left it aside for himself in his thicket dwelling. Saying to himself, 'I will eat this at the meal time,' he lay down and reflected on how virtuous he was! The jackal also left in search of a feeding ground and saw at the hut of a single field watchman two pieces of meat on a spit, a lizard and a pot of milk curds. 'Who is the owner of these?' he asked. When he had shouted out three times and not spotted an owner he strung on his neck a rope that he had found for the pot of curds, and biting into the pieces of flesh and the lizard took them in his teeth back to his own thicket and laid them aside, thinking 'I'll eat these when it is meal time.' He then lay down and [53] reflected on how virtuous he was. The monkey entered a forest grove and fetched a bunch of mangoes and put them aside in the thicket where he lived. 'I'll eat these when it is time' he said. He then lay down and reflected on how virtuous he was.

The Bodhisatta, however, set out at the right time for a meal intending to eat jungle grass. As he rested in the thicket where he lived he thought, 'Near me mendicants come by: I cannot give them grasses. I have no sesame oil or rice grain and if any mendicant comes up to me I will give him the flesh of my own body.' By the power of his virtue the golden throne of Sakka gave the appearance of heat.[5] He considered this and saw the reason for it and decided. 'I will test the hare king.' He went first to the dwelling place of the otter and stood in the disguise of a brahmin. 'Brahmin, why are you standing there?' asked the otter. 'Wise one, if, while keeping the *uposatha*, I should receive any food, I could perform my recluse's duties.' The other replied, 'Very well, I shall show you some food'. Talking with the priest the otter recited this verse:

1. 'I've got seven red fish, which I pulled out from the water on the dry ground
   This, Brahmin, is mine; and when you have eaten this, stay in the forest.'

The priest said, 'Leave it be; it is rather early. I will find it out later.' Then he went up to the jackal. The jackal said, 'Why are you standing there?' When he had spoken he gave just the same reply. The jackal said, 'You are very welcome! I'll give you some food.' In discussion with the priest, the jackal spoke a second verse:

2. [54] 'I have done wrong: I took the field watchman's food for the night:
   the piece of flesh, the two lizards and one pot of curds.
   This, Brahmin, is mine: and when you have eaten this, stay in the forest.'

The brahmin said, 'It is rather early now, I'll come and search it out later.'

Then he went up to the monkey, who asked, 'Why are you standing there?' When he had spoken he gave just the same reply. The monkey said, 'You are very welcome; I'll give some food to you.' In discussion with the priest, the monkey recited a third verse:

3. 'Ripe mango, refreshing water and cool shade are a delight
   for the mind:
   This, Brahmin, is mine; and when you have eaten this, stay
   in the forest.'

The brahmin said, 'It's too early now, I'll search it out later.'
He then went up to the wise hare. When asked why he was
standing there he gave the same reply. At what he heard from
the brahmin the Bodhisatta was delighted. 'It is so good that
you have come to me to find food. Today I will give a gift that has
never been given before. But you, a virtuous man, will not cause
any harm. Go sir: collect some wood, kindle the embers, and
then let me know. [55] I am going to give up myself and jump
within the hot embers; you can eat the flesh from my body when
it is cooked, and you can perform your recluse's duties!' Then,
in his discussion with the priest, the hare uttered a fourth verse:

4. 'The hare has no sesame, nor kidney beans nor rice.
   When you have eaten me, cooked in this fire, stay in the forest!'

Sakka heard what he had to say and by his own power created
a heap of cinders and informed the Bodhisatta. The Bodhisatta
rose from his jungle grass bed and went there and said: 'May no
living beings that live in my coat die because of me.' He then
shook his body three times and, giving his entire body into the
mouth of generosity, he hopped up just like a royal goose into a
pile of lotuses and with a delighted mind leapt on the heap of
embers. But the fire could not scorch even the tips of the hairs of
the Bodhisatta's body, as if he had entered into the birthplace of
the snow.[6] Then he called to Sakka and said: 'Brahmin, the fire
you made is too cool and cannot make heat even to the tips of
my hair: why is this?' 'Wise one, I am not a brahmin. I am Sakka,
and have come in order to test you.' 'Sakka, however long you
stay there, you would not see in me any reluctance to be eaten,

even if all the people in the world were to test me in generosity.'
The Bodhisatta roared the roar of a lion. So then Sakka said,
'Wise hare, may your virtue be known for the entire aeon.' So,
pressing a mountain, he took the essence of mountain and painted
the shape of a hare on the moon. Then he summoned the
Bodhisatta and, in the forest grove just by the forest thicket, he
caused him to lie down by some tender jungle grasses and went to
his own heavenly realm. [56] The four wise creatures lived in
harmony and with courteous minds, fulfilling virtue and keeping
the *uposatha* day, until they went in accordance with their deeds.

The Teacher introduced this account to reveal the noble truths
and explained the connection with the birth: at this explanation
of the truth the householder, who was generous with everything
to do with the requisites, obtained the fruits of stream-entry. 'At
that time Ānanda was the otter, Moggallāna the jackal, Sāriputta
the monkey and I was the hare.'

Notes

¹ *The Story of Gotama Buddha*, p. 25 (J I 20).

² Cone and Gombrich, *Perfect Generosity*, pp. 75ff., section 568ff.

³ H.C.P. Bell, Archaeological Survey of Ceylon, Annual Report, 1909.

⁴ Oddly enough, Thompson's *Motif Index* makes no mention of
this story, which seems to travel with Buddhism. For comment, see
Winternitz, *History of Indian Literature*, II, p. 145, n.3. See also
L. Alsdorf, *Śaśa-Jataka und Śaśa-Avadāna*, wiener Zeitschrift fur die
Kunde Sud-und Ostasiens, Wien, 1961; Francis and Thomas, *Jātaka
Tales*, p. 229; and, for extensive overview on literature on the subject,
L. Grey, *A Concordance of Buddhist Birth Stories*, Oxford: PTS, 2000,
pp. 365–70 (dittography in this section). For *Jātakamālā* story, see
Khoroche, *Once the Buddha was a Monkey*, pp. 37–45 (story 2).

⁵Sakka is king of the gods of the heaven of the Thirty-Three Gods,
where one can be reborn through acts of generosity, faith or by keeping
the precepts. In the Jātakas an undertaking or an act of great virtue—

such as the gift of King Vessantara of his wife and children—causes
Sakka's seat to become hot, and King Sakka goes to protect the one
who has enacted great virtue from any disastrous result of such a
courageous volition.

  6 *Himagabbhaṃ*: the clouds, as in the story from the present in
Jātaka 1.

19

The story of Nandiya the deer
Nandiya Jātaka (385)

Vol. III, 270–4

When the Bodhisatta makes his vow to become a Buddha he is told by the last Buddha, Dīpaṅkara, 'Just as water suffuses with coolness good and bad people alike, and washes away dust and dirt, so you too, cultivate loving kindness for friend and enemy alike.'[1] Although this is not one of the stories attributed by the *Cariyāpiṭaka* to the ninth perfection, of loving kindness (*mettā*), following I.B. Horner's example I have chosen it for its simplicity in expressing the great potency which this quality is said to possess.[2] Loving kindness has a worldly and a meditative application. In the worldly sense, it can be present at any moment or activity in daily life and ensures that wisdom is not harsh or cruel.[3] This worldly application is how it commonly appears in Jātaka stories where the Bodhisatta acts to protect or save the life of other beings. In the meditative sense it is regarded as a divine abiding (*brahmavihāra*): if loving kindness is extended to all beings, in all directions, it becomes immeasurable and may be developed into an object of concentration that can then be used as a means of attaining the first four meditations (*jhāna*s), that bring rebirth in a Brahma heaven. The four divine abidings are frequently taken as meditation subjects in Jātaka stories (9, 106).

Throughout Buddhist countries legends are constantly related of abbots or meditative monks who appease raging tigers, quell other wild animals and even keep insects at bay through the practice of loving kindness. The famous twentieth-century forest meditation teacher Maha Boowa, for instance, is said to have had a miraculous ability to empty dangerous places of tigers, and on one occasion, it is reported, calmed and formed a distant friendship with one.[4] The practice of loving kindness is probably the most commonly taught meditation practice in Sri Lanka and it is taught to children in schools. The *Mettā Sutta*, considered amongst the most auspicious texts of the Buddhist tradition, says that one wishing for, or even who has obtained, 'that tranquil condition', *nibbāna*, should cultivate loving kindness to all beings, in all directions, as a mother guards the life of her only child.[5] This text is thought to dispel all kinds of bad luck or unhappiness and is considered to have almost magical properties in Theravāda Buddhist countries, being chanted at major events such as a wedding, the birth of a child, starting a new building or moving house. It is striking that Jātakas in which the Bodhisatta is reborn as a deer usually involve him practising and acting upon loving kindness. Perhaps the appealing manner and soft eyes of the species make this the most obvious association.[6] In Indian stories generally deer are noted for their gentleness and are associated with the peace of forest hermitages, though often, as in this story, threatened by a hunter.[7]

Story from the present
'If, Brahmin, you are going to the Añjana Forest'

While staying in the Jetavana Grove the Teacher told this story about a monk who cared for his mother. The Teacher asked him, 'Is it true what they say about you caring for householders?' 'It is, sir.' 'Who are they?' 'My mother and father, sir,' he said. 'Well done! It is very good that you protect your family. In times long past you also protected your family. Even though they had taken an animal rebirth, the wise of old also protected the life of their mother and father.' Saying this he narrated this story about the past.

Story from the past

Once upon a time when the king of Kosala was ruling over the kingdom of Kosala in Sāketa the Bodhisatta took rebirth as a deer. When he grew up, the deer, called Nandiya, or Delight, was endowed with virtuous conduct and looked after his mother and father. At that time the kingdom of Kosala was rich in deer and the king used to go every day with a large retinue to hunt for them, going over men's ploughed fields and agricultural land. The men met together for discussion: 'Worthy friends, this king of ours destroys our crops and our livelihood will be destroyed. Why don't we encircle the Añjana Forest park, fix a gate to it, dig out a lotus pond and grow grasses. Then we'll enter the wilderness with sticks and clubs in our hands and beat the thickets. We'll drive the deer and surround them so that they go into the park and cover the gate as if they were cattle in a cow pen. After that we'll see that the king is informed and we may go about our business. This is our plan.' And as they were all in agreement, they prepared the park, entered the wilderness and encircled a space that measured a yojana. [271]

At that moment Nandiya had taken his mother and father into one of the small thickets and was lying down on the ground. Men carrying a variety of planks and weapons in their hands pressed down upon them and, shoulder to shoulder, surrounded the thicket. Some entered the thicket looking out for deer. Nandiya saw them and thought, 'Today I'll give up my life; it is necessary to offer it for the sake of my mother and father.' With this thought he roused his parents and paid homage to them: 'Dear ones, when these men come into the thicket they'll see three of us, but with this trick you should survive. It is better that you have life

and that I make a gift of my life to you. I'll stay in the thicket
while men surround it and then, as soon as they beat it, I'll leave.
And then they will think that there must have been only one deer
in this clump of trees. Be careful!' And, asking his mother and
father for forgiveness, he stood ready to go. He stayed in the
thicket and as soon as the men surrounding it and shouting started
to beat it, he left. Thinking that there must have been only one
deer in the thicket they did not go any further in. Nandiya went
and entered into the midst of the herd. The men surrounded all
the deer and made them go into the garden then closed the gate.
They informed the king and then returned to their own homes.
From that time the king went himself, shot and killed one deer
with an arrow and went taking it with him, or he sent orders and
had it brought. The deer drew lots. The chosen deer stood to one
side. Releasing the arrows, the king's men killed him. Nandiya
drank water in the lotus pond and ate the grasses, but still the
lot did not fall to him.

Now, after many days his mother and father longed to see
him and thought, 'Our son Nandiya, the king of the deer, is as
strong as an elephant and in good health. If he is alive he will
certainly leap over the fence and come and see us. [272] We'll
send him a message.' Standing beside the road they saw a brahmin
and said, 'Sir, where are you going?' They asked in human speech.[8]
'Sāketa,' he replied. They spoke the first verse, sending a message
to their son.

1. 'If, Brahmin, you are going to the Añjana Forest in Sāketa,
   please would you say to our own dear son, Nandiya by name,
   "Your mother and father are old, and they wish to see you".'

'Certainly', he agreed. He went to Sāketa and on the next
day entered the garden. 'Which is the deer called Nandiya?' he
asked. The deer went up to him and stood there. 'I am', he said.
The brahmin related the matter to him. Nandiya heard him and

said, 'I could go, Brahmin, but even if I could leap over the fence I would not leave, for my food is the fodder and water I have been given from the king. This places me in his debt; in addition, I have dwelt amongst these deer for a long time. So it is not fitting to leave without bringing him good fortune, and them too, or without showing my strength. When my turn comes I'll ensure their safety and will come happily.' And in explanation he spoke two verses:

2. 'The food and drink consumed by me is the gift of the king;
    This royal food [would be] wrongly eaten,[9] Brahmin, so I will not act.
3. I will expose my side to the king, with a sharp weapon in his hand.
    Then I may see my mother, happy and set free.'

[273] When he heard this, the brahmin left. Some time later it was the day for Nandiya's turn and the king came into the grove with a large retinue. The Great Being stood to one side. The king said that he would kill the deer and notched a sharp-edged arrow. While the other animals fled in fear at the risk of death the Great Being did not run in this way. Without fear, putting loving kindness before everything else, he exposed the ribs of his great side and stood motionless. Through the power of this loving kindness the king could not release the arrow. The Great Being said, 'Why do you not release the arrow, great king? Release it!' 'I cannot, king of the deer,' he replied. 'Through this know the excellence of excellent creatures, great king.' Then the king, delighted with the Bodhisatta, threw down the bow and said, 'Even this insentient wooden arrow recognizes excellence: how can I, a conscious man, not recognize it! Forgive me, I grant you freedom from harm.' 'Great king, you grant me freedom from harm but what will this herd of deer in the grove do?' 'I grant it

to them too,' he replied. In this way the Great Being, according to the way told in the Nigrodha Jātaka,[10] ensured that safety was granted to all the deer in the forest, to the birds that fly in the sky and to the fishes that move in the water. He established the king in the five precepts: 'Great king, now that you have abandoned following evil courses of action you should rule your own kingdom according to the ten ways of the king, with evenness, without anger and in accordance with *dhamma*.'

4. '"Generosity, virtue, giving up, uprightness, mildness, asceticism, lack of anger, lack of cruelty, forbearance and lack of enmity":
5. I see these good things established in the self, and joy and happiness arise in me, in no small degree.'

The Bodhisatta spoke in this way, teaching the ways of a king in verse form, and after he had stayed a few days near the king he had a golden drum beaten, announcing the gift of freedom from harm for all beings. 'Be vigilant, great king,' he said and left to see his mother and father.

6. 'In times past I was the king of the deer in the house of Kosala. My name was Delight, and so was my four-footed nature.
7. Kosala came: he had made his bow ready
   and notched an arrow to kill me in the Añjana Forest, his royal gift.
8. I exposed my side to the king, sharp weapon in his hand,
   And then I, happy and set free, went to see my mother.'
   These verses were spoken by the Fully Awakened Buddha.

The Teacher gave this talk, explained the truths and made the connections with the birth. (At the conclusion of the truths the monk who had cared for his parents was established in stream-entry.) 'At that time members of the royal family were the mother and the father, Sāriputta was the brahmin, Ānanda the king and it was I who was the king of the deer.'

Notes

¹ 'The Far Past' (J I 24).

² I.B. Horner, *Ten Jātaka Stories*, 1974, pp. 82–9.

³ Loving kindness accompanies the first skilful consciousness (*kusala citta*) accompanied by knowledge (*Dhammasaṅgaṇi* 36). A negative in ancient Indian languages has a much more active force than in English: so the absence of hatred (*adosa*) is explained by the commentary as the positive quality of loving kindness (*Atthasālinī* 129, Pe Maung Tin trans., 2 vols, *The Expositor*, I, PTS, 1920, pp. 169–71).

⁴ This is told in S. Buddhasukh trans., *The Venerable Phra Acharn Mun Bhūridatta Thera, Meditation Master* (Bangkok: Mahamakut Rajavidyalaya Press, 1976), p. 95 and pp. 253–9.

⁵ Sn 143–52.

⁶ See Jātakas 12, 482 and 483. In the Sāma Jātaka (540) the Bodhisatta is not a deer, but is always accompanied by them. Speaking of the Nigrodha Jātaka (12), Winternitz notes the similarity of the theme of a deer swaying a king through loving kindness with the Christian legend of St Placidus, converted to Christianity by a deer (Winternitz, *A History of Indian Literature*, p. 145).

⁷ See Patrick Olivelle, *Pañcatantra*, p. xxiii and, for instance, the opening lines of Act I in Kālidāsa's *The Recognition of Śakuntalā* (W.J. Johnson trans., Oxford: OUP, 2001, pp. 7–9).

⁸ Animals that converse with humans in their own speech are ancient features of Indian literature, of which there are many examples in the Vedas. See also Jātaka 476.

⁹ I have taken the word *avabhuttaṃ*, used by one of the Burmese manuscripts (Bd), on the suggestions of DP I 249 and CPD I 457. It means 'food eaten unlawfully'.

¹⁰ Jātaka 12: a story where the Bodhisatta as a deer protects a pregnant doe and receives a similar assurance from a king.

20

The story of the barleymeal sack
Satthubhasta Jātaka (402)

Vol. III, 341–51

The Ummagga Jātaka (546), mentioned in the story from the present here, describes the fully awakened Buddha as possessing 'great wisdom (mahāpañño), wide wisdom, smiling wisdom, swift wisdom, acute wisdom'.[1] In his last life the aspect of wisdom, essential not only as a perfection but for the attainment of enlightenment, also enables him to refute all kinds of different doctrines and to teach an enormous diversity of beings. As we see in the stories in this collection, even before the enlightenment the Bodhisatta is able to teach yakkhas (55), animals (316) and kings (476). The methods he employs vary and depend upon his use of skill in means (upāya kusala), but often, as is the case here, involve finding the answer to odd little puzzles. In this it follows the pattern of the Ummagga Jātaka, which illustrates the perfection of wisdom through the Bodhisatta's ability as a minister to solve endless riddles and practical difficulties, both domestic and state, for the king and his subjects. In the story here, the Bodhisatta, also a king's minister, works out the answer to a riddle that is causing great unhappiness for a wandering brahmin. Why is it that his wife will be killed if he goes home on that day and he will be killed if he goes home the next? In a manner reminiscent of modern detective fiction, the Bodhisatta works out the answer, using a variety of methods that include imaginative reconstruction, the logical listing of possibilities and direct questioning. In the end he teases out the correct solution: a snake in the brahmin's bag. But the Bodhisatta does not stop there. The brahmin, like other men of his caste in Indian folk tales, is something of a comic butt. He has been cuckolded by an unfaithful, younger wife, who has been the primary, if not immediate, cause of his problems. The Bodhisatta finds a way of bringing to light this other, hidden danger and takes steps to ensure that it does not threaten the brahmin's happiness again.

Jātaka stories are sometimes criticized for their worldly application of the Bodhisatta's skills, particularly in the area of wisdom. Solving this riddle is not obviously the product of wisdom as it is meant in the Buddha's teaching: the ability to see the marks of not-self (anattā), impermanence (anicca) and unsatisfactoriness (dukkha) in all areas of existence. Neither does it teach a path to freedom or give obvious spiritual guidance, though his investigations do rid the brahmin of his rather pressing immediate fear as well as its root cause. The story has, though, all the hallmarks of the way wisdom is described and enacted in early Buddhist discourses, where the Buddha is questioned and challenged by disciples and opponents about points of doctrine and practice. In the suttas the Buddha, confronted by a particular problem and person, uses discussion, close questioning and debate.[2] He eliminates possibilities in his elucidation of particular doctrinal points. He posits a variety of alternative situations and chooses the most suitable. Sometimes he suggests a practical solution to deal with the root of a problem that may not even be known to the questioner himself: a set of meditation practices are suggested, or a formulation of truth which elicits wisdom and enlightenment in the person ready to gain arahatship that day.[3] He constantly illustrates points prefixed by the words 'it is just as if' (seyyathāpi) when he creates new similes to explain a particular difficulty or to come up with an analogy.[4] With this creative mixture of imagination, logic, intuition and direct confrontation, painstaking care is used to dissect a problem and cater to specific individuals and their needs. The questioner is brought to confront the true situation and a way forward is given to help him address it.

Metaphor and simile also play an important and overt part of the Jātaka teaching method. Although the Bodhisatta does not make any analogies in his discussion here, the Buddha, in relating the story, does. The Bodhisatta follows the trail right back to the lethal source of the brahmin's problems with a simple pragmatism that is stressed within the story. His success, it is said, is achieved as if he had used the divine eye, one of the higher knowledges (abhiññās) that are sometimes developed by the Bodhisatta and used by the Buddha in his final life. This ability to see what is happening far away as if it were nearby is rendered unnecessary given the Bodhisatta's shrewd intellectual command of likely causes. It is a characteristic of early Buddhist texts that the psychic powers, although recognized and acknowledged as an important development in the path to Buddhahood, do not tend to be employed unless the situation requires it. For instance, when the aspirant Bodhisatta wishes to make the path smooth for the last Buddha he refrains from doing so through psychic powers, which he could, preferring to do the work by hand.[5] In his last life the Buddha often does employ the divine eye, but with the intent to instruct: he spots the difficulties of the struggling meditator, Moggallāna, for instance, whom he then visits and teaches.[6] In this story, such a feat is just not needed.

The story seems to have been popular historically. It is mentioned in the introduction to the Jātakas as exemplary of the fourth perfection, of wisdom, which the Bodhisatta is told to cultivate, 'Just as a monk, begging for alms, avoids neither low, middling nor high families, and takes his sustenance in this way, so you too, at all times ask questions of wakeful people'.[7] It is depicted on an outer wall in the eighteenth-century Kandyan style at Degaldoruva, Sri Lanka, though the surface of the mural is damaged.

Story from the present
'You are confused in mind'

The Teacher told this story while living in the Jetavana Grove about the perfection of wisdom. Later on the Ummagga Jātaka (546) makes it clear.[8]

Story from the past

Once upon a time a king called Janaka ruled the kingdom of Vārāṇasi. At that time the Bodhisatta had taken rebirth in a brahmin family, and they gave him the name young Senaka. When he became old enough he learned all kinds of skills at Taxilā and went back to Vārāṇasi and saw the king. The king established him in the post of minister and accorded great honour to him. [342] He governed practical affairs and spiritual matters for the king. He had sweet speech and spoke justly. He established the king in the five precepts and set him upon the beautiful path of generosity, the keeping of the *uposatha* and the ten skilful courses of action. It was as if the time of the Buddha had arisen throughout the kingdom. And on full-moon and new-moon days the king and his viceroys all met together in the *dhamma* assembly hall and decorated it. The Great Being delivered the teaching in the manner of a Buddha from the middle of an antelope-hide couch to the decorated *dhamma* hall: his speech was equal to the speech used for teaching by Buddhas. Then a certain old brahmin went for alms, collected a thousand punched coins,[9] deposited it with a brahmin family and then left saying that he would go for more alms. But before his return the brahmin family had used it up. When he returned he asked for the coins to be brought to him.

The brahmin could not give him the coins and gave him his own daughter as a wife. The old brahmin took her to a brahmin village near Vārāṇasi and set up house.

But his young wife, in her youth, was dissatisfied sexually and misbehaved with a young brahmin. For there are sixteen things that just cannot be satisfied. And what are the sixteen? The ocean is never satisfied by all the rivers. Fire is never satisfied with fuel nor a king with his kingdom, nor a fool with stupid things. A woman is never satisfied in matters to do with sex, with ornamentation and with childbirth. With these three things she cannot be satisfied. A brahmin is never satisfied with mantras, nor a meditator with the attainments, nor one who is training with the decrease of the possibility of rebirth.[10] The one with few wants is never satisfied with the virtue of ascetic practices, the one who loves effort with delight in effort, the one who expounds with conversation, the self-possessed person with people, the one with faith with attendance upon the order of monks, the generous man with his giving, the wise man with hearing the *dhamma*, and the four assemblies of monks, nuns, laymen and laywomen with the sight of the Thus-gone.[11]

Now the brahmin lady was dissatisfied with regard to sexual matters. [343] She wanted to get the brahmin out of the way in her desire to practise her base activities. One day, with mischief on her mind, she lay down. He said, 'What is it?' And she replied, 'Brahmin, I cannot do the work in your house. Fetch me a maid.' 'But my wife, we have no money. How shall I look for one and bring her back?' 'You'll have to go seeking for alms and search for money and bring her back.' 'Then wife, prepare some provisions for the journey for me.' She filled a skin bag with baked and unbaked meal and gave it to him. The brahmin travelled through villages, towns and cities and collected seven hundred coins, and then thought that he had enough money to get male and female slaves. So, turning back, he went towards his own town. At a

certain place where water was easy to find he opened the bag
and ate some barley. Without tying the opening to the bag he
went down to drink some water. Now a black snake in a certain
hollow tree smelled the odour of the meal and entered the bag.
Twisting himself into a coil he lay down and ate the barley. The
brahmin returned and, without checking inside, fastened the bag,
put it over his shoulder and went on his way. And while he was
on the road there was a spirit who lived in the cleft of a certain
hollow tree who said, 'Brahmin, if you stay on the road you will
die yourself. If you go home today your wife will die.' When he
had said this he disappeared. The brahmin looked but could not
see the spirit and was frightened, terrified with the fear of death.
Crying and grieving he reached the gate of the city of Vārāṇasī.
Now that day was a fortnight *uposatha* day, and the Bodhisatta
had sat down on a specially arranged teaching seat for the day's
dhamma talk. A large number of people had come in crowds,
with perfumes and flowers and suchlike in their hands, to hear
the *dhamma* talk. When he saw them the brahmin asked where
they were going. 'Brahmin, today the wise man Senaka will deliver
the teaching in the manner of a Buddha and with a sweet voice.
Do you not know?' At these words he thought, 'They say that a
wise man is going to teach. I am terrified with the fear of death.
But it is certainly the case [344] that a wise man can take away
great grief. It is right for me to go there and hear his teaching.'
The man, terrified with the fear of death, went there with them
and, when the assembly and the king had sat down in a circle in
the Great Being's retinue, he stood with the sack of barley on his
shoulder, not far from the teaching seat. The Great Being taught
as if bringing down the Ganga from the sky[12] or raining down
the rain of the deathless. The people in the crowd were delighted
and gave him a great ovation when he had spoken. Now wise
men can see very far. At that moment, the Great Being, whose
eyes had been purified by the five kinds of grace,[13] opened his

eyes and, looking all around the assembly, saw the brahmin and thought, 'This assembly is delighted and offers applause when they hear the *dhamma*. This particular brahmin is crying, in a state of anguish. There must be some private grief inside him that is giving rise to tears. I'll teach him, as if attacking a rusty stain with acid, or as if making a drop of water roll from a lotus leaf, so that his mind is pleased and free from grief.' So he addressed him: 'Brahmin, I am Senaka, the wise man. Now I will make you free from unhappiness. Speak openly.' And so, talking with him, he spoke the first verse:

1. 'You are confused in mind and shaken in faculties;
   Pools of water flow into your eyes;
   Come on and tell me. What has not come to any good?
   What did you wish for, that you have come here?'

[345] Then the brahmin told him the reason for his grief and uttered the second verse:

2. 'If I go home today my wife will die;
   But if I do not, the yakkha says it will be I!
   So I am trembling with this sorrow;
   Please explain the reason for this to me, Senaka.'

Then the Great Being, on hearing the brahmin's words, spread the net of knowledge as if throwing a net into the sea. 'There are many causes of death for beings: they die sunk into the sea; they are taken by predator fish; they fall into the Ganga or are taken by crocodiles; they fall from a tree or are pierced by a thorn, they are struck by various kinds of weapons, they eat poison or are hung or fall from a cliff, or die from extreme cold, or are overcome by various kinds of disease. So they die: and amongst these many causes of death from which one will this brahmin die if he lives on the road and which will his wife come upon and die from today?' So he pondered, and as he considered he saw the bag of meal on the brahmin's shoulder. 'There must be some snake that has entered into that bag. And he will have entered at breakfast time when the brahmin was eating his meal and left the opening of the bag unfastened and went to drink water. It will have gone in at the smell of the barley. And when the brahmin returned from drinking water he will not have realized that the snake had got in, tied the bag up and taken it [346] and gone on his way. Now, if he stays on the road he will, at a resting place, think of eating some meal, open the bag and put his hand in. The snake will bite his hands and he will die: this will be the cause of his death if he stays on the road. If he goes home, the bag will get into the hands of his wife. She will think, "I'll have a look at what goods are inside." She'll open the bag and put her hand in and then the snake will bite her and she will die: this will be the cause of his wife's death if he goes home today.' This he discerned with his resourceful knowledge. And then he thought, 'This snake must be a brave black snake. When the bag beats against the great ribs of the brahmin he does not show any movement or wriggling; he does not betray his presence even in the middle of such an assembly. This must be a brave black snake, a snake without fear.' He knew this with the knowledge of skill in means, as if he had seen with the divine eye. Thus in the middle of the royal assembly he determined accurately, with the knowledge of skill in means, just as if he had been a man standing there, that a snake had entered the bag. Then he uttered the third verse to the brahmin:

3. 'After considering over many possibilities
   I speak the one that is true to the situation:
   Brahmin, I think that, without you knowing,
   A black snake has entered your bag of meal.'

[347] When he had said this he asked, 'Brahmin, is there any meal in that bag of yours?' 'There is, wise man.' 'And did you eat some meal today at breakfast time?' 'I did, wise man.' 'Where were you sitting?' 'In a wood, at the roots of a tree.' 'When you

had eaten the meal and went to drink water, did you leave the bag fastened or unfastened?' 'Not fastened, wise man.' 'And when you had drunk the water did you check the bag?' 'I did not check it, wise man.' 'Brahmin, I think that when you went to drink water, without your realizing, the snake entered the bag because of the smell of the meal. This was the position. Go down and place your bag in the middle of the assembly, undo the opening, step back and, standing there, take a stick and hit the bag. Then, when a black snake with its hood fanned out emerges, hissing, there will be no doubt.' And he spoke the fourth verse:

4. 'Take a stick and hit the sack;
   See the snake, deaf and dumb and two-tongued.
   Cut today the doubt and worries.
   Open the bag and see the crooked one.'

The brahmin heard what the Great Being said and, with a sense of agitation and terror, did so. The snake, with his coil beaten by the stick, crept out from the opening of the bag and lay looking at all the people.

[348] Then, making the matter clear, the Teacher uttered the fifth verse:

5. 'Trembling with agitation in the middle of the assembly,
   The Brahmin has opened the meal bag.
   Then a creeping one, of terrible fiery power, emerged:
   The poisonous snake, fanning out his hood.'

When the questions had been asked by the Great Being, a certain snake charmer made a mouth band for the snake, seized it and set it free in the forest. The brahmin approached the king, wished him victory, made a gesture of añjali and spoke half a verse in praise of him:

6. 'It is a great gain, a great gain, for King Janaka,
   Who sees Senaka, the good, the wise.'

[349] Praising the king he took seven hundred coins from the bag and, praising the Great Being, he spoke a verse and a half, wishing to give a present in delight:

'You are the one who draws away the veil; yours, holy man, is a knowledge
that takes a terrifying form; the one with all-seeing eyes.
7. These seven hundred are mine; take them, I give them all to you.
Today, because of you, my life was won for me.
And more, for you have given my wife her safety.'

When he heard this the Bodhisatta spoke the eighth verse:

8. 'Wise men do not accept payment[14] for variegated verses, spoken with beauty.
Instead let them give wealth to you, Brahmin,[15]
And taking it with you, you can go back to your own abode.'

When he had said this the Great Being gave orders that the brahmin's bag be filled with a thousand pieces and asked him, 'Brahmin, who sent you on your alms round for money?' 'My wife, sir.' [350] 'Is your wife old or young?' 'Young, wise man.' 'Then she is being immoral with another and sent you away thinking that she would be safe. If you take these coins home she will give to her lover this money won by your hard work. Therefore, you should not go straight home but place the coins at the roots of a tree on the outskirts of the town or some such place, and only then return.' Saying this he sent him on his way. When the brahmin came near the town he left the coins at the root of a tree and went to his own house. At that moment his wife was sitting with her lover. The brahmin stood at the door and said 'Lady!' She recognized his voice and, putting out the light, opened the door. When the brahmin had entered she got the other to wait at the doorstep. She then went back into the house and did not see anything in the bag. 'Brahmin, what did you win after your alms round?' she asked. 'I got a thousand,' he said. 'Where is it?' she asked. 'I left it at such and such a place. We'll get it tomorrow—don't worry!' She went and told her lover who went and seized it as if he had deposited it for himself.

The next day the brahmin went and, not seeing the coins, went up to the Bodhisatta. 'What is it, Brahmin?' he said. 'I can't see my coins,' he replied. 'Did you tell your wife?' 'Yes I did, wise man.' Knowing that she would have told her lover he asked him, 'Brahmin, does your wife have a friend who is a brahmin?' He replied that she did. 'And is he a friend of yours?' The brahmin said that he was. And then the Great Being ordered him to be given seven days' expenses and said, 'Go, and on the first day invite and entertain fourteen brahmins, seven chosen by yourself and seven by your wife. And on the next day leave out one from each group, and so on, so that on the seventh day you invite one and your wife invites one. Then if you see that the arrival of one brahmin is a regular event, tell me.' The brahmin did this and informed the Great Being, 'Sir, I have observed there is a brahmin who is a regular guest.' The Bodhisatta sent men with him to bring that brahmin and asked him, 'Did you take a thousand coins that belonged to the brahmin from the root of such and such a tree?' 'I did not,' replied the brahmin. 'You do not realize that I am Senaka, the wise man. I will make you bring me the coins.' He was terrified and confessed, 'I took them!' 'And then what did you do?' 'I stored them at such and such a place.' The Bodhisatta asked the brahmin, 'Brahmin, will your wife remain so or are you going to take another?' 'Let her stay mine, wise man,' replied the brahmin. The Bodhisatta told the men to fetch the coins and the wife, and had the thieving brahmin give him the coins from his own hand. He punished him by having him expelled from the city and punished the wife too. Then he gave great honour to the brahmin and had him live close by to him.

The Teacher gave a *dhamma* talk that revealed the noble

truths, and made the connections for the birth. At the end of the
truths, many attained the fruits of the first path, stream-entry. 'At
that time Ānanda was the brahmin, Sāriputta was the spirit, the
followers of the Buddha the men, and I was the teacher Senaka.'

Notes

[1] The Ummagga Jātaka (546), one of the last ten, also describes its
subject matter as the perfection of wisdom and involves the Bodhisatta,
as Osadha, answering a number of riddles. A minister called Senaka
also features in that tale, though not as the Bodhisatta.

[2] The *sutta*s of the *Dīghanikāya* give perhaps the best examples of
this approach. See Joy Manne, 'Case histories from the Pāli Canon: the
Sāmaññaphala Sutta, hypothetical case history, or how to be sure to
win a debate', *Journal of the Pāli Text Society*, XXI, 1995, pp. 1–34.

[3] See *Udāna* 4.1, for instance, for the allocation of meditation
subjects to a particular person to suit temperamental needs. The ceaseless
questioning of the Buddha's son, Rāhula, at the right moment, by his
father, culminates in the boy attaining enlightenment in S IV 105.

[4] This is too large a subject to be dealt with here, but for someone
new to the Buddhist *sutta*s some good examples of the Buddha's teaching
methods are: 'The Simile of the Cloth' (*Vatthūpama Sutta*, no. 7, M I
37–40), where one simile is explored to explain a particular meditation
teaching; *Mahāsīhanāda Sutta*, no. 12, M I 73–7, where a number of
images are used to describe different future rebirths, and the exhortation
given to Tissa, a struggling meditator (S III 106–9), who is cured of
listlessness by a barrage of possibilities, posited by the Buddha, that
are eliminated one by one.

[5] *The Story of Gotama Buddha,* pp. 15–16 (J I 12).

[6] A IV 84–8.

[7] 'The Far Past' (J I 21) and, for mention of story, *The Story of
Gotama Buddha*, p. 60 (J I 46).

[8] See note 1 above. Jātaka 546 (J VI 329–478), by far the longest
Jātaka in the whole collection, provides a much more comprehensive
account of the range of the Bodhisatta's wisdom, as he solves numerous

puzzles and problems for the benefit of others. Despite being set apparently impossible questions to unravel by ministers envious of his success, he overcomes all intrigues and remains pre-eminent.

⁹ The *kahāpaṇa* is a punched coin, usually silver (I am grateful to Dr Shailendra Bhandaraka, Keeper of Coins, Oriental Collection, the Ashmolean Museum, for discussion about this).

¹⁰ The subject of this clause, *sekho*, refers to anyone who has not yet reached arahatship but has attained one of the stages of path. Such a person would have eliminated doubt, but would still need to work on other defilements. For *apacayena*, see DP I 161.

¹¹ There appear to be eighteen here; the dissatisfaction of women must have been perceived as a single item, with a threefold manifestation.

¹² The idea is that the heavens have a Ganga too, though it is also the case that any river can be called 'Ganga'. The Buddha speaks in this way in the story from the present in Jātaka 1.

¹³ See PED 446 and J 1 319.

¹⁴ Following a variant reading in a Burmese manuscript (Bd), I have taken *vetanan*, 'wages', here, rather than *vedanaṃ*, 'feeling', which is given in the PTS edition.

¹⁵ I have changed *brahme* to *brahma*, following a Burmese manuscript (Bd).

21

The story of the monkey king
Mahākapi Jātaka (407)

Vol. III, 369–75

The selfless monkey has always been a great favourite
throughout South-East Asia. It is shown at Ajaṇṭā, Bhārhut
and in bas-relief on a first-century BCE gateway to the stūpa at
Sāñchī.[1] It features as one of the *Jātakamālā* stories, though with
some differences that highlight the simple directness of the Pāli
version of the tale. In the later and more ornately sophisticated
Sanskrit collection, the Bodhisatta is described with greatly
idealized hyperbole. He leaps up into a mountain peak from his
tree, performs his act of heroism with the king and the entire
court as his audience and makes nothing as 'human' as a
miscalculation in his assessment of the distance across the river.
He falls short simply because the chasm is just such a great distance,
even for the Bodhisatta.[2] The Pāli version, as for other stories
told in the two collections, shows the Bodhisatta, while still an
animal, as much more like a real 'person', a figure sympathetic to
a modern reader in that he is liable to mistakes of various kinds,
such as, in this case, simply misjudging the distance. One similarity
between the two versions is interesting: the Bodhisatta ties the
creeper to his legs, as in the older verse portion of the Pāli tale.
The prose part of the story, unlike the verses, puts the creeper
around the waist.

Story from the present
'You have made yourself a bridge'

While staying at the Jetavana Grove the Teacher told this story about acting for the benefit of relatives. The occasion will appear in the Bhaddasāla Jātaka.[3] At that time they started up a discussion in the *dhamma* hall: 'Friend, the Fully Awakened Buddha behaves well to his relatives.' [270] The Teacher came and asked them what they had been talking about while sitting together. When they told him he said, 'It is not just now, but before too, that the Thus-gone behaved well to relatives,' and he told this story of long ago.

Story from the past

Once upon a time in Vārāṇasi, when Brahmadatta was king, the Bodhisatta took rebirth in the womb of a monkey and when he reached maturity was of good height and breadth and had stamina and vigour. He lived in the Himālayan regions with a retinue of eighty thousand monkeys. There, upon the banks of the Ganga, there was a mango tree, though some say it was a fig tree, which had branches and forks, gave a deep shade, had thick leaves and had grown up like a mountain peak. Its sweet fruits, which had a heavenly smell and flavour, were as big as water jars.[4] From one branch the fruits fell to the ground, from another into the water of the Ganga, and from two branches fruits fell into the middle, to the roots of the tree. The Bodhisatta took the troop of monkeys there to eat the fruits and thought, 'At some time danger will come to us because the fruit is falling into the water.' So at blossom time he got them to eat the flowers or nip them in the bud so that not one fruit, even the size of a chickpea, would be left remaining from the branch over the water.

Despite this one ripe fruit, hidden by an ants' nest, did fall into the water, unseen by the eighty thousand monkeys. The king of Vārāṇasi, who was amusing himself playing in the water, had had nets put upstream and downstream: the fruit stuck fast to the upstream net. When the king had enjoyed a day of play and it was time to go in the evening, the fishermen drew in the net, saw the fruit and, not recognizing it, showed it to the king.

The king asked, 'What is this fruit?' 'We do not know, sire.' 'Who will know?' 'The foresters, sire,' they said. He had the foresters summoned and, hearing from them that it was a mango, he cut it with a knife and had the foresters eat it first and he ate it afterwards and gave some to his ladies [371] and to his ministers. The taste of the ripe fruit remained, suffusing his entire body. Captivated by desire for the taste he asked the foresters the location of the tree and they told him that it was on the banks of the river in the Himālayan region. He had a quantity of boats strung to one another and sailed upstream on the route explained by the foresters. The exact number of days it took has not been related, but in due course he reached the place and the foresters said, 'Sire, this is the tree'. The king stopped the boats and with a crowd of followers went on foot. He had a couch arranged at the roots of the tree, ate the ripe fruit and, after enjoying the various excellent flavours, went to sleep. They put a guard in each direction and lit a fire.

When they had fallen asleep the Great Being arrived in the middle of the night with his troop. Eighty thousand monkeys moved from branch to branch and ate the mangoes. The king woke up and, seeing the tribe of monkeys, roused his men and had them call the archers. 'Surround these fruit-eating monkeys so that they do not escape and kill them. Tomorrow we'll eat monkey flesh as well as mangoes.' The archers obeyed, surrounded the tree and stood with arrows ready. The monkeys saw them and, terrified with the fear of death, as they could not escape, went up to the Great Being. 'Sire, archers stand surrounding the tree saying they are going to kill the monkeys who are running away! What are we going to do?' And they stood shaking. The Bodhisatta said, 'Do not be afraid, I'll save your lives'. Reassuring the tribe of monkeys, he got up onto a high branch that was growing straight and from there went along a branch that stretched towards the Ganga. From the tip of the branch he leapt a distance of a hundred lengths of a bow and landed on a bush on the bank of the river. 'This will be the spot that is as far as I have reached,' he said and marked out a space [372]. Then he cut a single cane creeper at the root, stripped it, and said, 'This end will be bound to the root and this will go into the air'. He decided upon two places and did not take into account the attachment to his own waist. Then he took that creeper and tied one end to the fixed tree on the riverbank and the other end to his own waist and, with the speed of a thundercloud ripped by the wind, jumped a hundred bows' length to the spot. Because he had not reckoned on the bit that was bound to his waist he could not reach the tree and grabbed tight onto a mango branch with both hands. Then he gave a sign to the tribe of monkeys: 'Quickly, get to safety by treading on my back and climbing down the cane creeper.' The eighty thousand monkeys paid homage to the Great Being and, asking his forgiveness, went there.

Now Devadatta, who was a monkey and among their number thought, 'This really is my chance to see the back of my enemy!' Climbing to a higher branch he stirred up his resolution and jumped onto the monkey king's back. The Great Being's heart broke and a terrible pain arose in him. But Devadatta, who had caused such terrible pain, got away. The Great Being was alone. The king, who was not asleep, had seen everything that was going on with the monkeys and the Great Being. He thought, 'This animal has not given any reckoning to his own life and has brought the troop to safety,' and lay down. At daybreak, as he was very pleased with the Great Being, he thought, 'It is just not right that this monkey king should be killed. I'll bring him down by some means and look after him.' He had the boat steered down the Ganga and had a temporary platform tied to it, then gently brought the Great Being down. He had him clothed with a yellow robe, had him washed with Ganga water and induced him to drink sugared water. He had his body cleaned and anointed with oil that had been refined a thousand times. Then he put an oiled hide on the couch and laid the Great Being down there, while he, the king, sat on a low seat and spoke the first verse:

1. [373] 'You have made yourself a bridge so that anyone can pass to safety.
   What are you to them and they to you, great monkey?'

When he heard this the Bodhisatta gave advice to the king and spoke the remaining verses:

2. 'I, O king, have been a lord and chief to them,
   when they were grief-stricken and fearful because of you, victorious one.

3. I leapt a hundred bows' length when I had bound the creeper firmly to my hind legs.

4. As if thrust by a thundercloud torn by the wind I reached the tree.
   But I, coming short of it, held on to a branch by the finger tips.

5. And while I was stretched out by the creeper and the branch, the branch-living animals went to safety, walking along together on foot.

6. Bondage does not torment me; death will not torment me.
   I have brought happiness to those whom I have ruled.[5]

7. Take these examples as illustrations, O king.
   For a king, there is the kingdom, the vehicles, the army and the city:
   the wise warrior seeks for the happiness of all of these.'

In this way the Great Being gave advice to the king, instructed him and died. The king had his ministers summoned, 'Perform honours to the body of the monkey king as if he were a king!' And he told his ladies, 'Go to the funeral ground in red clothes and dishevelled hair, with torches in your hands and make a retinue for the monkey king!' The ministers made a funeral pyre with a hundred waggon-loads of wood. When everything had been done for the Great Being according to royal custom, they took his skull and brought it to the king. The king had a shrine built at his funeral ground, had lights lit there and made offerings of incense and garlands of flowers. He had the skull adorned with gold and placed it in front on the tip of a spear. Honouring it with incense and garlands he went to Vārāṇasi and had it put at the palace gate. He had the city decorated and paid homage to the skull for seven days. Then, taking it as a relic, he had a shrine built and he honoured it with incense and garlands for the rest of his life. Established in the Bodhisatta's teaching, he was generous and performed auspicious actions, ruling the kingdom in accordance with *dhamma*, so that he had his next birth in a heaven realm.

The Teacher gave this talk, revealed the truths and made the connections with the birth: 'At that time Ānanda was the king, the Buddha's followers were the troop of monkeys and I was the monkey king.'

Notes

[1] Winternitz notes the similarity with a Cymric legend in the Mabinogian in which a king makes himself into a bridge, but there is no evidence of any cross-influence (Winternitz, *A History of Indian Literature*, p. 146, n. 4).

[2] Story 27. See Khoroche, *Once the Buddha Was a Monkey*, pp. 244–52.

[3] Jātaka 465. The story from the present for this tale, many pages

148

THE JĀTAKAS

long, tells of a king who did not support the monks and, wondering why they were not his friends, hopes to marry a Sakyan girl, from the family into which the Buddha had been reborn, to remedy the situation. The Sakyans, torn between desire to appease the king and their reluctance to send one of their own to him, trick him into accepting a daughter whose father was indeed a Sakyan, Mahānāma, but whose mother had been a slave. The child of this union is slighted by the Sakyans for his birth and, after many twists and turns, becomes king himself and decides to avenge his humiliation. On three occasions the Buddha mollifies the new king, but in the end realizes that the Sakyans cannot escape their *kamma*: the king kills them all. The Buddha cites this story as an instance of his attempts to protect his own family.

⁴ I have used the word *kumbha*, 'a jar', here, as does the modern Burmese version (VRI).

⁵ This and the next verse pose some difficulties: even with the commentary's help is not easy to translate, though the interpretation has been based upon it.

22

The story of the swift goose
Javanahaṃsa Jātaka (476)

Vol. IV, 211–18

Throughout India and South-East Asia the goose, rather like the Western swan, is a symbol of spiritual aspiration and meditation. The god Brahma is shown mounted on a goose and lines of geese are engraved in moonstones set at the doors of Sri Lankan temples as emblems of the Brahma heavens. There are several Jātaka stories involving geese, the most famous being the story of Dhataraṭṭha depicted at Ajantā (told in Jātakas 502, 533 and 534). The story chosen here is little known but has been selected for its particularly Buddhist subject matter and its suggestion of the influence of *abhidhamma* philosophy, at least in the narrative portions of the text. It involves the use of speed, as revealed in the magnificent display of the Bodhisatta as a goose, which is then turned to dramatic effect by the goose's *dhamma* talk that describes the great rapidity of the breakdown of conditioned things. According to the *abhidhamma*, the sign of *anicca*, or impermanence, may be discerned in all consciousness and matter. In the early *abhidhamma* system, consciousness is said to arise in an uninterrupted flow of infinitesimal moments coloured by the characteristics of the state of mind present at the time. Continuity from one moment to the next is provided by the relationship between states of mind in thought processes, by the association of these with the arising of material form and by the predisposition of mind to follow certain patterns in accordance with *kamma* that affect both mind and matter. For the human, choice exists all the time in the decision as to whether, for instance, to practise generosity and to live in accordance with the path, an intention leading to fortunate rebirths, or to cultivate unwholesome states of mind which lead, at death, to unfortunate rebirths. Matter is likewise involved in a dynamic movement of constant change, influenced by mind. Comparatively speaking, a moment of material form endures for slightly longer than a moment of mind, but that too is made up of endlessly changing entities, separate from, yet closely dependent upon, consciousness in their arising and ceasing. In anticipation of the theories of modern physics, this rate of change is also so rapid that it cannot even be perceived by the naked eye. It is a curious feature of Jātaka stories that we do find from time to time quite precise formulations of *abhidhamma* philosophy couched in technical terms, suggesting that this kind of analysis may have had a more popular appeal than is now supposed. Is it possible that the same group of monks who committed the *abhidhamma* to memory recited the Jātakas, and influenced their evolution? We simply do not know. This story uses little technical language, but the rapidity of decay attributed to the arising and ceasing of the constituents of life make it one of the few Jātakas where the story itself seems shaped by contact with *abhidhamma*, or at any rate ideas associated with it.

Story from the present
'Fly down right here, goose'

While living in the Jetavana Grove the Teacher told this story about the 'Strong Teaching *sutta*'.[1] The Exalted One said, 'It is just as if, bhikkhus, four good strong men, well trained in archery, dextrous and skilled in their craft, should stand in the four

directions. A man might come along and say, "If these four good
strong men, well trained in archery, dextrous and skilled in their
craft, [212] release arrows from the four directions, I will go
and catch them before they reach the ground." Would you not
think, bhikkhus, that this was a very swift man, endowed with
the greatest speed?' 'Say no more: it is so, sir.' 'So much, bhikkhus,
as the speed of that man is fast, so much as that of the sun and
moon is fast, so much as the gods run even in front of the sun and
the moon; yet there is something, bhikkhus, which is faster in
this than the gods: the constituents of life decay faster than these.
Therefore, bhikkhus, you should train yourselves in this way:
be vigilant; this is the way you should train yourselves, bhikkhus.'
On the second day after the day when this teaching was given
they talked about this in the *dhamma* hall. 'Sir, the Teacher,
standing himself in the particular sphere of the Buddha, makes
clear the fleeting, weak constituents of life in these beings, and
brings fear in abundance to ordinary men and monks. This indeed
is the power of a Buddha.' The Teacher arrived and asked them
what they were talking about. When they told him he said, 'It is
no wonder, bhikkhus, that having attained such omniscience in
these matters I have shown the fleeting nature of the constituents
of life and, having stirred the monks, given the teaching. For in
times past, even when I took a spontaneous rebirth as a goose,[2]
I showed the fleeting nature of the constituents of life. Arousing
the whole of the royal court, starting with the king of Vārāṇasi,
I delivered the teaching.' Saying this, he narrated this story of
long ago.

Story from the past

Once upon a time in Vārāṇasi, during the reign of Brahmadatta,
the Teacher took rebirth as a swift goose, and lived surrounded

by a flock of ninety thousand geese in Cittakūṭa. One day he went with his flock to the plains of Jambudīpa and ate the wild rice growing in a certain pool. Then he flew up into the sky back to Cittakūṭa with his great retinue in a leisured way as if in sport and as if stretching out a golden mat that extended the whole distance of length of the city of Vārāṇasi. And then the king of Vārāṇasi saw him and said to his ministers, 'This one must surely be a king, just like me.' Conceiving an affection for him he took flowers, garlands and ointments and looked out for the Great Being, causing all kinds of musical instruments to be played. When the Great Being saw the homage that was being paid he asked his flock, 'When a king pays such homage what does he expect?' They replied, 'He wants to be friends with you.' 'Then let the king be friends with me!' he said, and he went back and made friends with the king.

One day, when the king was in his leisure garden, he went to Lake Anotatta[3] and the bird arrived with water on one wing and sandalwood powder on the other. While everyone was watching, he sprinkled the king with the water and scattered the powder on him right there, and went back to Cittakūṭa. From that time on the king longed to see the Great Being and sat and watched the way he came, saying, 'Today my good friend will come.'

Now, two of the youngest goslings in the Great Being's flock decided that they would like to have a race with the sun, and asked the Great Being's permission. 'We'd like to race the sun!' But the Great Being replied, 'Children, the speed of the sun is very swift: you will not be able to race him but will perish on the way, so do not go.' They asked a second time and then a third time, and even on the third time he refused them. But they, stubborn in their pride, and without a true reckoning of their strength, decided to race the sun without informing the Great Being. So just before sunrise they went to the top of Mount Yugandhara and perched there. The Great Being, missing them, asked where they had gone. When he heard what had happened he thought, 'They won't be able to race the sun. They'll perish on the way: I'll go and save their lives.' And he too went to perch at the top of Mount Yugandhara. As the rim of the sun came up the goslings took off and flew alongside the sun. The Great Being flew with them. The youngest raced into the morning, and then felt exhausted, as if a fire had been started in the joints of his wings. Then he made a sign to the Bodhisatta, 'Brother, I cannot.' And the Great Being said, 'Don't be frightened: I'll save your life.' Enclosing him in his wing, as a cage, he soothed him and took him to the Cittakūṭa Mountain, settled him in the midst of the geese and then flew back again, caught up with the sun and accompanied the other. Now this one raced with the sun almost until noon, and then became tired, and it was as if a fire had been kindled in the joints of his wings. Then he made a sign to the Bodhisatta, 'Brother, I cannot.' And again the Bodhisatta comforted him, and, using his wing as a cage, went back to Cittakūṭa.

Now at that moment the sun reached its zenith in the sky. And the Bodhisatta thought, 'Today I'll put my bodily strength to the test.' With one swoop he flew up to the top of Yugandhara, perched there and then, with one swoop, caught up with the sun: at one point he was in front of it, at another behind. 'My race with the sun is pointless and has arisen from unwise attention. What is the sun to me? I'll go to Vārāṇasi and give my friend the king a talk about *dhamma*, that is suitable and to the point.' Then he turned, before the sun had passed the middle of the sky, and encircled the whole world from end to end, then, dropping his speed, he crossed Jambudīpa from one end to the other, and arrived in Vārāṇasi. It was as if for twelve leagues the entire city was under the shadow of the goose, and no chink could be discerned. As he gradually slackened his speed chinks could be seen in the sky. The Great Being slowed down his speed, descended from the sky and came to rest in front of a window. 'My friend

has come!' cried the king in happiness and laid down a golden
seat for the bird to perch upon. 'Come in, dear sir, sit here!' he
said, and spoke the first verse:

1. 'Fly down right here, Goose, your sight is dear to me
   You have become master here: make known whatever you
   wish.'

The Great Being sat on the golden seat. The king anointed his
wings with ointments a hundred or even a thousand times refined
and, offering him sweet rice and sugared water in a golden dish,
gave him a welcome of honeyed words. 'Friend, you have come
on your own. Where have you come from?' The bird gave him a
detailed account of what had happened. And then the king said,
'Show me a quick race with the sun.' 'Great king: it is not possible
to show this speed,' he replied. 'Then show me something like it.'
'Very well, great king. I'll show you something like it. Summon
some archers who are as swift as lightning.' The king summoned
them. The Great Being took four and went with them down
from the royal abode to the royal courtyard where he had set up
a stone pillar and had a bell tied around his own neck. Then,
perching on the top of the stone pillar, he set the four archers
facing the four directions and gave instructions, 'Great king, let
these four archers release their four arrows at the same moment
to the four directions. I will catch these arrows before they fall
to the ground and lay them at their feet. You'll know that I have
gone for the arrows by the sign of the sound of the bell, but I
won't be seen.' Then in the space of one moment he caught the
arrows that were released, laid them at their feet and was seen
still sitting on the stone pillar. 'You have seen my speed, great
king. Great king, this speed was neither my fastest nor my
middling. It was my very slowest. This is how fast my speed is,'
he said. And then the king asked, 'Sir, is there any other speed
which is faster than yours?' 'Yes, sir. Far faster than me, by a

hundred times, or even a thousand times, no, even by a hundred thousand times, are the lifespans of the constituents of these beings, which decay and break up as they come to an end.' And so he revealed the break-up of the elements of form, as they come to an end, moment by moment.

The king heard this talk from the Great Being, and, terrified with the fear of death, could not keep his senses, but fell to the ground. People were terrified and sprinkled water on the king to restore him to consciousness. And then the Great Being instructed him, 'Great king, do not be frightened: cultivate mindfulness of death. Practise the *dhamma*. Perform meritorious deeds such as generosity. Be vigilant.' Then the king said, 'Lord, I cannot live without a teacher endowed with knowledge, such as you. Do not go back to Mount Cittakūṭa, but stay here and be my instructor, teaching me the *dhamma*.' And he made his request in two verses:

2. 'By hearing of someone love is fed, but by seeing someone desire falls away.
   By both seeing and hearing love grows: O how dear you are to me, because I see you.
3. The sound of you is dear to me, and so much more the sight
   As you are so beloved to my sight, stay, goose, and be with me.'

The Bodhisatta said:

4. 'I would stay in your house forever, with homage paid to me,
   But you might, drunk one day, say the words,
   "Let the goose king be cooked for me!"'

And then the king said, 'But I certainly will not touch any strong drink'. To give him a promise he spoke this verse:

5. 'A curse be on any food or drink that is dearer to me than you.
   I'll not touch any drink while you live in my house!'

After this the Bodhisatta said six verses:

6. 'It is easy to understand the cry of jackals and vultures
   But the cry of men, much more that of a king, is far harder
   to divine.

7. A man might reckon "he is my kin, my friend",
   But the one who has been a friend before, might an enemy
   end.

8. The spirit that is kindred is near to you wherever he is,
   But the one that lives apart is so, even though he is near.

9. Wherever inside a friendly heart may be
   There is a friendly heart too, when across the sea.
   Wherever inside a corrupt heart may be
   There is a corrupt heart too, when across the sea.

10. Even though they live with you, O Lord of the chariots,
    enemies live apart:
    But, benefactor of the kingdom, even in remoteness, some
    may live near, in heart.

11. Even a dear one who stays too long may become a foe:
    So before I become hated by you, I'll take my leave and go!'

And then the king replied:

12. 'You do not register the añjali that pays homage thus and
    beseeches you.
    You do not speak a word to those who would attend on you.
    May we just beg of you this: that some time again you return.'

Then the Bodhisatta said:

13. 'If no accident comes to our lives!
    If you live, great king, and if I do too, benefactor of the
    kingdom!
    Then may it be we will see each other, after nights have passed.'

After he had said this to the king the Great Being went on his
way to Cittakūṭa. When the Teacher had given this teaching, he

said, 'Thus, bhikkhus, formerly, even though I was born amongst animals, I showed the fragility of the elements of life, and taught the *dhamma*.' Saying this he made the connections with the birth. 'At that time Ānanda was the king, Moggallāna was the youngest, Sāriputta was the next and the rest of the flock of geese were the followers of the Buddha; I was the swift goose.'

Notes

[1] This is a reference to a *sutta* which may be found at S I 265–6.

[2] *Ahetukaṃ* (see A I 82), referring to this kind of rebirth, is a technical term meaning 'without a cause', and has been taken here to mean 'without a natural cause': without the usual form of birth. This would mean a spontaneous birth, one of four kinds (*yoni*), which is usually associated with heaven realms or hells: the others are from an egg, a womb or from moisture. Birth from an egg was perhaps considered unsuitable by the ancient editors for a life in which wisdom and the ability to teach, as well as to behave, are such pre-eminent qualities. This is the only birth in the Jātakas described in this way.

[3] One of the seven great lakes of Himavā. It is surrounded by five mountains, including Cittakūṭa or Citrakūṭa. It is said to be one of the last to dry up at the end of the world (A IV 101). During periods when there is no Buddha, *paccekabuddha*s who dwell in Gandhamādana are said to come amongst men and wash their faces before starting on their journey to Isipatana. A sense of the auspicious accompanies offering water from this lake.

23

The story of Campeyya
Campeyya Jātaka (506)

Vol. IV, 454–68

After the enlightenment a black serpent king, Mucalinda, emerges from the river depths, opens his hood and shields the Buddha as he sits in contemplation, a scene often shown on images of the Buddha.[1] Magnificent and highly coloured nāgas can also be seen on gateways to temples in Thailand, where they are considered lucky and protective. In this story, the Bodhisatta is born as one of these fabulous creatures, which are half-serpent, half-human and can change their form at will. The Bodhisatta features in several nāga rebirths, which share a number of characteristics.[2] They involve the Bodhisatta acquiring wonderful powers through this rebirth, but also feeling shame at the form that he has taken—a sentiment recorded for none of his other rebirths in a 'bad destiny'. They involve his temporary emergence from the realm to keep the *uposatha*, a day when extra precepts are taken, above ground in his serpent-like form: this will ensure a fortunate rebirth in future. He is captured by a snake charmer and treated with some cruelty; despite his highly developed psychic powers, a feature of nāga existence, he does not use them to attack his captor.[3] He is then eventually freed and renews the aspiration to take a human birth. The stories are all attributed by the introduction to the Jātakas to the cultivation of the second perfection, of virtue (*sīla*).

All sorts of reasons have been posited as to why nāgas feature so markedly in early Buddhist texts. It has been suggested that they represent an earlier cult worship that predates the Buddha that is to a certain extent validated by appearing within Buddhist *sutta*s and the Jātakas.[4] They may anticipate the association of serpent power as a means of meditative practice. Curiously, a candidate wanting to become a Buddhist monk is still asked to this day whether he is a nāga, for there is an ancient rule that they are not allowed to assume the robe. This is perhaps a vestigial wariness of earlier cult practices in India, not felt to be suitable to one ordaining in the Buddhist order.[5] From the point of view of the stories, however, it is for their great splendour and character that they are memorable. They are like dragons in Western culture, though with auspicious rather than sinister connotations, and their palaces, fruitful trees, great treasure and good living provide a sumptuous world, hidden away from the outside world. The realm may be 'bad destiny' but it is fun too: all enjoy food, drink and music in endless supply. It is populated with nāga women who are beautiful and extremely free with their favours. Nāgas do emerge from the waters sometimes in Jātakas, and on land they either assume the form of a snake or take on a human appearance. Exhibiting their kinship with mermaids and merman, they never really seem at home there, as if they lack the solidity of body for a world where beings need to 'keep their feet on the ground'. In the Bhūridatta Jātaka (543) a nāga lady seduces an ascetic but, fearful of her own venomous power and jealousy, does not want to go with him to take his throne, and returns to her own realm.[6] When nāgas feature in stories they sometimes intercede in human events by passing on wish-fulfilling gems, guarding men from danger and, when venerated, presiding over wishes for children. Above ground, their existence is vulnerable, however, and they need to protect their young from their natural predator, the garuda bird, another mythical creature, who swoops down from the skies to attack them.[7]

For the Bodhisatta, a life in a nāga realm is for the development of virtue (*sīla*), for, he says, it is what he misses and craves for most. When the Bodhisatta is enjoined to cultivate this second perfection, he is told to protect it always as a 'camarī cow her tail'.[8] This involves keeping the five precepts (*pañca sīlāni*), the code of behaviour proper to a realm which has the wholesome mind (*kusala citta*) as its base. The five precepts that form the basis of Buddhist practice usually accompany the homage to the Triple Gem, described in the first story from the present (1). These are often chanted daily by Buddhists as part of their usual practice and involve five undertakings: first, to refrain from killing or harming other beings; second, to refrain from stealing; third, to refrain from harmful sexual conduct; fourth, to refrain from lying or harsh speech; and fifth, to refrain from intoxicants that muddle and confuse the mind. Within the Buddhist tradition, the simple practice of *sīla* is felt to be a protection against harm and dangers, both within the mind and in the outside world. On *uposatha* or *poya* days, lay people often take eight or ten precepts for a period of twenty-four hours: the usual five, with the third being replaced by the undertaking to refrain from sexual intercourse.[9] The others are refraining from activities such as eating after noon, going to shows or wearing adornments, and refraining from sleeping in a high and luxurious bed. The practitioner wears white, goes to a temple and spends the day there. As in medieval western Europe, virtue is considered a power that is proper to a particular species, plant, animal or jewel that constitutes its innate strength and even defines its identity. For humans, keeping the *uposatha* is, in *abhidhammic* terms, a way of finding and keeping the natural radiance of a birthright.[10] Lower rebirths do not have this base in skilfulness: for nāgas, it is the only way of being part of the world of men.

In this story, the nāga realm is described as a heaven of the Thirty-Three Gods, reflected on dark waters. The primeval shame that constantly clouds a nāga's existence, particularly on land, gives the rebirth here great poignancy. This reaches a climax in the Bodhisatta's retreat into the basket so that his wife cannot see his enslaved dance before the snake charmer and a large audience. In this story the place of the Bodhisatta's spouse is crucial. Sumanā is at first introduced as a typical nāga woman, intent on sexual pleasure and gratification, who alights upon the Bodhisatta because his good looks remind her of Sakka, the king of the heaven of the Thirty-Three Gods. She does, however, become an active and articulate defender of her husband in his time of need. Forsaking the familiarity of her home waters and acting on her own initiative, she too surfaces in the 'real' world. She argues on her husband's behalf, overrides the snake charmer's authority and releases the Bodhisatta from the confinement created by his refusal to misuse his great psychic power and thus break the precepts. In Jātakas, the interceding goddess, *dea ex machina*, personifies the power of femininity purified by virtue (538, 539 and 540). Here the Bodhisatta's spouse assumes this role: after the time of his shame she gives him the courage to stand with her, momentarily, freed and as a human, before they both return to fulfil their *kamma* in their life beneath the waters.

Nāga births are the only lower rebirths in which the Bodhisatta becomes desperate to assume the opportunities for self-control and purity offered by human status. A nāga realm is greatly auspicious and restorative for the occasional visit but is not considered, in Jātakas, a dignified place for the Bodhisatta to spend a whole lifetime. It is an intriguing and important contradiction that the perfection of virtue and valuable pearls emerge from the depths of such an existence. The story also, incidentally, says that because of the nāga's gifts the continent of India is covered with sand, the 'gold' that is given to the king. Another feature worthy of note is that this Jātaka should have had twenty verses to be placed in the section it is; now there are forty-four; so, as Oberlies points out, further verses must have been added at some time.[11]

The Campeyya Jātaka features widely in ancient Indian art. It is shown in mural paintings at Bhārhut, which show the Bodhisatta on his own, with Sumanā, with the snake charmer, and the scene of Campeyya hiding away when his wife appears. He is also depicted in a sculpted frieze with Sumanā. Both he and his wife have beautifully formed human bodies, but serpent hoods. The pictures can be seen produced digitally at the website of the Indira Gandhi National Centre for the Arts—Digital Slideshow. The story is depicted on painted murals in Cave 1 at Ajaṇṭā.

Story from the present
'Who is this shining like lightning?'

While staying in the Jetavana Grove, the Teacher told this story about keeping the *uposatha* day. At that time the Teacher said, 'It is good for you lay people to observe the *uposatha*. In times past, the wise abandoned the state of being a nāga just so that they could observe the *uposatha*.' And, when asked, he narrated this story of long ago.

Story from the past

Once upon a time, when Aṅga was king of the kingdom of Aṅga and Magadha was king of the kingdom of Magadha, there was a river between the two realms called Campā, in which there was a nāga realm; the king of the nāgas was called Campeyya. Now, sometimes the king of Magadha seized the kingdom of Aṅga and sometimes the king of Aṅga seized the kingdom of Magadha. One day the king of Magadha waged war against Aṅga and was defeated. Mounting his horse, he fled from the king of Aṅga and, followed by his warriors, reached the river of Campā, which was in full flood. Thinking that it was better to die by plunging

into the river than at the hands of others, he went down with his
horse into the river. At that time the nāga king, Campeyya, had
created beneath the water a jewelled pavilion and was drinking
deep of the water.[12] The horse, with the king on it, plunged into
the water in front of the nāga king. The nāga king saw the king
in all his regalia and conceived an affection for him. He rose
from his seat and told him not to be frightened, offering him his
own seat upon a couch and asking him his reason for plunging
into the water. The king told him everything that he could. Then,
encouraging him, the nāga king said, 'Do not be afraid, great
king, I will make you the lord of the two kingdoms.' When he
had entertained him for seven days in great splendour, on the
seventh day he left the nāga realm with the king of Magadha.
Through the power of the nāga king, the king of Magadha
captured the king of Anga, killed him and exercised kingship
over two kingdoms. From that time there was a firm friendship
between the king and the nāga king and the king of Magadha
had a jewelled pavilion built [455] on the shore of the river
Campā. Every year he made offerings to the nāga king with
great generosity. The nāga king used to leave the realm of nāgas
with a large retinue and accepted the offerings while a large
crowd watched his good fortune.

Now, at that time the Bodhisatta had been reborn in a family
of beggars. He used to go to the banks of the river with the king's
retinue and, seeing the good fortune of the nāga king, he came
to desire it and, standing near him, performed acts of generosity
and protected his *sīla*, his virtue. Seven days after the nāga king
died he died too and took rebirth in his palatial dwelling upon
the regal couch: his body was large and had the appearance of a
wreath of jasmine flowers. When he saw it, he was filled with
remorse. 'With the outcome of the good things that I have done,
lordship in the six heavens was laid up in store, like grain. But
I have taken rebirth in an animal form!'[13] And he considered

thoughts of death. Then a young nāga lady, named Sumanā, or
Jasmine, saw him and thought to herself, 'It must be that this
magnificent being is Sakka, who has taken rebirth!' She gave a
sign to the rest of the nāga women and they all went with various
kinds of musical instruments in their hands and gave offerings
to him. The nāga realm seemed like the realm of Sakka and the
thought of death subsided. He abandoned the body of a serpent
and, decorated with every kind of adornment, sat on the couch.
From that time on he lived with a great reputation and ruled the
nāga kingdom there. After some time though he became remorseful
and thought, 'What is this animal birth to me? If I keep the
uposatha, I'll be freed from this world and go in the paths of men.
I'll penetrate the truths and bring an end to suffering.' From that
time, he used to keep the day there in the palace but when the
adorned nāga maidens went after him, he broke his vows. So
from then on he left the palace and went into the garden, but the
women went after him there too and he still broke his keeping
of the *uposatha* day. So he thought, 'I'll really have to get out of
the nāga realm and go into the human world to live, keeping the
uposatha'. So from that time [456] onwards on *uposatha* days
he left the nāga realm and went not far from an outlying town
on top of a termite heap near the main road. With the thought,
'Let those who want my skin seize me, and those who want to
have me as a dancing snake do so,' he gave his body up into the
mouth of generosity and, winding himself in coils, lay down,
keeping the *uposatha*. Those who came and went on the main
road saw him and stepped forward to make offerings of
perfumes and suchlike. The inhabitants of the outlying village,
regarding him as a nāga king of great potency, constructed a
pavilion over him, spread sand all around and paid homage
to him with perfumes and suchlike. From that time on people
had faith in the Great Being, paid homage to him and made
their wishes for children. The Great Being kept the *uposatha*

on the fourteenth and fifteenth days of the month and lay on
top of the termite heap and, according to this method of practice,
returned to the nāga realm, having passed his time observing the
days in this way.

Now, one day his chief wife Sumanā said, 'Sire, you go to
the world of humans and keep the *uposatha*. But the world of
humans is risky and filled with danger; what if some danger
comes to you? Tell me a sign now by which we can know.' The
Great Being led her down to the shore of a lucky pool and said,
'Dear lady, if anyone harms me by hitting me the water in this
pool will become disturbed. If garuda birds seize me the water
will evaporate, and if a snake charmer captures me the water
will turn blood red.' In this way, he told her three signs. On the
fourteenth day he left the nāga realm, made a resolve for the
uposatha, and lay down on top of the termite heap. The termite
heap shone with the radiance of his body: his body was white like
a chain of silver and his head was like a bleached ball for playing.
In this Jātaka, the body of the Bodhisatta was the size of the beam
of a plough, in the Bhūridatta Jātaka the size of a thigh and in the
Saṅkhapāla Jātaka the size of a single trough-shaped canoe.[14]

At that time a certain youth from Vārāṇasi went to Taxilā to
be near a teacher that was renowned in all the directions [457],
from whom he had learnt a mantra with power over sense objects.
While he was travelling home on the road, he saw the Great Being
and thought, 'I'll capture this serpent, get him to dance in towns,
villages and royal cities and amass some wealth.' So he procured
some divine herbs and, reciting the divine mantra, went up to
him. From the moment he heard the divine spell the Great Being
felt as if red-hot needles had entered in his ears and his head was
as if wounded with the edge of a sword. He thought, 'Who can
this be?' and, lifting his head up from inside the coils, he looked
and saw the snake charmer and thought, 'This is strong poison
for me. If I become angry I'll snort the air out of my nostrils and

destroy his body as if it were a fistful of chaff.[15] Now, this would
be making a breach of *sīla*, so I won't look at him.' Shutting his
eyes, he retracted his head inside his coils. The brahmin snake
charmer ate a herb and, reciting the spell, spat upon the body of
the Great Being. By virtue of the power of the herbs and the
charm, wherever the spit touched him it was as if eruptions of
blisters arose. He then seized the nāga by the tail and stretched
him out so that he was full length. Then he squeezed him with a
stick forked like a goat's cloven foot until he was weak, grabbed
his head hard and crushed it. The Great Being opened his mouth
and the man spat into it and by the power of the herb and charm
broke his teeth so his mouth was filled with blood. The Great
Being, through fear of breaking his virtue, bore such suffering
patiently and did not open his eyes, even for one look. The Brahmin
thought, 'I'll make the nāga king weak!' and from tail to head he
trod on him as if crushing his bones to powder. Then he wrapped
him in strips of cloth and rubbed him with a rope rubbing, then
he caught him by the tail and beat him with a cloth beating.[16]
The entire body of the Great Being was smeared with blood but
he still bore the intense pain patiently. Recognizing the Great
Being's weakened state he made a basket out of creepers [458],
put him down into it and took him to the outlying town. He
made him perform in the middle of a great crowd: becoming blue
and other colours, in positions circling the four directions, [making]
small and large shapes: whatever the brahmin wished, the Great
Being danced exactly for him, even making his hood seem like a
hundred or a thousand hoods. The crowd were pleased and gave
the snake charmer a lot of money so that in one day he made a
thousand pieces and took requisites having the value of a thousand.
At first the brahmin had thought that he would release the nāga
when he had made a thousand, but when he had taken the money
he decided, 'I've earned this wealth in what is just an outlying
town. What a great amount I'll earn if I go near the king and the

king's ministers!' So he obtained a cart and a comfortable carriage, had the requisites put in the cart, sat in the comfortable carriage and, with a great following, had the Great Being dance through villages and towns. 'I'll let him go when I've got him to perform in Vārāṇasi for King Uggasena,' he thought. He killed frogs and gave them to the nāga king. However, the nāga king repeatedly refused to eat them, on the grounds that no creature should die on his account. Then he gave him honey and sweet corn but the Great Being did not eat them, thinking, 'If I take this as a feeding place death will only come to me inside a basket.' When a month had passed the brahmin arrived at Vārāṇasi and had the nāga perform at the villages outside the gates; he took a great deal of money. Then the king summoned him and ordered him to get the nāga to perform for him. The brahmin said, 'Very well, O king. I will get him to perform for you tomorrow, on the fifteenth day of the month'. The king had a drum beaten with the proclamation: 'Tomorrow the nāga king will dance in the palace courtyard; let a crowd gather together to see him!' The next day he had the royal courtyard decorated and called for the brahmin. He brought the Great Being in a jewelled basket and set the basket down on a multi-coloured rug, which he laid out. The king came down from the palace and sat down upon a royal seat, surrounded by crowds of people. The brahmin took the Great Being out and made him dance. The crowd simply could not stand still on their own; they twirled thousands of pieces of cloth in applause and rained a shower of the seven kinds of jewels down over the Bodhisatta. A full month had passed since his capture, and for all that time he had taken no food.

[459] Now Sumanā thought to herself, 'My beloved husband has been away a long time; it is now a full month in which he has not returned. What can the reason be for this?' So she went to the lotus pond to look there and saw that it had the appearance of blood. Realizing that a snake charmer must have captured him,

she left the nāga realm, went to the termite heap, and saw the spot where the Great Being had been seized and tormented. In tears she went to the outlying town and, asking, heard the news. So she went to Vārāṇasī and stood in the sky in the middle of the gathering in the royal courtyard, weeping. The Great Being, who had been dancing, saw her and was ashamed. He crept in the basket and lay there. At the moment when he had gone into the basket the king asked, 'What is the reason for this?' Looking round here and there he saw Sumanā hovering in the sky and spoke the first verse:

1. 'Who is this who has come, who shines like lightning or the healing star?[17]
   Goddess or heavenly minstrel? I cannot think that you are human.'

   Now the exchange between them is given in the verses:

2. 'I am not a goddess, nor a heavenly musician, nor a human. I am a nāga girl, revered sir, and I have come here with a purpose.'

3. 'You rage with a distracted mind. Streams of water flow from your eyes.
   What loss have you had? What is it that you yearn for? Lady, tell me this!'

4. 'He who is also called the snake of great power:
   This one the people call a nāga, O king.
   A man caught him and is making his living from him.
   So release him from bondage: he is my husband.'

5. 'How did a creature of such strength and energy
   come to fall into the hands of a travelling merchant?
   Explain the meaning of this, nāga girl.
   How can I know that he is a nāga that has been captured?'

6. [460] 'The nāga could reduce a city into ashes:
   in this he is endowed with strength and energy.

But the nāga reveres what is right
and therefore exerts himself and follows an ascetic path.'

The king asked, 'But how did this man catch him?' And then she explained:

7. 'On the fourteenth and fifteenth days, sire,
   the nāga king rests at the crossroads.
   But the man caught him and is making his living from him.
   So release him from bondage: he is my husband.'

And when she had said this she spoke two more verses, entreating him:

8. 'Sixteen thousand women, who wear jewelled earrings,
   and who live in the water, go to him as a refuge.
9. In accordance with what is right release him:
   not with hasty violence, but with a village, a gold ornament,
   a hundred cows.
   Let the snake go, with his body set free.
   Let the one who wished only for merit be released from
   bondage!'

[461] And then the king spoke three verses:

10. 'In accordance with what is right I'll release him:
    not with hasty violence, but with a village, a gold ornament,
    a hundred cows.
    Let the snake go, with his body set free.
    Let the one who wished only for merit be released from
    bondage!
11. I'll give a hundred gold ornaments, hunter,[18] and strong
    jewelled earrings;
    and a four-cornered bed, shining regally with flax flowers.
12. And two wives that are your equal, and a bull and a hundred
    cows.
    Let the snake go, with his body set free.

Let the one who wished only for merit be released from bondage!'

And the hunter replied:

13. 'Even without a gift, lord of men, but on your word,
    let me release this snake from bondage.
    Let the snake go, with his body set free.
    Let the one who wished only for merit be released from
    bondage!'

When he had said this he took the Great Being out of the basket. The nāga king came out and entered into a flower, abandoned his shape and, as if he had split the earth, emerged with the appearance of a young man, with body adorned, and stood there. Sumanā came down from the sky and stood by him. The nāga king stood paying respects to the king, making an añjali.

[462] In explanation the Teacher spoke two verses:

14. 'Free, the Campeyyan nāga said this to the king:
    "I pay homage to you, king of Kāsi, the one who brings
    prosperity to Kāsi.
    I hold out an añjali to you; I would see my own dwelling."

15. "They do indeed call it misplaced trust[19] for a human
    to place trust in a non-human.
    But if you are asking me about this—then let me see your
    dwellings."'

And then the Great Being, having made the king trust him, made an oath and uttered two verses:

16. 'Even if the wind were to carry off a mountain,
    the sun and earth were to fall to earth and all the rivers run
    against their stream,
    I, O king, would not tell a lie.

17. The sky might burst, the ocean dry up,
    the earth that bears all creatures and wealth might fall to pieces

and Mount Meru might pull up[20] its own roots, but
I, O king, would not tell a lie.'

When the Great Being spoke in this way, the king still did not
have faith and said:

18. 'They do indeed call it misplaced trust for a human
to place trust in a non-human.
But if you are asking me about this—then let me see your
dwellings!'

The king spoke the verse again, adding, 'You should recognize
the excellent thing that I have done. It is up to me to find out
whether [it is appropriate] to have faith in what is suitable, or
what is not.' Explaining this the king spoke another verse:

19. 'You are certainly large, extremely poisonous and of great
brilliance;
you are also quick to anger.
It is because of me that you have been freed from bondage;
you should recognize those who have done this.'

So, to arouse faith in him, the Great Being made an oath,
saying:

20. 'Anyone who does not recognize a deed done on his behalf,
like this,
should be cooked in a deep hell, should not take any pleasure
in his body and should go to his death imprisoned in a
basket!'

The Great Being spoke this verse and the king, now confident
in him, spoke his praise:

21. 'May this be a true promise from you.
Be free from anger and not resentful.
And may all your nāga tribe keep away from garudas
as men keep away from fire in the summer!'

The Great Being gave his praise in a verse:

22. 'You show compassion on the tribe of nāgas, lord of men,
    like a mother on an only son who is very dear to her.
    And so I, along with the tribe of nāgas, will do a great service
    for you.'

[464] When he heard this the king wished to go to the nāga realm
and ordered the army to be made ready, saying:

23. 'Let the well-trained Kambojan mules be yoked
    to the cheerfully coloured royal chariots,
    and the elephants with golden bridles too.
    Let us go and see the dwelling places of nāgas!'

Another verse was uttered by the Fully Awakened Buddha:

24. 'Kettledrums, cymbals, little drums and conches
    were played for King Uggasena.
    The king went, honoured and in great splendour,
    into the midst of the nāga people.'

Just at the time of their departure from the city the Great Being,
through his own power, made the nāga realms visible, with the
enclosing wall and the gate towers made of all kinds of jewels,
and he created an approach road to the nāga realm, made ready
with decorations. The king, accompanied by his retinue, entered
the nāga realm by the road and saw the delightful, well-laid-out
ground and palaces.

Explaining the matter the Teacher said:

25. 'The one who brings prosperity to Kāsi saw the ground
    heaped with gold
    and the golden palaces set out with lapis lazuli and crystal.

26. The king entered Campeyya's dwelling, a palace,
    which shone with the appearance of the sun and was as
    brilliant as brass-like lightning.[21]

27. He, the king of Kāsi, looked round Campeyya's dwelling,
    covered with various kinds of trees
    and filled with many varieties of perfumes.

28. And as the king of Kāsi entered Campeyya's abode
    heavenly instruments played and nāga girls danced.

29. [465] King Kāsi, with a trusting mind,
    went on his tour with a host of nāga girls.
    He sat down upon a seat that was made of gold,
    cushioned and polished with essence of sandalwood.'

As soon as the king had sat down they brought before him
heavenly food of many different flavours, and before the sixteen
thousand women and the rest of the retinue too. He and his
entourage stayed there for seven days and enjoyed heavenly food
and drink and other sense pleasures. He delighted in heavenly
sensual experiences and as he sat on the comfortable couch, he
praised the glory of the Great Being. And then he asked, 'Nāga
king, why do you abandon such good fortune as this and keep
the *uposatha*, lying on a termite heap in the human realm?' The
Great Being told him.

In explanation the Teacher said:

30. 'Enjoying himself and indulging in sensual delight
    the King of Kāsi said:
    "These, your excellent palaces, shine like the sun.
    There is nothing like this in the human world,
    so why then do you practise asceticism, O nāga?

31. These are beautifully dressed women:
    they wear gold bracelets and armlets and have rounded fingers
    and copper-red palms and soles of the feet.
    They are of unsurpassed beauty and stretch out their arms
    offering drinks.
    There is nothing like this in the human world,
    so why then do you practise asceticism, O nāga?

32. [466] The rivers are safe and peaceful with large, flat fish;
    their well-forded banks resound with birds that are free.
    There is nothing like this in the human world,
    so why then do you practise asceticism, O nāga?

33. Cranes, peacocks, heavenly geese and sweet-singing cuckoos
    fly together.
    There is nothing like this in the human world,
    so why then do practise asceticism, O nāga?

34. Mango, sāl, tilaka and roseapple trees,
    the cassia and the trumpet-flower tree are in full bloom.
    There is nothing like this in the human world,
    so why then do you practise asceticism, O nāga?

35. These are your royal lotus ponds;
    heavenly smells pervade them continually, all around.
    There is nothing like this in the human world,
    so why then do you practise asceticism, O nāga?"

36. "Not for the sake of children, nor wealth,
    nor even for long life, O lord of men.
    I have been longing for a human rebirth:
    that is why I exert myself and follow an ascetic path."'

When he had said this the king said:

37. 'You who are red-eyed, broad-shouldered, well dressed,
    with hair and beard groomed, well anointed with red
    sandalwood,
    illumine the directions like a king of the heavenly musicians.[22]

38. You, who have acquired the magical powers and great potency,
    have all the pleasures of the senses at your disposal.
    I ask you, nāga king, the meaning: why is the human world
    better than this world?'

[467] In reply to him the nāga king said:

39. 'Lord of men, nowhere but in the world of humans
    is there purity and self-control.

When I have attained a human rebirth I will make an end to
birth and death.'

When he heard this the king said,

40. 'It is truly the case that those who are wise,
     who have heard much and who think deeply about how
     things are,
     should be honoured.
     Now that I have seen the nāga ladies, and you, O nāga, I
     will make merit in abundance.'

And the nāga king replied to him:

41. 'It is truly the case that those who are wise,
     who have heard much and who think deeply about how
     things are,
     should be honoured.
     Now that you have seen the nāga ladies, and me, O king,
     make merit in abundance.'

When the nāga had said this Uggasena became eager to go.
'Nāga king, I have been here a long time. Let us go,' and he
asked permission to leave. And then the Great Being showed
him his wealth:

42. 'Here I have considerable wealth and a heap of gold,
     as high as a palmyra tree.
     Take from this world and have golden houses made
     and let them make also a wall of silver.[23]

43. [468] From this world take five thousand carts of pearls,
     mixed with lapis lazuli, and let them spread them on the
     floor of your ladies' apartment,
     and it will be free from stain and without dust.[24]

44. Live in such an excellent palace, that shines as brightly,
     O most excellent king.
     Rule your kingdom, the splendid city of Vārāṇasi, with
     peerless wisdom!'

The king heard his speech and assented. Then the Great Being had a drum beaten: 'All the king's entourage may take as much gold, money and other treasures as they wish!' He sent the treasure to the king in a hundred waggons of various kinds. Then the king, in great magnificence, left the nāga realm and went right back to Vārāṇasi. From that time, it is said, the entire surface of Jambudīpa (India) was gold.

The Teacher gave this talk and said, 'In this way the wise of old abandoned the state of being a nāga and lived keeping the *uposatha*.' And he made the connections with the birth: 'At that time the snake charmer was Devadatta, Sumanā was Rāhula's mother, Uggasena was Sāriputta and I was the nāga king, Campeyya'.

Notes

[1] J I 80.

[2] Most famous are Bhūridatta Jātaka (543) and Saṅkhapāla Jātaka (524).

[3] Nāgas, for instance, are said to remember past lives—perhaps in part a reason for the Bodhisatta's shame at this rebirth.

[4] For discussion on nāgas, see R.F. Gombrich, *How Buddhism Began, The Conditioned Genesis of the Early Teachings* (London: Athlone Press, 1996), pp. 70–4 and Collins, *Nirvana and Other Buddhist Felicities*, pp. 316–19.

[5] However, Gombrich notes that no one seems to know the reason for this. See ibid., p. 73.

[6] Jātaka 543 (J VI 160–1). In the Bhūridatta Jātaka a nāga lady seduces a human ascetic. They have a daughter, Samuddajā, who is brought up as a human princess. She is tricked into marrying a nāga king who has disguised himself as human. The product of their union is Bhūridatta, the Bodhisatta, who then determines to better his rebirth by keeping the *uposatha*.

[7] The mythical garuda birds are the traditional enemy of nāgas and seize them and their offspring whenever they can; only in the presence

of a completely awakened Buddha are they friends, and sing his praises together.

⁸ J I 21.

⁹ The *uposatha* is the full-moon, half-moon and sometimes quarter-moon day (the eighth, fifteenth and twenty-third day of cycle). In practice, this usually means the full-moon day, as in Jātaka 316.

¹⁰ The recollection of virtue, which includes the bringing to mind of occasions where these precepts have been observed, is one of the forty meditation subjects recommended by Buddhaghosa for bringing freedom from fear and a sense of contentment, as well as a happy rebirth. See *Path of Purification*, 240 (Vism VII 101–6).

¹¹ For this translation I have been greatly aided by Thomas Oberlies's recent work on this story, in 'A Study of the Campeyya Jātaka, including remarks on the text of the Saṅkhapāla Jātaka', *Journal of the Pāli Text Society*, XXVII, 2002, 115–46.

¹² Lit. 'was drinking a large drink.'

¹³ Although nāgas themselves are considered auspicious the nāga realm is technically a bad destiny, like an animal realm.

¹⁴ Bhūridatta Jātaka (543) and Saṅkhapāla Jātaka (524) are both nāga rebirths.

¹⁵ The air expelled from a nāga's nostrils was thought to be poisonous.

¹⁶ Perhaps this refers to the way cloth is beaten when it is laundered.

¹⁷ Osadhī is Venus, the morning star, used as an example of constancy, purity and whiteness (D II 111). Some accounts attribute its name to the fact that people drink medicines under its light, others to healing properties in its rays.

¹⁸ This verse and the following piece of prose refer to a 'hunter'. This section may represent a later addition to the text; the word 'snake charmer' has been substituted.

¹⁹ See Thomas Oberlies, 'A Study of the Campeyya Jātaka', p. 127, n. 41.

²⁰ I have followed DP I 499 for this translation.

²¹ DP I 604 gives this translation.

²² In ancient India red eye make-up was worn, which is perhaps why it is used as a term of approbation here.

[23] There are no variants, so the meaning or relevance of the wall of silver or even the agent responsible for making it are unclear. Oberlies describes the linguistic problems in this passage as 'insurmountable'. Ibid., p. 135.

[24] Pearls and jewels generally were felt to be the special province of nāgas (see Oberlies, ibid., p. 137). Pearls are in many cultures associated with the female and with chastity. Perhaps here they are also felt to have a magical purifying property that reflected and was a harbinger of sexual virtue, as was the case in medieval and Renaissance Britain. See Beverly Moon, 'The Pearl', in Mircea Eliade ed., *The Encyclopedia of Religion*, XI, London: Macmillan, 1987, pp. 224–5.

24

The story of Temiya, the dumb cripple Mūgapakkha Jātaka (538)

Vol. VI, 1–30

This story is considered one of the most important in Myanmar and is renowned throughout Buddhist countries. As the first of the last ten Jātakas (in Thai, *Tosachat*) it is also constantly depicted throughout temples in Thailand as amongst those representing the summation of the Bodhisatta path.[1] It describes a prince who feigns deafness, dumbness and the inability to use his limbs in order to escape the terrible *kamma* of being a king. Temiya, the Bodhisatta in this story, sees the terrible punishments inflicted by his father upon criminals. He recollects his own past life as a king, and the terrible hells he had experienced as a consequence. Urged on by a kindly goddess that lives in the white parasol, the symbol of kingship, the prince makes a resolve to feign disability. He deceives his parents and the subjects of the kingdom for sixteen years, causing them great distress until he finally convinces them all that he is unfit to assume the throne. He is condemned to death and a charioteer instructed to take him and kill him in a charnel ground outside the city limits. Even though the prince is consigned to an unlucky carriage, a sense of the auspicious accompanies his departure. The charioteer, told to leave by the unlucky gate, leaves by the fortunate eastern one; 'a lovely spot' is mistaken for the charnel ground where the prince is supposed to be killed. While the charioteer is digging his grave the boy rises, speaks and announces his intention to take up the holy life. The last part of the tale is taken up with dramatic interchanges of various kinds, largely in verse, in which the prince's resolve is described, explored and tested through a series of dialogues between pairs of central characters. At the end we are given a gloriously implausible finale, in which the court and the entire population of three countries forsake palace, city and the lay life to live and meditate in an idyllic ascetic community in the woods.

In other contexts in the Pāli Canon, the Bodhisatta employs regal authority to distribute gifts and bring material benefits to his subjects.[2] Here the role of king is presented as unequivocally damaging, certainly to oneself, and, in the case of the treatment of thieves and criminals, to others too. As Steven Collins notes: 'It is difficult to imagine a more explicit denunciation of kingship.'[3] The story has none of the public display of generosity associated with the famously munificent kings, Mahāsudassana (95) or Makhādeva (9); no indication is given that it is possible to reconcile kingship with adherence to the precepts and a skilful way of life. The kingdom is not being ruled with unusual cruelty or injustice: the punishments administered by the king to the four criminals, in the young Bodhisatta's presence, are characteristic of the ancient Indian punitive system.[4] It is royal office itself which is at fault. So the beginning of the story is imbued with a curious sense of paralysis. King, queen, court, and Temiya himself are all unable to behave freely, crippled by the mystifying and frustrating deadlock that can be resolved only away from court and palace life, out of the city gates, where Temiya takes up the renunciate life. The story does not, however, rest upon a code of denial or rejection. Temiya's purpose is an active one: in Thai temple art he is most popularly shown raising his chariot above his head to show his strength.[5] The tale posits a thoroughly Buddhist and a traditionally Indian ideal that is seen in so many tales: the authority of the holy life, which brings the simple happiness of spiritual practice and meditation, over that of king and state. For the ancient Indian, life in the city and in populous areas is associated with the lay life and the busy concerns of commerce, politics and business.[6] The world outside the city gates, the uncharted wilderness, needs treading with care. Its terrain includes the forest, the wasteland and the desert. It is the place for society's rejects, wild animals and the site of inauspicious areas where bodies might be dumped in charnel grounds—as is nearly the case for Temiya. But it is also an area where it is possible to live freely, either as *sannyāsin*, in the last stage of life, or as ascetic, who can roam where he pleases.[7] Renunciation (*nekkhamma*), the third perfection, is associated with giving up the lay life and taking the holy life: or, in the Bodhisatta vow, as an escape from prison.[8] In this sense it is described as the subject of the tale in 'the story from the present' and can be seen as the object of the Bodhisatta's single-minded dedication. Desire for renunciation gives us the simplicity of the tale's neat, uncluttered construction and steers the action with a crisp momentum, to give an end result of a meditative utopia, in the rural community of ascetics who live off the various fruits and natural produce growing around them.

The way that this goal is achieved, however, would probably have seemed as odd in ancient times as it does now. It involves another perfection, that of resolve (*adhiṭṭhāna*), with which this story is most commonly associated: the introduction to the Jātakas and the *Basket of Conduct* (*Cariyāpiṭaka*) takes the tale as the prime example of its cultivation in the Bodhisatta path.[9] In this story resolve might seem at first sight a kind of stubbornness— particularly when we hear of the agonies inflicted upon the Bodhisatta's parents because of it—but it was by such means that the Bodhisatta established himself on the path to enlightenment. Resolve, as the eighth perfection, is crucial in providing the basis whereby the Bodhisatta vow is set in motion. The Bodhisatta's vow to cultivate the perfections uses the verb connected with it.

'Having thus realized the fact of their being established in the heart, he firmly resolved on them (adhiṭṭhāya); and grasping them fully again and again he mastered them in their progressive and regressive orders.'[10] In the injunction to practise these he is instructed to cultivate resolve, 'just as a mountain, a rock, unwavering, is well established, and does not tremble in rough winds but remains in its own place'.[11] Resolve also features on the night of the enlightenment, when, as Gotama, the Bodhisatta makes the decision not to leave the Bodhi tree until he has found a way to freedom. Despite the immense weight attached to this perfection at the beginning of the tales, it occurs rather rarely in Jātaka stories themselves. We have seen one in Jātaka 20, when the Bodhisatta ensures that the cane stalks have no knots. There is also a resolve which is treated in an unusual way which occurs in the Mataṅga Jātaka (497), when the Bodhisatta is reborn as an untouchable.[12] In this story the Bodhisatta sets his heart on a high-caste girl and determines to marry her. He waits outside her house for days, and despite her rebukes and the violence of her attendants, eventually obtains her, for, as the story points out, the resolve of Bodhisattas cannot be deflected. It should also be said that the Bodhisatta in this tale ascends to a Brahma heaven in order to be worthy of his wife, and, out of respect for her caste, never makes love to her, but conceives their child by placing a finger upon her stomach. One of the points being made is that resolve is a neutral quality and one which we all use for all kinds of outcomes. More typically, in the Bhūridatta Jātaka (Jātaka 543), the Bodhisatta as a nāga is said to be fulfilling the perfection of resolve by keeping the uposatha.[13] In the Mūgapakkha Jātaka the silent resolve that instigates the drama of the first part of the tale seems excessively lonely and rigid at first: by the end it has borne fruit and has a happy and even festive outcome for all concerned. The tale seems, indeed, a marriage between this perfection and that of renunciation, the stated subject of the tale.

Linked to the intent to be free, resolve purifies not just the Bodhisatta himself, but those around him too.

Other features of this drama are worth exploring. The first part, with its testing of the Bodhisatta's will through comparison with other children, gives us a delightfully graduated account of Indian attitudes to children. It also gives us a curiously modern perspective on childhood decision making: all children, to a certain extent, undergo something of this 'refusal' process, a feature which reinforces the sense that resolve is neutral in itself, but may take a skilful or an unskilful course. The rejection of the father, the bitterness of the struggle of wills between parent and child and the child's unwillingness to fulfil parental expectations are all examined here in a manner that strikes chords with the methods of modern psychotherapeutic analysis. The story is a powerful study of these impulses with what is, however, a radically different orientation from the usual childhood battles. The resolve that is being tested is the Bodhisatta impulse; the conclusion the vindication of this impulse in the renunciate life. It is tested further through a series of dramatic set pieces after the Bodhisatta has left his parents' world and stands on his own ground outside the city gates. In the first, the interchange between the charioteer and the prince, the prince gives his apologia for his past actions and explores ways of taking up the life that he wants that will cause the minimum of trouble to the king and his kingdom. The second gives the movement back within the kingdom and the interchange between the charioteer and the mother as the happy news is delivered. The third returns outside the city limits, to the interchange between his father and the prince as the king fails to persuade the boy to return to the kingdom; his son then convinces the king of the superiority of the holy life. These dialogues, which dramatize stances exemplified by each of the characters, involve the kind of explorations of motive and doctrine found in epic drama and Greek tragedy. They also provide some strikingly

excellent poetry, including some of the most simply expressed
and satisfying lyrical passages in the Jātakas as a whole. The verses
in honour of friendship (vv. 12–21), the eulogy to the benefits of
the holy life (vv. 87–90) and Temiya's arguments against the king,
his father, are all justly renowned. The two short verses (vv. 30–
1) on the benefits of not being in a hurry, an underlying theme
within the tale, have a startlingly modern ring, and could usefully
be pasted on modern motorway service stations and bus depots.

Character is also examined with painstaking precision through
the events of the story. The charioteer, a particularly crucial figure,
occupies a role kin to that of a Greek tragic chorus, voicing in the
midst of heroic struggle the immediate concerns of the common
man. His removal of the boy from his mother is touchingly
poignant: he carefully extracts the boy from his mother by trying
not to touch her, '. . . with the heel of his palm he removed the
queen, who was lying in an embrace with her son, lifted the boy
like a bunch of flowers and left the palace'. He exhibits disbelief
that the boy has the use of his faculties, then straightforwardly
expresses self-seeking concern that he will lose out on gifts from
the royal family by not bringing the boy back alive (vv. 20–3).
After such speeches as the Bodhisatta's graceful and unadorned
eulogy to friendship (vv. 12–21), he develops the conviction that
he too should become an ascetic, though, after discussion with
the prince, he sees the pitfalls which must be negotiated first. When
he returns to the queen he is sensitive to her distress but careful
to ensure that he will not be punished for any account of events.
In all these encounters the charioteer's sense of diplomacy and
pragmatism gives a non-heroic counterpoint to the unfolding drama,
that allows a link to be made between two uncompromisingly
opposed kinds of life. His is the ordinary response of the subject
in the kingdom, obliged to obey orders such as in the command
to execute the prince, yet also kindly in the fulfilment of his duty

and ready to be convinced, in the end, of the happiness of the ascetic path once that duty has been discharged.

The other principal characters are treated with a sensitivity and care that ensure that our sympathies are maintained in the drama of the testing of will. The mother's love for her son is movingly portrayed in her spoken entreaties and attempts to awaken his intelligence. Her terrible grief, despairing castigation of the charioteer on his return and her restoration to happiness are all conveyed with a skilled lightness of touch. It is a subtle and well-crafted feature of the story that her relief at hearing that her son is alive and well is not recounted, in a manner which would delay the plot, but simply assumed. Her lonely, bitter questions in verse (vv. 54–5) confront the charioteer on his return; but when the news is delivered the story cuts back to Temiya, back in the forest, without further mention of her. We meet her again when a suitable time has elapsed for her complete restoration to happiness and vitality, after the journey outside the city gates in the company of the king. She can then embrace her son and comment in a mundane and plausibly maternal manner on the austerity of the ascetic's food: a domestic detail that shows her established to good humour well before the crisis of the confrontation between king and son begins and the final departure of the court from the city.

It is, however, in Temiya's relationship with his father that we see the real dramatic tension of the plot and the testing of the Bodhisatta's resolve. This is voiced through the polarization and ensuing dialogue between the way of life embodied by the palace and city and that of the woods outside the city limits. In the unmapped countryside lies the possibility of change and of real exploration of the mind. It is the place where people are 'not in a hurry', which can provide a space for meditation and the Bodhisatta path. Within the terms of thiss story, at any rate,

such freedom is denied the king. As minister of justice he has had
to perpetrate cruelties so that the rule of order can be sustained.
He has had to deny his paternal feelings in the expulsion of his
only son from his home. He even refuses, despite an earlier
promise, all the initial requests of the promised boon from his
queen. So when he first visits his son after the restoration to life
he acts initially as an ambassador for the royal throne. But even
in the interchange between them when he first arrives at the
pleasing spot outside the city, the Bodhisatta's authority is
established as pre-eminent, acknowledged by the king himself
in his avoidance of taking the higher seat. The confrontation is
on the Bodhisatta's own ground, not the king's. In the loving
dialogue of reunion, when their intimacy and friendship is
suggested by lines which echo verbally one another's speech (vv.
75–82), the Bodhisatta enquires not only about the king's health,
but his virtue too. Despite the king's attempts at persuasion,
with promises of the delights of sensory pleasure and of sons, the
battle is already half lost. Gradually, through their discussion,
the appeal of the holy life, outside the city limits, is seen to exert
an inexorable pull. The king, at first determined to bring his son
back, is convinced into becoming an ascetic too and his court and
subjects follow likewise.

A sense of cheerful momentum draws the story to its end. The
freshness of the queen's response and that of the ladies to the
idyll outside the kingdom is communicated with great immediacy
and vigour; the king embraces his new life with delight and his
subjects follow him with good heart. Despite the uncompromising
insight of the Bodhisatta's teaching, which voices his rejection of
the unsatisfactoriness of the lay life, nothing is allowed to detract
from making the movement of the court to the woods a natural
and happy consummation of the plot. Court and city move to the
place, supposed at first to be a charnel ground, which proves to
be a 'lovely spot' (ṭhānaṃ phāsukaṃ), an oasis in the wilderness.

The trees give fruit; the gods come down to protect and offer shelter where it is needed, sustenance is obtained without effort and even the animals ascend to a higher rebirth on death. Here, however romantically and implausibly, the Buddhist renunciate path is established for everyone, in what is intended to be an utterly delightful world of meditation practice, virtue and goodwill. As in the *Mahāsudassana sutta*, unruly behaviour, a reminder of the irrepressibly degenerate possibilities of the mind, is represented by the amiable drunks: though in this Jātaka one or two, in the absence of good drinking companions, even become ascetics too.[14] The fact that these trailers take a little longer to reach their goal gives some continuity for the lineage in the future, recorded in the lines at the end of the tale.

Despite the odd passivity of his resolve, the Bodhisatta's skilful intention brings happiness for himself, the king, the court and subjects too. This final vision provides a highly adventurous enactment of Buddhist ideals in the world of humans. It voices a revolutionary, even subversive, message which perhaps explains the story's popularity in countries such as Burma, where the state has, historically, been viewed with some suspicion. Whereas the Makhādeva Jātaka (9) and the Mahāsudassana Jātaka (95) leave monarchy intact, in Temiya's pastoral idyll no king, court, state or ministers are needed at all: it is a landscape where the real kingdom can be the mind itself. It seems unlikely that a genuine social utopia is being posited as an alternative to monarchic rule. Renunciation and resolve do produce external consequences but, as is the case with so many aspects of early Buddhist thought, their real arena is internal. The space where people 'are not in a hurry' and the 'lovely spot' which others perceive as a charnel ground, is, for the Buddhist, the space created by the practice of the eightfold path.[15] It is not bound solely by laws of king or state, inspires others to pursue it too, and leaves tracks that are to those interested in power and status—the kings of other realms—

at first bemused. In such a world, and within the spacious perspective of the resolve of the Bodhisatta vow, even the most officious state or state official cannot find a hold.

The last ten Jātakas are constantly depicted in temples in Thailand and this, as the first, is accorded a certain pre-eminence. The story is shown at Wat Yai Intharam at Chonburi in a spectacular painted mural that shows several events from Temiya's life, culminating in the visit from his father when he has become an ascetic.[16] Its popularity seems to have been long-standing. At Bhārhut it features in a sculpted plaque, which incorporates different elements from the story in an arrangement on one roundel. This shows the Bodhisatta as a child on his father's lap, grown up standing behind Sunanda as he digs his grave and then delivering a discourse as an ascetic.[17] In Myanmar it is on one of the earliest extant depictions of a Jātaka story, shown in a large terracotta plaque dating from the fifth century CE at Khinba mound, Thayekhittaya, and also features at the eleventh-century temple at Pagan.[18] In Sri Lanka it appears on the vestibule of the Tivanka shrine.[19]

Story from the present
'Do not show intelligence'

While staying in the Jetavana Grove the Teacher told this story about the higher renunciation. One day the monks were sitting together in the *dhamma* hall praising the nature of the great renunciation, as practised by the Blessed One.[20] The Teacher came and asked, 'What subject have you been discussing, while sitting together, bhikkhus?' When they had described it he said, 'No, bhikkhus, this renunciation, of leaving my kingdom, which I practised once I had fulfilled the perfections, was not marvellous. For when my knowledge was still unripe, and I was attaining the perfections, I left a kingdom then and renounced the world.' When he had said this, at their request he narrated this story of long ago.

Story from the past

Once, long ago, a king called Kāsi ruled justly in Vārāṇasi. He had sixteen thousand wives, but not one of them had conceived a son or a daughter. The citizens met together in the same way as in the Kusa Jātaka[21] and said, 'Our king has no one to protect his lineage. Please pray for a son.' The king ordered his sixteen thousand wives to pray for a son, but although they prayed and worshipped the moon and other deities, they did not conceive. But the chief queen, daughter of the king of Madda, called Queen Candā, was endowed with great virtue, and the king asked her to pray for a son too. So on the full-moon day she kept the *uposatha* and while lying on her little bed she reflected upon her own good conduct and made a declaration of truth: 'If my good conduct is unbroken, by this truth may a son be born to me.' [2] By the power of her virtue Sakka's dwelling became hot. Sakka noticed and realized the cause of this. 'Queen Candā prays for a son; I'll give her a son!' he said. When he looked around he saw the Bodhisatta as suitable for her child. Before that time the Bodhisatta had been king in Vārāṇasi for twenty years. After his death he had taken rebirth in an Annex hell (literally, 'adjunct hell') and suffered there for twenty thousand years and had then been reborn in the heaven of the Thirty-Three Gods. He remained there as long as his life lasted and, on dying, he wished to go to a higher heavenly world. Sakka went up to him though and said, 'Dear sir, if you take rebirth in the human world the perfections will be fulfilled, and it will be a great benefit for people. The king of Kāsi's chief queen, called Candā, prays for a child. Take rebirth

in her womb.' He listened and assented and died, with five
hundred shining gods, and took rebirth in her womb, while the
gods took rebirth in the wombs of the ministers' wives. The
queen's belly seemed as if it were filled with diamonds and when
she knew that conception had occurred she informed the king.

The king had every care given to the growing baby and when
the pregnancy was complete she gave birth to a son endowed
with the auspicious marks. And on that day five hundred children
were born in the ministers' households. At that moment the king
was sitting in the great hall surrounded by his ministers and
they informed him, 'A son is born to you, sire.' When he heard
the announcement affection for his son arose in him which
pierced through his skin and the rest of his body and touched his
very marrow. Joy arose within him and his heart was refreshed.
He asked the ministers, 'Are you pleased at the birth of my son?'
They replied, 'What are you saying, sire? Before we were without
a protector and now we have one, and have found a ruler.' The
king gave orders to his minister of war, 'My son should have a
retinue. Look around for as many children as have been born
today.' The minister saw the five hundred children and went and
informed the king. The king ordered five hundred ornaments
for the young nobles, and five hundred wet nurses too. For the
Bodhisatta he gave sixty-four wet nurses, who were free from
defects such as being too tall [3], who had breasts that did not
hang down and who gave sweet milk. For if a child sits on the
hip of a woman that is too tall and drinks her milk his neck will
be long. If he sits on the hip of one who is too short his shoulder
bone will be stunted. If he sits on the hip of one who is too thin
his thighs will hurt. If she is too fat[22] he will be bow-legged. If
she is too dark he will be cold and if she is too pale he will be too
hot. If children drink from a woman whose breasts hang down
the tips of their noses will get squashed. Some women give sour
milk, some bitter and so on. Therefore, avoiding all these faults,

he provided sixty-four nurses, whose breasts did not hang down and who all gave sweet milk.

Paying great honour to the boy he also granted a wish to Queen Candā. She accepted it and kept it. On the naming day he paid great homage to the brahmins who were experts in reading the marks and asked them if there were any dangers ahead. They saw the good fortune of his marks and said, 'Great King, the prince has auspicious marks of wealth and fortune. He is capable of ruling not just one continent but also four. No danger can be discerned.' The king was delighted with them and they gave a name to his son. Now, on the day of the prince's birth it had rained throughout the whole kingdom of Kāsi, and he was born wet: therefore the king called him Prince Temiya (the Wet One).[23] When he was a month old they adorned him and brought him into the presence of the king. The king looked at his beloved son, embraced him and, setting him on his lap, sat playing with him. Now, at that moment four thieves were led in. For one of these he ordered a thousand lashes with whips barbed with thorns; for another; admission into prison in chains; for another, the striking of a blow with a sword; and for another, impalement. The Great Being heard his father speak and, terrified, thought to himself, 'O no, my father, because of being king, is generating the grave *kamma* that brings rebirth in the Niraya hell!'

On the next day he was put to lie down on a regally arrayed bed under a white parasol. He slept just a little and when he woke up he opened his eyes and saw the white parasol and looked at the magnificent royal splendour. Even though he was already frightened, a terror arose that was still greater. He thought, [4] 'From where have I come to this royal household?' Remembering, with the knowledge of past lives, that he had come from a heaven realm he looked where he had been before and saw that he had been tormented in hell. Looking where he had been before that he saw that he had been king in that very city and considered, 'I

ruled the kingdom for twenty years, but was tormented in the
Ussada hell for eighty thousand years. Yet again, I have taken
rebirth in this house of thieves. My father gave such a harsh
sentence to the four thieves that were brought in that he has
ensured a hellish rebirth for himself. If I rule the kingdom I will
take rebirth in hell and experience terrible suffering.' As he turned
this over in his mind great terror arose and his golden coloured
body became pale like a withered lotus crushed in the hand.
Worrying as to how he could escape from the house of thieves he
lay himself down.

Now in the parasol there lived a shining goddess who had
been his mother in an earlier life. She comforted him, saying,
'Dear Temiya, do not be frightened. If you wish to go free from
this world, although you are not a cripple, be a cripple. Although
you are not deaf, be deaf. Although you are not dumb be dumb.
Assuming these three characteristics, appear to be without
intelligence.' And she spoke the first verse:

1. 'Do not show intelligence; seem foolish-minded to everyone.
   Let everyone treat you with contempt
   and in this way there will be benefit for you.'

Through her words he derived comfort and so replied:

2. 'I will follow the advice which you have given to me, O goddess.
   You are a well-wisher to me and want me to be safe, O goddess.'

When he had spoken the verse he resolved upon these three
characteristics. For the sake of his son's happiness the king had
the five hundred nobles brought into the boy's presence. When
they cried for breast milk the Great Being, terrified with the fear
of hell, did not cry, thinking, 'Death from thirst is better than
kingship.' The nurses informed Queen Candā [5] about what
had happened and she informed the king. The king called for
the brahmins who read signs and consulted them. The brahmins
said, 'Sire, after the natural time for milk has passed it should be

given to him. Then he will cry and take the breast eagerly and drink for himself.' From then on they let the natural time elapse and gave him milk and sometimes they let one time period elapse and sometimes they let the whole day go and did not give him milk. Although he was thirsty he did not cry for milk, through fear of hell. Then his mother, thinking that her son was hungry, gave him her breast, as did the nurses, even though he did not cry for it. The other children cried when they did not get their milk but he did not cry nor sleep nor bend his hands and feet nor listen to a sound. The nurses pondered this: 'His hands and feet are not like those of cripples; the end of his jaw is not like those that are dumb and the shape of his ear is not like those that are deaf. There must be a reason for this; let's test him.' So they decided to test him with cow's milk and for the whole day they did not give him any milk. Although thirsty, he made no sound for milk. And then his mother said, 'My son is thirsty, give him milk,' and she had them give it. In this way, from time to time, they gave him milk and for one year they tested him and found no chink.

Then they said, 'Children love eating cakes and pastries: let's try him out with that.' They sat the five hundred children near him, offered various pastries saying, 'Take whatever pastries you like!' and stayed hidden. The other children had quarrels and hit each other, grabbing the food and eating it. The Great Being thought, 'Temiya, wish for cakes and pastries and you wish for hell!' Through fear of hell he did not look at the pastries and though they tried him out in this way for a year they did not see a chink. Then they thought, 'Different kinds of fruit are dear to children,' and they brought various fruits to test him, whereupon [6] the other children squabbled and ate them, but he did not even look. In this way they tried him out with various kinds of fruit for a year. Then they thought, 'A toy is dear to children', and they brought elephants made of gold and other things and set them near him. The other children grabbed them as if plundering them but the Great Being did not look, and in this way they also tested him with toys for a year. 'There is a food for four-year-olds—let's test him with that,' and they put various kinds of food near him. The other children ate it bit by bit but the Great Being thought, 'Temiya, there is no counting your past births when food was not to be found.' And through fear of the Niraya hell he did not look, and his mother, with her heart unable to bear it, fed him herself.

Then they thought, 'Five-year-olds are frightened of fire; let's test him with that.' They had a big house made with lots of doors and covered it with palm leaves, sat him down in the middle of his entourage of children and started a fire. The other children fled shrieking. The Great Being thought, 'This is better than cooking in the Niraya hell.' And he was as motionless as if he had attained cessation[24] so they took him from the encroaching fire and led him off. And then they thought, 'Six-year-olds are frightened of mad elephants.' So they had trained a well-instructed elephant in rut and, sitting the Great Being down in the royal courtyard surrounded by the other children, they set it free. The elephant roared a trumpeting roar and beat the ground with his trunk, spreading alarm as he approached. The other children, terrified with the fear of death, fled in all directions but the Great Being, afraid of the Niraya hell, sat right where he was. The well-trained elephant picked him up and dandled him to and fro without harming him and then left.

When he was seven years old, at one time he was sitting with the other children around him. They released some snakes which had had their teeth pulled and mouths bound. The other children ran away shrieking but the Great Being reflected upon the fear of hell and thought, 'Destruction from the mouth of a fierce snake is better.' And he was motionless and the snakes twisted around his entire body and remained spreading their hoods over his head, but even then he did not move. In this way they tested him from time to time but saw no chink. [7] Then they thought, 'Children love shows.' So they sat him in the royal courtyard and organized a dancing show. The other children saw the show and said it was wonderful, chuckling with laughter, but the Great Being thought, 'There is not a moment for laughter or happiness in a rebirth in hell.' Reflecting upon the fear of hell he stayed motionless and did not look. In this way they tested him from time to time but did not find a chink. And then they thought, 'Let's test him with a sword'. And they set him down in the royal courtyard with the children. While the children were playing, a man jumped up brandishing a sword the colour of crystal shouting, 'They say that the king of Kāsi has a son that is ill-starred. Where is he? I'll chop off his head!' He rushed at them and when the others saw him they ran off screaming, but the Bodhisatta considered the terror of hell and sat as if uncomprehending. The man then touched him on the head with the sword, threatening to cut it off, but although he was indeed terrifying he could not terrify him and just went off. In this way from time to time they tested him, but could not find a chink.

When he was ten years old they tested his hearing and draped his bed with a curtain of hemp, making holes on the four sides. Without him seeing, they sat conch blowers under the bed. They got them to sound the conches all at one go and there was a single blast of sound. Ministers stood at the four sides and looked at the Great Being through the holes in the hemp and for the whole day they did not see any forgetfulness, or movement of the hands and feet, or the flicker of a tremble. After a year had passed they tried him again with the sound of a drum but still found no chink. Then they thought, 'Let's test him with a lamp.' That very night they decided to see whether he moved a hand or a foot in the dark. They lit some lamps in jars, put out the other lamps for a bit and sat him down. All at once they lifted the lamps from the jars, made it light and watched his posture. They tested him in this way for a year but could not find the slightest trembling.

Then they thought [8] they would smear his entire body with molasses and laid him down in a place where there were a lot of flies and roused the flies. These surrounded his entire body and bit him as if piercing with needles but he still remained motionless as if in the attainment of cessation: in this way they tested him for a year but could not find a chink. Then when he was fourteen they said, 'This boy loves cleanliness and hates lack of cleanliness. Let's test him with what is unclean.' From that time they did not wash him or rinse his mouth and when he passed urine and faeces he just lay there sunk in it. In this foul smell from his intestines it was as if he had had a ruptured hernia.[25] Flies bit him and surrounded him and people reviled him saying, 'Temiya, now you are a young man, who is going to care for you all the time? Why are you not ashamed, why do you lie down? Get up and look after your body!' but he, although sunk in unpleasant faeces, reflected upon the foul smell of the Mire hell,[26] which stretched for a hundred leagues in its foulness, and which could split the heart of those stuck there; and he was equanimous. And in this way they tested him for a year but could not find a chink.

Then they put fire pans under his bed thinking, 'Surely when he is oppressed by the heat he will be unable to bear the pain and betray some flinching.' It was as if blisters erupted on his body, but the Great Being thought, 'In the Avīci hell the fire spreads for a hundred leagues and there the pain is a hundred times, no, a thousand times worse.' And he endured it and did not move. And his mother and father, with their hearts breaking, called the men back and got them to take him from the heat of the fire and beseeched him, 'Dear Temiya, our son, we know that you are not a cripple by birth, because they do not have the feet and mouth and ears that you do. We got you as our child after praying for you; do not destroy us but release us from the reproach of kings throughout Jambudīpa.' Although begged in this way, it was as if he did not hear and he lay motionless. Then his mother and father left weeping, [9] and sometimes his father came alone to implore him and sometimes his mother. In this way for a year from time to time they tested him, but could not find a chink.

Then when he was sixteen they thought, 'Let him be a cripple and let him be deaf and dumb: is it not the case that those reaching this age like things which arouse lust, and do not like things which arouse aversion? These things are natural for this time, like the opening of a flower. We'll test him by bringing in some dancers.' So they summoned some women, endowed with charm, who had the most beautiful bodies, like heavenly maidens. 'Whoever can make the prince laugh or become entangled in desire[27] will be his chief queen.' Saying this, they bathed the prince in perfumed water, and arrayed him as if he were a shining god and placed him on a royal bed, set up in a regal private chamber, like that in a palace of the gods. They made the inner room one mingled perfume of wreaths of perfumed plants and flowers, incense, scents, intoxicating drinks and spirits and suchlike and left. And then the women surrounded him and made an effort to seduce him with song and dance and all kinds of mellifluous words, but in his great wisdom he just looked at them. 'May these women not find any contact with my body.' And he stopped the inbreath and the outbreath and his body was stiff and they did not have any contact with his body. They informed his mother and father: 'His body is stiff. He is not human but must be a yakkha.' So from time to time his mother and father tested him but could not find a chink. In this way for sixteen years they tested him with sixteen various great tests and many lesser tests and could not catch him out.

Now the king was extremely sorrowful and summoned the experts in the marks. 'At the time of the birth you told me that this was the mark of wealth and auspiciousness and that there was no obstacle. But he is a deaf and dumb cripple; what you said does not agree with this.' 'Great king, it was not undetected by the teachers. It is just that it would have been painful for you if we had said that the child, obtained after prayers by the royal family, was [10] accursed and so we did not say it.' 'What should we do?' 'Great king, if the prince lives in this house three dangers will be seen: to your life, your regal parasol and your queen. Yoke an unlucky carriage to an unlucky horse and lie him down in it.[28] Send it out by the western gate: you should bury him in a charnel ground.' The king, terrified at hearing of the danger, agreed. Queen Candā heard what had happened and went up to the king. 'Sire, I was granted a wish by you. I accepted it and kept it. Give it to me now.' 'Take it, my lady.' 'Give the kingdom to my son.' 'It is not possible my lady; your son is accursed.' 'If you cannot give it for life, then grant it for seven years.' 'It is not possible, my lady.' 'Then give it for six, for five, for four, for three, for two, for one year. For seven months, for six, for five, for four, for three, for two, for one month or half a month.' 'It is not possible, my lady.' 'Then give it to him for seven days.' 'Very well; take it,' he said.

She had her son arrayed, had the city decorated and a drum beaten announcing that the kingdom belonged to Prince Temiya. She seated him on the shoulders of an elephant and raised the white parasol over his head and had him make a circumambulation of the city. When he returned she had him laid on the royal bed and implored him all night. 'Dear Prince Temiya, because of you I have not slept for sixteen years. My eyes have dried up through crying and my heart is as if broken by grief. I know that you were not born a cripple: do not make me without a protector.' On the following day and the day after that she implored him in this way, for five days. On the sixth day the king summoned the charioteer, called Sunanda, and said 'My man, early tomorrow lie the prince down in an unlucky chariot to which you have yoked an unlucky horse. Take him out by the western gate and dig a hole with four walls in the charnel ground. Throw him in it, hit him on the head with the back of the spade and kill him. Shovel dirt over it, [11] make a heap of earth and then wash and come here.' On the sixth night the queen beseeched her son and said, 'Dear one, King Kāsi has given the order to bury you in a charnel ground. My son, tomorrow you are going to die.' When he heard this the Great Being thought to himself, 'Temiya, you have made an effort for sixteen years and now it has reached a head'. Joy arose within him though his mother's heart was near to breaking. But even though this was the case he did not speak to her, thinking that if he did he would not attain the head, his desired object.

Then, when night had passed and it was dawn, Sunanda, the charioteer, yoked the carriage, set it at the gate and entered the royal chamber. 'My lady, do not be angry with me, it is the order of the king.' Saying this, with the heel of his palm[29] he removed the queen, who was lying in an embrace with her son, lifted the boy like a bunch of flowers and left the palace. Queen Candā beat her breast and with a great wail cried out and fell down upon the ground. And the Great Being looked at her and thought that if he did not talk she would die of a broken heart: and he wanted to speak out. But he was patient, reflecting, 'If I speak, the effort made for sixteen years would be in vain. But if I do not speak I will be a support for myself and my parents.'[30] And then the charioteer placed him on the chariot thinking that he would drive it in the direction of the western gate and drove it instead in the direction of the eastern gate, hitting the chariot wheel on the threshold. The Great Being heard the noise and thought, 'My heart's desire has come to pass!' His happy mind was still more delighted. By the power of the gods the carriage left the city and went a distance of three yojanas, and a woodland thicket appeared to the charioteer as if it were a charnel ground.[31] 'This is a lovely spot,' he thought and, pulling his chariot off the road, he got down and took off the Great Being's possessions,

made them into a bundle and set them aside. Then, taking his
spade he started to dig a hole nearby.

Then the Bodhisatta thought, 'It is the time for me to apply
effort. I have not moved my hands or feet for sixteen years.[32] I
wonder if they are under my control or not?' Standing up he
rubbed his left hand with his right hand [12] and his feet with
both hands and brought into being the thought to leave the
chariot. As his feet touched the ground the great earth rose and
met the end of the chariot and stayed there like a leather bag
filled with air. He got down and walked several times backwards
and forwards and saw that he had the strength to go a hundred
yojanas in one day in this way. Then he thought, 'If the charioteer
were to engage me in a fight would I have the strength to oppose
him?' He took hold of the end of the carriage and lifted it up as
if it were a toy for children and realized he did have the strength
to oppose. After deliberation he conceived a desire for suitable
clothing. At that moment Sakka's dwelling became hot. Sakka
recognized the cause and said, 'Prince Temiya's heart's desire
has been realized. The wish has arisen for suitable clothing. What
is human dress to him?' And he gave orders to Vissakamma to
have heavenly dress taken to him: 'Go, and deck the King of
Kāsi's son'. He agreed and with ten thousand pieces of cloth
made a garment and dressed him up like Sakka, with divine and
human clothing. Then, with the grace of the king of the shining
gods, the Great Being went up to the charioteer as he was digging
the pit. Standing at the edge of the hole he said the third verse:

3. 'Why are you in such a hurry to dig a pit, charioteer?
   Answer my question, sir, what will you do with the pit?'

When he heard this, the charioteer, digging the pit, looked up
and spoke the fourth verse:

4. 'The king's son was born dumb, a cripple, without intelligence.
   I have been instructed by the king to bury his son in the wood.'

And then the Great Being said to him:

5. 'I am neither deaf, dumb, nor a cripple, nor even lame.
   It would be a wrongful act, charioteer, to bury me in the forest.

6. [13] Look at my thighs and arms and listen to what I say.
   It would be a wrongful act, charioteer, to bury me in the forest.'

Then the charioteer thought, 'Who is this? Has he been speaking for himself since he came?' He gave up digging the hole and looked up and saw the magnificence of the Great Being's appearance. Unsure whether he was a man or a god he spoke this verse:

7. 'Are you a god or a heavenly minstrel, or indeed Sakka, once a great giver of gifts?[33]
   Who are you and whose son are you?
   How may we know you?'

And then the Great Being revealed himself and taught the *dhamma*:

8. 'I am neither god nor heavenly minstrel, nor even Sakka, once a great giver of gifts.
   I am the son of the king of Kāsi—
   the one that you are going to bury[34] in a pit.

9. I am the son of that king under whose sway you gain your livelihood.
   It would be a wrongful act, charioteer, to bury me in the forest.

10. If I were to sit or lie in the shadow of a tree,
    I should not break its branch, and be an evil one, one who harms a friend.

11. Just like the tree, so is the king. Just like the branch, so am I.
    And just like the man who comes into the shade, so are you, charioteer.
    It would be an wrongful act, charioteer, to bury me in the forest.'

[14] Even when the Bodhisatta had said this, the charioteer still had no faith in him. And the Great Being thought, 'I will gain his confidence.' And making the forest ring with the approval of the gods and the sound of his own voice he recited ten verses:

In honour of friends

12. Food is plentiful for him when he is away from home:
    he lives in abundance,
    Who is loyal to his friends.

13. Whatever country he visits, in city or town,
    he is an honoured guest everywhere,
    Who is loyal to his friends.

14. Thieves do not harm him, nor warrior despise him:
    he goes past all his enemies
    Who is loyal to his friends.

15. He returns to his home without anger and is welcomed in council;
    foremost amongst his relatives is one
    Who is loyal to his friends.

16. Respectful to others, he is respected, valuing others, he is valued.
    He is spoken well of,
    Who is loyal to his friends.

17. Honouring others, he is honoured; paying respect, he is respected.
    He obtains fame and good repute,
    Who is loyal to his friends.

18. He shines like the fire and is radiant like a deity:
    he does not lose his lustre,
    Who is loyal to his friends.

19. Cattle are born to him and the seed sown in his fields flourishes:

    he enjoys the fruit of seeds sown,
    Who is loyal to his friends.

20. Torn[35] from a mountain or a tree, a man finds a safe spot,
    Who is loyal to his friends.

21. Just as the wind does not harm a banyan, grown with spreading roots,
    so enemies do not harm him,
    Who is loyal to his friends.

[15] Even though he gave the *dhamma* in so many verses Sunanda did not recognize him, asking who he was and going back to the chariot. When he could not see the chariot and the bundle, though, he returned, looked again and, recognizing him, fell at his feet, making an añjali and imploring him with this verse:

22. 'Go, I will lead you back to your home, O prince.
    Rule the kingdom, dear sir, for what will you do in the forest?'

    The Great Being replied:

23. 'O, enough of kingdom, of relatives, or of wealth,
    since my kingdom would only be obtained through wrong behaviour, charioteer.'

    The charioteer replied:

24. 'When you go from here you will get a full cup for me, O prince.
    At your return your mother and father will be generous to me.

25. Ladies of the court, princes, merchants and Brahmins,
    delighted at your return, will be generous to me, O prince.

26. Mahouts, bodyguards, charioteers and foot soldiers,
    pleased at your return, will be generous to me, O prince.

27. A crowd of country people, and people from the city too, will meet together.
    They will be generous with presents when you return, O prince.'

[16] The Great Being replied:

28. 'I have been given up by my father and mother,
    and by all the princes too, deprived of kingdom[36] and the city.
    I do not have any home of my own.

29. My mother acquiesced; my father cast me off.
    I am a recluse in the forest, and do not wish for sense pleasures.'

In this way joy arose in the Great Being as he brought to mind his own excellencies,[37] and, moved by joy, he gave an ecstatic utterance:

30. 'Truly, for those who are not in a hurry, it is the aspiration for good that succeeds.[38]
    Know this, charioteer, as for me the holy life is fully ripe.

31. Even the highest aim ripens for those who are not in a hurry.
    For me the holy life is fully ripe, and, having renounced,
    I have nothing to fear, anywhere!'

The charioteer said:

32. 'In this way your speech is beautiful and your words friendly.
    Why did you not speak when you were with your father and mother?'

Then the Great Being said:

33. 'I was not a cripple without the use of thighs, or deaf through lack of hearing.
    I was not dumb through lack of a tongue; do not take me as dumb!

34. I remember a former birth where I ruled a kingdom,
    And when I had ruled the kingdom, because of the evil I had done,
    I fell into a terrible hell.

35. For twenty years I ruled a kingdom,
    But for eighty-four thousand I roasted in hell.

36. [17] I am terrified of kingship, and being anointed in kingship.
    Because of this I did not talk when with my father and mother.

37. When my father placed me on his lap he gave orders:
    "Kill that one! Imprison that one! Torture with wounds and
    caustic substances!
    Impale that one on a spike!"[39] This is what he ordered.

38. When I heard this harsh speech uttered by him,
    although not dumb, in the guise of dumbness,
    although not crippled, in the guise of a cripple,
    I lay, completely sodden in my own urine and faeces.

39. Who would come to this life, so miserable, short
    and connected with suffering, and do harm to anyone?

40. Who, through not knowing wisdom and not seeing justice,
    would come to this life and do harm to anyone?

41. Truly to those who are not in a hurry, the desire for fruit
    succeeds.
    I am living the fully ripe, holy life: know this, charioteer.

42. Truly to those who are not in a hurry even the highest aim
    ripens.
    I am living the fully ripe holy life, and having renounced,
    have nothing to fear, anywhere.'

[18] Sunanda heard this and thought, 'This prince has thrown
away royal splendour such as this as if it were a corpse. He
entered the wood, not breaking his resolve to become an ascetic.
What meaning is there for me in this miserable life? I'll go with
him and become an ascetic too.' And he spoke this verse:

43. 'I'll become an ascetic, prince, with you.
    Summon me, dear sir, for it is the going forth that pleases me.'

When the Great Being was beseeched by him in this way he
thought, 'If I make him become an ascetic now my mother and
father will not come here, and they will lose out. The horses, the
chariot, the garments will be destroyed and blame will come to

me: they will think, "He is a yakkha, he must have eaten the charioteer".' Considering how to extricate himself from blame and to provide for his parents' welfare he gave the horses, chariot and adornments to the charioteer and spoke this verse:

44. 'Go, charioteer, and take the chariot back, as you are not free from debt.
    Going forth is for the one who is free from debt; this is praised by wise men.'

When he heard this the charioteer thought, 'If, when I have gone to the city, he goes anywhere else, his father will hear the news, ask me to show him his son, come here and not lay eyes on him: then he'll punish me. Because of this I'll explain the situation myself and extract a promise from the prince.' And he said two verses:

45. 'Just as I have done what you have asked,
    so you, dear sir, requested by me, could do what I ask.
46. Please stay right here while I bring the king.
    And then when your father has seen you he'll be happy and delighted.'

[19] Then the Great Being said:

47. 'Charioteer, I'll do what you ask of me.
    I would also like to see my father coming here.
48. Go, sir: return and wish health to my relatives.
    Give greetings from me to my mother and father.'

The charioteer accepted the instruction.

49. The charioteer clasped him by the feet and paid homage to him.
    He mounted the carriage and went up to the palace gate.

At that moment Queen Candā opened her window and asked, 'What news is there of my son?' She looked at the charioteer returning on the road and when she saw that he came back alone she grieved.

In explanation the Teacher said:

50. 'His mother saw the carriage empty and the charioteer returning alone.
    With her eyes filled with tears she wept and watched for him:
51. "This charioteer comes and has killed my own child.
    My son has now been killed and increases the soil in the earth.
52. Now bitter enemies rejoice, delighted.
    But I see the charioteer returning after killing my own child."
53. A mother sees an empty chariot and the charioteer returning, alone.
    With eyes filled with tears she weeps and implores:
54. "Was he deaf, was he crippled, did he wail when you struck him on the ground?
    Tell me this, charioteer.
55. How did a deaf cripple ward you off with his hands and feet, when struck on the ground? I have asked: tell me this!"'

[20] The charioteer said:

56. 'I will tell you, lady, but you must grant me my immunity, for what you hear and see from me about my time with the prince.'

And then Queen Candā said:

57. 'I grant you immunity, sir. Speak without fear, charioteer, about what you heard and what you saw when you were with the prince.'

Then the charioteer said:

58. 'He was not dumb, not crippled, but clear in speech.
    He said that he was frightened of kingship and so practised many ruses.

59. He remembers an earlier birth in which he ruled a kingdom,
    and after he had ruled this kingdom he fell to a terrible hell.
60. For twenty years he ruled the kingdom,
    but for eighty thousand he cooked in hell.
61. He was frightened of his kingdom and not wanting a royal
    anointment;
    because of this he did not speak when in the presence of his
    father and mother.
62. Endowed with all his limbs, of good height and girth, clear
    in speech,
    he stands, wise, on the path to heaven.
63. And if you wish to see the prince, your own child,
    go and I will bring you to where Temiya does his practices.'

[21] Now, when the prince had sent the charioteer off, he wished
to live as an ascetic. Knowing his intention Sakka gave an order
to Vissakamma,[40] 'Sir, Prince Temiya wishes to become an ascetic:
go and create a leaf hut for him and the requisites for an ascetic'.
He agreed and went with speed and created a hermitage in a
woodland thicket three yojanas in length. He made it so that it
had a place for the night and one for the day, a bathing pool, a
well and fruit-bearing trees. He created the requisites for an
ascetic and then went back to his own abode. The Great Being
saw it and, realizing it was a present from Sakka, entered the
leaf hut, took off his clothes, dressed himself in inner and outer
garments made of red bark and put on the hide of a black antelope,
making it go over his shoulder. He tied his braided hair into a
bun. Putting a carrying pole on his shoulder and taking a walking
stick he left the leaf hut; he walked up and down, making a
display of the glory of being an ascetic. He made a joyful utterance,
'Ah, the happiness, the happiness!' Then he entered the leaf hut
and, sitting on a mat of sticks and twigs, attained the five
knowledges.[41] In the evening he left and gathered some leaves
from a kāra tree, situated at the end of the walkway, soaked them

in water in a vessel given by Sakka, without salt or buttermilk or flavouring, and enjoyed eating it as much as if it were ambrosia. Then he cultivated the four divine abidings and arranged his dwelling there.

Now the king of Kāsi heard Sunanda's report and summoned the general, telling him to prepare for the journey.

64. 'Yoke the chariot horses; tie the belt to the elephants,
Sound the conch horns and cymbals, beat the drums.

65. Let the fastened kettle drums roar and the bass drum sound,
Let the city people come with me,
I will go to speak with my son!

66. Ladies, princes, merchants and Brahmins:
Have their chariots yoked quickly,
I will go to speak with my son!

67. Mahouts, bodyguards, charioteers and foot soldiers:
Have their carriages yoked quickly;
I will go to speak with my son!

68. A crowd of country people, and a crowd of people from the city too:
Have their carriages yoked quickly;
I will go to speak with my son!'

[22] Just as the king had ordered, the charioteers had the horses yoked to the chariots, stood them at the royal gate and informed the king.

The Thus-gone in explanation as Teacher said:

69. 'Sindh horses are yoked to swift vehicles and
charioteers approach the palace gate: "these horses are yoked, sire".'

Then the king said:

70. 'Fat horses fall behind in speed, scrawny ones fall behind in staying power.'

(They said to the charioteer, "Do not bring such horses!")
The horses were harnessed together, avoiding the fat and
the scrawny.'

So the king went into the presence of his son after he had
assembled the four castes, eighteen guilds, and the entire body
of his army. He took over three days to bring together the entire
force. On the fourth day he left, having brought together all those
to be collected, and went to the hermitage. Welcomed by his son,
he gave him his greetings.

In explanation the Teacher said:

71. 'The king, rushing, mounted the yoked chariot;
    He addressed his apartment of women: "all of you, follow
    me!"

72. [With] chowrie, turban, sword and white parasol
    Let the royal slippers, adorned in gold, mount the carriage.[42]

73. And then the king set out, accompanied by his charioteer,
    and came quickly to the place where Temiya practised.

74. When he saw him approach, in glory, as if on fire,
    surrounded by his assembly of warriors, Temiya said:

75. "Dear father, I hope you are well, I hope that you are in
    good health!
    I hope that all the queens, my mothers, too are well."

76. "I am indeed well, my son; I am in very good health
    and all the queens, your mothers, are well."

77. "I hope you do not drink, father, I hope that spirits are not
    dear to you.
    I hope that your mind delights in truthfulness, just actions
    and generous gifts."

78. "Indeed I do not drink, my son, and spirits are not dear to me.
    And moreover I do delight in truthfulness, just actions and
    generous gifts."

79. "I hope your oxen are in good health, and the animals that
    pull the waggon too.
    I hope there is no illness in you, that affects the body."

80. "My oxen are in good health and the animals that pull the
    waggon too.
    There is indeed no illness in me, nor torment in the body."

81. "I hope the borderlands are prosperous, and that the midlands
    are crowded too.
    I hope the treasury and the granary are quite full.

82. Welcome to you, great king, you are not unwelcome.
    Let them set up a couch where the king will sit."'

[23] And then the Great Being said, 'If he sits cross-legged let
them provide a rush mat,' and gave a verse upon that which had
been prepared.

83. 'Sit right here upon this seat that has been set:
    They will bring water from there and bathe your feet.'

The king, out of respect, did not sit upon the rush mat but sat
on the ground. The Great Being entered the leaf hut and took
out a kāra leaf and with this invited the king, and spoke a verse:

84. 'I have cooked this leaf of mine without salt: eat it great king,
    You have come as my guest.'

And then the king said:

85. 'I do not eat[43] leaves, it is not my food:
    I eat fine rice, boiled rice, white,
    with a curry of pure meat poured over it.'

At that moment Queen Candā came surrounded by her ladies.
She clasped the feet of her son and paid homage to him, and
with her eyes filled with tears sat down to one side. And then the
king said, 'Dear lady, see this food of our son's!' and put a bit
of the leaf into her hand and then gave it to the other ladies bit

by bit. They all said, 'My lord, how do you eat such food!' They took it, and said, 'You are going through great hardship, my lord!' and sat down. The king said, 'Dear son, this is just extraordinary to me.' And spoke a verse:

86. 'It appears extraordinary to me:
    that even though you are alone and secluded, eating such food,
    your complexion is bright!'

[25] And then he gave an explanation to him and said:

87. 'I lie alone, sire, on a laid-out mat.
    Through my solitary bed, sire, my complexion is bright.
88. No royal guards stand over me, armed with swords.
    Because of my happy bed, sire, my complexion is bright.
89. I do not grieve over the past; I do not yearn for the future.
    I live in the present, and so my complexion is bright.
90. By yearning for the future and regretting the past:
    Through this, the strong wither, like a fresh reed cut down.'⁴⁴

    The king thought, 'I'll anoint him right here and take him with me.' So he spoke these verses inviting him to the kingdom:

91. 'My army of elephants, my army of chariots, horses, foot soldiers,
    armoured soldiers and my delightful palaces I give to you, my son.
92. My women's quarters, adorned in every way, I give to you, my son.
    Go into them, my son, for you will be our king.
93. Beautiful and skilled women, expert in song and dance, will make love to you:
    O what will you do in the forest?
94. I will bring you adorned girls from enemy kings:
    When you have produced sons from these
    then you can go afterwards as an ascetic!

95. You are young and strong, in the first part of life, a boy.
    Rule the kingdom, dear one:
    O what will you do in the forest?'

In response to this the Bodhisatta gave words of teaching:

96. 'A young man should lead the holy life:
    The one who leads the holy life should be youthful.
    Going forth as a young man: this is praised by the wise.

97. [26] A young man should lead the holy life:
    the one who leads the holy life should be youthful.
    I will live the holy life and do not want the kingdom.

98. I watch as a young boy, obtained with difficulty,
    says 'dear dad', then, not even reaching old age, dies.

99. I watch as a young daughter, lovely to behold,
    wasting away, like a cut bamboo shoot, is broken down in
    death.

100. Even the young die, men and women;
    As to that you would trust in life, saying, I am young?

101. For surely, the lifespan of a youth may be very short,
    like the lifespan of fishes in little water.

102. The world is constantly attacked and constantly surrounded,
    As things pass by unfailingly;
    Why would you anoint me in kingship?

103. By whom is this world afflicted?
    By whom is it surrounded?
    What passes by,[45] unfailingly?
    Now I have asked, answer me this.

104. By death the world is afflicted.
    By old age it is surrounded.
    The passing of nights goes unfailingly.
    Know this, warrior.

105. Just as whatever is to be woven by a stretched thread,
    O king, is limited, in this way our mortal life is to be woven.

106. Just as a full, water-carrying river moves and does not go
     backwards,
     So the lifespan of mortals goes by and does not return.

107. Just as a full, water-carrying river moves
     and takes with it the trees sprung up at its bank,
     So living beings are surely taken by old age and death.'

[27] When king heard the *dhamma* talk from the Great Being
he wished to become an ascetic and leave the household life. 'I
will not go back to the city, I will become an ascetic right here.
And if my son should go to the city I'll give him the white parasol.'
So to test him he invited him to the kingdom again:

108. 'My army of elephants, my army of chariots, horses, foot
     soldiers
     armoured soldiers and my delightful palaces I give to you,
     my son.

109. My women's quarters, adorned in every way, I give to you,
     my son.
     Go into them, my son, for you will be king.

110. Beautiful and skilled women, expert in song and dance,
     will make love to you:
     O what will you do in the forest?

111. I will bring you adorned girls from enemy kings:
     when you have produced sons from these
     then you can go back as an ascetic!

112. A storehouse, a treasury, powerful vehicles and delightful
     palaces
     I give to you, my son.

113. Surrounded by circle of cows and accompanied by a retinue
     of slaves,
     Rule the kingdom, dear one,
     For what will you do in the forest?'

And then the Great Being, in explanation of his lack of desire for kingship, said:

114. 'What is the point of wealth, which does not last?
    What is the point of a wife who will die?
    What is the point of the lustre of youth,[46] which old age will overcome?

115. And in that, what delight is there, what sport, what sexual pleasure,
    and what wealth?
    What are young sons to me, O king?
    For I am free from ties.

116. But I do know this: death does not pass me by.
    What is sexual pleasure and wealth
    for the one who has fallen to the end maker?

117. [28] Just as the danger of falling to the ground
    is always there for fruit that is ripe,
    for those that are born as mortal men
    there is always the danger of death.

118. At night some are not seen, but by morning all are visible.
    Then in the morning some are seen, but at night they are seen no more.

119. And so exertion should be made today;
    for who knows the time of his own death?
    There is no truce with that great general, Death.

120. Thieves steal wealth, but I, O king, am free from ties.
    Go king and return; but I have no desire for the kingdom.'

So the Great Being's discourse, and its application, reached its conclusion. When they had heard it the king and Queen Candā at the start, and then the sixteen thousand wives, all wished to become ascetics. The king had a drum beaten in the city: 'Whoever wishes to become an ascetic with my son may do so!' [29] And he had the doors of all the treasuries of gold opened. And he had inscribed on a golden plate: 'At this spot here, and at this spot there, are big pots of treasure which people may take for themselves,' and had it attached to a big bamboo pillar. And the people of the city left shop doors wide open, abandoned their houses and gathered round the king. The king, with a great crowd of people, became an ascetic with the Great Being. The hermitage, given by Sakka, was three yojanas long. The Great Being wandered around the leaf huts, assigning the leaf huts in the middle to women, as their natures were timid, and giving the leaf huts on the outskirts to men. And on the *uposatha* day they all stood on the ground by the fruit-bearing trees which had been created by Vissakamma, gathered the fruits and ate them, following the practice of the ascetic life. The Great Being sat in the sky, and knowing the mind of anyone whose thoughts went to desire, or hatred or violence, delivered his teaching. As soon as they heard it they quickly attained the higher knowledges and the attainments in meditation.

Now, a neighbouring king heard that the king of Kāsi had become an ascetic and decided to seize the city of Vārāṇasi. He entered the city and, seeing it all decorated, went up into the king's palace and looked at the seven different kinds of excellent jewels that were there. Thinking that there must be some danger associated with the wealth, he summoned some drunkards and asked them by which gate the king had left. They told him that it had been the eastern one, so thereupon he left by the same gate and went down to the banks of the river. Seeing his approach the Great Being went up to him, sat in the sky and delivered a discourse. The king then went with his retinue to become an ascetic, as did another king in the same way. Three kingdoms were now abandoned, and the elephants became wild, forest elephants and the horses wild, forest horses. The chariots just rotted away in the woods. The coins in the storehouses were

treated as sand and scattered, and everyone reached the eight
attainments in meditation. At the end of their lives they were
bound for the Brahma heavens, and even the animals and elephants
and horses, their minds calmed in the company of the wise, attained
the six heavens of the sense sphere.

The Teacher gave this discourse and said, 'Not just now,
bhikkhus, but in past times too, I renounced and abandoned a
kingdom.' He made the connections with the birth: 'Uppalavaṇṇā
was the goddess that lived in the parasol, Sāriputta the charioteer,
members of the royal family were the mother and the father, the
Buddha's followers were the retinue. And I was Mūgapakkha'.

They reached the island of Sri Lanka: the elder Khuddakatissa
from Maṃgaṇa, the elders Mahāvaṃsaka and Phussadeva
from Kaṭakandhakāra, the elder Mahārakkhita from
Uparimaṇḍakamāla, the elder Mahātissa from Bhaggari, the
elder Mahāsiva, from Vāmattapabbhāra, and the elder
Mahāmaliyadeva, from Kāḷavela.[47] These elders are known as
latecomers into the assembly of Kuddāla, the assembly of
Mūgapakkha, the assembly of Ayoghara and the assembly of
Hatthipāla.[48] But the elder Mahānāga from Maddha and the
elder Maliyamahādevā commented on the day of the
parinibbāna, the complete enlightenment of the Buddha: 'Well
friend, today the company of those who were in the assembly of
Mūgapakkha has come to an end.' They asked why and this
was the reply: 'Sir, I then was a drunkard. And when I could not
get the others to come with me for a drink, because they had all
renounced, I became an ascetic too.'

Notes

[1] See S. Leksukhum, with photos by G. Mermet, 'The Ten Great
Jātakas', *Temples of Gold: Seven Centuries of Thai Buddhist Paintings*
(London: Thames and Hudson, 2001), pp. 136–59.

[2] See this book, discussion for Jātaka 95, p. 76.

[3] Steven Collins, *Nirvana and Other Buddhist Felicities* (Cambridge: OUP, 1998), p. 433ff provides illuminating discussion of this story as a Buddhist utopian vision.

[4] It was the duty of a king to inflict punishment on his subjects (*Mahābhārata*, XII, 15). Punishments in ancient India were unbelievably harsh: see A.L. Basham, *The Wonder that was India*, London: Sidgwick and Jackson, 1967, pp. 118–22.

[5] Ibid., p. 139. In the Ayutthaya period, this scene adorned the walls of the pavilion of the Somdet Phra Buddha Kosacharn at Wat Buddhaisawan. It is depicted in temples throughout Bangkok and, in the provinces, in Wat Ta Khu at Nakhon Ratchasima and at Wat Yai Intharam at Chonburi (north wall, west panel), where he twirls the chariot above his head.

[6] See Basham, *The Wonder that was India*, pp. 191–233.

[7] For the forest dweller's life, see W. Doniger and B.K. Smith, *The Laws of Manu* (Harmondsworth: Penguin, 1991), chapter 6, pp. 117–27.

[8] See 'The Far Past' (J I 21).

[9] *Basket of Conduct*, 36–8 (*Cariyāpiṭaka* III, 1–19) and J I 46.

[10] *The Story of Gotama Buddha*, 31 (J I 25).

[11] J I 23.

[12] J IV 377

[13] J VI 184.

[14] See D II 172 for some gamblers and dancing drunkards.

[15] It is not yet 'the beautiful place' that is *nibbāna*, but it is on its way. See *Path of Purification*, 215 (Vism VII, 33) *sundaraṃ thāṇaṃ* and, for discussion of *nibbāna* as a 'place', Collins, *Nirvana and Other Buddhist Felicities*, p. 224.

[16] E. Wray, C. Rosenfield, and D. Bailey, with photographs by J.D. Wray, *Ten Lives of the Buddha: Siamese Temple Paintings and Jātaka Tales* (New York: Weatherhill, revised paperback edn, 1996), pictures, pp. 27–8, comment, pp. 134, 136.

[17] This can be seen on the Indira Gandhi National Centre for the Arts website, at http://ignca.nic.in/asp/showbig.asp?projid=jtk2.

[18] Mentioned in http://www.azibaza.com/lectures_burm_arts.htm.

[19]'Buddhist paintings in Sri Lanka', Albert Dharmasiri, http://www.artslanka.org/buddhistart/body.html.

[20] This is the final renunciation, when Gotama leaves his family in the quest for Buddhahood.

[21] Jātaka 531. This is usually thought to mean that the wives of the king are sent on to the street in order to conceive from any man there. In the Kusa Jātaka (531) the virtuous chief queen leaves the palace, is kidnapped by Sakka, masquerading as an old man, and is taken to a heaven realm where she conceives a son, called Kusa after the grass she brings back as proof of her visit and her fidelity. There are some problems, though, with the idea that the women went out and slept with any man. Traditionally, Indian culture regards barrenness as the problem of the woman concerned, not a male difficulty, which would be implied by the practice of going on to the street: though they were perhaps just been realistic about the problem. Another difficulty is that unless the succession was matrilineal, which is certainly possible, the product of the union would not technically be the heir. So could it be the case that the women used to go out as mendicants for a while, to adopt an ascetic life? This is a less sensational interpretation, but one that is supported by the usual Indian literary convention that women wanting a child go into the forest, live as ascetics in a forest and are granted their wish by a god. In the Kusa Jātaka the women leave the palace on *uposatha* days.

[22] DP I 756 suggests *balaṅkapāda* here—having crow's feet—but this sounds a bit like the marks on a face.

[23] There seems to be more than one meaning to this name, however, which as we shall see proves significant. PED 306–7 notes, 'There is an ancient confusion between the roots *tim*, *tamas*, etc. (to be dark), *tim*, *temeti* (to be wet), and *stim* to be motionless.'

[24] *Nirodha samāpatti* is considered the highest stage of meditative attainment.

[25] See DP I 151; *antaruddhi*: hernia rupture.

[26] The Mire hell is described in Jātaka 541 (J VI 111).

[27] See DP I 693–4 on *kilesa* for sexual passion or desire.

[28] Certain features, such as different-coloured eyes, would be regarded as bringing bad luck in a horse; the chariot or carriage would perhaps be in a colour considered inauspicious, or one which

had been used for inauspicious purposes, such as the removal of a
dead body.

²⁹ This would be a way of moving the queen without touching her
with the whole of his hand.

³⁰ The word *paccayo*, 'cause, condition, ground' here is interesting.
The strong supporting condition, *upanissaya paccayo*, the ninth cause
in the list of twenty-four causes that constitute the seventh book of the
Abhidhamma, the *Pāṭṭhāna*, is associated with conditions that help to
elicit a change in state: the right food, lodging or teacher. The Bodhisatta
hopes that his actions will be the 'strong supporting condition' for
spiritual change both in himself and in his parents. The term was used
widely by this time in all Buddhist systems, not just the Theravāda.

³¹ All attempts to associate the Great Being with the inauspicious
meet with failure, presumably through the good offices of the gods: the
chariot leaves by the lucky eastern gate and the charioteer thinks a
beautiful woodland is a charnel ground.

³² Emending *hatthapādena* to *hatthapāde na* (literally, 'not hands
or feet') which makes the sentence a negative one, with 'hands and feet'
then the object of the verb.

³³ The word *purindada* is a distortion of the Vedic word meaning
'breaker of fortresses'. Through the punning wordplay beloved of
ancient Indians (*nirukta*) the term was taken by Buddhist commentators
to mean 'formerly a giver' (*pure + dā*).

³⁴ I am following the suggestion of W. Geiger, B. Ghosh trans., K.R.
Norman revised, *A Pāli Grammar* (Oxford: PTS, 1994), p. 29 in
translating *nighaññasi* as a future of *nikhanati* ('dig into, bury').

³⁵ This is the only place the word *darito* occurs. It could have been
misread by a scribe so it is emended to *dalito*, split or torn.

³⁶ I have emended *rathassa* (of the chariot) to *raṭṭhassa* (of the
kingdom) as presumably it is kingdom rather than chariot which the
prince has lost.

³⁷ The recollection of one's own virtues always seems odd to the
modern mind! Calling to mind one's own good behaviour is, however,
a Buddhist meditative exercise (*sīlānussati*), intended to allay fear and
bring happiness in daily life. It is one of the forty subjects for meditation
recommended by Buddhaghosa, in *The Path of Purification*.

38 The commentary says that this refers to the fact that he was prepared to wait for sixteen years before success.

39 For *accetha* ('neglect'), read *appetha* ('fix', 'fasten', and hence 'impale'). See 'acceti' DP I 25.

40 Vissakamma is artist, designer and decorator to the gods! (DPPN II 906–7).

41 The five higher knowledges (*abhiññā*) are: 1) the psychic powers, with ability to become many, become invisible, walk through a wall as if it is air, etc., 2) the Divine Ear that hears sounds far and near, heavenly or human, 3) penetration of the minds of others, 4) memory of past lives and 5) the Divine Eye that sees the arising and falling of beings in different conditions (D I 78–83).

42 Something is wrong with this passage: it is not possible to construe. See DP I 484; Be: *upādhī rathaṃ āruyha[ntu] suvaṇṇehi alaṃkatā.*

43 At the suggestion of the Sinhalese manuscript (Cks) I have put *bhuñjāmi*, 'I eat' rather than *buñje*, 'I would eat', which is given in the PTS text.

44 See S I 5 for a *sutta* in which the Buddha utters a strikingly similar verse to a shining god on the benefits of the ascetic life.

45 Reading *gacchanto* ('going' and hence, for the context here, 'passing by'), Bd. These lines are curious; the riddling tone is clear though the exact meaning is not.

46 Reading *vaṇṇena* here, to give 'complexion' or 'lustre', following a Burmese manuscript (Bd). See PED 596.

47 This is an odd reference that links this story to the Kuddāla Jātaka (70; J I 315), the Ayoghara Jātaka (510; J IV 499), and the Hatthipāla Jātaka (509; J IV 490)—all of which involve the Bodhisatta taking family and friends outside the city to live a renunciate life. No proper explanation as to how the arrival of these elders is linked to earlier events is given in any of the tales. Possibly this description of earlier rebirths of some elders who were thought to visit Sri Lanka after the death of the Buddha represents an attempt to posit an ancient lineage with a longstanding connection with the Bodhisatta.

48 These refer to the Kuddāla, this story, Ayoghara and Hatthipāla.

25

The story of Mahājanaka
Mahājanaka Jātaka (539)

Vol. VI, 30–68

Discussion about the story

The condition of all beings, *saṃsāra*, is often described as an ocean in ancient Indian thought. The codifier of law, Manu, categorizes those that have undertaken a sea journey with those who should be excluded from rituals: purification would be required after any voyage.[1] Buddhism, however, travelled with mercantile interests that crossed oceans and so depended upon sea travel for its dissemination.[2] This story is most widely known through a maritime image, of the Bodhisatta being rescued by a goddess after swimming for seven days on his own after a shipwreck. It is one of the most frequently depicted scenes in the temple art of Sri Lanka and Thailand, both seafaring nations. Despite the story's link with renunciation, the scene in the ocean prompted ancient sources to associate it with the perfection of vigour or effort (*viriya*), a word cognate to the Latin word for 'man' (*vir*) and hence English words such as virility and virtuosity. The introduction to the Jātakas says, 'All the men died in the middle of the ocean, with no shore in sight; but there was nothing at variance in my mind (*cittassa aññathā*) and this is the perfection of effort.'[3] Mahājanaka's valiant attempts to survive are treated in the tradition of the last ten Jātakas as representing this perfection too: in some depictions his effort looks as light as air, as if he is being lifted from the wreck by Maṇimekhalā as he falls.[4]

The story's exploration of the nature of appropriate effort, 'with nothing at variance', is communicated with considerable dramatic skill. Winternitz says of its 'overwhelming power' that it could only have been inspired 'by the deepest inner conviction and no less poetical talent'.[5] Split into two distinct sections, the tale nonetheless represents a unified sequence from the heroic quest of a prince to regain his throne, to the king's subsequent efforts to adopt the renunciate life. In the first part, the Bodhisatta shows a combination of courage and inventiveness characteristic of a folk hero. The taunting of the brahmin boys about his birth when living in exile and the interchange with his mother in which he resists her advice not to go to sea show his strength before the ordeal of his survival for seven days after the shipwreck. This, however, along with his display of shrewd common sense to avoid death, is the real test of the Bodhisatta's mettle. After his long swim of seven days which culminates in his eloquent debate with the goddess, Maṇimekhalā, he is tested by situations where the correct placing of effort lies in acquiescence, not action. He lets the goddess carry him to safety, the magical carriage that chooses a king goes straight to him while he sleeps and the kingship is offered to him rather than being claimed. When the two protagonists come together, tests of wit and skill are needed. In this, many features are recognizable from the ordeals and romantic courtships of folk traditions around the world, particularly where a throne is concerned.[6] Sīvalī seems to represent the glories of the city of Mithilā. She herself has imposed a quick and gruelling test on the earlier candidates for her hand—a ruthless piece of character assessment whose shaming echoes the routing of Penelope's suitors and the abasement of the sailors by Circe in the Odyssey. This is the first time that she herself has been tested. The prince parries her demands, by paying attention to the palace rather than her, and changes the rules of engagement. Unlike the other humiliated suitors, he proceeds at his own pace, does not search her out, but waits for her to choose him, which she does, by accepting him with her hand. Throughout this part of the story we see the need for different kinds of effort, not all requiring obvious strain or 'brawn'. Mahājanaka's silent recognition of his subjects while lying on the stone, his regal response to the tests of the princess, and his careful measuring of what is necessary as, for instance, in the stringing of the bow, a task that he performs with an ease compared to women carding cotton, are all achievements that contribute to his suitability to be king.

With the solving of the riddles another key influence in the tale is introduced. Riddle-solving forms a central part of the accumulation of wisdom in Jātakas (as in Jātaka 402). In Sri Lanka, they are still, to this day, a popular means of encoding medical, psychological and esoteric knowledge.[7] The riddles here have a particular significance: the earlier king had oriented his life by waiting upon the *paccekabuddha*s, ascetics who lived on his generosity in alms, every day at dawn and sunset. By recognizing the honour they were paid by the last king, and hence the true spiritual alignment of Mithilā, the new king discovers the secrets encrypted in the old king's riddles. In the time when there is no Buddhist path, there is no means for obtaining arahatship, which requires the teaching of a fully awakened Buddha. This curious shadow or absence hangs like a backdrop over all the Jātakas, but *paccekabuddha*s, barely mentioned in other *nikāya*s, are a reminder that it is a temporary one, and that spirituality can never be lost completely.[8] Many stories describe them and their path to enlightenment.[9] It is the yearning for their reassuring presence after they leave that leads the Bodhisatta to renunciation: the three simple and lyrical verses (vv. 22–4) in which he expresses his sense of loss at their departure—unexplained in the narrative— are a testament to the values they represent. In the last part of the story, striking images associated with *paccekabuddha*s in other

Jātakas govern the Bodhisatta's effort as he tries to take up the holy life. The tree that is beautiful but which bears no fruit, an analogy for the life of the recluse, and the girl with a solitary bangle are both images famously described elsewhere as instigating the enlightenment of those who become *paccekabuddha*s.[10] *Paccekas*, in the absence of a teacher, were thought to find freedom through the teaching of a meaningful event. The Bodhisatta can never become a *paccekabuddha*: his ultimate aim is to become, in his last lifetime, a fully awakened Buddha, who can teach a complete way to others. Even up to his final departure, however, with the obliteration of footprints that might find him, his efforts to take up the holy life are punctuated by a series of memorable events and encounters that align him with these often silent and mysterious figures, the *paccekas*; like them he finds his path on his own, but others cannot follow him.

Key events in the story are resolved in an almost palpable silence. While there is great poetry, skilled debate between protagonists and an extensive eulogy to the city of Mithilā (vv. 25–115), major agreements are unspoken. Mahājanaka's assessment of the crowd as his subjects while lying on the stone, Sīvalī's acceptance of him as her husband and her placing of the golden pin to help him answer the riddle about the head of the bed, all take place without discussion. The populace complain of the king's silence when he has assumed the attitude of a *paccekabuddha* (v. 21). The king copies their walk and behaviour, not their speech, to prepare himself for his departure. When he passes down from the palace Sīvalī silently and symbolically frees him to renounce his kingship by paying respects to the man she thinks is a *paccekabuddha*: though the fact that she thinks it is such a figure who has been teaching shows that these enlightened beings do teach sometimes. The little girl's bangle is a silent teacher (vv. 157–9). The fletcher is silent when he has given his advice (vv. 165–7). Unlike the Vessantara Jātaka (547), where the

Bodhisatta revives his swooning wife, Mahājanaka disappears
without a word into the forest when she is unconscious: his
strenuous attempts to dismiss her, and hence the crowds that
follow her, have been to no avail.[11] Although the king's rejection
of Sīvalī in this story seems cruel, those who heard the story
would have seen it as part of the Bodhisatta's larger search, which
culminates in Buddhahood, at a time when he can teach Sīvalī
to find enlightenment for herself. In this story she seems
to represent the lay life and her people; his is a particularly
lone way.

As if to highlight the power of silence, a special place is also
accorded to the role of noise and music in this Jātaka. Musical
instruments accompany the wonderful carriage and roar like
the sea to greet the Bodhisatta. Songs and music at his first festival
are like the roar of the Yugandhara ocean. The first thing people
notice about him when he becomes a recluse is that he does not
listen to songs or music (v. 20). The renunciate king remembers
the music before the visual beauty that had accompanied his
entrance to the garden where he saw the two trees (vv. 144–9). The
twofold structure of the story seems to create a parallel between
Mahājanaka's lone escape from the waters and his attempts to
become an ascetic. A noise, compared to village games, is produced
by the streaming crowds that surround him as he leaves Mithilā
(v. 129). In the vow that opens this book the Bodhisatta describes
himself as one who will take others across the sea of existence.[12]
Perhaps because it is a tale about the development of heroic effort,
however, the most famous scene in this story is the rescue by the
goddess of a man on his own. It is a curious and even contradictory
image for this perfection—and apt in a story so influenced by
the *paccekabuddha*s, who find enlightenment for themselves
(*sāmaṃ*). The hero, as Bodhisatta, cannot find complete release
in this lifetime and so does not become one of their number, but
this Jātaka bears the stamp of their solitary path.[13]

Story from the present
'*Who is this in the middle of the ocean?*'

While staying at the Jetavana Grove the Teacher told this story about renunciation. One day the monks sat down in the *dhamma* hall and were praising the great renunciation of the Thus-gone. The Teacher came in and said, 'So what then, bhikkhus, have you been discussing while you have been meeting together?' They told him the subject. 'This, bhikkhus, is not the first occasion that I have made a great renunciation.' And he narrated this story about times long past.

Story from the past

Once upon a time at Mithilā, in the kingdom of Videha, a king ruled called Mahājanaka.[14] He had two sons, Ariṭṭhajanaka and Polajanaka. The king handed over the viceroyship to the elder of these and the position of leader of the army to the younger. In course of time Mahājanaka died and Ariṭṭhajanaka became the king and gave the viceroyship to the other. A certain foot servant of his went into the presence of the king and said, 'Sire, the viceroy wishes to kill you.' When he heard this story from him again and again the king became divided from Polajanaka and had him placed in chains and put in a house near the royal palace. He ordered him to be put under guard. The prince made a declaration of truth:[15] 'If I have been an enemy to my brother, may my chains not become loosened and may the door not open; if I have not, may my chains loosen and may the door open.' Sure enough the bonds [31] broke, chain by chain, and the door opened. So he left and went to a border town and set up house; the inhabitants of the border town recognized him and waited upon him. The king could not manage to get him captured. Polajanaka eventually went to the borderland that had come into his possession, with a large retinue, saying, 'I was not my brother's enemy before, but I certainly am now.' So he went to Mithilā with a large following of people and settled his army outside the city. The city dwellers heard, 'Polajanaka has come,' and almost all went, with elephants and other vehicles, to join him; and other cities also came. He sent a message to his brother: 'I was not your enemy before, but now I am. Give me the royal parasol— or battle.' The king went to give him battle and warned his chief queen: 'Dear lady, it is impossible to know in war whether there will be victory or defeat, or if I should meet with a fatal injury. Please guard our unborn child.' Saying this, he left. Then, in battle Polajanaka's warriors killed him.

When it was reported that the king was dead there was confusion in the entire city. The queen heard of his death and as quickly as possible she laid gold and other treasures into a basket, spread a small cloth over it and sprinkled husked rice over that. She then dressed herself in a stained garment and, making her body look unattractive, put the basket on her head and left early in the day, so that no one would recognize her. She left by the northern gate. As she had not been anywhere before she did not know the road and could not work out the directions, but she had heard that there was a city called Campā. So she sat down and asked if there were people going to Campā.

Now, the child in her womb was not just anyone, but the Great Being, who had taken rebirth and was filled with the perfections; the world of Sakka shook with his glory. And Sakka, wondering, realized the cause of this: 'In this lady's womb a being of great merit has taken rebirth; I must go.' When he had decided this he conjured up a covered chariot and prepared a couch in it and, as if he were an old man driving the carriage, stood at the door of the house where she was sitting and asked if there was anyone wanting to go to Campā. 'I would like to, sir.' [32] 'Then, good lady, get up into my carriage.' 'But sir. I am very far gone in my pregnancy and it is not possible for me to get into the carriage. I'll go behind, just give me space for this basket.' 'What are you saying, dear lady? For sure, there is no one as strong in the skill of driving a carriage as me. Don't worry, just get up into the carriage and sit down.' Through his powers he caused the earth to rise just at the moment when she was getting into the carriage so that it joined the back of it. Realizing that this was a god she got on the couch and lay down. And the moment that she lay down on the divine bed, she fell fast asleep. When Sakka had gone a distance of thirty yojanas and come to a river, he woke her up. 'Madam, get down and bathe in the river. At the head of the bed there is a cloak. Put it on. There is a pan-cooked cake at the front of the carriage; eat that,' he said. As soon as she had done so she fell fast asleep again. When it was evening they reached Campā and she saw the gate, the watchtower and the walls. 'What is this city?' she asked. He replied that it was the city of Campā. 'How do you explain this, sir? Surely the distance from our city to Campā is a good seven yojanas?' 'Certainly lady, but I know a direct route.' He then got her to get down by the southern gate. 'Lady, my village is further on—you enter the city here.' When he had said this Sakka went on ahead and then vanished and went back to his own realm.

The queen sat down in a certain hall. At that moment a certain citizen of Campā, a brahmin reciter of verses with a retinue of five hundred young attendants, was on his way to bathe and saw her sitting there, lovely and restored to beauty. The moment he saw her, by the power of the being in her womb, he conceived the great affection that one feels for a younger sister. Seeing that the youths remained standing there he entered the hall alone, addressed her as sister and asked her in which city she lived. She replied that she was the principal queen of King Ariṭṭhajanaka of Mithilā. 'Why have you come here?' he asked. 'The king has been killed by Polajanaka, and I was frightened, thinking that I must escape to protect my baby.' 'Have you any relative in this city?' he asked. 'None, sir,' she said. 'Then do not worry, I am a brahmin of the north, a teacher from a great house whose fame is widespread. I will install you as my sister and look after you. Call me brother and clasp my feet in grief.' She fell at his feet and made a great lament, and they each grieved over the other. [33] His attendants ran up and asked, 'What is going on, teacher?' 'This is my younger sister; she was born at a certain time when I was not there,' he said. They replied, 'Do not be troubled as from now on you will be able to see her.'

So he brought a large covered carriage and sat her in it. Saying to the driver, 'Good man, tell my wife that this is my sister and tell her to take care of everything,' he sent her home. His wife saw that she bathed in hot water, had a bed prepared for her and got her to rest. When the brahmin had bathed and come home at the time of the meal he said, 'Sister, please dine with me.' And he ate together with her and continued to watch over her within his house. Not long afterwards she gave birth to a son, and he was called Prince Mahājanaka, after his grandfather. And as he grew up he played with other boys, and when they teased him with their own pure and high-caste birth he would hit them hard on account of his great strength and stout heart. They used to wail with a loud noise and when asked who had beaten them used to say that it was 'the widow's son'. The prince wondered why they kept on calling him 'the widow's son' and decided to consult his mother. One day he asked her: 'Mother, who was my father?' She deceived him and said, 'My child, the brahmin is your father.' When they hit him on another day and called him 'the widow's son' he replied, 'Actually, I am the brahmin's son'. They said, 'What has the brahmin to do with you?' So he thought about this. 'They ask me what the brahmin has to do with me, and my mother does not explain the reason and will not do so out of pride in herself. I'll make sure she does explain it to me.' While drinking at her breast he bit her there and said, 'Tell me about my father, or I will cut your breast off.'[16] This time she was unable to deceive him and explained, 'You are the son of king Ariṭṭhajanaka of Mithilā. Your father was killed by Polajanaka. I came to this city so that I could protect you. The brahmin installed me as a younger sister and took care of me.' And from that time on he was no longer angry when he was called 'the widow's son'.

Before he was sixteen he had learnt the three Vedas and all kinds of skills [34] and by the time he was sixteen he had become surpassingly handsome. Then he thought, 'I will seize the kingdom that belonged to my father.' He asked his mother, 'Mother, have you got any wealth to hand? If you do not, I will make some money and then seize the kingdom that belonged to my father.' She said, 'I did not come here empty-handed. There is a quantity of pearls, jewels and diamonds of great value for taking the kingdom.[17] Take it and claim the kingdom: do not ply any trade.' He replied, 'Mother, give me the wealth here, but I will take only half now. I will go to the Beautiful Land and bring back a large fortune and then seize the kingdom.' He got her to bring him half, collected his merchandise and put it on board a ship with some merchants setting out for the Beautiful Land. Then he said goodbye to his mother. When he told her where he was going she said, 'My son, there is not much success to be found at sea but there is a great deal of danger. Do not go, there is plenty of wealth for you to claim the kingdom.' He said, 'I must go, mother.' And so, bidding her farewell, he went on board the boat. On that very day an illness struck Polajanaka's body and he could not rise from his bed.

On board there were seven hundred legs[18] and in seven days the boat went seven hundred yojanas, but it sailed so fiercely that it could not hold out and its boards split. The water rose higher and higher and the boat plunged into the midst of the ocean, while all the passengers and crew moaned and cried and invoked various gods. The Great Being, however, did not moan or cry or pray to deities but, seeing that the boat was about to sink, he beat together some ghee with sugar, ate a bellyful and then smeared two outer garments with sesame oil, tied them on tightly and stood leaning against the mast. When the boat did sink the mast stayed upright. The people on board became food for the fishes and tortoises while the water all around became red with blood. The Great Being, standing at the mast, determined the direction in which Mithilā lay and leapt from the mast, passing beyond the fishes and tortoises so that he fell one hundred and forty cubits from the boat. On that very day Polajanaka died. From then the Great Being went through the crystal-coloured waves and crossed the ocean like a heap of gold, and he spent seven days as if they were one. [35] Then he saw the shore, and washed his mouth out with salt water[19] as it was an *uposatha* day. Now, a daughter of the gods called Maṇimekhalā, or Jewelled-girdle, had been appointed by the Four Guardian Kings as the protector of the oceans and told, 'It is not right for those who have reverence towards the mother and other such qualities to fall into the sea: look out for them.'[20] She did not watch the ocean for seven days, for it is said that her mindfulness had been forgotten while she enjoyed the results of bliss; though some say that she had met up with some shining gods. At any rate she said to herself, 'It has been seven days since I have kept watch on the sea. I wonder who has come by?' When she looked she saw the Great Being. She thought, 'If Prince Mahājanaka should perish in the ocean I would not keep my admission into the assembly of shining gods'. She assumed a well-adorned appearance and stood in the air not far from the Bodhisatta. As a test of his mettle she uttered the first verse:

1. 'Who are you, struggling, out of sight of the shore, in the middle of the ocean?
   What aim do you pursue, and, knowing this, are making an effort so manfully?'

Then the Great Being said, 'Today is the seventh day that I have been crossing the ocean. I have seen no other being before. Who is it who is speaking to me?' As he gazed into the air and saw her he uttered a second verse:

2. 'Careful of my vow to struggle in the world, O Goddess: because of this I struggle, out of sight of the shore, in the middle of the ocean.'

Wishing to hear a *dhamma* talk she spoke a third verse:

3. 'In the deep and measureless [sea] where no shore can be seen your human struggle is useless, you will not reach the shore and you will die!'

Then the Great Being replied, 'What are you saying? If I die making all this effort I will be free from any blame.' And he uttered this verse:

4. [36] 'He that does things that should be done by humans is free from debt,
   to relatives or to shining gods or to ancestors, and feels no regret afterwards.'

And then the goddess spoke this verse:

5. 'What is the point of effort if the deed cannot be achieved, is fruitless and exhausting, and has death as the product?'[21]

When she had said this the Great Being bewildered her by speaking more verses:

6. 'Whoever considers the deed ever unattainable, O Goddess, will not protect his own life; he will know this if he gives up.

7. Some in this world, Goddess, undertake deeds for the fruit
   of their intention;
   some deeds prosper and some do not.
8. Do you not see, Goddess, the visible fruit of deeds?
   for others have sunk; I am crossing and I can see you near me.
9. So I will struggle according to my ability and strength
   and go towards the shore of the ocean;
   I will do what is to be done by men.'

[37] The goddess heard his brave speech and spoke a verse
extolling him:

10. 'You who go on in this measureless sea,
    endowed with strength and rightness, and are not worn
    down by the task:
    go to the place where your heart takes delight.'

When she had said this, she asked, 'Wise man, who has made
such a great effort: where can I take you?' He replied, 'To the city
of Mithilā'. So she picked him up like a bundle of garlands and,
taking him in both arms, got him to lie at her breast and sprang
up into the air, carrying him as if he were her dear child. His body
inflamed with salt spray, the Bodhisatta slept soundly for seven
days, touched by the divine contact. Then she brought him to
Mithilā and laid him down on his right side on an auspicious
stone[22] in a mango grove. There she left him under the protection
of the goddesses of the garden and went back to her own home.

Now Polajanaka had not had a son, but he did have just one
daughter, a wise and accomplished girl called Princess Sīvalī.
And they had asked him as he lay on his deathbed: 'Great king,
when you have gone to the state of being a god, to whom shall we
give the throne?' He replied, 'Give it to one who is able to please
my daughter, princess Sīvalī, or who can tell which is the head
of the square bed, or who can string the bow that takes the strength
of a thousand men or who can bring out the sixteen great treasures.'

They said, 'King: tell us a verse about the treasure.' The
king said:

    11. 'At the rising of the sun there is treasure and at its
        setting too.
        Inside there is treasure and outside there is treasure;
        but there is also a treasure that is neither inside nor
        outside.
    12. [38] Climbing up there is a great treasure
        and there is also a treasure in coming down.
        At the four sāl trees all around for a yojana there is
        treasure.
    13. At the tips of the teeth there is a great treasure, at the
        tips of the tail, and in the 'kebuka'.
        There is a great treasure at the tips of the trees: sixteen
        are the great treasures.
        There is [that which takes] the strength of a thousand
        men[23] and a bed for the winning of Sīvalī.'

He gave an utterance about other treasures as well as these.
After the king's death the ministers performed the funeral rites
and on the seventh day they met for discussion. 'The king has
said that his kingdom should be given to the man able to please
his daughter. Now who will be able to please her?' They agreed
to summon his favourite, the general of the army. He assented,
and in order to gain the kingdom, came to the door of the palace
and had his presence announced to the king's daughter. She
knew why he had come and thought to herself, ' I wonder if he
has the firmness of character to bear the royal parasol?' So in
order to test him she had him asked in. He heard her instruction
and, anxious to please her, went with great haste up from the
foot of the stairs and stood in her presence. In order to test him
she said, 'Race quickly up on the flat roof of the palace!' Thinking
that he would please the princess, he sprang forward. Then she

said 'Come here!' and he immediately did so. Recognizing his absence of strength she said: 'Massage my feet!' He, in order to please her, sat down and massaged her feet. At this she struck him on the chest with her foot and made him fall over so that he was lying prone on his back. She then gave a sign to her maids, 'Beat this blind and stupid fellow, who is devoid of strength: then grab him by the throat and throw him out.' They then did this. He was asked by the ministers, 'How did it go, general?' He said, 'Just don't talk about it. That woman is not human.'

Then the keeper of the stores came, and she shamed him in the same way. Then too the treasurer, the guardian of the royal parasol and the swordsman: she shamed them all as well. Then the people at large discussed it, 'No one can please the king's daughter; give her to someone who can prepare the bow that needs the strength of a thousand.' But there was no one who could do this. So then they said, 'Give her to the one who knows the head of the square bed'. But no one could determine it. So then they said, 'Give her to the one able to find the sixteen treasures.' But no one could find them. [39] Then they deliberated, 'A kingdom is not protected without a king: what is to be done?'

Then the king's priest said, 'Do not worry: we will send out the wonderful royal carriage.[24] A king that is picked up by the royal carriage is able to rule the whole of Jambudīpa.' They agreed and had the city decorated, yoked four horses the colour of white lotuses onto the auspicious carriage and spread a coverlet over them. They arranged there the five emblems of royalty[25] and surrounded the carriage with a fourfold army.[26] Now musical instruments are sounded in front of a chariot with a driver but behind for a chariot without one: so for this case the royal priest said, 'Sound musical instruments behind!' He sprinkled the strap of the chariot and the goad from a golden water jar and said, 'Go where there is someone of sufficient merit to rule the kingdom.'

The chariot encircled the royal palace and then went up the Kettledrum street. The general and all the others thought, 'The

wonderful chariot is coming up to my house!' But it went past all
their houses and encircled the city until it left by the eastern gate.
It then went on towards the park. When they saw it proceeding
so quickly they cried out, 'Stop it!' But the priest said, 'Do not try
and stop it; let it go a hundred yojanas if it wants.' The chariot
entered the park and circled around the auspicious stone and
stopped as though ready for someone to get onto it. The priest
saw the Great Being lying there and spoke to his ministers, 'Sirs,
someone can be seen lying down on the stone. We do not know if
he has the strength of character suitable for the white parasol or
not. If he is worthy he will not look at us; but if he is an unlucky
person he will get up in fright and look at us, trembling. Quickly:
sound all the musical instruments.' So they immediately played
all the kinds of musical instruments and the roar was like that of
the sea. The Great Being woke up at the noise, uncovered his
head and looked out at the mass of people and thought that it
must be that they had come for him with the white parasol. So he
covered his head again and turned over and lay on his left side. The
priest uncovered his feet and inspected the marks that were there:[27]
'Let it be him: this man could rule four continents, let alone one.'
So he ordered them to sound the musical instruments again.

[40] The Bodhisatta uncovered his face and turned around so
that he lay on his right side and looked at the mass of his people.
The priest comforted the people and then made an añjali gesture
of respect and, kneeling face down, said, 'Rise, sire, the kingdom
has come to you.' 'Where has the king gone?' asked the Bodhisatta.
'He is dead.' 'Is there any son or a brother?' 'There is not, sire.'
'Very well, I will take up the kingdom.' Rising up from the stone
he sat down cross-legged and was anointed there and then. He
was named King Mahājanaka. He then mounted up into the
chariot and, having entered the city in royal glory, went to the
palace, arranged the general and the others in their positions and
then went up to the roof of the palace.

Now, the princess, wishing to test him on first impressions,
gave some instructions to one of her attendants: 'Go to the king,
approach him and then say that Princess Sīvalī summons him,
and that he should come as quickly as possible.' The wise king
appeared not to hear her words and commented on the
appearance of the palace: 'Ah! Very beautiful.' So the attendant
informed the princess that he had been unable to get the king to
listen to him. 'Lady, the king heard your message but just praised
the palace and did not count your words even as straw.' She
thought to herself, 'This must be someone of great character.'[28]
So she ordered him back a second and a third time. But the king
just pleased himself and went up to the palace at his normal pace,
stretching like a lion.

Because of the power of his self-confidence the princess could
not keep steady as he approached and she gave him her hand to
lean on. He took her by the hand and sat down on the royal
couch under the raised white parasol. He asked his ministers,
'Sirs, did the king leave any instructions to you when he died?'
'Yes sire,' they said. 'So tell me,' he said. 'He declared that Princess
Sīvalī should be given to the person who could please her.'
'Princess Sīvalī gave me her hand to lean on when I came near;
that means that I please her. Tell me another of the instructions.'
'Sire, the instructions was to give the kingdom to the one who
can determine the head of the square bed.' The king thought to
himself, 'This is difficult to work out. But by a trick it should be
possible.' So he took a golden hairpin from his head and put it
into the princess's hand, saying to her, 'Put this where it belongs.'
[41] She took it and placed it at the head of the bed—and just as
the proverb says, she gave him the sword.[29] For then, through
this sign, he knew which was the head. As if he had not heard
their discussion about this, he asked what people were saying,
and when he had heard, he assured them that it was not wonderful,
'For this is the head of the bed.' He then asked for another

instruction. 'The king ordered that the kingdom should be given to the one who can string a bow needing the strength of a thousand men.' 'Bring it here,' he said. He ordered them to bring the bow and strung it while sitting on the couch, as if it were a woman's bow for carding cotton. 'Tell me another instruction,' he said. 'Sire, the king said the kingdom should be given to the one who can find the sixteen treasures.' 'And what utterances were given about them?'[30] he asked. They repeated the verses that have been given earlier, that start with the rising of the sun. When they told him the meaning was as clear as the moon on the surface of the sky. And then he said, 'There is certainly not time today: we'll get the treasure tomorrow.'

The next day he called together the ministers and asked them. 'Did your king feed *paccekabuddha*s?'[31] They said that he did. He thought to himself, 'The sun that was spoken of is not this sun; *paccekabuddha*s are called rising suns because they are like them. The treasures must be at the place where he met them.' Then the king said, 'When the *paccekabuddha*s came, where did he go to meet them?' They told him that it was at a particular place. So he ordered them to dig at the spot where they ate and bring out the treasure: this they did. He then asked, 'When he followed them and it was time to go where did he stand before he left?' They specified a spot and again he ordered them to dig there and they found some treasure. All the people there sent out a thousand shouts, for at the instruction about the sunrise they had been wandering around digging where the sunrise was; at sunset they had been wandering around where the sun went down. 'But this is the wealth and the wonderful thing is right here.' They gave vent to their joy and happiness. For the 'treasure within' he got them to look at the threshold stone within the main gate of the palace. For the 'treasure outside' he got them to look at the threshold stone outside. And for the treasure 'neither inside nor outside' he got them to look underneath the threshold.

[42] For the 'alighting' he got them to look at the place where
they positioned the golden ladder at the time for mounting the
state elephant. For 'the dismounting' he had them look at the
spot where they dismounted from the elephant's shoulders: 'the
four great sāls' were the four great feet, made of sāl wood, at
the foot of the platform where they paid homage. He got them
to dig treasure pots 'all around for a yojana': now a yojana is
the length of a chariot,[32] so he had them bring out treasure pots
from around the area where they paid respects. 'A great treasure
at the tips of the teeth': at the place where the state elephant
stood he had them bring out two treasures from the place which
faced his two tusks. 'At the ends of the tail': for this he got them
to dig up at the place where a state horse stood, at the place
facing his tail. 'In the kebuka': this is a name for water, so he had
the water of the royal lake drained where a treasure was revealed.
For 'the great treasure at the end of the trees' he got them to find
treasure pots in the park at the circle where the great sāl tree left
a shadow at midday. When he had got them to find sixteen
treasures, he asked if there were any other instructions—and
they said there were not. The general populace were delighted
and the king announced, 'I will throw this wealth into the mouth
of generosity!' So in the middle of the city and at the four gates
he had five halls for giving built and arranged a great act of
giving. And then he called for his mother and the brahmin from
the city of Campā and accorded the highest honour to them.

In the youthful days of his reign the son of King Ariṭṭhajanaka,
King Mahājanaka, ruled over the entire kingdom of Videha. The
whole city was agog to have a look at him and said, 'The king is
said to be wise: let's go and see him.' They came from here and
there with many presents and arranged a big festival in the city.
They covered the palace with elephant rugs and suchlike,[33]
arranged perfumes, wreaths and garlands, and soon made a dark

cloud of cooked grain, flowers, perfumes and incense. They prepared all kinds of food and drink. Then, in order to make offerings to the king, they brought [43] different varieties of foods such as soft and hard foods and drinks and fruits in bowls of silver and gold and stood surrounding him on all sides. The circle of king's ministers sat on one side, the group of brahmins on another, on another such people as wealthy merchants, and on another the most beautiful of the dancing girls. Brahmin chanters of blessings, who sang auspiciously and were skilled in songs for festivals, sang beautiful songs and suchlike and played all kinds of instruments. The king's palace resounded with one roar, like the depths of the Yugandhara ocean, and everywhere one looked the palace trembled. The Great Being sat on the royal throne beneath the white parasol and, regarding the great splendour like the glory of Sakka, remembered his own great struggle in the ocean, and thought, 'Effort is the most suitable thing to be cultivated. If I had not shown such effort in the ocean I would not have acquired this glory.' And joy rose up in him at the recollection of that effort, and with a surge of joy he made this inspired utterance:

14. 'The wise man should take hope and should not become discouraged.
    I look at myself; for what I wished for has come to be.
15. The wise man should take hope and should not become discouraged.
    I see my own self, who was brought out of the water to dry land.
16. A wise man should work on and not become discouraged.
    I look at myself; for what I wished for has come to be.
17. A wise man should work on and not become discouraged.
    I look at myself, who was brought out of the water to dry land.

18. The man who possesses wisdom, even though overcome with
    suffering, should not destroy hope on his way to happiness.
    There are many kinds of contacts, both beneficial and harmful:
    those which are not reflected upon lead towards death.[34]
19. That which was not even thought of has come into being;
    that which has been thought of will be destroyed.
    There is no possession consisting of pure thought, for man
    or woman.'

[44] After that he ruled the kingdom and was unswerving in the
ten royal qualities,[35] and attended upon the *paccekabuddhas*. After
some time Queen Sīvalī gave birth to a son endowed with
fortunate and auspicious marks, and they gave him the name
Prince Dīghāvu, or Longlife. When he came of age the king gave
him the viceroyalty. Now, one day the gardener brought the king
various kinds of fruits and flowers. When he saw them he was
delighted, paid the gardener the greatest respects and told him
to have the garden decorated and that he would come and see it.
The gardener agreed, did as he was asked and had the king
notified. The king arrived at the gate of the garden, seated on
the shoulders of a fine elephant and surrounded by a large retinue.
Now there were two mango trees there, of a lustrous dark colour.
One of these did not have any fruit and the other had fruit that
was extremely sweet. Because the king had not tasted the mango
fruit no one had ventured to pick them. The king, riding by on
his fine elephant, picked one fruit from it and ate it, and at the
moment it touched the tip of his tongue a taste that seemed divine
arose. He thought to himself, 'I'll eat a good amount when I
come back.' But when the people realized that the king had eaten
the first fruit, from the viceroy right down to the mahouts they
picked and ate the fruit, and those who did not get fruit broke
the branches with sticks and left the tree plucked bare. So the
tree stood, broken and split up, while the other remained with
its existing beauty, like a mountain of jewels.

When the king left the garden he saw it and asked his ministers what had happened. 'When everyone saw that the king had eaten the first fruit they plundered it, sire,' came the reply. 'But the other has lost no leaf or colour at all,' he said. 'It did not lose anything because it did not have any fruit,' they replied. At this the king received a sense of urgency. 'This tree stands [45] with its dark lustre because it has no fruit; the other is broken and split because it had fruit. The kingdom is just like a fruitful tree; the life of an ascetic is just like the tree with no fruit. It is the one who has property who has fear, not the one without. I will become like the tree without fruit, not like a fruitful one: so I shall renounce and abandon my worldly success and become a recluse.'[36] Making his mind firm he made a resolve and entered the city, stood at the gate of the palace and called for the general of the army. 'Great general, from this day onwards do not let anyone see me except for the servant who brings food and fetches water for my mouth and a toothbrush. Gather my oldest and most eminent ministers and take charge of the kingdom. From now on I am going to live the life of an ascetic on the roof of the palace.' After giving these instructions he duly went up to the roof of the palace and lived an ascetic life alone. As time went by the people met together in the palace courtyard but did not catch sight of the Great Being. 'This is not like our king of old,' they said, and uttered these two verses:

20. 'Alas, our king, the lord of all directions of the earth, is not the one that was of old,
    Today he pays no attention to dances nor does his mind turn to songs.
21. He does not even look at the deer in the garden nor the geese,
    He remains silent and dumb and does not take charge of anything.'

They asked, it is said, the man who brought food and the attendant whether the king had talked to them or not. They replied that he had not. At this they said, 'The king, through non-attachment to sense pleasures, with a mind immersed in seclusion, remembers the *paccekabuddha*s associated with his family. He says to himself, "Who will tell me the dwelling place of those beings who possess all excellences such as virtue, and who live possessing nothing?" So he utters these three verses:

> 22. "Loving happiness, keeping hidden,
>   ceasing from punishments and imprisonments:
>   in whose wonderful garden today are they, young and
>   old?
> [46] 23. I pay homage to these wise men.
>   Firm, and having crossed over the thicket of desire,
>   they live without longings, in a world that is longing.
> 24. They have cut through the net of death and the tough
>   knot of illusion;
>   They go, with desire cut through: O who will show me
>   where they have gone?'"

After he had been practising the life of an ascetic for four months in his palace he applied his mind intently on going forth. His home seemed like the Niraya hell between the worlds and the three worlds appeared as if on fire.[37] With his mind intent upon the prospect of going forth, he embarked upon a eulogy of Mithilā, 'When will the time come for me to be able to leave behind this Mithilā, that is adorned and dressed up like the realm of Sakka, and go into the Himālayas in the dress of an ascetic?

> 25. O when shall I leave Mithilā, that is so splendid,
>   spacious and bright on all sides?
>   When shall I take the going forth, O when is the time
>   that shall be?[38]
> 26. O when shall I leave Mithilā, so splendid and divided
>   into such even parts?
>   When shall I take the going forth, O when is the time
>   that shall be?

27. O when shall I leave Mithilā, so splendid, with its great ramparts and gateways?
When shall I take the going forth, O when is the time that shall be?

28. O when shall I leave Mithilā, so splendid, with its strong, polished storehouse?
When shall I take the going forth, O when is the time that shall be?

29. O when shall I leave Mithilā, splendid, with its beautiful divisions and magnificent roads?
When shall I take the going forth, O when is the time that shall be?

30. O when shall I leave Mithilā, with its well-arranged bazaars?
When shall I take the going forth, O when is the time that shall be?

31. When shall I leave Mithilā, splendid with it throngs of horses, cows and chariots?
When shall I take the going forth, O when is the time that shall be?

32. When shall I leave Mithilā, splendid with its garlanded groves and woods?
When shall I take the going forth, O when is the time that shall be?

33. When shall I leave Mithilā, splendid with its garlanded parks and forests?
When shall I take the going forth, O when is the time that shall be?

34. When shall I leave Mithilā, splendid with its garlanded palace orchards?
When shall I take the going forth, O when is the time that shall be?

35. When shall I leave Mithilā, splendid with its three turrets,

filled with kinsmen[39] of the king, established in glory by
Somanassa the Videhan?
When shall I take the going forth, O when is the time that
shall be?

36. When shall I leave the splendid throngs of the Videhans,
    the protectors of justice?
    When shall I take the going forth, O when is the time that
    shall be?

37. When shall I leave the Videhans, splendid, invincible,
    protectors of justice?
    When shall I take the going forth, O when is the time that
    shall be?

38. O when shall I leave the harem, so delightful and divided
    into such even parts?
    When shall I take the going forth, O when is the time that
    shall be?

39. O when shall I leave the harem, so delightful, with lime-
    washed clay
    When shall I take the going forth, O when is the time that
    shall be?

40. O when shall I leave the women's quarters, with its sweet
    smells that delight the mind?
    When shall I take the going forth, O when is the time that
    shall be?

41. O when shall I leave the peaked roofs, so splendid and
    divided into such even parts?
    When shall I take the going forth, O when is the time that
    shall be?

42. O when shall I leave the peaked roofs, with lime-washed clay?
    When shall I take the going forth, O when is the time that
    shall be?

43. O when shall I leave the peaked roofs, with their sweet smells
    that please the mind?

When shall I take the going forth, O when is the time that shall be?

44. O when shall I leave the peaked roofs, smeared with sprinkled sandalwood?
When shall I take the going forth, O when is the time that shall be?

45. O when shall I leave the golden couches, covered with brightly coloured woollen rugs?
When shall I take the going forth, O when is the time that shall be?

46. O when shall I leave the cotton and silk, the fine linen and every kind of cloth?
When shall I take the going forth, O when is the time that shall be?

47. O when shall I leave the delightful lotus ponds, filled with the sound of ruddy geese,
and covered with water plants and lotuses of blue, red and white?
When shall I take the going forth, O when is the time that shall be?

48–9. O when shall I leave the troops of elephants, adorned in every way, decked with golden ribbons; the perfumed golden harnesses mounted with village chiefs with kusa grass spears in their hands?
When shall I take the going forth, O when is the time that shall be?

50–1. O when shall I leave the troops of horses, adorned in every way,
the noble, thoroughbred sindhs with swift chariots, mounted with village chiefs who carry short swords and bows?
When shall I take the going forth, O when is the time that shall be?

52-3 [48]. When shall I leave the military chariots,
            decked, with banners flying, covered in tiger skin
            and adorned in every way,
            mounted with village chiefs clad in armour with
            bows in their hands?
            When shall I take the going forth, O when is the
            time that shall be?

54-5. When shall I leave the gilded chariots, decked with
       banners flying,
       and chariots covered with panther and tiger skin,
       adorned in every way, mounted with village chiefs
       clad in armour with bows in their hands?
       When shall I take the going forth, O when is the
       time that shall be?

56-69. When shall I leave . . . [same formula for] buffalo-
        led chariots, bull-led chariots, goat-led chariots,
        ram-led chariots and deer-led chariots.

70. O when shall I leave the brave men on elephants,
     adorned in every way,
     clad in black armour, brave with kusa spears in
     their hands?
     When shall I take the going forth, O when is the
     time that shall be?

71. O when shall I leave the brave men on horses,
     adorned in every way, clad in black armour, with
     short swords and bows in their hands?
     When shall I take the going forth, O when is the
     time that shall be?

72. O when shall I leave the brave archers, adorned in
     every way, clad in black armour, carrying quivers
     and with bows in their hands?

When shall I take the going forth, O when is the
time that shall be?

73. O when shall I leave the brave royal sons, adorned
in every way, clad in many-coloured armour,
wearing golden garlands?
When shall I take the going forth, O when is the
time that shall be?

74. O when shall I leave the troop of Ariyans, wrapped
in cloth, with limbs anointed with yellow
sandalwood, dressed in fine Benares linen?
When shall I take the going forth, O when is the
time that shall be?

75. O when shall I leave the seven hundred wives,
adorned in every way?
When shall I take the going forth, O when is the
time that shall be?

76. O when shall I leave the seven hundred wives with
beautiful hips and tiny waists?[40]
When shall I take the going forth, O when is the
time that shall be?

77. O when shall I leave the seven hundred wives, who
are loyal and with loving speech?
When shall I take the going forth, O when is the
time that shall be?

78. O when shall I leave the fine bronze dish and the
pure gold plate?
When shall I take the going forth, O when is the
time that shall be?

79–80.[41] O when will the troops of elephants, adorned in
every way,
decked with golden ribbons and the perfumed
golden harnesses

mounted with village chiefs with
kusa grass spears in their hands, not follow me as I go?
O when is the time that will be?

81–2. O when will the troops of horses, adorned in every
way,
the noble, thoroughbred sindhs with swift chariots,
mounted with village chiefs who carry short swords
and bows, not follow me as I go?
O when is the time that will be?

83–4. O when will military chariots, decked with banners
flying,
covered in tiger skin and adorned in every way,
mounted with village chiefs clad in armour with bows
in their hands,
when will they not follow me as I go?
O when is the time that will be?

85–6. O when will the gilded chariots, decked with banners
flying,
and chariots covered with panther skin and tiger
skin,
adorned in every way, mounted with village
chiefs clad in armour with bows in their hands, not
follow me as I go?
O when is the time that will be?

87–100. O when will the . . . [same formula for] buffalo-led
chariots, bull-led chariots, goat-led chariots, ram-led
chariots and deer-led chariots
O when is the time that will be?

101. O when will the brave men on elephants, adorned in
every way, clad in black armour, brave, with kusa spears
in their hands, not follow me as I go?
O when is the time that will be?

102. O when will the brave men on horses, adorned in every
     way, clad in black armour, with short swords and bows in
     their hands, not follow me as I go?
     O when is the time that will be?

103. O when will the brave archers, adorned in every way, clad
     in black armour, carrying quivers and with bows in their
     hands, not follow me as I go?
     O when is the time that will be?

104. O when will the brave royal sons, adorned in every way,
     clad in many-coloured armour, wearing golden garlands,
     not follow me as I go?
     O when is the time that will be?

105. O when will the troop of Ariyans, wrapped in cloth, with
     limbs anointed with yellow sandalwood, dressed in fine
     Benares linen, not follow me as I go?
     O when is the time that will be?

106. O when will the seven hundred wives, adorned in every
     way, not follow me as I go? O when is the time that will be?

107. O when will the seven hundred wives, with beautiful hips
     and tiny waists, not follow me as I go?
     O when is the time that will be?

108. O when will the seven hundred wives, who are loyal and
     with loving speech, not follow me as I go?
     O when is the time that will be?

109. O when shall I take the bowl, and with head shaved and
     dressed in the robe wander in search of alms?
     O when is the time that will be?

110. O when shall I wear the robe, made from discarded rags,
     on the great road?
     O when is the time that will be?

111. O when shall I wander, in seven days of storms, rained
     upon and with robe wet, in search of alms?
     O when is the time that will be?

112. O when shall I spend the whole day at a spot at the roots
of a tree, in the woody forest, free from longing?
O when is the time that will be?

113. O when shall I live in the mountain heights, with fear and
dismay abandoned, without a second person, free from
longing?
O when is the time that will be?

114. O when shall I make my mind straight, like a lute player
[tuning] his lovely seven-stringed lute?
O when is the time that will be?

115. O when shall I, like a chariot maker[42] cutting the edges[43]
for sandals, cut the bonds to the senses, both divine and
human?'

[52] Now it is said the king was born at a time when the human
lifespan was ten thousand years. He spent seven thousand years
ruling the kingdom, and became a recluse when he still had three
thousand years to live. For four months since the time when he
had seen the mango trees at the gate of the park he had lived in
his house, thinking, 'It would be better to take the going forth
and leave this house.' So he secretly ordered an attendant to go
to the market, without anyone else knowing, and bring him back
some yellow-brown robes and an earthenware bowl; which he
did. The king then ordered his barber to cut his hair and dismissed
him. Then he dressed himself with one garment, covered himself
with another and wrapped another one over his shoulder. He put
the earthenware bowl in a bag and strung that over his shoulder
too. Then, taking a walking stick, he walked on the roof of the
palace several times backwards and forwards with the carriage
of a *paccekabuddha*. That day he remained there, but on the next
day at sunrise he began to go down from the palace. Queen Sīvalī
sent for seven hundred of his concubines and said. 'We have not
seen the king for a long time—a good four months have passed.
But today we will see him, so go and adorn yourselves and, using

your female wiles and most charming behaviour, try hard to entangle him in the knots of passion.' So she went up with them, all dressed up and adorned, determined to see the king. But although she did meet him as he was coming downstairs, she did not recognize him: instead she paid respects and stood to one side as what she thought was a *paccekabuddha*, who had come to give instruction to the king, passed by. And so the king came down from the palace.

When she had ascended to the top floor of the palace she saw the king's hair, the colour of bees, and pieces of his regalia lying by the royal bed. 'That was no *paccekabuddha*! It must have been our dear lord. Come, I'll go and plead with him to come back.' So she came down from the top of the palace and reached the royal courtyard. Then she and the other ladies released their hair so that it tumbled down their backs and beat their chests with their hands. They followed the king, wailing with great emotion, 'O how can you do such a thing, great lord?' The entire city was shaken and they followed the king weeping, 'It is said that our king has gone forth! How will we ever find such a just ruler again?'

Then the Teacher, describing the wailing of the women and how the king left them and went on his way, said:

116. 'Seven hundred wives, adorned in every way, stretched out their arms, crying, "O why are you going to forsake us?"

117. Seven hundred wives, with beautiful hips and tiny waists, stretched out their arms, crying, "O why are you going to forsake us?"

118. Seven hundred wives so loyal and with such loving speech, stretched out their arms, crying, "O why are you going to forsake us?"

119. Seven hundred wives, adorned in every way:
     "The honoured king has left us and run away to take the going forth!"

120. Seven hundred wives, with beautiful hips and tiny waists:
     "The honoured king has left and run away to take the
     going forth!"
121. Seven hundred wives so loyal and with such loving speech:
     "The honoured king has left and run away to take the
     going forth!"
122. Leaving behind the fine bronze bowl and the pure gold plate,
     he has taken up the earthenware bowl, for his second
     anointment.'

The weeping Queen Sīvalī could not prevent the king from
going, so she settled on a stratagem, sent for the general of the
army and gave him some instructions. 'Sir, start a fire in the old
houses and buildings ahead, in the direction in front of the king.
Fetch grasses and leaves to that spot and get some smoke going.'
He had this done. She then went to the king and, falling at his
feet, informed him that Mithilā was burning, and spoke two verses:

123. 'There are terrible pyres, and the stores are burning bit by
     bit:
     silver and gold, and many pearls and gems.
124. Crystals, mother of pearl, cloth, yellow sandal,
     antelope skin, ivory goods, copper and much black iron.
     Go king and turn back, and do not destroy this wealth of
     yours!'

And then the Great Being said, 'Queen, what are you saying?
Those who have something can have it burnt. But I have nothing.'
In explanation he recited this verse:

125. 'We live happily, those who have nothing.
     Mithilā might burn, but nothing has burnt of mine!'

[55] After he had said this the Great Being left by the northern
gate and then his wives also left. Then Queen Sīvalī thought up
a trick and gave instructions to them: 'Make it appear as if villages

have been destroyed and that the land is being wasted'. So they explained to the king how, all at the same time, armed men were living by plundering and were running around here and there. Some had sprinkled essence of lac on their bodies and were being laid down on boards, as if wounded, or dead. The people upbraided him with the words, 'Great king, while you are taking care of your affairs they are ransacking the kingdom and killing the people!' And then the queen paid her respects to the king and uttered this verse to persuade him to turn back:

126. 'The wild men have risen up, they are laying waste to the kingdom,
     Come, O king, and turn back: do not destroy this kingdom!'

The king thought to himself, 'It just is not true that while I have been taking care of my business thieves have risen up and are devastating the kingdom. This must be Sīvalī's doing.' And he said this to make the matter clear:

127. 'We live very happily, those who have nothing.
     Even though the kingdom is being wasted, nothing is destroyed for me.

128. We live very happily, those who have nothing;
     we exist feeding on joy, like the Gods of Streaming Radiance!'[44]

Even though he had said this, the crowd still followed the king. So then he thought, 'The crowd do not wish to turn back: I'll have to make them.' When he had gone a length of about two miles[45] he turned back and, standing on the main road, he questioned his ministers, 'Whose kingdom is this?' They replied, 'Yours, King.' [56] 'Make a royal decree to keep a distance from this line,' he said. So with his ascetic's staff he drew out a line across the road and because of the king's power no one could cross the line he had made. The crowd wailed with a great lament as they stood under the head of the line. The queen, also unable to cross the line, saw the king going away with his back to her and could not restrain her grief. She beat her breast and then fell prone across the main road and so, by moving forward, went over the line. The crowd said, 'The line has been broken by those that guard it!' and followed where the queen had led. The Great Being went towards the north, to the foothills of the Himälayas. The queen went too, taking with her the army and waggons. The king, still unable to turn back the crowd, went on for sixty yojanas.

Now, at that time there lived an ascetic called Närada, who lived in the Golden Cave in the Himälayas and practised the five higher knowledges.[46] After seven days in the happiness of meditation he emerged from it and was exclaiming out loud, 'O, the happiness, the happiness! I wonder if there is anyone in the whole of Jambudīpa searching for this happiness?' With his divine eye he looked around and saw Mahäjanaka, and that he was bringing about Buddhahood. 'The king cannot make a great renunciation and turn back the people who are following in Queen Sīvalī's wake. They make an obstacle for him, so I'll give him something to say to them that will strengthen his resolve all the more.' By the power of his supernatural abilities he went to the king and appeared before him, standing in the sky, and said this, to produce energy in him:

129. 'What is this great noise, like games in a village?
      We ask the ascetic: why is a crowd of people streaming
      around?'

The king replied,

130. 'The crowd are streaming round as I have left and renounced.
      I have gone beyond the boundary, for the attainment of
      truth;
      my departure is mixed with pure delight. Why do you ask,
      as you must know this?'

[57] And Nārada said this in order to stir up his strength:

131. 'Do not think you have crossed over while you still carry a body;
    this *kamma* cannot have been crossed over, and there are still many obstacles ahead.'[47]

Then the Great Being said:

132. 'What danger in this is there for me
    as I live in such a way that I do not wish for pleasures in this world or in the next?'

And Nārada explained the danger by speaking a verse:

133. 'Sleep, laziness, weariness, discontent, drowsiness from food:
    for the one living in the bodily frame, there are many dangers.'

[58] Then the Great Being uttered this verse, praising him:

134. 'Certainly the venerable sir, the brahmin, has given lovely advice.
    And so I ask the brahmin: Who are you, sir?'

At this Nārada said:

135. 'Nārada is my name; they knew me as Kassapa.
    I have come before you, sir; it is good to meet with noble men.

136. May you enjoy a completely joyful abiding in this:[48]
    and may you supplement anything that is missing with forbearance and peace!

137. Give up any sense of inferiority and any sense of haughtiness[49]
    and, as you go forth, honour the work to be done, wisdom and the way that is right.'[50]

In this way he gave advice to the Great Being and returned through the air to his own abode. When he had gone, another ascetic, called Migājina,[51] who had just emerged from meditation, looking around saw the Great Being and thought he would give him some advice that would turn the great crowd back. He showed himself in the sky above him and said:

[59] 138. 'You have forsaken, Janaka, the crowds of elephants and horses,
the city dwellers and the countrymen
and, as an ascetic, you have gone for delight in the earthenware bowl.

139. Perhaps countrymen, friends, colleagues or relatives have performed some treachery against you?
Why has it pleased you to do this?'

Then the Great Being said:

140. 'No, Migājina, I have never at any time, in any way,[52] overpowered any relative unjustly nor have they overpowered me.'

When he had refuted Migājina's question he spoke revealing his reason for becoming an ascetic:

141. 'When I saw the world turning, being devoured and made muddied
and that ordinary people were harmed and bound here, where they had sunk.
That is when I compared myself to them and became a mendicant, Migājina.'

[60] The ascetic, wishing to hear him expand upon his reason, spoke this verse:

142. 'Who is your lord, your teacher, from whom does this pure statement come?
They say that an ascetic who passes beyond suffering does not reject precepts, or theory, or giving up,
O lord of charioteers.'

And then the Great Being replied:

143. 'No, Migājina, I have never at any time, in any way,
     honoured an ascetic or brahmin nor approached one
     for instruction.'[53]

When he had made this statement, he spoke explaining right
from the beginning his reason for going forth:

144. 'As I proceeded, shining in great pomp and majesty,
     songs were being sung, lovely music was being played.
     The garden resounded with the play of musical
     instruments
     and was filled with the finest sounds of percussion.

145. I saw, Migājina, a mango tree,
     outside the protective wall [of the garden],
     destroyed[54] by people who wanted the fruit.

146. So then I abandoned pomp, Migājina, got down,
     and approached the root of the mango tree that was
     fruitful and the one without fruit.

147. The fruitful mango tree was destroyed and broken,
     with stalks removed,
     while the other mango tree was shining, with a dark
     colour and delightful.

[61] 148. So in this way we kings are beset by many thorns;
     our enemies will destroy us just as the fruitful mango
     tree is harmed.

149. A panther is harmed for its pelt, an elephant for its tusks,
     a rich man is harmed for his wealth:
     for me, without house or friendship,
     the fruitful mango tree and the one without fruit were
     both teachers.'[55]

When Migājina heard this he exhorted the king to be vigilant
and then went back to his own realm. When he had gone Queen
Sīvalī fell at the king's feet and said:

150. 'Elephant drivers, royal guards, charioteers and foot soldiers:
the people are all frightened, exclaiming, "the king has gone
forth!"'

151. When you have set up protection for the people and
established your son as king: only when you have come
back and done this should you take the going forth.'

Then the Bodhisatta said:

152. 'I have given up countrymen, friends, ministers and relatives.
[62] The Videhans have sons: Longlife is the good luck of
the kingdom;
They will look after the kingdom of Mithilā, great queen.'

The queen said: 'Sire, you are becoming an ascetic; what shall
I do?' He said, 'I will tell you: do what I say,' and he said this:

153. 'Go, I will teach you a description of what pleases me.
If you take charge of the kingdom,
you will do great evil in body, speech and mind and go to
an unfortunate rebirth.[56]
So keep yourself going with almsfood, given by others
and prepared by others:
this is the teaching of the strong.'

So the Great Being advised her in this way. And the sun went
down as they conversed with one another. Now the queen set
up her camp at a suitable spot; the Great Being meanwhile went
to the root of a certain tree and stayed there, and on the next day
took care of his bodily needs and went on his way. The queen
ordered the army to follow behind, and she also went behind
him. At the time for going on the alms round they reached a city
called Thūṇa. Now at that moment, inside the city, a certain man
had bought a large piece of meat from a slaughterhouse and had
cooked it on a spit over embers. He then placed it on a board to
cool and left it. But while he was occupied with something else

a dog came and ran away with it. When the man realized he followed the dog to outside the southern gate of the city, but became fed up with searching and went back. The king and the queen, separately, were coming up in front of the dog, which dropped the meat in fright and ran off. When the Great Being saw this he thought, 'This dog has dropped the meat and run off without regard, but no other owner can be seen. You could not find such a blameless piece of almsfood.[57] I'll eat it.' So he took out his earthenware bowl, took the piece of meat, wiped it, put it on the dish, found a pleasant spot where there was water and ate it. The queen saw this and thought, 'If this man were worthy of a kingdom he would not eat such detestable leftovers dropped by a dog. Well, he is not my husband now.' She addressed him, 'Great king, are you eating such disgusting food?' 'Queen, through your blindness you cannot recognize the excellence of this piece of almsfood.' And he contemplated the spot right where it had fallen, ate the food as if it were ambrosia and then rinsed his mouth and washed his hands and feet. At that, the queen addressed him in reproach:

154. 'Whoever does not eat by the time of the fourth occasion for eating
    dies from starvation through not eating;
    nonetheless a worthy man of good family should not resort to ignoble, dirty almsfood;
    this is not good, this is not well done, that you eat the leavings of a dog.'

The Great Being said:

155. 'Sīvali, it is not unfitting to eat what has been discarded by a householder or a dog.
    Any food that is obtained in accordance with what is right is completely suitable for eating.'

[64] As they debated with each other in this way they reached the gate of the city. There some children were playing and a little girl was pummelling some sand in a little winnowing basket. On one of her wrists there was one bracelet, and on the other two; the two bracelets clinked against each other while the other one made no noise. The king saw the cause of this and said, 'Sīvalī follows behind me; a woman is a stain for a recluse. People will reproach me, regarding me as someone who takes the going forth but cannot leave a woman. If this girl is wise, she will be able to explain a reason for Queen Sīvalī turning back. I'll listen to what she has to say and then send Sīvalī away.' Thinking this he said,

156. 'Little girl, always the darling of your mother, adorned with bracelets,
        why does one of your arms make a sound and the other does not?'

The little girl replied,

157. 'Ascetic, on this arm are fastened two bangles.
        From their jangling together the sound arises:
        this event happens from the second one.

158. Ascetic, on this arm is fastened one bangle.
        This, without a second, does not produce a sound.
        It remains silent, a sage.[58]

159. The second is a bringer of dispute;[59]
        What can a single thing quarrel with?
        Solitude brings you happiness in your wish for heaven.'

He heard this statement from the girl and, understanding the cause, explained it to the queen.

160. 'Listen, Sīvalī, to the verses declared by the little girl.
        The servant girl reproaches me, for this is what happens with a second person.

161. This path, good lady, that is walked by travellers, divides
in two.
You take one and I'll take another.
Do not call me husband, and do not say "I am your wife"
again.'

She listened to his words and, saluting him, said, 'Sire, you take
the higher, the right hand path and I'll go on the left'. But after
she had gone a little way she could not suppress her grief and
went back to the king. And she entered with him into the city.

Explaining the matter the Teacher gave half a verse:

162. 'Conversing in this way they reached the city of Thúṇa.'

[66] After they entered, the Great Being went round for alms and
reached the door of an arrow maker. Sívalí stood to one side. At
that time the arrow maker was heating an arrow on a heap of
embers, had moistened it with rice water and was making it
straight by looking at it with one eye after closing the other. When
he saw this the Great Being thought, 'If this is a wise man he'll tell
me the reason for this; I'll ask him.' And he approached him.

In explanation the Teacher said,

163. 'When it was time for food at the storehouse of the arrow
maker:
there the arrow maker closes one eye and looks sideways
with the other.'

And then the Great Being said,

164. 'Listen to me, arrow maker.
It is good that you look in this way,
whereby you look sideways with one eye after closing the
other.'

And he, answering him, replied,

165. 'Ascetic, with two eyes, the bow appears as if diffuse.

The arrow maker cannot find the best feature and does not smooth it to straightness.

166. For the person who looks askance with one eye and closes the other,

the arrow acquires the best feature and becomes suited to straightness.

167. The second is the bringer of dispute; what can a single thing quarrel with?

Solitude brings you happiness in the wish for heaven.'

When he had given this advice he was silent. The Great Being went for alms and, having collected some food mixed together, he left the city and sat down in a place which was pleasant and had water. And when he had done everything that he had to do, he put away the bowl in the bag and addressed Sīvalī:

168. 'Listen, Sīvalī, to the verses taught by the arrow maker.

The servant reproached me; this is what happens with a second person.[60]

169. This is a divided path, good lady, for the traveller to follow.

You take one and I'll take another.

Do not you call me husband, and do not say "I am your wife" again.'

They say that although he had asked, 'do not call me husband', she followed the Great Being but could not persuade the king to turn back and the crowd followed her. Not far away there was a forest. The Great Being saw a dark streak of woodland and, wishing to get her to turn back, he broke a reed off from some muñja grass he saw on the roadside. 'Look at this Sīvalī; this cannot be joined together again. So your association with me cannot be joined together again either.' And he said this half verse,

170. 'Live alone, Sīvalī, like a muñja grass reed that has been pulled out.'

She heard this, and cried 'From now on there is no more association with King Mahājanaka for me!' Unable to bear her grief she beat her breast with both hands and fell senseless on to the main road. The Great Being, seeing that she was unconscious, entered into the forest, obliterating his footprints. Ministers came and sprinkled her body with water and massaged her hands and feet to bring her back to consciousness. 'Oh where has the king gone?' she asked. 'Don't you know?' they replied. 'Find him, sirs!' she ordered. But although they ran around here and there they could not see him. She poured forth her grief and had a shrine built at the spots where the king had been, which she honoured with offerings such as flowers and incense, and then turned back. The Great Being entered the Himālaya region and in the course of seven days he cultivated the higher knowledges and the attainments.[61] And he did not go again into the ways of men. The queen had shrines made at all the places he had been: the spot where he had spoken with the arrow maker, the spot where he had spoken with the servant girl, the spot where he had eaten the piece of meat, the spot where he had conversed with Migājina and the one where he had spoken with Nārada. She paid homage to them with incense and flowers and then, surrounded by the army, she went to Mithilā. She had her son anointed in the mango grove and told him to enter into the city surrounded by the army. And then she took the going forth and lived in the grove. She did the preparations for *kasiṇa* practice and attained the meditation, destined for rebirth in a Brahma realm.[62]

The Teacher gave this teaching and said, 'Not just now, but in times past the Thus-gone made a great renunciation.' And he made the connections in the births: 'At that time Uppalavaṇṇā was the sea goddess, Sāriputta was Nārada, Moggallāna was Migājina, the nun Khemā was the little girl, Ānanda the fletcher, Rāhula's mother was Sīvalī, Rāhula was prince Dīghāvu,

members of the royal family were the mother and the father and
I was Mahājanaka.'

Notes

[1] Someone who has travelled by sea is ranked with arsonists, poisoners
and adulterers. See W. Doniger with B.K. Smith, *The Laws of Manu*
(Harmondsworth, Middlesex: Penguin, 1991), p. 60 (3.158).

[2] See H.P. Ray, *The Archaeology of Seafaring in Ancient South Asia*
(Cambridge: CUP, 2003), p. 63 and M. Winternitz, *History of Indian
Literature* (Srinivasa Sarma revised), 2 vols. (Delhi: Motilal, 1983), II,
p. 127, n. 2. Seafaring Jātakas include 196, 360 and the Suppāraka
Jātaka (463), a famous tale where the Bodhisatta is a skilled mariner.

[3] J I 60.

[4] At the shrine hall at Wat Yai Intharum, Chonburi. See S. Leksukhum,
with photos by G. Mermet, 'The Ten Great Jātakas', *Temples of Gold:
Seven Centuries of Thai Buddhist Paintings* (London: Thames and
Hudson, 2001), p. 140. Also at Wat No, Suphanburi, Thailand. See E.
Wray, C. Rosenfield, D. Bailey, with photographs by J.D. Wray, *Ten
Lives of the Buddha: Siamese Temple Paintings and Jātaka Tales* (New
York: Weatherhill, 1996, rev. edn), p. 35.

[5] *History of Indian Literature*, p. 142.

[6] See Thompson, *Motif Index*, 'suitor tests/quest', H336 and H1200–
H1399. See also S. Thompson and J. Balys, *The Oral Tales of India*
(Bloomington, Indiana: IUP, 1958), motif index nos H 305–88.

[7] The Ummagga Jātaka (546) is particularly popular in Sri Lanka.
For the use of riddles there, see Nandasena Ratnagalle, *Folklore of Sri
Lanka* (Colombo: State Printing Corporation, 1991), pp. 125–33.

[8] It should be noted that the verses do not mention the *paccekabuddha*
by name. At the time of the first composition of Jātakas it seems that
the term had not been developed fully. On *paccekabuddha*s in the canon,
see DPPN II 94–6, Winternitz, *History of Indian Literature*, p. 141,
n. 3, and J. Garrett Jones, *Tales and Teachings of the Buddha: The Jātaka
Stories in Relation to the Pāli Canon* (London: Allen and Unwin, 1979),
pp. 166–70. The Pāli *sutta*s place less emphasis on these figures than

the later tradition. They do not feature in any Jātaka verses. For fuller studies of the subject, see K.R. Norman, 'The Pratyeka-Buddha in Buddhism and Jainism', *Selected Papers*, Vol. II (Oxford: PTS, 1991), pp. 233–49, and R. Kloppenborg, *The Paccekabuddha: a Buddhist ascetic. A study of the concept of paccekabuddhas in Pāli canonical and commentarial literature* (Lieden: Brill, 1974).

[9] Other Jātakas where they appear include 408, 420, 421, 424, 442, 459 and 529.

[10] See Kumbhakāra Jātaka (408). These two incidents feature in Jain and Buddhist texts, suggesting an earlier strain of spiritual practice absorbed by both traditions. See K.R. Norman, 'The Pratyeka-Buddha'.

[11] See Cone and Gombrich, *Perfect Generosity*, p. 73 (J VI 565–6).

[12] See 'The Bodhisatta Vow: the far past'.

[13] A famous poem, 'The Rhinoceros Horn', also eulogizes a solitary spiritual existence (Sn 35–75).

[14] Mithilā, the capital of the Videhan country, is mentioned in 22 Jātakas (see, in this volume, 'The Story of Makhādeva', 9). Mahājanaka's eulogy to the city provides us with its fullest description. It is said to be seven yojanas long and was visited by the Buddha. It is usually identified with Janakapura, a small town within the Nepal border region (DPPN II 635).

[15] A *saccakiriyā*, a statement of truth with magical efficacy, features in Jātakas 20 and 75.

[16] An example of the Bodhisatta's less than exemplary behaviour when the occasion demands!

[17] Reading *rajjaggahaṇappamāṇo* with a Burmese manuscript (Bd) so that 'for taking the kingdom' is in the nominative.

[18] That is, 350 people.

[19] Amending to *loṇodakena*, 'with salt water'.

[20] The Four Great Kings are the protective deities of the Buddhist tradition. They rule the heaven realm above the humans, though take their place also as inhabitants in the realm above that, the heaven of the Thirty-Three Gods (*Tavatiṃsa*). As guardians of each cardinal direction they are thought to protect anyone who keeps the *uposatha* day. The intervention of the goddess is a kind of overdetermination that

vindicates the power of the *uposatha*: for the seven days before she does not notice the Bodhisatta, but decides to look after he has kept it. Maṇimekalai is the heroine of a Tamil folk epic, written by Sattanar in the fifth to the sixth century CE. Buddhism flourished in Tamil Nadu and it seems she was adopted as a protective goddess of the sea. See H. P. Ray, *The Archaeology of Seafaring*, pp. 270–1.

21 Reading *abhinippannaṃ*, 'produced', 'accomplished' with Bd, as suggested by PED 65, to give 'product'.

22 I have been unable to find any account of these auspicious slabs, though they feature elsewhere in the Jātakas (J 1 59).

23 We see a few lines later that this is a bow.

24 The word *phussa* means speckled, then brightly coloured and festive (PED 480). This wonderful state carriage is also described in J II 39 and J III 238.

25 These are a sword, the white parasol, the turban, slippers and a yak's tail fan, mentioned in Jātaka 538.

26 An army that extends on four sides, a traditional term, here perhaps meaning that the army has flanks in front of, behind, and on both sides of the carriage.

27 In his last birth thirty-two auspicious marks were discerned on his body which meant that he would be either a wheel-turning monarch or a Buddha. (See *Lakkhaṇa Sutta*, D III 142–79.) Although this is not his last birth, as a royal human in this birth he probably displays some. The marks pertaining to the feet are that his feet are well planted, so that he walks evenly and with level tread, that the mark of a wheel appears on the feet (and palms of his hands) and that he has extended heels. He has long fingers and toes that are like a net, and his hands and feet are soft and tender.

28 *Mahājjhāsayo*: motivation, disposition.

29 The Jātaka trans. (PTS), VI, p. 26, n. 1 refers the reader to the *Kathāsaritasāgara*, *The Ocean of Story*, sections 72, 47 and 54, where the snake maiden gives the hero a sword and horse. See Thompson, 'Bride helps suitor perform his tasks', *Motif Index*, H 335.01 for counterparts in Irish, Icelandic, German, Italian and Japanese folk tale.

30 *Udāna*: literally an inspired or joyful utterance (PED 134 and DP 421–2).

31 *Paccekabuddha*s are fully self-enlightened (*sāmaṃ*), but do not teach the full path to awakening.

32 A yojana has two meanings: the yoke of a carriage, used as the length meant here, and a measure of a distance of about seven miles, used earlier in the story from the past.

33 See DP I 77.

34 According to the *Abhidhamma* system, contact (*phassa*) is the first universal mental factor (*cetasika*) common to all mental states and sensory experience. We are experiencing such contacts all the time. According to the same system, *vitakka*, initial thought or the bringing of the mind to an object, is the first factor involved in the attainment of the first *jhāna*, the first meditation. Where *vitakka* occurs in such a state and indeed in any good, skilful state of mind, it is associated with the second factor of the eightfold path, right intention. Contacts 'which are not reflected upon' (*avitakkitā*) are therefore those which have not been investigated with mindfulness and skilful attention. The word *vitakka* does sometimes have a negative connotation in the *sutta*s (M I 211–14) and indeed in the *Abhidhamma*, in consciousness where attention is wrongly placed. Here, however, *vitakka* is clearly meant to have a positive association as the correct application of the mind in response to any contacts that arise (See DhS 1, 2, 7 and 21).

35 These are given in Jātaka III 274 as generosity (*dāna*), virtue (*sīla*), letting go (*pariccāga*), straightness, gentleness, asceticism, lack of anger, non-harm, forbearance (*khanti*), and non-opposition. Three of these, generosity, virtue and forbearance, are the same words used for three of the perfections to be developed by the Bodhisatta. Lack of anger is considered to be the same as a fourth, loving kindness.

36 The same story is given about a king in Jātaka 408: the king becomes a *paccekabuddha*, an option not chosen by the Bodhisatta given his vow to attain Buddhahood. The similarity, however, reinforces the constant evocation of the *pacceka* path suggested in this story.

37 The three worlds refer to the sense sphere, the heavens above that (*brahmaloka*) and the formless (*arūpa*) realms.

38 These verses are very repetitive: like all bardic and oral literature they depend heavily on repetition and stock formulae. A particular force would accompany the chanting of this section by, as would be usual, a

group of monks who have all themselves chosen to renounce the worldly life. The lay life is described here in what would be perceived as its most glorious form: the wording of the eulogy of the city of Mithilā is very like that used to describe the palace and city of the universal monarch in the *Mahāsudassana Sutta* (D II 190–2). As with many verses of this type the repetitions are not rigidly mechanical: a group of chanters would need to be alert to catch the variations. The second line is the same for each verse from verse 25 to verse 47.

[39] For *bandhunī*, 'kinsmen', used here, see commentary and entry for *bandhunī* in PED 482.

[40] See PED 715 for 'hips', here *susoññā* rather than 'of good understanding' (*susaññā*): as this feature is linked with small waists, this translation seems more likely!

[41] Verses 79–108 follow the same pattern as for verses 48–77, with the people and animals being left in Mithilā becoming active in the questions as the ones who will no longer follow his movements. The break between the two sections is marked, crucially, in the impersonal objects left behind in verse 78, 'the fine bronze dish and the pure gold plate'. They of course cannot follow the king and, in verse 109, the third section of this extended lyrical outburst moves to the contrasting eating accoutrement associated with the going forth: the earthenware bowl of the mendicant. The 'fine bronze bowl and golden plate' are not forgotten: they recur in verse 122, uttered by the Buddha, as signs of the royal, lay life, this time directly contrasted with the earthenware bowl, the emblem of the monastic.

[42] The text has a chariot maker (*rathakāro*), an odd choice of profession. Skills tend to be transferable amongst Indian craftsman so perhaps the man who carved the wood for a chariot was also called upon to make the templates for sandals?

[43] On the suggestion of the Sri Lankan manuscript (Cs) and PED 421 (under *parikanta*) I have read *pariyantaṃ*, ('limit', 'border') here to give 'edges'.

[44] A Brahma heaven realm where those are born who have attained the second meditation, characterized by joy, happiness and one-pointedness. See Jātaka 99.

[45] It says a *gāvuta*, which was about two miles (PED 250).

[46] This Nārada features in *Sudhābhojana Jātaka* (Jātaka 535), where he is also said to be Sāriputta in an earlier birth as is the case in this tale. The higher knowledges are the psychic powers (*iddhi*s), said to become available to the practitioner after he has attained the fourth meditation (*jhāna*). Sometimes the list appears with a sixth (D III 281), the destruction of the corruptions (*āsava*s), associated with the attainment of enlightenment. As Nārada has himself made a vow to become the chief disciple of the Buddha, he would not have taken this option.

[47] This passage poses a number of linguistic difficulties; it appears to rest both upon an inference that the Bodhisatta is claiming to be enlightened and Nārada's almost brahminical interpretation that while there is still a body there can be no freedom from defilements. In Buddhist terminology the one who has 'crossed over' (*tiṇṇo*) is enlightened and has left behind defilements, though here this would be an inappropriate term as the Bodhisatta has postponed his enlightenment until his final lifetime. While the Bodhisatta claims in verse 130 only to have stepped over the town boundary, he clearly regards this as a step symbolic of the freedom of the ascetic life and perhaps Nārada felt he was underestimating the inner dangers ahead. At any rate Nārada's use of the word seems to be a satiric play incorporating some or all of these levels of meaning. He is saying that the Bodhisatta might have crossed over the town boundary, that symbolizes his movement to the ascetic life, but he still needs to be vigilant. The Bodhisatta accepts the admonishment with good grace (verse 134).

[48] Lit. 'may a completely joyful abiding come to pass for you'. The commentary says that he refers to the four divine abidings (*brahmavihāra*s) of loving kindness, compassion, sympathetic joy and equanimity. This verse is a free translation of lines which would be stilted if translated literally.

[49] For the translation 'haughtiness', see *unnataṅ* (DP I 434–5).

[50] *Kammaṃ vijjam ca dhammaṃ*. The commentary, in perhaps a rather cumbersome manner, relates the first to the ten skilful kinds of action, the second to the five higher knowledges and the meditative attainments and the third to the preparatory work for the *kasiṇa* practice.

⁵¹ Migājina is identified at the end with the arahat Moggallāna, the other chief disciple of the Buddha in his last life.

⁵² PED 282 suggests that *na jātucca* in the text should be *na jātu ca*, 'not at all', 'never'.

⁵³ This verse follows almost exactly the same grammatical pattern as verse 140.

⁵⁴ Reading *hatamānaṃ*, 'damaged', 'harmed', with a Burmese manuscript (Bd).

⁵⁵ These verses pose difficulties, but I have by and large followed the commentary's suggestions.

⁵⁶ *Rajjaṃ tuvaṃ kārayantī* (*kāreti*, DP I 652). It is not clear whether the king is advising his queen not to administer the kingdom or discouraging her from installing their son. I have taken it as advice for the queen herself, given perhaps because she is a woman, or because she personally will generate unfortunate *kamma* by being a monarch. The commentary takes it to mean that there will be an unfortunate outcome from installing their son as king and taking charge herself too. It is unlikely to be a warning against her installing the son. The conclusion of the story does not suggest that the son's assumption of the throne is anything other than desirable. Given her attitude towards the king at the end of the story it is improbable that Sīvalī would encourage her son to be king if her husband had disapproved of it (for *kārayantī* see DP I 652).

⁵⁷ Literally 'such a blameless piece of alms food does not exist'.

⁵⁸ *Munibhūto*. A *muni* meant originally a teacher who has taken a vow of silence.

⁵⁹ Here, as in verse 167, I have followed a Burmese manuscript (Bd) to read *vivādappatto*, 'full of' or 'with' dispute.

⁶⁰ The Pāli is very unclear here and gives 'servant' in the feminine, as in the comparable verse after the little girl has spoken (v. 160). As the arrow maker is mentioned, however, I have taken him as the servant (taking *pessiyo* with a Sri Lankan manuscript, Cks) and adjusted the text to the masculine, to create what seems to be an intended parallel between this and verse 160. The verse seems to be corrupt, however, and it may be that the 'servant' once referred to the girl with the bangle (for an emendation based on this supposition, see VRI).

61 The attainment (*samāpatti*) are the eight meditations (*jhāna*) with, sometimes a ninth—the attainment of cessation (*nirodha samāpatti*), only obtainable by stream enterers. This should not be accessible to a Bodhisatta, who postpones his enlightenment though, as the next story (540) demonstrates, he does appear to attain such a state even when not a stream enterer.

62 *Jhānaṃ.* It does not say which meditative state. The *kasiṇa* practices are meditations on one of the elements, or a colour, for which a device is constructed.

26

The story of Sāma
Sāma Jātaka (540)

Vol. VI, 68–95

The story of Sāma is beloved throughout South-East Asia
for its portrayal of loving kindness (*mettā*), the ninth
perfection.[1] Here, as was suggested in Jātaka 385, this quality
is imbued with a magical power beyond even that of the higher
knowledges (*abhiññās*) in Buddhism. It apparently achieves the
impossible: the revival of the dead. It tells of a couple, recently
descended from a Brahma heaven, who eschew sexual passion
and live as ascetics in woods in the Himālayas, suffusing the area
around with loving kindness. They have a child, with the help of
Sakka, to whose care they devote themselves completely. Sheltering
from a storm, however, they stumble on a termite mound, are
poisoned by an enraged snake and become blinded. Their son
Sāma, finds them and cares for them until he too is attacked, by
the arrow of a hunter king, and apparently dies. A local goddess
intervenes to ensure that she and the parents return to the 'body'
and revive him. They each make statements of truth, Sāma is
revived, his parents have their sight restored and the errant king
returns to his kingdom. In the *Rāmāyaṇa* version of the same
tale, recounted on Dasaratha's deathbed, the man who has been
shot does not recover.[2] A sense of the beauty of loving kindness
animates this rural idyll, however: it is a paean to the transformatory
power of *mettā*, both in daily life and as a meditative practice,
which seems almost boundless in its effect.

The story is fuelled by the drama of a harsh dose of realism. The protagonists learn through starkly brutal circumstances the difficulties of finding and balancing the practice of loving kindness with awareness of the forces that militate against it. This can be seen firstly in the story of the couple. Their decision to practise an ascetic life is not criticized and is explained by their recent descent from a Brahma heaven, which has made them distasteful of the 'way of the world'. It has the support of the gods of the heaven of the Thirty-Three, who aid any active pursuit of virtue in the world. Ancient Indians, however, placed a high value on sexual happiness (kāma) as a means of ensuring well-being and the continuation of the family line. The couple have not considered the possibility of needing care themselves and have to be persuaded by that great champion of common sense, King Sakka, to beget one, a son conceived through his powers. The parents also seem oversolicitous to the child once born: with that unerring psychological accuracy that one finds sometimes in Jātaka narrative, the Bodhisatta's nagging fears when they are out of his sight seem justified. The vengeful bite from the snake is attributed to a combination of the couple's own past kamma, their lack of awareness and the spite of another being. The immediate cause is also that they smell of sweat, according to Indian literary convention one of the distinguishing features of humans, as opposed to gods.[3] By trying to isolate themselves from the outside world and their human physicality, the parents have made themselves open to attack. They have created around themselves an enclave that reminds them of a Brahma heaven, but become blinded, literally, by inappropriate love. For the one pursuing loving kindness as a meditation practice, the commentator Buddhaghosa, warns against hatred on the one hand and unbalanced affection on the other.[4] Through the events of the story both worm their way into the couple's pastoral world.

The development to maturity of the Bodhisatta, despite the

oddity of his upbringing, has a universal applicability. Protected
in a cocoon for the first part of his life, he cries to see his parents
blinded but laughs too: he is delighted that he can now look
after them, with their roles reversed. He has to construct bridges
everywhere for his unseeing mother and father, an image strikingly
suggestive of all children's attempts to build up an identity
acceptable to their parents. He creates a world that they can live
in and, as they had done for him, dedicates himself to their care
and protection. The domestic details of his daily routine in looking
after them are practical and well realized, down to the complicated
rituals involving carrying heated pots of water to bathe their feet
and keep their limbs warm. However, as his parents had done
before him, he lives in a familiar, inner world that does not
prepare him for life outside his protected space. Surrounded
wherever he goes by animals tamed by kindness alone, he has
no expectancy of attack and, when spotted by the king, is
mistaken for a god or a nāga, but not a man. As the first verse
indicates, he also loses the quality of alertness to the outside
world which is the hallmark of Buddhist practice: he is 'careless'
(*pamattaṃ*), despite his remarkable ascetic bearing. We are told
that he re-establishes mindfulness (*sati*), with impressive poise
and presence of mind, even though apparently fatally wounded.
It is suggested, however, that he too has been insufficiently aware
of danger in the world around.

These might seem harsh judgements of what is depicted as a
sanctuary, but the charmed forest also provides the means
whereby the threats are overcome. The local goddess, Bahusodarī,
the *dea ex machina*, sees the situation and comes to the family's
aid, knowing that their intervention could save the son from death.
But is Sāma really 'dead'? Both the narrative and the verses of
the Bodhisatta hint that he has been keeping himself barely alive
after attack, through meditative practice (vv. 396–7). To the king

it looks like death, because Sāma has no in or out breath or
outward sign of consciousness. These are also, however, features
of some higher meditative states.[5] Careful rules guard entry in
these states that are described by the great commentator on
meditation, Buddhaghosa.[6] In two verses Sāma explains after
his revival 'the nature of non-dying': that just because the usual
mental activity has stopped does not mean a being is not alive; it
is possible that even when the breathing has stopped, a person
can have entered the state of cessation, a state usually associated
with enlightened beings.[7] His response to the attack seems to have
been to enter a meditation where he seemed 'dead' to the world.

As a rule, Jātakas tend to be literal and less highly coloured
than Indian myths, in that wonderful occurrences, even those
involving gods and the supernatural, are all explained in terms
that accord with Buddhist cosmological theory and the doctrine
of *kamma*. The king of Kāsi goes straight to a hell from this life
through the force of his actions, for instance.* In a similar
incident to Sāma's 'death' in another Jātaka, the poison has not
yet killed the Bodhisatta and is dispelled.[8] No other story has a
being completely revived from the dead. This Jātaka gives a
happy ending—but still provides a thoroughly Buddhist
explanation for it all. Nonetheless, the Bodhisatta needs the
simple statement of truths from his parents and the intervention
of the local goddess to awaken. The goddess, like the parents,
declares the truth of her love for him and makes a simple statement
of truth. The sense of smell, which had instigated the blinding of
the parents, is again invoked, by her declaration that all the trees

---

*It might seem puzzling that the king in this story also does not plunge
into hell immediately for his action. The shooting of the Bodhisatta here, in
one act of casual violence, was presumably not considered so weighty as to
warrant immediate rebirth in a hell realm. Indeed at the end of the story he
manages to redeem himself.

around have their own perfume. This simple acknowledgement of the senses and the external circumstances of the wood end the long dark night of Sāma's 'death'. In one moment of breaking dawn, Sāma is restored to consciousness, a teacher and an adult. His parents are freed from the blindness that has prevented them from standing as beings capable of looking after themselves. The king, now willing to acknowledge his confusion, is able to learn from the Bodhisatta, whose virtues he has at last come to recognize, and returns to act as monarch in his own kingdom. The whole episode communicates the sense of waking from a bad dream, or a spell: by bearing witness to the separate identity of each tree the local goddess has ensured that each human is mindful of where he stands, his place in the forest and his own identity too.

An important figure in the drama is the hunter king, who introduces into the story the gravitational weight of the outside world and a life governed entirely by greed, hatred and delusion. He casually destroys the peace of the renunciates' lives, at all times boorishly repeating the *leitmotiv* that boasts his fame and skill (vv. 5, 26, 45 and 60). In striking contrast to Sāma, he has neglected his kingdom and left it with his mother. On his own admission he has been overcome with simple greed (*lobha*), described by Buddhaghosa as a 'near enemy' to loving kindness, and cannot recognize the Bodhisatta for what he is.[9] Even when abashed at his crime he blunders his way into the hermitage, to announce himself to the parents with his usual absence of tact. He is not shown just as a villain: he is genuinely grieved by his actions and solicitous of the parents' welfare. He does, however, embody human nature at its most self-centred and, it has to be said, amusing. Through the events of the story, Sāma and his parents have to become reconciled to him and his coarse perception of events around him. He is also tamed by them. Bewildered by Sāma's revival, the parents' goodwill even in adversity and the qualities he has found in the enchanted woods he finally takes refuge in the Bodhisatta, his guide and teacher. He returns to fulfil his duty in the lay life, as a just king, while the Bodhisatta returns to fulfil his. So through the power of the loving kindness of the others, even this comic buffoon practises generosity and becomes destined for a heaven realm.

The story lacks the obvious linguistic stature of some of the verse portions of other Jātakas, though the apparently endless refrain of the long night chorus of Sāma's 'death' would be particularly effective in a chanted recitation: the text was not intended to be read to oneself. The depiction of the situation in the wood is exquisite in its evocation of the beauties of the practice of loving kindness. It also shows the way that even this redemptive quality has its own pitfalls if pursued to the neglect of awareness. But the 'enemies' of this perfection, within and without, are overcome when it is linked to the acknowledgement of truth, the awareness which allows all the protagonists to fulfil their appropriate duties as free agents. As a vindication of the importance of the simple qualities of tenderness and care for one's own family the tale makes a suitable conclusion to this anthology. The frame story, from the present, describes the Buddha's approval of a monk's apparent neglect of his rules in looking after his own parents, an example of the practical approach to individual cases the Buddha exhibits throughout his teaching career. That it is good to care for parents is undoubtedly the story's message, but its subtlety of construction suggest the need for alertness and flexibility in all situations. All those in the tale have to learn to use loving kindness well.

The story is shown in Cave 17 at Ajaṇṭā and on a relief at Sāñchī. The favourite depiction in temple art of this story shows Sāma, surrounded by deer, as he is hit by the king's arrow.[10] This scene is painted at Wat Yai Intharam and Wat Bang Yikhan in Thailand. The story features in Gandhāran art.[11]

Story from the present
'*Who has struck me with an arrow?*'

While staying at the Jetavana Grove the Teacher told this story
about a certain brahmin who supported his mother. It is said
that at Sāvatthi there was a certain merchant who was worth
eighteen crores. He had one son, who was dear and loving to his
parents. One day this son went up to the roof of the palace and
opened a window from the top of the palace. Looking out on to
the street he saw a crowd of people with perfumes and garlands
in their hands going to Jetavana to listen to *dhamma*. [69] He
thought he would go too, had some perfumes and garlands
collected and went to the monastery. He saw that clothes,
medicines and drinks were given to the monks, paid homage to
the Exalted One with perfumes and garlands and sat down to
one side. He listened to the teaching, heard about the danger of
the sense desires and the blessings arising from a holy life. When
the assembly rose he asked the Exalted One for ordination. The
reply was that the Thus-gones do not ordain those without
parental permission. So he went away, living for seven days
without food, got his parents to grant their approval and then
asked for ordination. The Teacher sent a monk who ordained
him. When he had taken the ordination he practised with great
achievement and honour. He pleased his preceptors and teachers
and five years after his full ordination had learnt the teaching
thoroughly. Then he thought, 'I am distracted living here. It is not
suitable for me.' Wishing to fulfil the responsibility of insight[12]
he obtained a meditation object from a teacher in a hermitage
and went to a certain outlying town and lived in the forest. There
he set up a course of insight and worked hard for twelve years,
making an effort, but could not attain any distinction.

As time went by his mother and father also became poor:
those that hired land or engaged in trade with them thought, 'In

this family there is no son or brother, who will demand payment of a debt and seize it.' So they took anything they could lay their hands on and fled. The household servants and workers grabbed the gold and the silver and suchlike and also fled. In the course of time the two were destitute and did not even have a jug to pour out water. In the end they sold their house and became homeless. In a state of wretchedness they begged for support, dressed in rags, with an alms bowl in their hands.

Now at that time a certain monk left the Jetavana Grove and went to stay at the monk's dwelling place. The son performed his hospitable duties and, as he sat comfortably, asked the monk where he was from. The monk replied that he was from Jetavana. He asked after the health of the Teacher and his disciples and then asked for news of his parents. 'Tell me, bhante, about the health of such and such a merchant's family in Sāvatthi.' 'Sir, do not ask for news about that family,' the monk replied. 'Why, bhante?' he asked. 'They say that there was a son in the family, but he became a monk in this time of teaching. Since the time of his ordination the family has been badly reduced and now the two parents beg for alms in a state of destitution.' When he heard the description from him the son was unable to keep his composure. He began to weep, with his eyes full of tears. 'Why do you grieve, sir?' the other monk said. 'These are my parents, bhante, and I am their son!' 'Sir, your mother and father have come to ruin because of you. Go and look after them.' The son thought, 'I have struggled for twelve years putting in effort, and have not been able to attain the path and fruit. [70] I am useless. What is ordination to me? I'll become a layman and care for my parents. I'll practise generosity and be one bound for heaven.' So when he had reflected, he handed over his forest dwelling to the elder and left on the next day. By stages he reached the monastery behind Jetavana near to Sāvatthi. There were two paths: one to Jetavana and one to Sāvatthi. He stood there and thought, 'Shall

I go and see my parents first, or the Ten-Powered One? I saw my mother and father for a long time once but from now on it will be difficult to get a sight of the Buddha. So today I'll see the Fully Awakened One and hear his teaching and then tomorrow I'll go and see my parents.' Leaving the road to Sāvatthi he arrived at Jetavana in the evening.

On that very day, at dawn, the Teacher, looking out at the world, had seen the strong predisposition of the monk.[13] When the son arrived the Teacher extolled the praise of parents in the *Mātiposaka Sutta*.[14] When the son heard this *dhamma* talk, standing in the assembly of monks, he thought, 'As a layman I can support my parents. But the Teacher says a son who is an ascetic can be a support too. I went away before without seeing the Teacher and I was deficient in such an ordination. I will maintain my parents, without becoming a layman, while still being an ascetic.' He took his wooden ticket,[15] his ticket food and his rice gruel and felt as if for twelve years he had been committing a grave offence against the rules for monks.[16] In the morning he went to Sāvatthi and wondered if he should collect rice gruel first of all, or go and see his parents. He thought it would not be right to visit them in their wretched state empty-handed, so he collected some rice-water gruel and went to the door of their former house. After he had gone in search of gruel he approached the wall and saw his mother and father sitting down. Grief welled up in him and with tears streaming from his eyes he stood near them. They saw him and did not recognize him. His mother thought that he must be standing there to collect alms and said, 'Bhante, there is nothing here that is fit to give you. Please go on.' He heard her words and, catching the grief which filled his heart, stood right there with tears streaming from his eyes. Even when he was addressed a second and a third time he still stood there. Then the father said to the mother, 'Go, can this be your son?' She got up, went to him and recognizing him, fell at his feet and wept, and his father did so too, and there was a great outpouring of sorrow. When he saw his parents he could not hold his composure and burst into tears. After he had given vent to his grief he said, 'Do not worry, I will look after you.' [71] When he had comforted his parents he gave them rice gruel and got them to sit to one side. Then he went on an alms round for more food and gave it to them, and then went to get alms for himself. When he had finished his meal he made a dwelling for himself to one side. From that time he supported his parents by this method. The almsfood he had obtained for himself, even on half-moon days and suchlike, he gave to them. Then he went for alms for himself and ate what he had obtained. Whatever food he received for the rainy season he gave to them, and ate his own. He took old cloth strips that had been used by them and then dyed them and used them himself. Days when he received alms were few and days when he received none were frequent. His inner and outer clothing became very rough.

As he looked after his parents, in time he became very thin and pale. His friends and companions asked him, 'Sir, your bodily complexion used to shine before and now you are thin and pale. Has some sickness come to you?' 'Sir,' he replied, 'there is no sickness in me but there is an obstruction for me.' And he told them what had happened. 'Sir, the Teacher does not allow us to waste what is offered by those with faith. It is not right for you to give to laymen what is offered by those with faith.' When he heard what they said he shrank back, ashamed. They were not content with this and informed the Teacher what he was doing. He called for the son of the family and asked him, 'Is it true what they say, that you are looking after laymen?' He said it was. The Teacher, wishing to praise his good action and to tell a story about his own practice in the past asked him, 'And what laymen are you supporting, bhikkhu?' 'My parents, bhante.' The Teacher, wishing to encourage him further, said, 'Very good, very good!'

He said this three times. 'You are on a path that I was on. In times past I used to beg for alms and support my parents,' he said. At the monks' request, he gave this explanation of the matter to them.

Story from the past

Once upon a time, not far from Vārāṇasi, on the near bank of the river, was a village of hunters and on the far side there was another village. Five hundred families dwelt in each. The two hunter chiefs who lived in the two villages were firm friends. When they were young they made an agreement: 'If we have a daughter and a son, let a marriage be arranged between them.' Then [72] a son was born to the chief who lived in the near-bank village. The boy was called Dukūlaka, one who wears fine cloth, because he was lifted with a fine cloth at the moment of birth.[17] In the other house a daughter was born, and they gave her the name Pārikā, the girl of the far shore. Both were good-looking and of golden complexion. Although they were born in hunter families, they did not take life.

In the course of time, when the boy Dukūlaka was sixteen, his parents said, 'Son, let us bring you a wife.' But as he had just come down from a Brahma world the pure being shut both his ears. 'I do not want to live in a household. Do not speak of such a thing.' Though they spoke of it three times, he did not want it. The girl Pārikā was addressed by her parents, 'Dear one, our good friend has a son who is good-looking, with a golden complexion, we'll give you to him.' She shut her ears as she had come down from a Brahma world too. Dukūlaka sent her a message in secret. 'Go and live in the house of another, if you want a sexual relationship. I do not have any desire for sex.' She sent just the same message to him. But despite their unwillingness their parents arranged the marriage. As they had both crossed over the ocean of sexual passion they lived apart, like two great Brahmas.

Dukūlaka did not kill fish or deer and did not even sell animal
flesh that was brought to him. And then his mother and father
said, 'Son, you have come to a hunter family but you do not wish
to live in a house or to kill living beings. What will you do?' 'My
dear parents, with your approval I'll become an ascetic this very
day.' 'Go on then,' they said and let both of them go.

They saluted his parents and left entering the Himālayan
region along the banks of the Ganga, at the place where the river
Migasammatā flows down from the Himālayas. Then they left
the Ganga and climbed up in the direction of the Migasammatā.
At that moment, Sakka's dwelling appeared hot. Sakka realized
the reason and spoke to Vissakamma. 'Dear Vissakamma, two
great individuals have left and entered the Himālayan region.
There ought to be a dwelling place for them. Go and see that a
leaf hut [73] and the necessaries for an ascetic life are created for
each of them about half a mile from the river Migasammatā.'[18]
He said, 'very well', and he made everything ready in the same
way as described in the Mūgapakkha Jātaka (538). He drove
away the creatures that made unpleasant noises, created a single-
track footpath and went back to his own abode. They saw the
path and followed it towards the hermitage. Wise Dukūlaka
entered the leaf hut and saw all the necessities for an ascetic life.
'These are gifts to us from Sakka,' he said, seeing they were like
things given by him. He took off his outer clothes, put on a robe
of red bark, threw a black antelope hide over his shoulder and
tied his hair into a bun: he put on the dress of a sage. Then he
gave the ordination to Pārikā too, and they both cultivated loving
kindness to all the beings of the sense sphere that lived around.
Through the power of their loving kindness all the beasts and
birds entertained a mind of loving kindness towards one another
and no creature harmed another.[19] Pārikā brought food and water,
swept the hermitage and did all the housework. Both collected
various kinds of fruit and ate them. Then they each entered the

hut on their own and lived performing the duties of an ascetic life. Sakka came and looked after them. One day he looked and saw that they would lose their sight. Perceiving the danger he approached wise Dukūlaka, greeted him and sat down to one side. He said, 'Bhante, a danger is on the cards for you. You ought to have a son to care for you. Follow the way of the world.' 'Sakka, what are you saying? Even when we were in the midst of household life we gave up the way of the world disgusted, as if at a heap of worm-infested dung. How can we start on such a course now that we have entered the forest and have taken up the life of a sage?' 'Oh well, bhante, if not, then at the right time you should touch the ascetic Pārikā's navel with your hand.' Dukūlaka agreed and said this could be done.[20] Sakka took his farewell and went to his own abode. Dukūlaka explained the matter to Pārikā and touched her navel with his hand.

At that time the Bodhisatta fell away from a divine realm and took rebirth [74] in her womb. After ten (lunar) months she gave birth to a son with golden skin, and because of this they called him Suvaṇṇasāma, Golden Sāma. They both bathed the Bodhisatta, laid him to sleep in the leaf hut and went in search of various fruit. At that moment some kinnaras took the boy and had him washed in their caves. (Kinnara women from another mountain had been wet nurses for Pārikā.)[21] Going up to the top of the mountain, they decorated him with various kinds of flowers and made marks on him with yellow ointment, red arsenic and other such things. Then they took him back to the leaf hut and put him back to bed. Pārikā came back and gave the child her breast. In the course of time he grew, cared for by his parents, and when he had reached about the age of sixteen they used to leave him in the leaf hut sitting on his own and go out to collect various fruits and roots from the woodland. The Great Being was convinced that one day some accident would happen and used to watch the path that they had taken. Then, one day, as they were bringing back roots and fruits from the woodland in the evening, not far from the hermitage, a great storm cloud arose. They took shelter at the roots of a tree and stood on a termite mound. Inside it there was a poisonous snake. Water dripped from their bodies and, mixed with the smell of sweat, it entered into the snake's nostrils. He was furious and attacked them with the breath from his nostrils. The two became blind and could not see one another. Wise Dukūlaka said to Pārikā, 'Pārikā, my eyes have gone. I cannot see you.' She said the same to him. As they could not see the path they thought their life was over and wandered around, crying. 'What did we do in the past for this to happen?' they asked. Now, it is said that formerly they had been a doctor and his wife.[22] The doctor had treated a very wealthy patient for a disease of the eyes but he had not paid his fee to him. The doctor, enraged, had told his wife and asked her what they should do. She had also been angry and suggested, 'There is no point in getting any fee from him. Give him a preparation, saying that it is his medicine and make him blind in one of his eyes.' The doctor agreed and, following her suggestion, did just that. And through this action of a past life both eyes, for both of them, became blind.

Now the Great Being thought, 'On other days [75] my parents have come back by this time. Now I just do not know what has happened. I'll go on the path.' So he followed the path, making a noise. They recognized his voice and made an answering call. In their affection for their son they said, 'Dear Sāma, there is danger here! Do not come near!' But he gave them a long pole to hold and told them to catch hold of it. They took hold of the end of it and went up to him. He asked them what it was that had destroyed their eyes. 'Dear son! When the rain came we went to the roots of a tree and stood on a termite mound; this was the cause.' When he heard this he realized, 'There must have been a poisonous snake there. He must have released poisonous breath in anger.' As he looked at his parents he cried and also laughed. So then they asked him, 'Why do you cry and laugh?' 'Dear parents, I cried because your eyes have been destroyed while you are still young. But I laughed because now I will care for you. So do not worry, I will look after you.' So he led them back to the hermitage and tied ropes all over the place, at the spots where they spent the day, where they spent the night, the walkways to the leaf hut and the areas for excretion and the areas for urinating. And from that time he kept them in the hermitage and he gathered roots and fruit from the woodland. In the morning he used to sweep the dwelling, go to the Migasammatā River, draw water and prepare their food. He used to get the water for washing and cleaning their teeth and gave them all kinds of sweet fruit. When they had rinsed their mouths he used to eat his own food. After he had eaten, he used to salute his parents and go into the forest in search of different fruits, surrounded by a troop of deer. When he had gathered fruit from the mountain with a retinue of kinnaras in tow, he went back in the evening. He took some water in a pot, heated it up and let them wash and bathe their feet in the hot water as they pleased. Then he bought a pot for burning charcoal and warmed their limbs. As they sat there he gave them various kinds of fruit and after all this he ate his own food and stored up what was left. In this way he looked after his mother and father.

Now at that time a king called Piliyakkha ruled in Vārāṇasi. He conceived a great desire for venison and left the kingdom in the care of his mother. He entered the Himālayan region armed with five kinds of weapons, killed deer and ate their flesh.[23] [76] He came to the Migasammatā River and in due course reached the fording place where Sāma used to draw water. He noticed deer tracks and made a hide with branches the colour of jewels. Taking his bow he notched a poisonous arrow and lay hidden. The Great Being came back from gathering fruits in the evening, stored them in the hermitage and saluted his parents. 'I'll get some water for washing and come back.' He took a water jug and singled two deer out from the herd that surrounded him. He set the water jug on their backs, led them with his hand and went down to the fording place at the river.

The king in his hide saw him and thought, 'In all the time that I have been travelling I have never seen a human here before. Is he a god? Is he a nāga? If I approach him to ask he will fly up in the air if he is a god and sink into the ground if he is a nāga. But I'm not always going to be staying in the Himālayas. I'll go back to Vārāṇasi and there my ministers will ask me, "So, great king, while you were visiting the Himālayas did you see anything extraordinary, that no one has ever seen before?" And I'll say, "Well, yes, I did see a strange being." And they'll ask me what it was, and if I say I don't know, they'll look down their noses at me. So I'll shoot him with an arrow to disable him and then ask him.' The deer crossed first at that point and drank some water. The Bodhisatta, like a great elder who had thoroughly grasped his rules, went down to the water sedately, delighting in complete tranquillity. He came out again, put on his bark garment and draped the antelope hide over one shoulder. He lifted the water jug, filled it with water and set it upon his left shoulder.

At that moment the king decided it was time to shoot and released an arrow dipped in poison. He wounded the Great Being on his right side and the arrow went out of the left side. Seeing that he had been struck the herd of deer fled in terror. Wise Golden Sāma, even though he was wounded, did not upset the water jar in any way, re-established his mindfulness and emerged slowly.[24] He dug up some sand, heaped it up in one direction and placed his head in the direction of his parents' dwelling. [77] He lay down, like a golden image on a silver plate in the sand, and set up mindfulness. 'In this Himālayan region I do not have an enemy. Nor am I an enemy to anyone else.' As he said this he vomited blood from his mouth. Without seeing the king, he spoke this verse:

1. 'Who has struck me with an arrow, a careless water carrier?²⁵
   What warrior, brahmin or businessman lay in wait to wound
   me?'

When he had said this, he spoke another verse to show the
unsuitability of his body as food.

2. 'My flesh can't be used as food; there is no value in my skin.
   So what advantage did you think there would be in wounding
   me?'

Saying the second verse, he asked him his name and such things.

3. 'Who are you and whose son? How do I know you?
   Tell me, sir, now I have asked:
   Say why you lay in wait to wound me.'

The king heard this and thought, 'Even though my poisonous
arrow has wounded this man he does not blame or reproach me.
He converses with a kind voice as if soothing my heart. I'll go
near him.' He went up and stood by him.

4. 'I am the king of Kāsi, I am known as Piliyakkha.
   I left my kingdom through desire and I wander, searching for
   deer here.

5. I am skilled in archery, strong in the bow and famous.
   An elephant would not escape me if he came in my arrow's
   range!'

[78] Praising his own strength in this way he asked him his family
name and said,

6. 'And whose son are you? How may I know you?
   Make known your own and your father's name.'

When he heard this the Great Being thought, 'If I said that I
were a god, a nāga, a kinnara or something like that, or that I

was a warrior, or something like that, he would believe it. But it is better to tell the truth.' So he said:

7. I am a hunter's son, my friend, called Sāma.
   Relatives called me this when I was alive,
   but today I have come to this and lie here.

8. I am wounded, with a broad poisoned arrow, like a deer.
   See, king, I lie here, drenched in my own blood.

9. My skin is pierced through. See where the arrow has gone;
   I vomit out blood.
   Afflicted, I ask you, why did you lie in wait to wound me?

10. A leopard is killed for its hide, an elephant for its tusks,
    So what advantage did you think there would be in wounding me?'

The king heard what he said. He did not say how things really were, but spoke a lie:

11. A deer was nearby and had come in arrow range.
    When it saw you, Sāma, it fled; no anger for you entered me.

[79] And then the Great Being said, 'What are you saying, great king? In this region of the Himālayas no deer is frightened of me.' And he said this:

12. 'As long as I can remember, as long as I have had knowledge,
    No deer has been scared of me, or footed animal in the forest.

13. As long as I have been wearing a bark dress,
    as long as I have been in my youth,
    No deer has been scared of me, or footed animal in the forest.

14. O king, timid kinnaras in the Gandhamādana mountains:
    We meet, in the mountains and in the woods, and are friendly to one another.
    For what reason would a deer have fear for me?'

When he heard this the king thought, 'I have wounded this innocent man and I have told a lie. I'll come clean.' He said,

15. 'Sāma, no deer saw you: I spoke a lie to you about this.
    Overcome with violence and desire, I shot an arrow at you.'

[80] When he had said this, he thought, 'Sāma here will not die alone in this forest. There must be some relatives: I'll ask him'. And he said this,

16. 'Where have you come from? Who did you leave behind,
    when you came to the Migasammatā River as a water carrier?'

[80] Sāma heard this and felt a great pang as blood poured out of his mouth.

17. 'My parents are blind, I look after them in the wild woods,
    For them I came to the Migasammatā River.'

When he had spoken he started to weep for his parents,

18. 'Their life is just an ember: blind, they'll die through lack of
    water, I suppose.

19. This [wound] is not too painful for me: this is to be expected
    for a man.
    But that I won't see my mother, that is more painful than this.

20. This [wound] is not too painful for me: this is to be expected
    for a man.
    But that I won't see my father, that is more painful than this.

21. My mother will cry throughout the night, wretched,
    In the middle of the night and at the end; like a river she
    will dry up.

22. My father will cry throughout the night, wretched,
    In the middle of the night and at the end; like a river he will
    dry up.

23. When they want their feet rubbing to get up and wander
    around.
    They'll cry out, 'Sāma' and roam in the wild woods.

24. It is this second arrow that pierces my heart;
    That I shall not see them, blind, and that I will not be alive.'

[81] The king listened to his lament and thought, 'This man, remaining holy in the teaching up to the end, supports his parents. He grieves for his misfortune on their account. This is the excellent man I have harmed. How can I comfort him? What use will a kingdom be when I am in hell? I'll look after his parents in the way he has done. His death will be deathless.' Making this resolution he spoke,

25. 'Do not grieve to excess, Sāma, the one who is beautiful to look at.
    I will be an attendant to your parents in the wild woods.
26. I am skilled in archery, strong in the bow and famous.
    I will be an attendant to your parents in the wild woods.
27. Searching for deer's leftovers, various roots and fruits from the woodland,
    I will be an attendant to your parents in the wild woods.
28. Which is the wood, Sāma, where your parents are?
    I'll look after them there, just as you have done.'

Then the Great Being said, 'Well done, great king; you look after them.' Saying this he showed the path,

29. 'This is the single track, king, where my head is pointing,
    Go from here; their dwelling is about half a mile away.[26]
    There are my parents; go and look after them.'

Indicating the way [82] to him, he felt such a powerful affection to his parents, that he experienced great pain. He offered the king an añjali and asked him again, saying

30. 'I pay homage to you, king of Kāsi,
    I pay homage to you, the luck of the Kāsis,[27]
    My parents are blind; please would you support them.
31. I offer an añjali to you, king of Kāsi,
    Convey the greetings to my parents that I have given to you.'

The king agreed and the Great Being, having sent his greetings to his parents, lapsed into unconsciousness.

Then the Teacher said this:

32. 'Saying this, the youth Sāma, beautiful to look at,
    fainted through the power of the poison and became unconscious.'

Until now he had spoken as if speaking on one out breath. Now, through the power of the poison, his speech, dependent on the continuity of his underlying consciousness, heart and bodily form, was distressed and cut short.[28] He closed his mouth, shut his eyes, and his hands and feet became stiff. His entire body was wet with blood. The king exclaimed, 'Just now he was talking with me; why has he held the in and out breaths? They have stopped; his body has become stiff; now Sāma has gone.' Unable to control his grief, he put both hands on his head and made a loud lament.

Then the Teacher spoke:

33. 'This king grieved with intense wretchedness;
    "I am going to get old and die! I did not know this before but now I do.

34. Seeing Sāma, who replied to me when afflicted with poison, dead,
    I know there is no return from death.

35. [83] Today, at his death, he did not utter any reproach to me.
    And now I will go to hell; there is no doubt about this in me.

36. For a long time they will speak in villages of the evil done then as a stain;
    and they will speak of the one who brought the stain.
    Who can speak to me in the forest, where there are no men?

37. In villages people come together and remind each other of crimes;
    Who will remind me in the forest, where there are no men?"'

Now, at that time a goddess, named Bahusodarī, lived in the Gandhamādana Mountains. She had been the Bodhisatta's mother seven lifetimes before this one. She always turned her mind with great affection towards her son. But on that day, while enjoying her heavenly good fortune, she did not turn her mind to him: actually people said that she had gone to a gathering of shining gods. At the moment he lapsed into unconsciousness however, she wondered how things were going with her son, and did see him. 'King Piliyakkha has wounded my son with a poisoned arrow! He lies on a sandbank on the shore of the Migasammatā River while the king makes a loud lament. If I do not go, my son Golden Sāma will perish. The king's heart will break and Sāma's parents will be without food, will not get any water and will die of thirst. If I go, though, the king will take a jug of water and go to Sāma's parents. They'll hear what he says, and [84] he'll lead them to their son. Then they and I will make a declaration of truth. This will dispel the poison and, in this way, my son will regain his life, his parents will regain their sight and the king will hear a *dhamma* talk from Sāma. He'll make a great act of generosity and become bound for a heavenly rebirth. So I'll go there.' She went to the shore of the Migasammatā River and, standing in the sky, unseen, she spoke to the king.

The Teacher explained the matter:

38. 'The goddess, invisible, above the Gandhamādana Mountains
    out of compassion for the king, spoke these words.

39. "The offence that you have committed, great king, is a serious
    crime.
    For with a single arrow you have killed three: the unhating
    parents and their son.

40. Go, and I'll train you so that there might be a happy destiny
    for you.
    Look after the blind ones in the wood, as is right,
    A happy destiny might, I think, then come your way."'

He heard the goddess's words and took confidence. 'It is said that if I look after the parents I'll go to heaven. What is a kingdom to me? I'll look after them.' He made a strong resolve and, giving vent to a great outpouring of grief, allayed his sorrow. Thinking that Sāma must be dead he honoured the body with various flowers, sprinkled it with water and walked around it three times. He paid homage at the four points, took the jar which had been blessed by him and, with a heavy heart, turned his face to the south.

The Teacher explained the matter:

41. 'After an outpouring of grief the king, filled with misery,
    took the water pot and went towards the south.'

[85] The king, by nature a man of great stamina, took the water jug and entered the hermitage as if breaking into it. He reached the door of wise Dukūlaka's hut. The wise man, sitting inside, heard the sound of his footstep. 'This is not the sound of Sāma's step: whose is it?' Asking, he spoke a double verse:

42. 'Is this the footstep of a human coming?
    It is not the sound of Sāma; who are you, sir?

43. Sāma walks softly, he places his feet softly;
    It is not the sound of Sāma; who are you, sir?'

When he heard this the king reflected, 'If I do not reveal to them my royal status and tell that that I have killed their son, they will be angry and speak bitterly to me. I will become angry with them and I might harm them. This would not be skilful for me. No one is unafraid when they hear the word "king" so I'll reveal my royal status.' He set the water jug down in the stand for it and waited at the door of the leaf hut.

44. 'I am the king of the Kāsis, known as Piliyakkha.
    Through desire I have left my kingdom and wander in search of deer.

45. I am skilled in archery, strong in the bow and famous.
    No elephant would escape me if he came in my arrow's range!'

The wise man made a friendly welcome and said,

46. 'Welcome to you, great king, and a very great welcome!
    You are a great lord to have come here.
47. The tiṇḍuk tree, the piyal tree, the honey tree and the
    kāsmarī:[29]
    Their fruits are few and small; but eat the best that there is.
48. This cool water has been brought from a mountain cave;
    drink from this, great king, if it is your wish.'

[86] After such a welcome the king thought that it would not be
right to say, in the first instance, that he had killed his son. He
decided to speak as if he did not know and then tell him. He said,

49. 'Blind, you cannot see in the woods, so who brought your
    fruit?
    Such a complete range of food must have come from someone
    with good sight.'

When he heard this the wise man explained to the king that
they had not fetched the various fruits but their son had done it
for them. He spoke two verses:

50. 'Our young son, Sāma, is not very tall but is very beautiful
    to look at.
    His long black hair curls like the tail of a dog.
51. He brings fruit and goes down to the river with a ewer to
    bring back water.
    I don't think he's far away.'

Then the king spoke.

52. 'I have killed your Sāma, who was a helper for you,
    the boy that you have described, Sāma, beautiful to look at.
53. His long black hair that then curled like the tail of a dog:

he lies now with this smeared in blood: Sāma has been killed by me.'

Not far from the wise man was Pārikā's leaf hut. She was sitting there listening to the king's words. Wanting to know what had happened [87] she left it, feeling her way with a rope, went near to Dukūlaka and said,

54. 'Tell me, Dukūlaka, who is this saying that Sāma has been killed?
    When I heard the words, "Sāma has been killed" it pierced my heart.

55. Just a tender shoot from a bodhi tree, a young branch fanned by the breeze:
    When I heard the words, "Sāma has been killed" it pierced my heart.'

Then the wise man admonished her,

56. 'This is the king of Kāsi, Pārikā.
    He shot an arrow in anger at Sāma, in the Migasammatā Mountains.
    Do not wish evil to him.'

Pārikā said,

57. 'With difficulty! A dear son is taken,
    who looked after the blind in the forest.
    How can my heart not be angry
    towards the murderer of an only son?'

Dukūlaka spoke:

58. 'With difficulty! A dear son is taken,
    who looked after the blind in the forest.
    But wise men teach lack of anger,
    even towards the murderer of an only son.'

Saying this both beat their breasts with their hands and praised the virtues of the Great Being, grieving with great passion. Then the king comforted them.

59. 'Do not grieve excessively with the words, "Sāma is killed!"
    I will be your servant and look after you in the wild wood.
60. I am skilled in archery, strong in the bow and famous.
    I will be your servant and look after you in the wild wood.
61. Searching for the leavings of deer and roots and fruits from the woodland,
    I will be your servant and look after you in the wild wood.'

[88] Conversing with him they said,

62. 'But it is not right, great king, it is not suitable for you.
    You are our king; we pay homage at your feet.'

When he heard this the king was greatly relieved. 'This is wonderful: there is not the slightest harsh speech towards me, the one who has done the harm. They give me welcome.' Thinking this, he spoke this verse,

63. 'You have spoken the *dhamma*, hunter, and have given great honour.
    You are my father; and you, Pārikā are my mother.'

They offered an añjali and made a request to the king. 'Great king, there is nothing that needs doing for us, but please take a staff and, guiding us, show us Sāma.' And they spoke two verses:

64. 'Homage to you, king of Kāsi, homage to the luck of the Kāsis.
    We offer you an añjali in the hope that you will lead us to Sāma.
65. Falling at the feet of the one whose face is beautiful to look at,
    Beating our breasts, we will go to our death.'

[89] As they were talking the sun went down. Then the king

considered, 'If I take them there now and they see him, it will break their hearts; then it will be the death of three people and I will go to the lowest hell. So I won't show them.' He spoke four verses:

66–9. 'He's to be seen at the end of the sky: a wild region, filled with beasts of prey:
That is where Sāma lies, killed, as if the moon had fallen to the ground.
That is where Sāma lies, killed, as if the sun had fallen to the ground.
That is where Sāma lies, killed, covered with blood.
He's to be seen at the end of the sky: a wild region, filled with beasts of prey:
That is where Sāma lies, killed; stay in your hermitage.'[37]

They then spoke a verse, to show that they had had no terror of wild beasts and suchlike.

70. 'Even if a hundred, thousand or a myriad of wild beasts were there,
what could cause us harm in the forest?'

The king, unable to dissuade them, took their hands and led them there.

In explanation the Teacher said,

71. 'Then the king of Kasi took the hands of the blind ones in the wild wood
and went to the place where Sāma had been killed.'

[90] Leading them near him he stopped and said, 'This is your son'. His father took the head, his mother the feet and they sat down and wept.

In explanation the Teacher said,

72–5. 'Perceiving their son Sāma, fallen, covered with blood,

Abandoned in the wild forest, as if the moon had fallen
to the ground.
Abandoned in the wild forest, as if the sun had fallen to
the ground.
Perceiving him abandoned in the wild forest, they grieved
with great passion.
Perceiving their son Sāma, fallen, covered with blood,
They stretched out their arms and cried, "Sir, it is not right!"

76–81. "Sāma, the beautiful one, are you asleep?
You who went to your death in this way, have you
nothing to say?
Sāma, the beautiful one, are you deeply intoxicated?
Sāma, the beautiful one, are you deeply indifferent?
Sāma, the beautiful one, are you deeply angry?
Sāma, the beautiful one, are you deeply arrogant?
Sāma, the beautiful one, are you deeply distracted?
You who went to your death in this way, have you
nothing to say?

82–5. Now, who will arrange our matted hair?
Sāma, the one who helps the blind, is dead.
Who will sweep the hermitage with a broom?
Sāma, the one who helps the blind, is dead.
Who now will wash us with both cool and heated water?
Sāma, the one who helps the blind, is dead.
Who will feed us with different roots and fruit?
Sāma, the one who helps the blind, is dead!"'

[91] When his mother had wept copiously, she hit her breast with
her hand and reflected on her torment. 'This is just grief for my
son. Through the power of the poison he might have entered into
an unconscious state. I'll make a declaration of truth.'

In explanation the Teacher said,

86–93. 'Seeing her son Sāma lying covered with blood,
         the grieving mother, in pain, spoke the truth.

Pārikā's declaration of truth

"Sāma lived rightly in the past:
By this truth may the poison in him be destroyed!
Sāma lived as a Brahma in the past:
By this truth may the poison in him be destroyed!
Sāma spoke the truth in the past:
By this truth may the poison in him be destroyed!
Sāma looked after his parents in the past;
By this truth may the poison in him be destroyed!
Sāma respected the elders in his family:
By this truth may the poison in him be destroyed!
Sāma was dearer to me than life:
By this truth may the poison in him be destroyed!
Whatever good thing I or his father have ever done:
By all this good may the poison in Sāma be destroyed."'

[92] And when his mother had delivered her seven verses in this way, her statement of truth, Sāma turned around and lay on the other side. His father said, 'My son lives. I will make a declaration of truth'. And he also made one.

In explanation the Teacher said,

94–101. 'Perceiving his son, Sāma, lying covered with blood,
          the grieving father, in pain, spoke the truth.

Dukūlaka's declaration of truth

"Sāma lived rightly in the past
[as above]

Whatever good thing I or his mother have ever done;
By all this good may the poison in Sāma be destroyed.'"

And when he had done this Sāma turned around again and lay on the other side. And then the goddess made her declaration. In explanation the Teacher said,

102–5. 'The goddess, unseen in the Gandahmādana Mountains,
Out of compassion for Sāma, spoke this truth:

The goddess's declaration of truth

"I have lived in the Gandhamādana Mountains for a long time.
There exists no one else dearer to me than Sāma:
By this truth may the poison in him be destroyed.
All the trees in the Gandhāmadana Mountains have a perfume;
By this truth may the poison in him be destroyed."
And while they wept with great feeling,
Quickly Sāma rose up, young and handsome.'

The Great Being's recovery, the restoration of his mother's and his father's sight and the first break of day: by the power of the goddess all of these four things were revealed in the hermitage in a single moment.

[93] The parents were still more delighted and exclaimed, 'We have found our vision and Sāma is cured.' And then wise Sāma delivered these verses:

106. 'I am Sāma, your dear one, and I have arisen safely.
Do not grieve greatly, but speak sweetly to me.

107. Welcome to you, great king, and a very great welcome!
You are a great lord to have come here.

108. The tiṇḍuk tree, the piyal tree, the honey tree and the kāsmarī:
     Their fruits are few and small; but eat the best that there is.
109. This cool water has been brought from a mountain cave;
     drink from this, great king, if it is your wish.'[31]

The king saw this wonderful thing and said,

110. 'I am dazed and amazed. All directions bemuse me.
     I saw you, Sāma, a ghost, who is now, Sāma, alive.'

Sāma said, 'This king called me dead. I will show to him the nature of non-dying.'

111. 'Great king, even a living man, who has a strong pain:
     they think him dead while living, when mental activity has stopped.[32]
112. Great king, even someone living, who has a strong pain:
     they think him dead while living, when he has gone to cessation.'[33]

He pointed out that the world considered him dead, even though he was alive. Wanting to teach the matter properly to the king, he spoke two more verses:

113. [94] 'The man who looks after his parents according to what is right:
     even the gods cure the one who supports his parents.
114. The man who looks after his parents according to what is right:
     in this world they praise him and, later, he delights in the heavens.'

When he heard this the king thought, 'This is a marvel. Even the gods cure the disease that arises in the one who looks after his parents. Sāma is greatly radiant. 'Offering an añjali, he said:

115. 'I am still more amazed. All directions bemuse me.
I go for refuge in you, Sāma,
You are my refuge.'

And then the Great Being said, 'If, great king, you want to go
to a heavenly realm and wish to enjoy divine happiness, observe
these ten just practices.' And he delivered ten verses on living well.

Ten ways of living well

116–25. 'Do what is right, great warrior king, for your parents.
Doing this, you will go to heaven, O king.
Do what is right, great warrior king, for your children.
Doing this, you will go to heaven, O king.
Do what is right, great warrior king, for your friends
and ministers.
Doing this, you will go to heaven, O king.
Do what is right, great warrior king, for your strong
pulling animals.
Doing this, you will go to heaven, O king.
Do what is right, great warrior king, for the villages
and towns,
Doing this, you will go to heaven, O king.
Do what is right, great warrior king, for the rural
people in the kingdom,
Doing this, you will go to heaven, O king.
Do what is right, great warrior king, for ascetics and
brahmins,
Doing this, you will go to heaven, O king.
Do what is right, great warrior king, for animals and
birds,
Doing this, you will go to heaven, O king.

> Do what is right, great warrior king and, acting in
> justice, bring happiness.
> Do what is right, great king, and with the shining gods
> and Brahmas,
> You will find heaven, through acting well.
> Do not, O king, neglect your duty!'

[95] When he had spoken in this way he taught the ten duties of
a king, advised him further and gave him the five precepts. The
king accepted the admonishment by prostrating with his head,
went to Vārāṇasi and did things to bring good fortune, such as
being generous and the like, and he was one that was bound for
a heaven world. The Bodhisatta attained to the higher knowledges
and the meditative attainments while with his parents, and was
reborn in a Brahma realm.

The Teacher delivered this *dhamma* talk: 'Bhikkhus, looking
after parents, this is the family tradition of the wise.' As he said
this he explained the four noble truths and, at the completion of
his talk, one monk attained to stream-entry. 'At that time, Ānanda
was the king, Uppalavaṇṇā was the goddess, Anuruddha was
king Sakka, Kassapa was the father and Bhaddākapilāni was
the mother. I was Golden Sāma.'[34]

Notes

[1] See, for instance, S. Leksukhum, *Temples of Gold*, pp. 139–42.
Caroline Rhys Davids has translated an abbreviated version of this
story in C. Rhys Davids, *The Stories of the Buddha, being Selections
from the Jātaka* (London: Chapman and Hall, 1929), pp. 206–19. As
Winternitz points out, there is a comparable story in *Rāmāyaṇa*, II, 63,
25ff (see *History of Indian Literature*, pp. 142–4).

[2] See S.I. Pollock, R.P. Goldman ed., *The Rāmāyaṇa of Vālmīki;
An Epic of Ancient India* (Princeton, New York: Princeton University
Press, 1986), Vol. II, 57–8, pp. 207–11. The story has interesting variations

from the Jātaka. The man is shot inadvertently, in the dark; he does not recover and both the victim and the parents reproach Dasaratha bitterly for what he has done.

3 In one famous story in the *Mahābhārata* Damayantī recognizes her husband Nala from among gods who look like him, partly because he sweats (*Mahābhārata*, III 53 1).

4 For the dangers of hatred, the 'far enemy' of loving kindness, see *Path of Purification*, pp. 321–33 (Vism IX 1–50). Also, see p. 344 (Vism IX 93): 'It (*mettā*) succeeds when it makes ill will subside, and it fails when it produces (selfish) affection.'

5 The fourth *jhāna* and the higher meditations are characterized by the absence of in and out breath. See *Path of Purification*, p. 305 (Vism VIII 209). *Saṃkappa*, the word used for the second factor of the eightfold path, is in *abhidhammic* thought associated with initial thought, which is dropped in all meditations after the first *jhāna*.

6 The preliminaries and practice of the first four *jhāna*s are described in *Path of Purification*, pp. 122–75 (Vism XII).

7 His use of the word *nirodha*, usually associated with *nibbāna*, is odd, as he is not yet enlightened. He is perhaps making a more general comment, not applicable to himself, or means, more generally, an advanced stage of meditation.

8 In Candakiṇṇara Jātaka (485), Rāhulamātā in an earlier birth revives the Bodhisatta through the intervention of Sakka and her declarations of love. These withdraw the effect of the poison but, like here, it does not seem to be the case that he is dead, just dying (J IV 282–8).

9 *Lobhā*, v. 4 and v. 15. This is desire or greed, the 'near enemy' of loving kindness (*Path of Purification*, p. 345, Vism IX 98).

10 See Leksukhum, ibid.

11 See Winternitz, *History of Indian Literature*, II, p.144, n. 1.

12 *Vipassanaṃ*: insight meditation.

13 *Upanissayaṃ*: literally, 'strong supporting condition'. This is the ninth condition in the twenty-four *paccayas*, or causal relationships. It denotes the condition whereby someone is ready to experience a change of state or insight, but needs the right circumstances, such as contact with a person, food or climactic conditions, for this to occur.

[14] See S I 181. In this short *sutta* a lay brahmin approaches the Buddha and asks if he is acting correctly by begging for food for his parents; the Buddha says that he is.

[15] Used for collecting alms. The ticket entitled him to the ticket food and gruel.

[16] This (*bhikkhuparājikaṃ*) refers to the grave offences performed by monks that warrant immediate exclusion from the order. This means here the offence of taking what is not given: he feels that having achieved so little in twelve years he had not deserved the alms food he had received.

[17] PED 384: *Dukūla*, fine woven cloth or silk.

[18] Vissakamma is the builder and designer for the gods (see DPPN II 906-7).

[19] Literally, 'even the animals received the consciousness associated with loving kindness' (*mettacittam eva paṭilabhiṃsu*). The idea is that loving kindness is contagious.

[20] I have made Dukūlaka the subject of this and the next sentence as the scribe seems to have got in a muddle here by referring to the Great Being, who has not yet appeared in the story at all. Dukūlaka is not the Bodhisatta; his son-to-be is.

[21] A kinnara is a mythical creature, half-bird and half-human. Their officiation reinforces the sense of the unworldly about the birth.

[22] The Burmese manuscript (Bd) says *te kira pubbe vajjakūle ahesuṃ*: 'it is said that formerly they were in a doctor's family', which I have taken to mean that he was a doctor and she was his wife.

[23] See Jātaka 55 which also describes five weapons.

[24] I have followed Margaret Cone, with a Burmese manuscript here (Bd), to read *anavasumbhitvā* ('not upsetting') for *anusumbhitvā* in the PTS text (see DP I 101).

[25] The commentary explains that he was cultivating loving kindness and so at that moment was careless (*pamattaṃ*) and without mindfulness (*sati*). The first word has pejorative associations: it is in the first verse of the story and there appears to be an implied criticism of the practice of loving kindness without the development of mindfulness (*sati*), which has to be re-established after the attack.

[26] *Aḍḍhakosa* is equal to half a measure of five hundred bow lengths.

27 Literally 'the one who increases the Kāsis'.

28 The continuity of the stream of underlying consciousness (*bhavaṅga*) is the resultant skilful *citta* that forms the basis of all human birth. It is the passive, radiant state to which the mind turns in deep sleep and at the completion of any given thought process (see R. Gethin, *Foundations of Buddhism*, pp. 215–16 and *Atthasālinī*, p. 279). At its ceasing, life is over. Sāma's 'death' is described with carefully observed detail and, as sometimes happens in Jātakas, with an *abhidhammic* formulation of the process of events. The *bhavaṅga* consciousness seems to be described as cut short. The way that the king expresses incredulity over the next few lines, observing the loss of apparent consciousness of the world and the ceasing of the in and out breath, prepares the way for Sāma's explanation of what has happened at the end of the story.

29 Tinduk, *Diospyros embryopteris*; piyāl, *Buchanania latifolia*; madhuka; (honey tree), *Bassia latifolia* and kāsmarī, *Gmelina arborea*.

30 As in the previous story (539), this and subsequent verse sequences make extensive use of repetition. While this technique is particularly suited to chanted performances, it is less effective in a story read to oneself. The first line of verse 66 is repeated for each verse; I have just put it in the first and the last verse to convey something of the repetitive effect. For verses 72–5 the same technique has been used. The first line, which should introduce each verse, is included only the first time it is used and the last (vv. 72 and 75). For verses 76–81 the second line is repeated in the original after each question. Again it has been included only in the first and last verse in the sequence. This is a compromise, but is better than leaving out whole sections, which the Cowell and Rhys Davids translations do. I think the repetitions would work well, in full, for reading out loud.

31 Sāma's verses are the same as the words of welcome given by his parents to the king in verses 46–8, one of many verbal echoes within the verses which betray underlying affinity of character.

32 Reading *saṃkappaṃ* with Cks. This word for thought is sometimes associated with initial thought (*vitakka*), the first factor of the first meditation which is dropped in subsequent *jhānas* (DhS 21). This line could mean that thought has stopped, as in meditation. Was

Sāma really dead? It appears not, though whether he was simply unconscious or had attained a profound meditative state is unclear.

33 The commentary takes this to mean that the Great Being is describing a state where there is no in or out breath, known here as cessation (nirodha). This state is usually associated with the attainment of nibbāna (PED 371). The Bodhisatta could not have entered nibbāna, as he has postponed his attainment of the path. He could be making more general comment on such states, hinting that he has been in meditation.

34 Ānanda, the Buddha's companion in the Bodhisatta's last life, features in many Jātakas. Uppalavaṇṇā, famed for her meditative ability and psychic powers, was the goddess of the white parasol in the Mūgapakkha Jātaka (538). Mahākassapa has not been a character in any of the other stories in this collection but features in some other Jātakas, such as the Saṃkhapāla Jātaka (524), the Cullasutosoma Jātaka (525) and the Mahāsutasoma Jātaka (537). In his last life he is one of the chief disciples of the Buddha, famous for his love of great asceticism and the kind of rural existence described in this story. He was chief amongst those who upheld niceties of form (A I 23). In his last life he entered into a marriage like the one described in this story, to the same woman, now called Bhaddākapilānī. They spent the wedding night separated by a chain of flowers and finally joined the order separately; both became enlightened (see DPPN II 476–83). Mahākassapa lived to be one hundred twenty years old. Bhaddākapilānī was Kassapa's wife for many rebirths and was described by the Buddha as foremost amongst the nuns who could recollect past lives (see DPPN II 354–5).

Further reading and bibliography

The text used, Jātaka, was established and transliterated in Roman script at the end of the nineteenth century in an edition still available from the Pāli Text Society (PTS): V. Fausbøll ed., *The Jātaka together with its Commentary*, 7 vols (London, 1877–96). Volume I begins with the *Jātakanidāna*, a separate work which includes the Bodhisatta vow, the search for the perfections and the life story of the Buddha. A recent Burmese version of the entire Pāli canon, called the *Chaṭṭha Saṅgāyana*, is now out on CD ROM (VRI). The disc is free and may be obtained from Vipassana Research Institute, Dhammagiri, Igatpuri 422 403, Dist. Nasik, India. See www.tipitaka.org.

Jātaka translations

E.B. Cowell ed., *The Jātaka or Stories of the Buddha's Former Births*, 6 vols (Cambridge: Cambridge University Press, 1895–1907 and index 1913). All reprinted by Pali Text Society in 3 volumes, 1990.

H.T. Francis and E.J. Thomas, *Jātaka Tales* (Cambridge: Cambridge University Press, 1916). Contains 114 tales.

C.A.F. Rhys Davids, *The Stories of the Buddha, being Selections from the Jātaka* (London: Chapman and Hall, 1929).

There has been one recent translation, M. Cone and R. Gombrich, *The Perfect Generosity of Prince Vessantara* (Oxford: OUP, 1977).

Jātakanidāna (Introduction to the Jātakas)

N.A. Jayawickrama, *The Story of Gotama Buddha* (Oxford: PTS, 1990) is used in this collection.

T.W. Rhys Davids, *Buddhist Birth Stories* (London: Trubner and Co., 1880). Translation of *Jātakanidāna* and a few stories.

Retellings

The stories are commonly told to children in Buddhist countries and a number of monasteries give shortened retellings which can be found just by typing the word 'Jātaka' into a search engine. There is, however, a curious dearth of full modern translations of the tales.

Pāli canon

The PTS keep most of their canonical translations in print. Editions of texts from the Pāli canon can be ordered from the Pāli Text Society, 73, Lime Walk, Headington, Oxford, OX3 7AD, UK. Email: pts@palitext.demon.co.uk. Their catalogue, available on request, is invaluable as a short introduction to the range of texts available. All Pāli texts used are PTS editions and referenced simply by name of text or abbreviation in notes.

How to look up references in Pāli Buddhist translations

As there are now sometimes two good translations for some of the collections I have given the PTS Pāli text in references. For those new to Pāli and early Buddhist studies this need not pose a problem for further research if the list of usual abbreviations, given here, is used to match the original with any translations available. So M I 36 means *Majjhimanikāya*, volume I, page 36. This may be found by taking the *Middle Length Discourses of the Buddha* (PTS/Wisdom trans.) and looking for this reference in the top right-hand corner of the left page or the top left-hand corner of the right page. In this case it is on pages 117–18. The page reference of the original is also given in square brackets within the text of the translation. If *The Middle Length Sayings* (PTS) translation is to hand, the same method is used, though you need the right volume, in this case volume I. For those texts which are entirely in verse form, reference is made to the verse number: so Sn 45 means *Suttanipāta*, or *Group of Discourses*, verse 45. For those who wish to look up a single *sutta*, good translations can now be found on the Internet, by typing the name of the *sutta* into the search engine. I found three translations of the *Makhādeva Sutta*, a counterpart to Jātaka 9, in this way.

All Pāli texts are PTS. Below is a list of all texts mentioned in this collection, with the title of some translations under each. The PTS translations are all still available, often as reprints.

Aṅguttaranikāya (A)
F.L. Woodward (Vols II and IV) and E.M. Hare (Vols I, III and V), *Gradual Sayings of the Buddha* (London: PTS, 1885–1910).

Atthasālinī
Pe Maung Tin, *The Expositor*, 2 vols (London: PTS, 1910).

Cariyāpiṭaka (Cp)
I.B. Horner, *Basket of Conduct, Minor Anthologies* (London: PTS and Routledge and Kegan Paul, 1975), III.

Dhammasaṅgaṇi (Dhs)
C.A.F. Rhys Davids, *Buddhist Psychological Ethics* (London: PTS, 1900).

Dhammapada
K.R. Norman, *The Word of the Doctrine* (Oxford: PTS, 1997).

Dīghanikāya (D)
T.W. Rhys Davids, *Dialogues of the Buddha*, 3 vols (London: PTS, 1899–1921) and M. Walshe, *Thus Have I Heard: The Long Discourses of the Buddha* (London: Wisdom, 1987).

Majjhimanikāya (M)
I.B. Horner, *The Middle Length Sayings*, 3 vols (London: PTS, 1957–9).
Bhikkhu Ñāṇamoli and Bhikkhu Bodhi, *The Middle Length Discourses of the Buddha* (Boston: Wisdom Books/PTS, rev. ed., 2001).
The Pātimokkha, W. Pruitt, ed., K.R. Norman, trans. (Oxford: PTS, 2001).

Paṭisambhidāmagga
Bhikkhu Ñāṇamoli, *The Path of Discrimination* (Oxford: PTS, 1991).

Saṃyuttanikāya (S)

Bhikkhu Bodhi, *Connected Discourses of the Buddha* (Oxford: PTS/ Wisdom, 2000).

C.A.F. Rhys Davids (Vols I and II) and F.L. Woodward (Vols III, IV and V) *The Book of the Kindred Sayings*, 5 vols (London: PTS, 1917– 30).

Suttanipāta (Sn)

K.R. Norman, *Group of Discourses* (Oxford: PTS, 1995).

Therīgāthā

C.A.F. Rhys Davids and K.R. Norman, *Poems of Early Buddhist Nuns* (*Therīgāthā*), revised joint reprint with section of *Elders' Verses* (Oxford: PTS, 1989).

Vibhaṅga

Vinaya piṭaka (Vin)

I.B. Horner, *The Book of Discipline*, 6 vols (Oxford, 1938–66). Rules for monks and nuns along with incidents which prompted their institution.

Other related texts

Āryaśūra: P. Khoroche trans., with foreword by W.Doniger, *Once the Buddha was a Monkey: Ārya Śūra's Jātakamālā* (Chicago: University of Chicago Press, 1989).

Āryaśūra: J.S. Speyer trans. and ed., *Jātakamālā: Garland of Birth Stories of Āryaśūra*, Sacred Books of the Buddhists, (London, 1895), I.

Bhikkhu Bodhi, trans., 'A Treatise on the Pāramīs', translation of the *Cariyāpiṭaka Aṭṭhakathā*, in *The Discourse on the All-Embracing Net of Views: The Brahmajāla Sutta and Its Commentaries* (Kandy: BPS, 1978), 242–317. This is the most comprehensive commentarial discussion on the ten perfections.

Buddhaghosa: Bhikkhu Ñāṇamoli trans., *The Path of Purification (Visuddhimagga)*, 2 vols (Berkeley: Shambala, 1976). This commentarial meditation manual is still in constant use in South-East Asian countries. It lists and gives instructions for 40 *samatha* (calm) meditation subjects, many of which are mentioned in Jātakas:

10 *kasiṇa*; recollections of Buddha, *dhamma* and *saṅgha*, 4 divine abidings (*brahmavihāra*). Pāli text abbreviated to Vism.

Sally Mellick Cutler, 'A Critical Edition, with translation, of selected portions of the Pāli *Apadāna*', D. Phil., Oxford, 1993.

P.S. Jaini trans., *Apocryphal Birth Stories: Paññāsa Jātaka*, 2 vols, (London: PTS, 1985–98). Some non-canonical Jātakas, now popular in Thailand.

P. Olivelle, *The Pañcatantra, The Book of India's Folk Wisdom* (Oxford: OUP, 1997).

Śantideva: S. Batchelor trans., *A Guide to the Bodhisattva's Way of Life* (Dharamasala: Library of Tibetan Works and Archives, 1979). Mahāyāna interpretation of the perfections and Bodhisatta path.

Śantideva: K. Crosby and A. Skilton trans., P. Williams intro., *Bodhicaryāvatāra* (Oxford: OUP, 1996).

Dictionaries

M. Cone, *Dictionary of Pāli* (DP), part I, A–Kh (Oxford: PTS, 2001).

F. Edgerton, *Buddhist Hybrid Sanskrit: Grammar and Dictionary*, 2 vols (Delhi: Motilal Banarsidass, 1953), Vol. II.

Sir M. Monier-Williams, *Sanskrit–English Dictionary* (Oxford: OUP, 1899).

T.W. Rhys Davids and W. Stede, *Pāli–English Dictionary* (PED), (Oxford: PTS, 1999; first published 1921–5).

Begun by V. Treckner, revised, continued and edited by D. Andersen, *Critical Pāli Dictionary* (CPD), 2 vols (Copenhagen: Royal Danish Academy of Letters and Sciences, 1924–48).

Works of reference

L. Grey, *A Concordance of Buddhist Birth Stories* (Oxford: PTS, 2000). Gives each story, short summary of its action and list of publications concerning it. It is particularly useful in tracing influences and similarities with tales in other cultures. It assigns Folk Index motif where appropriate.

G.P. Malalasekara, *Dictionary of Pāli Proper Names*, 2 vols (London: PTS, 1974; first published 1938).

S. Thompson, *Motif Index of Folk Literature:* a classification of narrative elements in folk tales, ballads, myths, fables, mediaeval romances, exempla, fabliaux, jest-books and local legends, 6 vols (Bloomington: Indiana University Press, 1957). A monumental work although rather weak on Indian and Asian material. Its attempt to classify tales under motif headings is always thought-provoking and provides surprising cross-cultural parallels.

S. Thompson and J. Balys, *The Oral Tales of India* (Bloomington, Indiana: IUP, 1958).

M. Yamasaki and Y. Ousaka, *Index to the Jātakas* (Oxford: PTS, 2003). Computer generated index of all words used in Jātakas; an important addition to Pāli studies.

Bibliography

D.C. Ahir ed., *The Influence of Jātakas on Art and Literature* (New Delhi: BR Publishing Company, 2000).

C. Allen, *The Buddha and the Sahibs: the men who discovered India's lost religion* (London: John Murray, 2002).

L. Alsdorf, *Śaśa-Jātaka und Śaśa-Avadāna*, wiener Zeitschrift für die Kunde Süd-und Ostasiens (Wien, 1961).

A.L. Basham, *The Wonder that was India* (revised edn., London: Sidgwick and Jackson, 1967).

K.R. Blackstone, *Women in the Footsteps of the Buddha: Struggle for Liberation in the Therīgāthā* (Richmond, Surrey: Curzon, 1998).

Bhikkhu Bodhi, *Dāna: the Practice of Giving; selected essays* (Kandy: BPS, 1990).

J. Bronkhorst, *The Two Traditions of Meditation in Ancient India* (New Delhi: Motilal, 1993).

S. Buddhasukh trans.,*The Venerable Phra Acharn Mun Bhūridatta Thera, meditation master* (Bangkok: Mahamakut Rajavidyalaya Press, 1976).

G. Bühnemann, *The Iconography of Hindu Tantric Deities*, 2 vols (Groningen, 2000–1).

R.F. Burton, *The Book of the Thousand Nights and a Night*, 12 vols (London: H.S. Nicholl, 1885).

J. Bunyan, Introduction and Notes W.R. Jones, *The Pilgrim's Progress* (Oxford: OUP, 2003).

K. Chaitanya, 'The Beast Fable', *A New History of Sanskrit Literature* (London and Bombay: Asia Publishing House, 1962).

W.A. Clouston, *Popular Tales and Fictions, their Migrations and Transformations*, 2 vols (Edinburgh and London: Blackwood, 1887).

N. Coghill trans., G. Chaucer, *Canterbury Tales* (Harmondsworth: Penguin, 1951, rept, 2001).

S. Collins, *Selfless Persons: Imagery and Thought in Theravada Buddhism* (Cambridge: CUP, 1982).

——, *Nirvana and other Buddhist Felicities: Utopias of the Pali Imaginaire* (Cambridge: CUP, 1998).

M. Cone and R.F. Gombrich, *The Perfect Generosity of Prince Vessantara: A Buddhist epic translated from the Pali and illustrated by unpublished paintings from Sinhalese temples* (Oxford: OUP, 1977).

A.K. Coomaraswamy, *Mediaeval Sinhalese Art* (New York: Pantheon, 1956).

L.S. Cousins, 'Pāli Oral Literature', in P. Denwood and A. Piatigorski eds, *Buddhist Studies: Ancient and Modern* (London: Curzon, 1983), 1–11.

——, 'Buddhist *Jhāna*, its nature and attainment according to the Pāli sources', *Religion*, 3 (1973), pp, 115–31.

——, *Samatha-Yāna* and *Vipassanā-Yāna*, G. Dhammapala et al. eds, *Buddhist Studies in honour of Hammalava Saddhātissa* (Nugegoda: Hammalava Saddhatissa Felicitation Volume Committee, 1984), pp. 56–68.

——, 'Good or Skilful? *Kusala* in Canon and Commentary', *Journal of Buddhist Ethics*, Vol. 3, 1996, pp. 136–64.

Sir A. Cunningham, *The Stūpa at Bharhut* (London: Allen and Co., 1879).

S. Cutler Mellick, 'The Pāli Apadāna Collection', *Journal of the Pali Text Society*, XX (1994), pp. 1–42.

A. Dante, *La Divina Commedia: Inferno* (Milan: Biblioteca universale, 1949).

_____, Introduction and Notes D. Higgins, 'Inferno' in *The Divine Comedy* (Oxford: OUP, 1993).

W. Doniger O'Flaherty and S. Kakar, *Vatsayana Mallanaga: Kamasutra; A new, complete translation of the Sanskrit text* (Oxford: OUP, 2002).

W. Doniger O'Flaherty and B.K. Smith, *The Laws of Manu* (Harmondsworth: Penguin, 1991).

P. Dundas, *The Jains* (London: Routledge, 2002).

M.L. Feer, *A Study of the Jātakas*, trans. of *Etudes Bouddhiques: Les Jātakas, Journal Asiatique*, May–Sept 1875 (Calcutta: Susil Gupta, 1963).

J. Garrett Jones, *Tales and Teachings of the Buddha: the Jātaka Stories in Relation to the Pāli Canon* (London: Allen and Unwin, 1979).

W. Geiger, B. Ghosh trans., *Pāli Language and Literature* (New Delhi: Oriental Books Reprint Corporation, 3rd reprint, 1978).

R. Gethin, 'The Mātikās: Memorization, Mindfulness and the List', in J. Ggyatso ed., *Reflections on Mindfulness and Remembrance in Indian and Tibetan Buddhism* (New York: Albany State University Press, 1992), pp. 149–72.

_____, *The Foundations of Buddhism* (Oxford: OUP, 1998).

R.F. Gombrich, *How Buddhism Began: the conditioned genesis of the early teachings*, (London: Athlone, 1996).

_____, *Theravada Buddhism, A Social History from Ancient Benares to Modern Columbo* (London: Routledge, 1988).

R.F. Gombrich and G. Obeyesekare, *Buddhism Transformed: Religion and change in Sri Lanka* (Princeton: Princeton University Press, 1988).

R. Graves, ed., *New Larousse Encyclopedia of Mythology* (London: Hamlyn, 1983).

S. Hamilton, *Identity and Experience: the constitution of the human being according to early Buddhism* (London: Luzac, 1996).

_____, *Early Buddhism: a new approach, the I of the beholder* (Richmond, Surrey: Curzon, 2000).

D.V.J. Harishchandra, Foreword by D.N. Atukorala, *Psychiatric Aspects of Jataka Stories* (Galle: Upuli Offset Printers, 1998).

J.C. Harris, 'The Wonderful Tar Baby', *Uncle Remus and His Legends of the Old Plantation* (London: Routledge and Co., 1881).

P. Harvey, *An Introduction to Buddhism: Teachings, History and Practice* (Cambridge: CUP, 1990).

O. von Hinüber, *A Handbook of Pāli Literature* (Berlin: Walter de Gruyter, 1996).

C.H. Holt, *The Religious World of Kīrti Śrī, Buddhism, Art and Politics in Late Medieval Sri Lanka* (Oxford: OUP, 1996).

J. Jacobs, *History of the Aesopic Fable*, Vol. I of *Fables of Aesop* in 2 vols (London: Nutt, 1889).

J. Keay, *India, a History* (London: HarperCollins, 2000).

D. Keown, *Buddhism, a Very Short Introduction* (Oxford: OUP, 1996).

R. Kipling, *The Writings in Prose and Verse of Rudyard Kipling*, 27 vols (London: Macmillan, 1897–1910).

K.K. Klaustermaier, *Buddhism: A short introduction* (Oxford: Oneworld, 1999).

R. Kloppenborg, *The Paccekabuddha: a Buddhist Ascetic. A study of the concept of paccekabuddhas in Pāli canonical and commentarial literature* (Lieden: Brill, 1974).

B.C. Law, *Heaven and Hell in Buddhist Perspective* (Delhi: Pilgrim Books, 1998).

S. Leksukhum, with photos by G.Mermet, 'The Ten Great Jātakas', *Temples of Gold: Seven Centuries of Thai Buddhist Paintings* (London: Thames and Hudson, 2001).

J. Manne, 'Case histories from the Pāli Canon: the *Sāmaññaphala Sutta*, hypothetical case history, or how to be sure to win a debate', *Journal of the Pali Text Society*, XXI (1995), pp. 1–34.

B. Moon, 'The Pearl', in Mircea Eliade ed., *The Encyclopedia of Religion* (London: Macmillan, 1987) II, pp. 224–5.

S. Murcott, *The First Buddhist Women: Translation and Commentary of the Therīgāthā* (Berkeley: Parallax, 1991).

K.R. Norman, *Pāli Literature, including the Canonical Literature in Prakrit and Sanskrit of All the Hīnayāna Schools of Buddhism* (Wiesbaden: Harrassowitz, 1983).

——, 'The Pratyeka-Buddha in Buddhism and Jainism', *Selected Papers*, Vol. II (Oxford: PTS, 1991), pp. 233–49.

Nyanaponika Thera and H. Hecker, Bhikkhu Bodhi ed. *Great Disciples of the Buddha: Their Lives, Their Works, Their Legacy* (Boston and Kandy: Wisdom/BPS, 1997).

T. Oberlies, 'A Study of the Campeyya Jātaka. Including Remarks on the Text of the Saṅkhapāla Jātaka', *Journal of the Pali Text Society*, XXVII (2002), pp. 115–46.

Anant Pai, *Jātaka Stories*, Amar Chitra Katha, 1003 (India Book House).

S. I. Pollock, R.P. Goldman ed., *The Rāmāyaṇa of Vālmīki: An Epic of Ancient India* (Princeton, New York: Princeton University Press, 1986).

W. Rahula, 'Humour in Pāli Literature', *Journal of the Pali Text Society*, IX (1981), pp. 156–74.

____, *What the Buddha Taught* (Oxford: Oneworld, 1997; first published 1959).

H.P. Ray, *The Archaeology of Seafaring in Ancient South Asia* (Cambridge: CUP, 2003).

A. Schimmel, *The Mystery of Numbers* (New York and Oxford: Oxford University Press, 1993).

A. Seneviratna, *King Aśoka and Buddhism: Historical and Literary Studies* (Kandy: Buddhist Publication Society,1994).

M. Southwold, *Buddhism in Life: The anthropological study of religion and the practice of Sinhalese Buddhism* (Manchester: MUP, 1983).

T. Tun, ed., *The Royal Orders of Burma, AD 1598–1885* (Kyoto: Centre for Southeast Asia Studies, Kyoto University, 1986), V, 1788–1806.

M. Winternitz, *A History of Indian Literature* (Srinivasa Sarma revised), 2 vols (Delhi: Motilal, 1983), II, 108–51.

P. Wongthet, S. Nathalang ed.,'The Jātaka stories and Laopuan world view', *Thai Folklore: insights into Thai culture* (Bangkok, 2000), 47–61. Originally published in *Asian Folklore Studies*, 48 (1989), 21–30.

E. Wray, C. Rosenfield, D.Bailey, with photographs by J.D. Wray, *Ten Lives of the Buddha: Siamese Temple Paintings and Jātaka Tales* (New York: Weatherhill, rev. ed., 1996).

W. Geiger, B. Ghosh trans., K.R. Norman revised, *A Pāli Grammar* (Oxford: PTS, 1994).

W. Doniger O'Flaherty, *Hindu Myths: a sourcebook translated from the Sanskrit* (London: Penguin, 1975).

Appendix A

The disciples of the Buddha

The Buddha's disciples frequently take rebirth with him in various forms in a number of stories, either as major players or in cameo roles. Most of them attain enlightenment, or arahatship, in his lifetime, after having made resolves comparable to that of the Buddha many lifetimes ago: Sāriputta, for instance, is said to have made a resolve to be his chief disciple and to attain enlightenment under his guidance. Having attained this goal, his death, like that of other arahats and *paccekabudhha*s, is called a *parinibbāna*, or entrance into *nibbāna*. Below is a list of followers and their identities in past lives in stories featured here.

Anuruddha: Sakka (243 and 540).

Ānanda: Pajjunna (75), tree spirit (121), king (243, 385, 407 and 540), otter (316), brahmin (402), king who protects goose (476), arrow maker (539).

Aṅgulimāla: yakkha (55).

Bhaddakāpilānī, Bodhisatta's mother (540).

Devadatta, foolish merchant (1), water yakkha (20), Kalābu, king of Kāsi (313), snake charmer (506).

Kassapa, Dukūlaka, the Bodhisatta's father (540).

Khemā, girl with bangle (539).

Moggallāna, elephant (37), jackal (316), youngest goose (476), Migājina (539).

322   THE JĀTAKAS

Rāhulamātā, the Buddha's consort in many lives: Subhaddhā (95), Sumanā (506), Sīvalī (539).

Rāhula, king's eldest son (95), Dīghāvu (539).

Sāriputta, monkey (37 and 316), chief disciple (99), general (313), brahmin (385), tree spirit (402), King Uggasena (506), second youngest goose (476), charioteer (538), Nārada (539).

Uppalavaṇṇā, the goddess of the parasol (538), the goddess Bahusodarī (540).

Other Buddha's followers:

Travellers (1), troop of monkeys (20 and 407), courtiers (95), flock of geese (476), the court (538).

Members of the royal family, father and mother deer (385).

Cosmology

There are thirty-one levels of existence in Buddhist cosmology, not all of which are mentioned in the stories in this collection. Those that do feature are listed here, with the story numbers in which they appear or are mentioned placed in parentheses.

Formless realms (arūpa)

These four realms are the highest kinds of existence, where beings take rebirth without any bodily form at all. The Bodhisatta never takes rebirth in these in Jātaka stories as his lifespan, of anything from 20,000 to 84,000 aeons, would be too long for him to be able to fulfil his vow (99). These realms correspond to the four formless meditations, the fifth to the eighth *jhāna*.

Brahma heavens (rūpa)

These are the heavens in which rebirth takes place on the basis of the meditation (*jhāna*). There are twenty-three in all, arranged in groups that correspond to the first four *jhāna* meditations. The Bodhisatta enters or leaves one of these realms in a number of stories. King Makhādeva is reborn in one for practising the divine abidings (9). The parents of Sāma are also reborn from such a realm (540). In Jātaka 99 the Bodhisatta is reborn in the Realm of Streaming Radiance (*ābhassara*), associated with the second meditation, characterized by strong joy (*pīti*).

Beings in these realms fill a universe with their bodies and only use the senses of sight and hearing. Their lifespans vary from a third of an aeon up to 16,000 in the very highest. There is no speech, action or dialogue in a Brahma heaven: no stories are set in these realms. If a being does wish to visit the realm of humans he needs to acquire a bodily form (99).

Deva realms (kāma)

These are the six heavens of the sense sphere, in which beings are reborn on the basis of generosity, keeping the precepts, faith and discussion about *dhamma*. The highest of these are not mentioned in the stories in this collection. Beings from the two lowest, the heaven of the Four Kings and the realm of the Thirty-Three Gods, are frequently involved in the action of Jātakas, though usually 'on the ground' when they visit animals and humans. The Four Great Kings are associated with protection. The goddess in Jātaka 539, for instance, acts on their behalf, to safeguard those lost at sea. The spirits of trees are associated with this realm (121). The realm of the Thirty-Three Gods is a place of music, games, entertainment and discussion and is ruled by King Sakka. Sakka, whose throne becomes hot when some act of virtue is about to take place, frequently intercedes in the human realm in disguise (316, 539 and 540). Vissakamma, the architect and designer from this realm, builds huts for ascetics (538 and 540). As in all the sense-sphere heavens, lifespans are very long (500–128,000 divine years), though not as long as in the Brahma realms. There is no old age, sickness or death in the human sense. Beings fall away from that heaven when their lifespan is over and take rebirth elsewhere.

The human realm

The lowest of the seven realms in which rebirth takes place on the basis of skilful consciousness (*kusala citta*). Buddhist *abhidhammic* sources say that the lifespan of a human is variable. The introduction to the Jātakas concurs with this but says that beings here have lifespans ranging from a hundred years to, in a golden age, 84,000 years! (9 and 95). This realm is regarded as a fortunate destiny (*sugati*), but humans do experience old age, sickness, death and hunger; in this regard they share features with the animal realms, to which they live in close proximity. This realm is said to be the best place to practise the Buddhist path. The Bodhisatta vow is taken here (the Far Past) and Buddhas always become fully enlightened as humans.

The bad destinies (dugatiyo)

These are seven *dugatiyo*: the four realms of animals, the jealous gods (*asura*s), hungry ghosts (*peta*s) and the hells. Many Jātakas take place in the higher animal realms, the destinies of those who do not keep the precepts. The nāga realm (506) is also considered a lower destiny, though the snake-like nāgas can assume human form. There are a number of hells, where lifespans may last for aeons. The king in Jātaka 313 is swallowed up by the Avīci hell, one of the lowest. The Bodhisatta is never born in a hell in the Jātakas, but remembers the Ussada hell in Jātaka 538. As for any other realm, existence in the hells is impermanent.

For tables of realms, see Collins, *Nirvana and Other Buddhist Felicities*, p. 298, Table 4.1 and Gethin, *Foundations of Buddhism*, pp. 116–17.

Appendix C

Indian sites that portray Jātakas

Indian sites that portray Jātakas translated in this collection

Ajaṇṭā, 75, 313, 506, 539, 540.
Bhārhut, 9 ('maghā deviya'), 316 ('sachha'), 407, 538 ('muga pakiya').
Buddha Gaya, 106.
Nāgārjunakoṇḍa, 316, 506.
Sāñchī, 407, 540.

Source: D.C. Ahir, 'The Jātakas in Indian Art', *The Influence of Jātakas on Art and Literature*, pp. 1–30.

Glossary and index of proper names

Does not include places and people mentioned only in passing. Number of story in this collection in which a character features, either in story from the present or in earlier life, in brackets. Although diacritics are used words are in Roman alphabetical order.

A

Abhiññā, the higher knowledges, obtained on the basis of the fourth meditation (*jhāna*).

Anāthapiṇḍika, a banker of Sāvatthi and lay disciple of the Buddha, famed for his outstanding generosity (1).

Anotatta, one of seven great lakes (476).

Anuruddha, cousin of the Buddha and one of his principal disciples, renowned both for his friendliness and his skill in the divine eye, which enables him to see the arising of beings in different realms (Sakka in 540).

Abhidhamma, Buddhist higher philosophy, in seven books, constituting one of three 'baskets', or collections, of the teaching.

Ājīvaka, naked ascetic.

Ānanda, one of the chief disciples and the Buddha's constant companion. He provides an unenlightened, human 'foil' to the Buddha, weeping at his death, *parinibbāna*, and making errors of various kinds during the Buddha's life, for which he is rebuked by the other monks. He commits to memory all the teachings of the Buddha so that they can be recorded at the First Council after the Buddha's death. His admission to this council of arahats is only obtained the night before the meeting, when he becomes enlightened on going to bed. Like the two chief disciples, Moggallāna and Sāriputta, he is constantly reborn alongside the Bodhisatta (75, 121, 316, 385, 402, 407, 539 and 540).

Aṅgulimāla, a robber who becomes a monk in the Buddha's order and attains arahatship. He made a necklace from the little fingers of his victims and hoped that the Buddha would give him the last; the Buddha converts him instead. A chant delivered by him, in which he says he has killed no being in the time since he was born as a Buddhist monk, is said to have saved the baby of a labouring woman and is still chanted today for women in childbirth (yakkha in 55).

Arahat, an enlightened being. This form of enlightenment is only possible in the time of a Buddha's teaching. Sometimes those listening to the stories told by the Buddha attain arahatship at the conclusion of a story and after the exposition of the four noble truths. More commonly, they attain the three stages of path that precede it: stream-entry, which means that arahatship will be obtained in seven lifetimes; one-return, which means that it will be obtained within one more rebirth, and never-return, which means that it will be obtained in this lifetime.

Ariṭṭhajanaka, son of king Mahājanaka, who assumes kingship but is killed by his brother *Polajanaka*, father of the Bodhisatta (539).

Avīci, the lowest of the eight great hells, probably the same as the Niraya hell. Ten thousand yojanas long, it is boiling hot and is the destination of those who have performed very grievous crimes. It is said to be the lowest point in the universe. Rebirth here may be for aeons, but is not permanent.

B

Bahusodarī, goddess of the mountain who used to be the Bodhisatta's mother (540). In last life is arahat, Uppalavaṇṇā.

Bhaddakāpilānī, an enlightened nun at the time of the Buddha, who had been the wife of Kassapa. As Pārikā she is the wife of Kassapa in his earlier rebirth as Dukūlaka, and mother of the Bodhisatta as Sāma (540).

Bhante, term of address for monks, still used today.

Bhikkhu, Buddhist monk. In this translation the word 'monk' is used in narrative, but the word 'bhikkhu' is retained as a term of address.

Bodhisatta, the awakening being, or the being bound for enlightenment, who has made a vow to develop the ten perfections and become a completely awakened Buddha; denotes the Buddha in the stories from the past.

Brahma, lord of the heaven realm attained by the first meditation or *jhāna*; also denotes beings in the form (*rūpa*) heaven realms.

Brahmadatta, king of Vārāṇasi. So many Jātakas take place during this king's reign that it is thought to be a dynastic title.

Brahmavihāra, divine abiding. One of the four illimitables of loving kindness, compassion, sympathetic joy and equanimity, which can be developed in the world in dealing with others or as meditations (*jhānas*) leading to rebirth in a Brahma heaven after death.

Buddha, literally, one who is awake. The fully enlightened being who can teach, as well as find, the eightfold path to freedom. It is a generic term, applied to Buddha Gotama, the most recent Buddha, whose past lives form the subject matter of the Jātakas. His predecessor and mentor was called Dīpaṅkara.

C

Campā, the city and river share the same name, after white campaka flowers on the riverside.

Campeyya, the Bodhisatta's name in a nāga rebirth (506).

Candā, daughter of Madda king and consort to ruler of Vārāṇasi (538).

Cetiya, one of sixteen regions (*Mahājanapadas*) in what is now India.

Cittakūṭa, a mountain, and the gateway to the heaven of the Thirty-Three Gods.

D

Deva/devatā, a shining god, or goddess, who is not immortal, but born for a long period in a sense-sphere heaven through the practice of generosity, keeping *sīla* and suchlike. Devas have happy existences and live in splendid palaces (*vimānas*) in heavenly realms, or sometimes they preside as benign, protective presences in trees and lakes. Such a goddess also lives in the royal white parasol in Jātaka 538. They can and do visit humans to converse with them and advise. Their homes are described in 'The story of Nimi' (541).

Devadatta, the chief villain of the Jātakas, dedicated to undermining the Bodhisatta in his aim. In his last life, as the Buddha's cousin, he becomes a dark parody of the Buddha. After trying to kill the Buddha when they both were young, he forms his own assembly and teachings, causing a schism in the Saṅgha, that ensures a hellish rebirth (1, 20, 313 and 407).

Dhamma, first, the Buddha's teaching, a refuge and meditation object as the second aspect of the Triple Gem in Buddha, *dhamma* and *saṅgha*; second, more general spiritual teaching when there is no Buddha's teaching available, as is the case in the stories from the past; third, justice, what is right, lawfulness; and fourth, how things are. The word has been retained in some contexts: *dhamma* hall, the meeting place of the monks and *dhamma* talk, in the *dhammadesanā*. Sometimes words such as 'teaching', 'justice' and 'what is lawful or fitting' have been used.

Dīghāvu, 'Longlife', Mahājanaka's son (539), an earlier rebirth of Rāhula, the Bodhisatta's son in his final rebirth.

Dīpaṅkara, the Buddha preceding the present one, Gotama. He predicts the eventual destiny of the Bodhisatta-to-be, the hero of the tales, who prostrates himself before Dīpaṅkara and makes the resolve to be a Buddha. Dīpaṅkara instructs him in the ten perfections (*pāramīs*).

Dukūlaka, Sāma's father (540) and an earlier rebirth of Kassapa, one of the Buddha's chief disciples.

G

Gandhamādana, one of the five mountain ranges that encircle Lake Anotatta (540).

J

Janaka, a king of Vārāṇasi, whose minister is Senaka (402).

Jambudīpa, one of four great continents which surround Mount Sumeru. It is the known world and is hence associated with India: it is the only place in which Buddhas are born.

Jetavana, a grove in Sāvatthi, bought by the lay disciple, Anāthapiṇḍika, for the Buddha's use, by covering its surface with coins. It is the scene of many talks and discussions between the Buddha and his followers.

Jhāna, one of eight meditative states or *samāpatti*s which bring rebirth in a Brahma heaven. The first four are called the form *jhāna*s: the first is accompanied by initial thought, sustained thought, joy, happiness and one-pointedness; the second by joy, happiness and one-pointedness; the third by happiness and one-pointedness; and the fourth by one-pointedness. The fourth meditation is the traditional starting point for the higher knowledges (*abhiññā*s), or the formless *jhāna*s. The fifth is the sphere of boundless space, the sixth the sphere of boundless consciousness, the seventh the sphere of nothingness and the eighth the sphere of neither perception nor non-perception. The four path moments, of stream-entry, one return, never return, and enlightenment, described in the conclusions of some stories, are known as *lokuttara jhāna*, meditations that transcend or are of a higher order than the world.

K

Kalābu, king of Kāsi (313).

Kālakañjaka Asura, a class of jealous god, a lower rebirth (94).

Kalpa, an aeon.

Kamma, literally, action; the activity and its effects which govern future circumstances and rebirths.

Kāra, a kind of tree.

Kasiṇa, device made of one of four elements, or four colours, or space or light, used to induce calm meditation (*jhāna*).

Kāsi, one of the sixteen *Mahājanapada*s, or countries, whose capital was Vārāṇasi.

Kāsmarī, kāsumāri tree = *Gmelina arborea*.

(Mahā) Kassapa, one of the Buddha's chief disciples in the Bodhisatta's last lifetime. In an earlier rebirth is husband of Pārikā and father of Sāma, the Bodhisatta (540).

Kiṃsuka, the *Butea frondosa* tree (lit. 'what's this?').

Kinnara, a mythical being, half-bird and half-man (lit. 'what man?').

Kora the Kṣatriya, a naked ascetic (94).

Kosala, country to the north-west of Magadha and adjacent to Kāsi, with which it seems to have been in prolonged struggle. One of the sixteen *Mahājanapada*s, or ancient territories of India.

Kuṇḍaka, red powder of rice husks; name for Bodhisatta as ascetic in Jataka 313.

Kusa, a kind of coarse grass with long pointed stalks used in brahminical ritual.

Kusāvātī, a city in the kingdom of the Mallas, later called Kusinārā, the scene of the Buddha's death.

Kusinārā, later name for Kusāvātī, the scene of the Buddha's death.

Ketakavana, a forest in Kosala where the Buddha relates Jātaka 20.

Khadira, the hardwood tree *Acacia catechu*.

L

Licchavi, warrior tribe of India, whose capital was Vesāli.

M

Madda, the name of a country and a people; birth place of Queen Candā (538).

Makhādeva, the Bodhisatta, king of Mithilā in Videha, who for successive periods of eighty-four thousand years each is prince, viceroy, king and then ascetic. Becomes an ascetic when his barber finds a grey hair (9).

Mahājanaka, king of Mithilā, who had two sons, Ariṭṭhajanaka and Polajanaka. Polajanaka becomes king when he kills Ariṭṭhajanaka, whose wife goes into exile and gives birth to a son, the Bodhisatta, also called Mahājanaka. After perils of sea journey and Polajanaka's death Mahājanaka reclaims Mithilā and marries Polajanaka's daughter Sīvalī (539).

(Mahā) Moggallāna, second of the Buddha's disciples, pre-eminent in the *iddhi*s, or psychic powers, which in his last lifetime are constantly

employed to locate, visit and encourage suffering meditators and practitioners, whatever their rebirth. Frequently reborn with Sāriputta, the Buddha's chief disciple, in the company of the Buddha (37, 316, 476 and 539).

Maṇimekhalā, Jewelled Girdle, a goddess placed by the Four Great Kings in Jātaka 539 to preside over the ocean and protect those who keep *sīla* from harm. Rescues Mahājanaka (539).

Manosilātala, a locality in the Himālayas.

Māra, sense-sphere god whose name, associated with death, aptly describes his embodiment of all the forces that militate against wholesomeness, happiness or the practice of meditation. In the *Jātakanidāna* he appears before the Buddha, assuming tempting and frightening forms in an attempt to challenge and dissuade him from his path. It is because of his challenge that Gotama brings the earth to witness for his great act of generosity in giving food to seven hundred ascetics as King Vessantara. Oddly enough, Māra features rarely in Jātaka stories, where malevolence is more commonly represented by Devadatta, the Buddha's cousin in his last life.

Migājina, ascetic, an earlier incarnation of Moggallāna, who emerges from meditation to encourage the Bodhisatta, Mahājanaka, in his going forth (539).

Migasammatā, a river which rose in the Himālayas and flowed down to the Ganga (540).

Mithilā, capital of the Videha country, a city that features in many Jātaka stories, and is the subject of extensive eulogy in 'The story of Mahājanaka' (539). Also home of King Makhādeva (9).

Muñja, a sort of reed, *Saccharum munja*.

N

Nāga, legendary being, part-snake and part-human, that lives in underground palaces in caves or in the depths of rivers, lakes and seas. Endowed with supernatural powers and the ability to protect humans, nāgas can change form at will and are the possessors of various kinds of magical gems and treasures which they guard under water. The

Bodhisatta is reborn as a nāga on several occasions, though through shame at finding himself in what is a lower realm, keeps the *uposatha* day in the hope of a human birth (506).

Nandiya, the Bodhisatta as a deer (385).

Nārada, ascetic, earlier incarnation of Sāriputta, who gives advice to Mahājanaka when he renounces the kingship (539).

Nibbāna, literally means the 'quelled' or 'put out', as in a candle wick. The state of freedom and ease in which all suffering of any kind ceases, the goal of the Buddhist path.

Niraya, one of lowest hells, where rebirth may be for aeons, but is not permanent.

P

Paccekabuddha, one who has found enlightenment on his own (*sāmaṃ*), without hearing the teaching of a Buddha. During the time in which the stories from the past are told there are neither Buddhas nor arahats. Paccekabuddhas, or silent Buddhas as they are sometimes known, therefore feature as representatives of the spiritual path in Jātaka stories when the teaching is lost. They embody, but do not teach fully, the complete path to enlightenment.

Pajjunna, the god of rain, (75) at that time an earlier incarnation of Ānanda.

Pāramī, perfection. One of the ten qualities needing cultivation by a Bodhisatta so that he can become a Buddha in his final life.

Piliyakkha, a king of Kāsi who shoots the Bodhisatta with an arrow (540).

Piyāl, a kind of tree, *Buchanania latifolia*.

Polajanaka, son of king Mahājanaka and brother of Ariṭṭhajanaka, from whom he seizes the kingship. Father of Sīvalī, who becomes consort to Mahājanaka, Polajanaka's nephew and the Bodhisatta (539).

R

Rāhula, name means literally a 'fetter'. The Buddha's son, who became an arahat in his lifetime (95).

Rāhulamātā, name given in texts for Rāhula's mother and consort of Gotama; she is called Yasodharā in northern texts. She usually features as Bodhisatta's consort. Becomes enlightened in Gotama's last life (95, 506 and 539).

Rājagaha, capital city of Magadha.

S

Sāketa, a town in Kosala, which was possibly its older capital. One of six great cities of the Buddha's time, along with Campā, Rājagaha, Sāvatthi, Kosambi and Vārāṇasi.

Sakka, king of the heaven of the Thirty-Three Gods, the realm above the heaven of the Four Kings, which is just above the human realm. As the lord of a heaven where beings are reborn through such activities as generosity or keeping the precepts, he notices and sometimes helps humans who are trying to cultivate these virtues or follow a spiritual path. In such instances his attention is alerted by a sudden increase in heat in his heavenly throne. Sakka denotes the office rather than the individual: the king of this realm is always called Sakka, though different beings can occupy his position. His name is said to derive from the fact that he gives generously and thoroughly (*sakkaccaṃ*).

Sāl, national tree of the Sakyans, *Shorea robusta*.

Saṃsāra, literally, 'wandering', the condition of all living beings.

Sasa, a hare, the Bodhisatta (313).

Sāvatthi, capital of Kosala.

Sīla, moral virtue associated with keeping of five precepts (*pañca sīlāni*) of not killing, not stealing, not indulging in sexual misconduct, not lying and not becoming intoxicated.

Sīvalī, daughter of Polajanaka, and the Bodhisatta's consort in 'The story of Mahājanaka', associated with Rāhulamātā (539).

Subhaddā, wife of King Mahāsudassana, Rāhulamātā in an earlier life (95).

Sumanā, Jasmine, the Bodhisatta's nāga consort in 'The story of Campeyya', associated with Rāhulamātā (506).

Sunakkhatta, Licchavi prince of Vesāli. Erstwhile member of the Buddha's order of monks whose departure was prompted by the Buddha's failure to use and display the psychic powers (*iddhi*s) or to explain the beginnings of things (94).

Sunanda, charioteer to King of Kāsi, associated with Sāriputta (538).

Suttas, Buddhist texts, one of three 'baskets', or collections of the teaching, mostly composed of talks and discussions given on specific occasions.

Senaka, Bodhisatta as minister of Madda (402).

T

Taxilā/Takkasilā, capital of Gandhāra, a centre of education (in the Punjab).

Temiya, Wet One, prince, name of Bodhisatta in Mugapakkha Jātaka (538).

Thūṇā, city mentioned in 'The story of Mahājanaka' (539).

tiṇḍuk, a kind of tree, *Diospyros embryopteris*.

U

King Uggasena, king of Vārāṇasi, an earlier incarnation of Sāriputta, who witnesses Campeyya's dance (506).

Uposatha, The days of the full moon, new moon and days midway between: the fourteenth–fifteenth and/or the eighth day of the moon's cycle. A day of purification in which lay disciples take extra precepts and wear white. Often spent at monasteries for offering food to monks, chanting, listening to *dhamma*, etc. Called *poya* day in modern Sri Lanka. Along with more general injunctions to be generous and to guard virtue, *sīla*, its observance is frequently recommended in Jātaka stories.

Uppalavaṇṇā, in Buddha's lifetime a nun renowned for her meditative skill and psychic powers. Born as the goddess of the white parasol (538) and the goddess of the mountains (540).

Ussada, one of the lowest Niraya hells (538).

V

Vārāṇasi (Benares), capital of Kāsi.

Vesāli, capital of the Licchavis.

Videha/Videhans, a country and its people, whose capital was Mithilā, ruled by Makhādeva (9) and Mahājanaka (539).

Vipassī, the nineteenth of the twenty-four Buddhas (94).

Vinaya, the Buddhist monastic code, one of three 'baskets', or collections, of the teaching.

Vissakamma, chief designer and architect of the heaven of the Thirty-Three Gods who arranges leaf huts and requisites for virtuous humans too (538, 540).

Y

Yakkha, non-human, rather like a goblin. Often depicted as protective deities in doors of temples, they are generally regarded as benign in a Buddhist context. Although some feature in the heaven of the Thirty-Three Gods, they are more usually considered to be inhabitants of the realm of the Four Great Kings. In Jātakas, however, they are often malevolent and feature as man-eating spirits in Jātakas 1, 20 and 55, where their rebirth is regarded as a descent. As the first story tells us, they can be spotted by their red eyes and failure to cast a shadow.

Yojana, measurement of distance. As much as can be travelled with one yoke of oxen, so about seven miles. Often translated as 'league'. In Jātaka 539, it refers in the riddles to the length of an oxen cart.

Yugandhara, one of seven mountain ranges that surround Mount Meru.

Frequently used technical terms

attainments (samāpatti): the eight meditations or *jhāna*s.

'bound for a heaven realm': term used to describe someone who has made great merit and will be reborn in a heaven on death.

declaration or statement of truth (saccakiriya): a statement of a single true fact, usually with regard to one's own virtue, that produces a magical effect in the world around (20, 75 and 540).

divine abidings: the four *brahmavihāras*: the meditations on loving kindness, compassion, sympathetic joy and equanimity. These four qualities can occur in daily life. When they are practised as meditations they lead to rebirth in a Brahma heaven.

higher knowledge (*abhiññā*): The six higher knowledges are the miraculous powers described in the *Sāmaññaphala Sutta*. They are first, the psychic powers, with the ability to become many, become invisible, walk through a wall as if it is air etc; second, the Divine Ear that hears sounds far and near, heavenly or human; third, the penetration of the minds of others; four, the memory of past lives; five, the Divine Eye that sees the arising and falling of beings in different conditions; and six, the destruction of the corruptions (*āsavas*). In Buddist thought described as becoming available to one who has practised the fourth meditation. In Jātakas usually only five are mentioned: the sixth brings enlightenment.

ten powers: ten powers possessed only by a Buddha. These include skills such as the recollection of past lives, the ability to discern the past lives of others and the ability to understand the laws of *kamma*.

four noble truths: formulated by the Buddha in his first sermon, are usually taken as the distillation of his path: the truth of *dukkha*, suffering or dissatisfaction; the truth of the origin (*samudaya*) of suffering, the thirst or craving that gives rise to suffering; the truth of the cessation (*nirodha*) of suffering; and the truth of the path (*magga*) that leads to the cessation of suffering. The truths are usually taught together: to understand one is to understand them all. One cannot truly understand the first truth—for instance of suffering or dissatisfaction—and not also come to see the path to the freedom from that. It is not commonly observed that in the *suttas* this teaching is usually reserved for those near one of the stages of path themselves. We are told at the end of many stories that a number of those who heard the Jātakas when they were first given attain one of the four stages of enlightenment through hearing these truths when their minds are ready to understand them.

five percepts: associated with *sīla*: undertakings stated or chanted by the Buddhist practitioner when he takes 'refuge' in the Triple Gem: the

Buddha, the *dhamma* (the teaching) and the *saṅgha* (the community of those that follow the teaching). They are 1) I undertake the rule of training not to take life; 2) I undertake the rule of training not to take what is not given; 3) I undertake the rule of training not to indulge in sexual misconduct; 4) I undertake the rule of training not to speak falsely; and 5) I undertake the rule of training not to become intoxicated. When they are maintained they are felt to protect the practitioner from inner and outer harm.